Strategic Alliances in a Globalizing World

A volume in
Research in Strategic Alliances

Series Editor:
T. K. Das, *City University of New York*

Research in Strategic Alliances

T. K. Das, Series Editor

Researching Strategic Alliances: Emerging Perspectives (2010)
edited by T. K. Das

Strategic Alliances in a Globalizing World (2011)
edited by T. K. Das

Strategic Alliances in a Globalizing World

edited by

T. K. Das
City University of New York

IAP

Information Age Publishing, Inc.
Charlotte, North Carolina • www.infoagepub.com

Library of Congress Cataloging-in-Publication Data

Strategic alliances in a globalizing world / [edited by] T.K. Das.
p. cm. -- (Research in strategic alliances)
Includes bibliographical references and index.
ISBN 978-1-61735-378-9 (pbk.) -- ISBN 978-1-61735-379-6 (hbk.) -- ISBN 978-1-61735-380-2 (e-book)
1. Strategic alliances (Business) 2. International business enterprises.
3. International trade. I. Das, T. K. (Tushar Kanti), 1938-
HD69.S8S7757 2011
338.8'7--dc22

2011001319

Printed and bound by CPI Group (UK) Ltd, Croydon, CR0 4YY

CONTENTS

Foreword to the Series . . . .*vii*

About the Series . . . . *ix*

1. Expanding to Institutionally Different Countries: Reasons, Firm International Experience, and Entry Mode Choice
Xavier Castañer and Mehmet E. Genç *1*

2. Smarter Mover Advantage: A Longitudinal Analysis of International Joint Ventures in China's Auto Market
Qingjiu Tao, John E. Prescott, and Sean Tsuhsiang Hsu. *27*

3. A Shift in the Wind?: Strategic Alliances Versus Wholly Owned Units in Global Industries
Ravi Madhavan *53*

4. Contractual Alliance Governance: Impact of Different Contract Functions on Alliance Performance
Dries Faems, Rutger Alberink, Gjalt de Jong, Aard Groen, and Rosalinde Klein Woolthuis. *67*

5. Governance Structure Choice in Strategic Alliances: The Roles of Alliance Objectives, Alliance Management Experience, and International Partners
Bing-Sheng Teng and T. K. Das *93*

6. Turning Experience Into Alliance Capability: Alliance Evaluation in Rolls-Royce
Ard-Pieter de Man, Mike Nevin, and Nadine Roijakkers *117*

7. The Formation of International Strategic Alliances by Born Global Firms: A Theory-Grounded Review
Robert Gannon and Noushi Rahman *139*

8. The Containment of Opportunism in the Post Formation Period of Interorganizational Relationships
Kerstin Neumann and Reinhard Bachmann 159

9. Relationship Management in International Strategic Alliances and Networks
Poul Houman Andersen 185

10. Sensemaking in Cross-National Alliances
T. K. Das and Rajesh Kumar 219

11. National Culture and Legitimacy in International Alliances
Rajesh Kumar and T. K. Das 243

About the Contributors 263

Index 273

FOREWORD TO THE SERIES

Relationships have been important to commercial activity and economic transactions for thousands of years. Yet, the development of a global competitive landscape has substantially enhanced the importance of partnerships between economic entities. These partnerships, referred to as strategic alliances, provide access to resources and capabilities that allow firms to gain economies of scope and to increase their productivity and innovation. The economies, productivity, and innovations are necessary to at least maintain competitive parity and especially to achieve a competitive advantage in the often highly competitive global markets. Strategic alliances have also become a prominent means of entering new markets, especially foreign markets. Therefore, alliances and the networks of firms of which they are a part have become essential for the conduct of business for all types of firms, large, small, established, and new.

Because of their growing importance, research on strategic alliances has increased markedly in the last 2 decades. Yet, there is need for an authoritative compendium of strategic alliance research and knowledge. This book series on *Research in Strategic Alliances* fills this critically important gap in our field. It provides a thorough examination of significant topics that provide complete and up-to-date knowledge on strategic alliances. This book series will serve as a catalyst for more effective management of strategic alliances and will guide future research on them. I commend it to you.

—Michael A. Hitt

Distinguished Professor and Joe B. Foster Chair in Business Leadership at Texas A&M University, and Past President of the Academy of Management and the Strategic Management Society.

ABOUT THE SERIES

The globalization of markets has led to increased interdependence among business firms, leading to an explosion in the number of strategic alliances. Strategic alliances, briefly, are cooperative arrangements aimed at achieving the strategic objectives of two or more partner firms. These interfirm arrangements can range from joint R&D to equity-based joint ventures. However, the scholarship relating to strategic alliances remains largely dispersed in the literatures of traditional academic disciplines such as strategic management, marketing, economics, and sociology. This book series on strategic alliances will cover the essential progress made thus far in the literature and elaborate upon fruitful streams of scholarship. More importantly, the book series will focus on providing a robust and comprehensive forum for new scholarship in the field of strategic alliances. In particular, the books in the series will cover new views of interdisciplinary theoretical frameworks and models (dealing with resources, risk, trust, control, cooperation, learning, opportunism, governance, developmental stages, performance, etc.), significant practical problems of alliance organization and management (such as alliance capability, interpartner conflict, internal tensions, use of information technology), and emerging areas of inquiry. The series will also include comprehensive empirical studies of selected segments of business, economic, industrial, government, and nonprofit activities with wide prevalence of strategic alliances. Through the ongoing release of focused topical titles, this book series will seek to disseminate theoretical insights and practical management information that will enable interested professionals to gain a rigorous and comprehensive understanding of the field of strategic alliances.

CHAPTER 1

EXPANDING TO INSTITUTIONALLY DIFFERENT COUNTRIES

Reasons, Firm International Experience, and Entry Mode Choice

Xavier Castañer and Mehmet E. Genç

We examine entry mode choice and its consequences when a multinational enterprise (MNE) expands into an institutionally different country. We argue that discussions of entry mode should distinguish between informal (e.g., culture) and formal (e.g., laws) institutions, and should take into account not just the home country of the MNE and its distance to the focal host country, but the MNE's overall footprint and experience across the world in general, especially in countries with an institutional structure that is similar to that of the focal host country. Specifically, we argue that firms with experience in countries with different informal institutions will be more likely to enter via acquisitions than firms without such experience, that such experience will not matter as much in the case of formal institutions, and that such firms will exit more quickly when they enter via equity alliances than through full acquisitions. We also distinguish between balanced and

Strategic Alliances in a Globalizing World, pp. 1–25

unbalanced alliances and argue that balanced alliances will be more enduring, but only when the host country is culturally (not legally) different from the other countries where the MNE has experience. Our arguments suggest that entry mode should be conditioned on a firm's experience in other markets, and that intercountry differences in formal versus informal institutions have distinct influences on entry mode.

INTRODUCTION: PURPOSE, KEY CONCEPTS, AND STRUCTURE

Thanks in large part to the liberalization and development of emerging markets—such as Brazil, Russia, India and China—firms are expanding in these markets at a rapid pace. In fact, recent data on foreign direct investment (FDI) suggests that for the first time ever, emerging markets are likely to attract more FDI inflows than developed countries (Kekic, 2009). Moreover, even though global FDI flows decreased by 17% in 2008, FDI flows to emerging markets increased by 10% during the same year. Further, it is likely that the majority of growth in the future will come from developing country markets. Many of these countries however, are markedly different from the Triad countries (i.e., United States, Europe, and Japan), both in terms of formal institutional structure and their cultural values (House, Hanges, Javidan, Dorfman, & Gupta, 2004; Kaufmann, Kraay, & Mastruzzi, 2003).

Expanding into institutionally different countries can help firms obtain several benefits. In addition to the growth opportunities mentioned above, these countries can provide multinational enterprises (MNEs) valuable experience they can then leverage in other, similar countries. Furthermore, these different environments can allow MNEs to learn new business models, and offer unique chances for process and product innovations, which MNEs can then leverage throughout the world (e.g., Immelt, Govindarajan, & Trimble, 2009). Differences provide diversity, which can be harnessed to generate new, unique knowledge.

Although expansion into institutionally different countries—developing or developed—can present lucrative long-term opportunities, such countries are unfamiliar territories for many firms; this is especially true for firms from the industrialized world expanding into emerging markets. As mentioned above, many of these emerging markets have different institutional systems compared to western countries. Hence, serving these markets is likely to generate a considerable liability of foreignness, especially for western MNEs with little experience in these markets (Hymer, 1976; Zaheer, 1995). Even if the country to be entered is economically advanced, its institutional structure may be very different than those with which the MNE has experience. The difficulties Japanese firms face in the United States (e.g., Hennart & Zeng, 2002) is just one example.

This chapter discusses the value of expansion into an institutionally different country and the choice of entry mode to enter that country, taking into account the foreign firm's overall international footprint and experience, and using a theoretical framework that includes differences not just in culture but also in the formal institutional environment.

Institutions can be defined as formal and informal rules that promote order in a society and constrain human behavior (North, 1990; Scott, 2001). Scott mentions three institutional pillars: regulatory, normative, and cognitive. Regulatory institutions refer to laws and regulations that explicitly promote certain behaviors and restrict others. Normative institutions refer to a set of widely shared values and norms about appropriate behavior. Cognitive institutions refer to shared cognitive structures such as cognitive schemas and frames that shape how people process and interpret information. Similarly, North distinguishes between formal and informal institutions. Formal institutions refer to written rules that constrain and promote behavior such as laws and regulations. Informal institutions refer to unwritten but widely shared rules, such as norms of behavior and codes of conduct that guide human action in a society. Hence, entering an institutionally different country means stepping into a society which has either different formal or informal institutions, or both. Given that earlier studies of foreign entry have emphasized the role of culture (e.g., Kogut & Singh, 1988), it is useful to evaluate how culture relates to the notion of institutional environment. Culture refers to the norms of appropriate behavior and values and assumptions that are largely taken for granted by members of a society (Hofstede, 2001). As such, culture can be considered part of the normative—and to a lesser extent cognitive—set of institutions, but not of the regulatory set. A focus on culture thus misses an integral part of the institutional environment. Hence, in this study we consider both formal and informal institutions.

Previous literature on the proper entry mode has considered national culture (Erramilli, 1996; Hennart & Larimo, 1998) as well as the cultural distance between the source and destination countries (e.g., Barkema, Bell, & Pennings, 1996; Kogut & Singh, 1988). However, as Tihanyi, Griffith, and Russell (2005) report, the results of such studies are inconclusive. Whereas some studies have found that cultural distance between host and home countries increases the likelihood to use joint ventures (JVs) over acquisitions (Kogut & Singh, 1988), others found either no impact or a negative relationship between cultural distance and entering via equity alliances (see Tihanyi et al., 2005, for a review). Similarly, some studies have considered the effect of cultural distance between home and host country on joint venture longevity (e.g., Barkema & Vermeulen, 1997; Park & Ungsson, 1997). However, these have also produced conflicting results (Hennart & Zeng, 2002).

These studies have two shortcomings. First, by only considering the distance between home and host countries, they ignore the firm's experience in other countries where it operates and the possibility of learning from, and subsequently leveraging, such experience. However, a MNE can learn from its experience in other institutionally different countries (e.g., Barkema et al., 1996) and transfer knowledge across subsidiaries as well as from subsidiaries to the headquarters (e.g., Bartlett & Ghoshal, 1989; Gupta & Govindarajan, 2001). The host country may be institutionally distant from the MNE's home market, but if the firm already operates in another country that is similar to the host country, it may transfer resources (including knowledge) from there. As a result, the distance between the source and destination countries does not necessarily correspond to the distance between the firm's home country and the host country. Experience in markets similar to the host country can provide valuable knowledge (Barkema et al., 1996). This knowledge can be transferred to the new host country and help the firm establish itself faster than it would be able to otherwise. Managers from institutionally similar countries where the firm already has operations can be assigned to manage the new subsidiary. These managers will be more attuned to the market and nonmarket conditions in the host country. For example, Carrefour's operations in mainland China are headed by the president of their unit in Taiwan, a market where Carrefour had been present for 18 years. In the words of this manager:

> We discovered Chinese culture and the way to work with the Chinese in Taiwan when the retail sector in mainland China was totally closed. International companies that decided to enter Taiwan—not Hong Kong—15 or 20 years ago have a fantastic advantage in China, and that was the case for Carrefour. (Child, 2006)

By international experience we refer to the cumulative experience of the firm in all the countries in which it operates. Obviously, firms may have entered and subsequently exited some countries. In such cases, the relevance of the experience in these locations will depend on how long the firm operated there and how long ago it exited the market. The longer it has been since the exit, the more difficult it will be able to retrieve the experience, since organizational memory may not exist and individuals involved in those experiences may have left the firm. Hence, we focus on current or recent experience.

Second, the studies' focus on cultural distance ignores other institutional elements such as regulatory and to lesser extent cognitive institutions. In addition to cultural similarity to other geographic locations, a firm also can and should consider how similar the laws and regulations in the host country are to those at other locations where the firm is present, and whether employees in the host country have the ability to correctly interpret the organizational practices it is likely to transfer (Kostova, 1999). Therefore, in understanding the proper choice of entry mode, we argue one has to consider distances in formal (regulatory) as well as informal (normative) institutions. Thus, we claim that in entering an institutionally different host country, the appropriate entry mode for a company will depend on (1) the distance between not just the home and the host country, but also on the MNE's other foreign operations as well as its overall experience in similar institutional settings, and that (2) such distance should encompass both informal and formal institutions. To the extent that an MNE already has experience in countries that are similar to the host country in question, it faces a lower liability of foreignness, which gives it more flexibility in choosing its entry mode.

Furthermore, we claim that formal and informal institutions may have different implications for entry mode. Although experience in similar *cultural* settings can help the firm overcome cultural problems in the host country, having experience with *formal* institutions similar to those in the host market may not matter as much for entry mode choice because regardless of its experience in a similar market, the firm may still have to ally with a local partner for legitimacy reasons or simply because the laws force it (Yiu & Makino, 2002).

Although there have been several studies of international JVs in institutionally different countries, most focus on the value foreign partners contribute in transition economies (Brouthers, Brouthers, & Werner, 2008; Steensma, Tihanyi, Lyles, & Dhanaraj, 2005), the likely evolution of such alliances (Steensma, Barden, Dhanaraj, Lyles, & Tihanyi, 2008) or the host country institutional conditions that favor joint ventures over acquisitions and greenfield investments (Meyer, 2001). These studies consider neither the impact of formal and informal institutional distance, nor the MNE's experience in diverse institutional settings and its ability to transfer resources from countries other than its home country.

The remainder of the chapter is structured as follows. First, we discuss the value of expanding to institutionally different countries, noting both the potential benefits and risks. Next, we assess the likely consequences of choosing among two different entry modes (full acquisitions vs. alliances) when entering such countries. We conclude by reflecting on our contribution and offering implications for theory and practice.

THE VALUE OF EXPANDING TO INSTITUTIONALLY DIFFERENT COUNTRIES

International business researchers generally see differences between countries as a hurdle (e.g., Hymer, 1976; Ghemawat, 2001). For instance, Johanson and Vahlne (1977) conceptualized these differences as generating psychic distance, which they define as "the sum of factors preventing the flow of information to and from the market. Examples are differences in language, education, business practices, culture, and industrial development" (p. 24). They further argued that when the firm moves into an institutionally different country, much of the knowledge managers developed in their home country has limited applicability. Hence, mistakes will be made and new knowledge has to be developed through experience, which is costly and time consuming (Dierickx & Cool, 1989). As a result, the more different the host country is from the home country, the bigger the disadvantage the firm faces.

The natural reaction of firms would be to try to reduce these costs. Therefore, the firm would first expand into psychically similar countries. Further, firms would enter these countries using less risky entry modes such as exporting or licensing (Johanson & Vahlne, 1977), a nonequity alliance or, if entering firms' resources are subject to market failure (Hennart, 1988), through an equity alliance with a local firm. If the firm entered through an alliance, once it accumulates sufficient experience and knowledge, it might rely less on its partner and gain more control of its activities, and start expanding into more distant countries in a sequential manner.

Some studies have attempted to test these propositions with inconclusive results. Whereas some studies show a negative relationship between home-host country cultural distance and firm performance (Luo & Peng, 1999), others show no relationship at all, or even a positive relationship (Evans & Mavondo, 2002; Morosini, Shane, & Singh, 1998). In a meta-analysis of 67 studies, Tihanyi et al. (2005) do not find any robust effect of cultural distance on entry mode choice or firm performance. This could be because expansion into different countries provides opportunities to improve performance, as well as the well-known risks. Perhaps some companies are able to capitalize on the differences between countries (Ghemawat, 2003).

We argue that there are three reasons why firms can improve their performance and their knowledge stock by expanding into institutionally different countries. First, expanding only into institutionally similar countries can lead to overconfidence (March, 1991). Firms that expand only into similar countries are likely to have a higher chance of survival and success due to low risks and familiarity of the environment. Paradoxically, this success however can lead them to think that they have mastered international expansion and that their capabilities would be valuable anywhere (Haleblian & Finkelstein, 1999). As a result, when the firm expands to institutionally distant countries, it struggles (e.g., Ghemawat, 2001; Khanna, Palepu, & Sinha, 2005).

Second, instead of relying only on their home-grown resources and products, firms can tap into their subsidiaries' knowledge to enhance innovation and broaden their knowledge base (Bartlett & Ghoshal, 1989; Kogut & Zander, 1993). Although this can be done to some extent with subsidiaries in institutionally similar countries, the diversity of knowledge the firm can gain there is limited. When the firm expands into an institutionally different country, it is more likely to get exposed to new and different business models. We view international expansion as a series of exploitation and exploration moves. Each new foreign expansion involves some exploration. However, we argue that going into institutionally similar countries entails less of an exploration than going into institutionally different countries where the environment is very different and there is much to learn (e.g., an American firm expanding to Canada vs. to Japan). Such exploration in turn increases the firm's knowledge stock and, if successful, its ability to adapt to different conditions around the world. For instance, Das (1993) cites the example of Vicks India, where the company developed a new package size that made its products affordable for local people, and devised an efficient way to distribute it. It then used that distribution system in other, similar countries (to India). Similarly, Immelt et al. (2009) describe how GE innovates in subsidiaries in less developed countries and applies the innovation at home. Thus, firms can benefit from engaging in international exploration to learn different things and develop new products which can then be exploited in other countries.

More generally, drawing from the learning literature, we argue that in order to be successful and adaptive firms need to balance international exploitation and exploration (Levinthal & March, 1993; Luo, 2002). Firms that only engage in international exploitation limit their adaptive and absorptive capabilities (Cohen & Levinthal, 1990; March, 1991), whereas firms that only engage in international exploration cannot exploit the knowledge they learn and take undue risk.

Third, expansion into institutionally different countries can help managers develop a global mindset (Doz, Santos, & Williamson, 2001; Gupta & Govindarajan, 2002; Murtha, Lenway, & Bagozzi, 1998). MNEs tend to have assets that are superior to those of local firms, which enable them to earn returns on those resources when they expand abroad (Hymer, 1976). However, this self-perceived superiority tends to result in a worldview that their practices are the best. Perlmutter (1969) called this ethnocentrism. Expanding into institutionally similar countries is unlikely to challenge these assumptions whereas expanding into institutionally different countries might, which in turn can help managers gain a broader perspective, appreciate the value of local knowledge and integrate the best aspects of different systems. It may also allow managers to develop a deeper understanding of what can and cannot be transferred across countries (Gupta & Govindarajan, 2002). Thus,

> **Proposition 1:** Firms that engage in international exploration and subsequently exploit the newly acquired knowledge will perform better than firms which only engage in international exploitation.

> **Proposition 2:** Firms that are present in institutionally different countries are more likely to (a) develop a global mindset, and (b) perform better in subsequent international expansion moves.

Some empirical research is consistent with this view. For example, Goerzen and Beamish (2003) find that the most profitable MNEs in their sample are those that are present in a large *and* institutionally diverse set of countries. Similarly, Genç and Castañer (2009) find that institutional (especially cultural) diversity in the firm's country portfolio exerts a positive influence on multinational bank performance, especially if the firm has a large geographic scope.

RELEVANCE FOR ENTRY MODE RESEARCH

As we mentioned above, studies of entry mode choice focus mostly on the cultural distance between the home country and the host country. Almost all studies on the effect of cultural distance on entry mode choice or alliance longevity look at cultural distance between the home and host country, and in general do not control for a firm's presence in other countries (Barkema & Vermeulen, 1997, 1998; Hennart & Larimo, 1998; Kogut & Singh, 1988; Park & Ungson, 1997; see Barkema et al., 1996, for an exception). As we mentioned above, however, having operations in other countries, especially in countries that are institutionally similar to the host country, raises the possibility that the firm already possesses the requisite knowledge to operate there. As such, the firm may be less likely to revert to local partners, for example. Further, the diversity of the environments a MNE operates in should not be evaluated solely on the cultural dimension. Home and host countries may be similar culturally but different in terms of laws and regulations. For example, the United

Kingdom and the United States both belong to the Anglo-Saxon cultural cluster (House et al., 2004), but their laws govern firms' activities quite differently (Hart, 1992). Existing literature generally overlooks this formal dimension of institutional distance. Moreover, the few studies that consider the effect of formal institutions (e.g., extent of property rights protection, regulations) on entry mode choice have only considered the host country conditions (e.g., Brouthers & Brouthers, 2003; Lee & Mansfield, 1996; Meyer, 2001; Yiu & Makino, 2002). However, MNEs may perceive a lower risk posed by poor formal institutions in the host country if their home country also has poorly developed formal institutions or if they have had experience in other countries with that characteristic. A limited number of studies show that such experience gives less-developed country firms an edge over firms from developed countries when they both enter a host country with less developed formal institutions (e.g., Cuervo-Cazurra & Genç, 2008; Khanna & Palepu, 2006). Therefore:

Proposition 3: Entry mode is a function of the formal and informal institutional distance between the host country and the entering firm's overall international geographic footprint and experience.

So far we have considered why expanding into institutionally different countries may be beneficial, at least in the long term, and how this is relevant for deciding on the appropriate entry mode choice. However, this does not answer the question of which entry mode firms should choose entering institutionally different countries to the firm's experience. In the next section, we address this question.

THE CHOICE OF APPROPRIATE ENTRY MODE IN INSTITUTIONALLY DIFFERENT COUNTRIES

Once a firm decides to enter an institutionally different country than the firm's geographic portfolio, the question becomes which entry mode the firm should choose. The extant literature suggests that managers should choose a mode which (1) allows quick access to local resources, and (2) helps the firm reduce risks in the host country. Both acquiring a local firm and allying with one can theoretically offer these benefits (e.g., Hennart & Reddy, 1997; Kogut & Singh, 1988). Both of these means are considered preferable to a wholly-owned greenfield investment when entering an institutionally distant country, because knowledge of the local market is crucial. Since such knowledge is usually subject to market failure (Hennart, 2009), the firm has to access it either through an alliance with a local partner, or by purchasing a local firm. Therefore, in this chapter we focus on acquisitions and alliances. This does not mean that greenfield entry is always an inferior choice. Rather, greenfield entry tends to be driven by firm-specific resources such as R&D intensity (Hennart & Park, 1993), whereas in this chapter we are more interested in country-level factors and in the resources local firms can provide.

We make several arguments. First, we argue that from a learning perspective, managers might see expanding into an institutionally different country as an opportunity to learn (e.g., Matthews, 2006). The firm uses this expansion as a way to learn about a particular environment which it can then exploit in countries characterized by similar institutional environments. Therefore, the firm's motive for international expansion should play a role in the selection of entry mode.

Second, both digestibility and implementation (in acquisitions) and rent appropriation (in alliances) concerns will be more acute when the firm expands into an institutionally different setting. On the one hand, it is often not possible to acquire the assets that the foreign firm seeks separately from the other assets of the local firm (Hennart, 1988). For example, a foreign firm seeking knowledge of the local market cannot just buy that asset from the local firm; it would have to buy the firm itself. However, a full acquisition of the local firm creates digestibility and post-acquisition integration problems, which are likely to be more severe in institutionally different countries (Morosini et al., 1998). On the other hand, in institutionally different countries, the foreign firm is more likely to perceive its partner's behavior suspiciously due to cultural and legal differences. Further, the foreign firm cannot accurately evaluate the relative contribution of the local firm since it lacks the knowledge required to make that evaluation (Arrow, 1962), especially if the contribution of the local firm is tacit, as in the case of dealing with local suppliers, customers and the government. Conversely, the local firm may be suspicious that the foreign partner, once it acquires the experience, will terminate the agreement (e.g., Reich & Mankin, 1986).

Third, the net effect of experience in institutionally different markets on the preferred entry mode is not obvious. MNEs with extensive experience in other institutionally similar countries may effectively bridge the distance between the home and the host country by tapping into those subsidiaries that have the most relevant skills and resources. Therefore, they may be better able to both handle postacquisition integration problems as well as communicate and build trust more effectively with a local partner.

Moreover, formal and informal institutions exert powerful but distinct influences on entry mode choice. For instance, formal institutions such as regulations may force a foreign firm to partner with a local firm, even if this would not be the most preferred choice for the foreign firm. Formal institutions can push a foreign firm to engage in an alliance for legitimacy reasons (Yiu & Makino, 2002). Foreign firms may prefer alliances over acquisitions to avoid a nationalist backlash or xenophobia (Hennart & Larimo, 1998). In addition, when the industry is politically sensitive, formal institutions may favor partnering with a local firm (Gomes-Casseres, 1989). For example, when Dubai Port wanted to buy a port in the United States, it was denied permission. Opting for a partnership with a U.S. firm might have increased its chances of approval. In general, the lower the quality of formal institutions in a host country, the more likely firms are to enter the country through partnering with local firms to reduce their risks (Brouthers & Brouthers, 2003; Meyer, 2001; Yiu & Makino, 2002).

The choice between acquisitions, greenfield investments and alliances revolves around risk, resource access speed, legitimacy, control and organizational costs (see also Collis & Montgomery, 1998). Speed refers to a firm's ability to quickly access local resources (e.g., Garrette, Castañer, & Dussauge, 2009) and establish itself in a short period of time. Studies show that speed is especially important when the industry has a high growth rate, and when the firm is a follower in its industry (Caves & Mehra, 1986; Hennart & Zeng, 2002). Control relates to the firm's control over assets and decisions about its operations in the foreign country. Risk refers to the potential for failure or poor performance due to possible rent expropriation by the potential partner, and resource imitation (Gomes-Casseres, 1989; Gulati & Singh, 1998; Hamel, 1991). For instance, in partnering with Chinese firms, Korean and American-headquartered semiconductor firms worried that the Chinese investors will access critical technology and emerge as future competitors (Siegel & Chang, 2008). In the international context, risk also includes political risk, which reflects the possibility that once an investment is made to enter the country, the firm becomes vulnerable to hold-up or outright nationalization by the host country government (Henisz, 2000; Kobrin, 1979). Table 1.1 summarizes the value we assigned to each of the main entry governance modes along these variables, based on the literature. Since access to local market knowledge and managing risks become even more important in institutionally different countries, and since alliances and acquisitions are preferable to greenfield investments in these two regards, we focus on these two entry modes. Below, we consider acquisitions and alliances in more detail and discuss how the MNE's geographic experience affects their relative attractiveness when entering institutionally different countries.

Table 1.1. Control, Risk, Organizational Costs and Access Speed by Entry Mode

	Ownership Form			
	Hierarchy			
Key Factors Determining Entry Mode	*Greenfield Investment*	*Full Acquisition*	*Hybrid (JV, Equity Alliance)*	*Quasi-Market (Nonequity Alliances)*
Control	Very high	Very high	Substantial	Little
Fast access to local resources	Low	High	High	High
Risk of rent appropriation	None	None	Low	High
Political risk	High	High	Moderate	Low
Legitimacy	Low to Moderate	Low	High	Moderate
Organizational costs (e.g., integration/coordination)	Low	Very high	High	Low

Full Acquisition

Full acquisition of a local firm entails full ownership and hence total control over operations. Although one of the supposed advantages of full acquisitions is quickness in accessing the required resources, there are two fundamental challenges to a foreign parent's ability to readily use its new subsidiary's resources. First, the liability of foreignness is still there despite the acquisition (Cohen & Levinthal, 1990; Morosini et al., 1998). While local employees are assumed to know and understand the local context, the foreign parent managers in charge of monitoring and managing the affiliate lack institutional intelligence (Ang & Inkpen, 2008). Thus, in a full acquisition, foreign managers have to rely on the local employees. Understanding, having a good rapport with and trusting them might not be an easy task however, especially if there are significant cultural differences. Differences in language in particular and culture in general can make communication and understanding difficult. In the case of language, the use of proficient translators might facilitate understanding but may also reduce the scope and intimacy of communication due to the presence of another person; besides, it is very difficult to translate nonverbal clues. Further, cultural differences might make communication styles incompatible in terms of tone, volume, gesticulation, and physical proximity and contact, creating a feeling of discomfort. Managers from low-context culture may have difficulties in communicating with managers from a high-context culture (such as Japan) where much communication is contextualized and cannot be effectively translated (Hall, 1959).

Even if foreign managers can use their authority to order local employees to perform a task, foreign managers might not know whether this is possible and may have difficulty in effectively monitoring its execution, given the institutional differences. Thus, in setting the objectives for the local subsidiary foreign managers need to rely on local employees' knowledge about what is feasible in this new institutional environment. Hence, foreign managers have to trust that local employees will behave in the best interest of the firm and reveal appropriate information. Thus by trust, we refer to one party's (let's call him A) belief that the other party (B) will (1) have A's best interest at heart and (2) satisfactorily collaborate, i.e., provide appropriate information to A. This is similar to Das and Teng's (1998) trust and confidence notions, respectively. They define confidence as "a firm's perceived certainty about satisfactory partner cooperation" and trust as "positive expectations about another's motives with respect to oneself in situations entailing risk." We argue that foreign managers ought to trust local managers but cannot be confident. This lack of confidence in turn makes smooth functioning of the local firm more difficult.

Second, as in any acquisition implementation, the retention and deployment of the target resources might be problematic (Jemison & Sitkin, 1986). The foreign firm probably acquires the target to access certain local resources which it intends to combine with its own resources to successfully sell its goods in the local market (Hennart, 2009). These resources are likely to be complementary assets (Teece, 1986) such as the local firm's marketing and distribution capabilities, or more generally, its understanding of the local market. However, if the foreign acquirer perceives its goods as superior to what is available on the local market, and relies on local managers solely for their knowledge of local market conditions, they are likely to treat local managers as technologically less sophisticated. This might prompt acquiring managers to replace the product and production processes of the target by those of the acquirer (Jemison & Sitkin, 1986), and to eliminate or significantly reduce target's own resources and capabilities (Capron, 1999). These actions might be exacerbated by cultural differences. Communication problems and misunderstandings might lead the acquirer to adopt a more directive and forceful approach. As a consequence, local target employees may feel marginalized and some might leave the company, taking their local knowledge with them (Hambrick & Cannella, 1993; Walsh, 1988), while the remaining ones may feel less motivated and exert less effort (e.g., Morosini et al., 1998; Very, Lubatkin, Calori, & Veiga, 1997; Zaheer, Schomaker, & Genç, 2003).

In addition to informal-cultural differences, formal differences may also disfavor acquisitions in relation to other forms of entry. Countries differ widely in terms of their antitrust laws, and acquisitions are subject to antitrust concerns (Capron & Guillén, 2009). Especially if the foreign firm is entering a concentrated or consolidating industry, a foreign firm buying a local firm can invite more scrutiny than local firms buying each other. In concentrated industries, acquisitions are preferable because they do not create additional capacity. However, this same motive will make them more likely to be subject to scrutiny.

Finally, the market for corporate control, like other markets, is subject to adverse selection and information asymmetry (Balakrishnan & Koza, 1993). Depending on the amount and quality of information on companies dictated by formal institutions, the market for control of local firms may be highly inefficient, and the buyer may end up with a "lemon" (Akerlof, 1970). Knowing this, the foreign firm may be less willing to engage in an acquisition. Despite the generic benefits advocated for full acquisitions over other development modes, the arguments above suggest that entering institutionally different markets via acquisitions is problematic in terms of accessing local resources. Therefore:

Proposition 4: Entering via a full acquisition into a country that is institutionally different from other countries where the firm has operations via a full acquisition is likely to result in poor performance.

Such problems with acquisitions may be tempered by a firm's experience in institutionally different markets. First, experience in other markets that are institutionally different from the home country allows MNE managers to appreciate intercountry differences, both in culture and in laws and regulations. Such experience heightens the managers' sensitivity to the applicability of their organizational practices and management styles in different countries. In other words, experience in diverse markets helps MNE managers develop a cosmopolitan and global mindset (Gupta & Govindarajan, 2002). In addition, employees of the local firm may be more accepting of a foreign manager who has extensive experience in diverse markets. Hence:

Proposition 5a: Firms that have experience in other countries with different informal institutional settings will be more likely to enter a host country via full acquisitions than firms who lack such experience.

Proposition 5b: A firm that has experience in other countries with different informal institutional settings will achieve better performance than a firm that lacks such experience, when both firms enter the host country via a full acquisition.

Even though the firm's deeper understanding of cultural differences can help it make acquisitions work, such experiences will matter less in the case of differences in formal institutions. Having been present in countries with different formal institutions is unlikely to be of much help in managing the acquisition process in an institutionally (legal) different environment since acquisitions are fraught with human issues, which are more cultural in nature (e.g., Jemison & Sitkin, 1986; Larsson & Finkelstein, 1999). Therefore:

Proposition 6a: Firms that have experience in other countries with different formal institutional settings will be more likely to enter a host country via full acquisitions than firms that lack such experience.

Proposition 6b: A firm that has experience in other countries with different formal institutional settings will not achieve better performance than a firm that lacks such experience, when both firms enter the host country via a full acquisition.

Alliances

In order to quickly gain access to valuable local resources and reduce risks of entering an institutionally different country, collaboration with a local partner is the alternative to a full acquisition of a local firm (e.g., Kogut & Singh, 1988). Here, we distinguish equity alliances or JVs from nonequity alliances, the former being a more hierarchical (hybrid) means of governance (Williamson, 1991). Within equity alliances, we further distinguish between balanced and unbalanced alliances. By balanced alliances we refer to arrangements where both parties have a more or less equal say or power, at least formally. Alliances or JVs with a majority owner are unbalanced.

A balanced alliance requires agreement among partners through a joint governance forum and hence does not give full authority to any partner. The lack of full authority and the resulting need for negotiation and compromise in balanced alliances might be a blessing in disguise in the sense that it prevents falling in the acquisition trap mentioned above. Given that partners in balanced alliances need to agree, none of them (in particular, the foreign firm) can improperly impose its way and thus alienate the other's employees. Hence, the balanced equity structure acts as a natural forbearance mechanism. Combined with high resource commitments by both parties, which market entry usually requires, such an alliance could lead to strong interpartner harmony (Das & Kumar, 2009). Consistent with this, Hennart and Zeng (2002) find that balanced ownership of joint ventures between Japanese and American headquartered firms have a significant and positive effect on the longevity of the JV.

If, however, the alliance is structurally unbalanced, then the same situation as in a full acquisition can emerge. This was the case in the Xerox-Fuji Xerox JV in Japan. Xerox, through its UK subsidiary, set up a JV with Fuji of Japan in order to commercialize Xerox's large copiers in Japan. After an initial period, Xerox managed to obtain the majority of the JV (51%). Seeing Fuji and the JV as a mere commercialization and distribution arm, Xerox stalled the technological development of the JV, whereas Fuji wanted to invest more in technological development, having realized that the Japanese and other Asian markets required smaller copiers. Therefore, partners had divergent goals, exacerbated by lack of cultural understanding. It took Xerox more than a decade to realize the marketing sense and technological prowess of its Japanese partner and benefit from its contributions (Gomes-Casseres & McQuade, 1991). Cultural differences partly explain why it took so long for Xerox to reverse its perception and treatment of the Xerox-Fuji Xerox JV. Due to their cultural values, Japanese managers didn't confront the US managers for a long time (high forbearance), which prevented an open discussion. These arguments suggest the following:

> **Proposition 7:** When entering into a country that is different in terms of informal institutions from the other countries where the firm is present, entry through a balanced alliance is more likely to endure and succeed than entry through an unbalanced alliance or a full acquisition.

Unlike cultural differences, when entry entails differences in terms of formal institutions, the relative benefits of balanced versus unbalanced alliances are not very clear. Cultural differences across countries have a significant bearing on organizational arrangements and issues such as forbearance and handling of conflict, which are crucial to alliance success. Differences in formal institutions however, tend to focus more on external constraints on the alliance rather than on internal constraints. Finally, the foreign firm may have to enter the country via alliances when the formal rules coerce it to do so, when the industry is politically sensitive so that a local partner may be required to fulfil formal institutional requirements, or in order to gain legitimacy in the eyes of key stakeholders (Yiu & Makino, 2002). Such legitimacy is likely to be even more important in countries with different formal institutions because the firm will be more dependent on resources from those key stakeholders in order to survive in that market. In such cases, the foreign firm will engage in forbearance and refrain from conflict, even if it has the majority stake in the alliance and is not happy with its local partner, simply because it fears losing support of key stakeholders. Therefore, we propose that:

> **Proposition 8:** When entering a country that is different in terms of formal institutions from the other countries where the firm is present, there will not be a significant difference in success or endurance between the balanced versus unbalanced alliances.

Even if alliances might prevent some of the full acquisition pitfalls, collaboration does not necessarily give the foreign firm immediate access to the local partner's resources. This is subject to negotiation which is costly and takes time (e.g., Doz, 1996; Zaheer, McEvily, & Perrone, 1998). Further, both parties are legitimately concerned with possible rent appropriation and resource imitation (Dyer & Singh, 1998). The local partner could learn about the foreign firm's superior product and underlying technology and become a stronger competitor in the future (Hamel, 1991). Similarly, the foreign firm might, over time, learn about the target's local competences (such as marketing and distribution) and dissolve the alliance when the local partner's skills are no longer needed (Reich & Mankin, 1986).

In such a context, it is likely that both parties might want to obtain greater contractual safeguards through equity and greater contractual detail or complexity (Dyer & Singh, 1998; Hennart, 1988; Reuer & Ariño, 2007). However, the very feeling and expression of distrust implicit in greater contractual safeguards may actually make collaboration more difficult (Das & Teng, 1998). Knowing that contractual safeguards (equity) give an option to exit (Kogut, 1991) may reduce firms' resource commitment and make exit more likely. Furthermore, cultural differences can exacerbate misunderstandings and communication problems, triggering conflict, delayed implementation, and ultimately lead to the premature dissolution of the alliance (Doz, 1996; Kogut, 1989). Even though acquisitions are fraught with similar difficulties, foreign firms are likely to keep acquired units longer even if they sustain losses, simply because they entailed larger investments and because they lack the option to exit embedded in alliance contracts (Kogut, 1991). Further, large resource commitments involved in acquisitions, coupled with subsequent losses can cause escalation of commitment (Staw, 1981). Therefore, we propose:

Proposition 9: A firm that has entered an institutionally different country via an equity alliance is more likely to exit sooner than a firm that has entered through a full acquisition, provided that neither firm has experience in other institutionally different countries, or in countries that are institutionally similar to the focal host country.

Managers of firms with experience in a variety of cultural and legal institutional settings are likely to have a high level of institutional intelligence or knowledge (Ang & Inkpen, 2008). This is due to the fact that in such global corporations, managers tend to be rotated among subsidiaries (e.g., Martínez & Jarillo, 1989). Managers in charge of leading such corporations or their subsidiaries are likely to have some personal or prior professional experience in dealing with a similar country, which makes negotiation and ensuing collaboration with local managers more positive. The same might apply if the local managers have had prior experience in interacting with people from the foreign firm's home country.

In addition, firms that have experience in institutionally similar countries can achieve a certain level of trust with managers of the potential local partner because these firms are more likely to be reputable partners, especially if they have engaged in successful alliances in those countries. Once such trust is built, it can reduce the perception of potential contractual hazards and thus lead to lower demands for contractual safeguards (Gulati, 1995; Ring & Van de Ven, 1992; Zaheer et al., 1998). In other words, preexisting trust can help establish interpartner legitimacy (Kumar & Das, 2007). This in turn will facilitate effective collaboration.

These arguments are valid not just for differences in informal institutions, but also but also for formal institutions. For instance, foreign managers will have a better idea of when these formal institutional differences will be more salient, and will have a deeper understanding of the implications of differences in formal institutions. Therefore, we propose:

Proposition 10: A firm that has entered an institutionally different country through equity alliances will not be more likely to exit sooner than a firm that has entered via an acquisition, provided that both firms have experience in other institutionally different countries.

CONCLUSION

In this chapter, we examined why entering into institutionally different countries is likely (because it can generate long term benefits), and considered the different likelihoods and consequences of entering via acquisitions versus alliances, conditioned on a firm's international experience in other markets. We put forward rationales about why a firm may want to enter an institutionally different country even though it is costly and fraught with interorganizational and political risks. Firms can enter these countries in order to engage in exploration and learning and achieve a more diverse base of knowledge that can be subsequently exploited.

Regarding entry mode choice, we first argued that in considering the appropriate entry mode, scholars and managers should take into account not just how different the host country environment is from the firm's home country environment, but the firm's operations and experiences elsewhere in the world, particularly in countries that are similar to the host country in terms of institutions (Genç & Castañer, 2009; Goerzen & Beamish, 2003). Furthermore, we distinguished between formal and informal institutions and argued that they may have different implications for entry mode. We then considered two different modes of entry: full acquisitions and alliances. Firms with experience in countries with similar institutions to the focal host country would be more likely to enter via acquisitions than firms who do not have such experience, but that such experience is likely to matter only in the case of cultural differences, whereas differences in formal institutions may still force a firm to enter via alliances, regardless of its experience in countries with similar formal institutions. Within equity alliances, we further distinguished between balanced and unbalanced equity alliances and argued that whereas balanced equity alliances are preferable for entering countries that are culturally different, such alliances do not have clear benefits in entering countries which differ in terms of formal institutions. Finally, we argued that for firms lacking experience in similar countries, those that enter via alliances will exit sooner than those that enter through acquisitions, the actual postentry performance notwithstanding. We proposed that for firms with experience in similar markets, there will not be any difference between entry modes in terms of time to exit.

Our chapter contributes to the literature on international expansion (e.g., Luo & Peng, 1999), MNE performance (e.g., Goerzen & Beamish, 2003), as well as on entry mode choice and alliance longevity (e.g., Hennart & Reddy, 1997; Hennart & Zeng, 2002). We build on these literatures by considering not only culture but also formal institutions such as regulations and laws. This is in accordance with studies showing that formal and informal institutions may have different impacts on the successful transferability of organizational practices (Kostova & Roth, 2002). Past studies that have examined formal institutions have tended to consider the host country institutions, ignoring the firm's home country or its worldwide experiences (e.g., Yiu & Makino, 2002). Further, past studies have limited themselves to distance between home and host country, ignoring the possibility that the firm has learned from its experiences in other countries or the transfer of that learning to other countries. In existing literature, the firm is a hostage of its home country heritage. We argue that explanations of strategic decisions such as international expansion and market entry mode should consider the entire MNE experience.

Our propositions have both theoretical and practical implications. Theoretically, explanations of entry mode and predictions of alliance or acquisition success have to take into account a firm's entire portfolio of operations across the world, not just its home country. Second, studies have to consider the possibility that firms may enter institutionally different countries in order to learn new knowledge which they can then exploit in other countries. Third, researchers have to move away from an exclusive focus on culture toward a broader understanding and conceptualization of a country's institutional environment which includes its formal-legal dimensions.

Practically, our arguments indicate that firms should enter new, institutionally different countries, even if such entry does not provide imminent financial benefits. As a more general principle, firms should not just enter institutionally similar countries to minimize risk and benefit from managerial scale economies; they should balance geographic exploration with exploitation (March, 1991). Moreover, in deciding on the appropriate entry mode, firms should scour their entire geographic coverage to find if they employ people who have knowledge that is applicable in the new host country, and transfer resources from the most appropriate country. They should also consider not just cultural differences between countries but also differences in formal institutions.

ACKNOWLEDGMENT

We would like to acknowledge the comments of J. P. Bonardi and J. C. Usunier to an earlier version of this manuscript. Part of this chapter also benefited from the feedback at different stages of J. F. Hennart, E. Ors, and participants and reviewers at the conferences of the Academy of Management and the Academy of International Business.

REFERENCES

Akerlof, G. A. (1970). The market for "lemons": Quality uncertainty and the market mechanisms. *Quarterly Journal of Economics, 84,* 488–500.

Ang, S., & Inkpen, A. C. (2008). Cultural intelligence and offshore outsourcing success: A framework of firm-level Intercultural capability. *Decision Sciences, 39,* 337–358.

Arrow, K. (1962). Economic welfare and the allocation of resources for invention. In K. Arrow (Ed.), *The rate and direction of inventive activity: Economic and Social factors* (pp. 609–626). Princeton, NJ: Princeton University Press.

Balakrishnan, S., & Koza, M. (1993). Information asymmetry, adverse selection, and joint ventures. *Journal of Economic Behavior and Organization, 20,* 99–117.

Barkema, H. G., & Vermeulen, F. (1997). What differences in the cultural backgrounds of partners are detrimental for international joint ventures? *Journal of International Business Studies, 28,* 845–864.

Barkema, H., & Vermeulen, F. (1998). International expansion through start-up or acquisition: A learning perspective. *Academy of Management Journal, 41,* 7–26.

Barkema, H. G., Bell, J. H. J., & Pennings, J. M. (1996). Foreign entry, cultural barriers, and learning. *Strategic Management Journal, 17,* 151–166.

Bartlett, C. A., & Ghoshal, S. (1989). *Managing across borders: The transnational solution.* Boston, MA: Harvard Business School Press.

Brouthers, K., & Brouthers, L. (2003). Why service and manufacturing entry mode choices differ: The influence of transaction cost factors, risk, and trust. *Journal of Management Studies, 40,* 1179–1204.

Brouthers, K., Brouthers, L., & Werner, S. (2008). Real options, international entry mode choice and performance. *Journal of Management Studies, 45,* 936–960.

Capron, L. (1999). The long-term performance of horizontal acquisitions. *Strategic Management Journal, 20,* 987–1018.

Capron, L., & Guillén, M. (2009). National corporate governance institutions and post-acquisition target reorganization. *Strategic Management Journal, 30,* 803–833.

Caves, R., & Mehra, S. (1986). Entry of foreign multinationals into U.S. manufacturing industries. In M. Porter (Ed.). *Competition in global industries* (pp. 449–481). Boston, MA: Harvard Business School Press.

Child, P. (2006). Lessons from a global retailer: An interview with the president of Carrefour China. *McKinsey Quarterly,* special edition, 70–81.

Cohen, W., & Levinthal, D. (1990). Absorptive capacity: A new perspective on learning and innovation. *Administrative Science Quarterly, 35,* 128–152.

Collis, D. J., & Montgomery, C. A. (1998). *Corporate strategy: A resource-based approach.* Boston, MA: Irwin McGraw-Hill.

Cuervo-Cazurra, A., & Genç, M. (2008). Transforming disadvantages into advantages: Developing country MNEs in the least developed countries. *Journal of International Business Studies, 39,* 957–979.

Das, G. (1993, March–April). Local memoirs of a global manager. *Harvard Business Review,* 38–47.

Das, T. K., & Kumar, R. (2009). Interpartner harmony in strategic alliances: Managing commitment and forbearance. *International Journal of Strategic Business Alliances, 1,* 24–52.

Das, T. K., & Teng, B. (1998). Between trust and control: Developing confidence in partner cooperation in alliances. *Academy of Management Review, 23,* 491–512.

Dierickx, I., & Cool, K. (1989). Asset stock accumulation and the sustainability of competitive advantage. *Management Science, 35,* 1504–1511.

Doz, Y. L. (1996). The evolution of cooperation in strategic alliances: Initial conditions, or learning processes? *Strategic Management Journal, 17,* 55–83.

Doz, Y. L., Santos, J., & Williamson, P. (2001) *From global to metanational: How companies win in the knowledge economy.* Boston, MA: Harvard Business School Press.

Dyer, J., & Singh, H. (1998). The relational view: Cooperative strategy and sources of interorganizational competitive advantage. *Academy of Management Review, 23,* 660–679.

Erramilli, M. K. (1996). Nationality and subsidiary ownership patterns in multinational corporations. *Journal of International Business Studies, 27,* 225–248.

Evans, J., & Mavondo, F. T. (2002). Psychic distance and organizational performance: An empirical examination of international retailing operations. *Journal of International Business Studies, 33,* 515–532.

Garrette, B., Castañer, X., & Dussauge, P. (2009). Horizontal alliances as an alternative to autonomous production: Product expansion mode choice in the worldwide aircraft industry, 1945–2000. *Strategic Management Journal, 30,* 885–894.

Genç, M., & Castañer, X. (2009). *Country institutional environments and multinational enterprise profitability: An empirical analysis in banking.* Unpublished working paper, Baruch College, City University of New York, New York.

Ghemawat, P. (2001). Distance still matters. The hard reality of global expansion. *Harvard Business Review, 79*(8), 137–147.

Ghemawat, P. (2003). The forgotten strategy. *Harvard Business Review, 81*(11), 76–84.

Goerzen, A., & Beamish, P. W. (2003). Geographic scope and multinational enterprise performance. *Strategic Management Journal, 24),* 1289–1306.

Gomes-Casseres, B. (1989). Ownership structures of foreign subsidiaries: Theory and evidence. *Journal of Economic Behavior and Organization, 11,* 1–25.

Gomes-Casseres, B., & McQuade, K. (1991). *Xerox and Fuji Xerox (case # 9-391-156).* Cambridge, MA: Harvard Business School Publishing.

Gulati, R. (1995). Does familiarity breed trust? The implications of repeated ties for contractual choice in alliances. *Academy of Management Journal, 38,* 85–112.

Gulati, R., & Singh, H. (1998). The architecture of cooperation: Managing coordination costs and appropriation concerns in strategic alliances. *Administrative Science Quarterly, 43,* 781–814.

Gupta, A. K., & Govindarajan, V. (2001). Converting global presence into global competitive advantage. *Academy of Management Executive, 15*(2), 45–56.

Gupta, A. K., & Govindarajan, V. (2002). Cultivating a global mindset. *Academy of Management Executive, 16*(1), 116–126.

Haleblian, J., & Finkelstein, S. (1999). The influence of organizational acquisition experience on acquisition performance: A behavioral perspective. *Administrative Science Quarterly, 44*, 29–56.
Hall, E. T. (1959). *The silent language*. Greenwich, CT: Fawcett.
Hambrick, D. C., & Cannella, A. A. (1993). Relative standing: A framework for understanding departures. *Academy of Management Journal, 36*, 733–763.
Hamel, G. (1991). Competition for competence and inter-partner learning within international strategic alliances. *Strategic Management Journal, 12*, 83–103.
Hart, J. A. (1992). *Rival Capitalists: International competitiveness in the United States, Japan, and Western Europe*. Ithaca, NY: Cornell University Press.
Hennart, J. -F. (1988). A transaction costs theory of equity joint ventures. *Strategic Management Journal, 9*, 361–374.
Hennart, J. -F. (2009). Down with MNE-centric theories! Market entry and expansion as the bundling of MNE and local assets. *Journal of International Business Studies, 40*, 1432–1454.
Hennart, J. -F., & Larimo, J. (1998). The impact of culture on the strategy of multinational enterprises: Does national origin affect ownership decisions? *Journal of International Business Studies, 29*, 515–538.
Hennart, J. -F., & Park, Y. R. (1993). Greenfield vs. acquisition: The strategy of Japanese investors in the United States. *Management Science, 39*, 1054–1070
Hennart, J. -F., & Reddy, S. (1997). The choice between mergers/acquisitions and joint ventures: The case of Japanese investors in the United States. *Strategic Management Journal, 18*, 1–12.
Hennart, J. -F., & Zeng, M. (2002). Cross-cultural differences and joint venture longevity. *Journal of International Business Studies, 33*, 699–716.
Henisz, W. J. (2000). The institutional environment for multinational investment. *Journal of Law, Economics, and Organization, 16*, 334–364.
Hofstede, G. H. (2001). *Culture's consequences: International differences in work-related values*. Beverly Hills, CA: SAGE.
House, R. J., Hanges, P. J., Javidan, M., Dorfman, P. W., & Gupta, V. (2004). *Leadership culture and organizations: The GLOBE study of 62 societies*. Thousand Oaks, CA: SAGE.
Hymer, S. (1976). *The international operations of national firms: A study of direct investment*. Cambridge, MA: MIT Press.
Immelt, J. R., Govindarajan, V., & Trimble, C. (2009). How GE is disrupting itself. *Harvard Business Review, 87*(10), 56–65.
Jemison, D. B., & Sitkin, S. B. (1986). Corporate acquisitions: A process perspective. *Academy of Management Review, 11*(1), 145–154.
Johanson, J., & Vahlne, J. -E. (1977). The internationalization process of the firm: A model of knowledge development and increasing foreign market commitments. *Journal of International Business Studies, 8*, 25–34.
Kaufmann, D., Kraay, A., & Mastruzzi, M. (2003). *Governance matters III: Governance indicators 1996-2002*. Working Paper 3106. Washington, DC. World Bank.
Kekic, L. (2009, October 8). The global economic crisis and FDI flows to emerging markets. *Columbia FDI Perspectives, No. 15*.
Khanna, T., & Palepu, K. (2006). Emerging giants: Building world-class companies in Developing Countries. *Harvard Business Review, 84*(10), 60–69.

Khanna, T., Palepu, K. G., & Sinha, J. (2005). Strategies that fit emerging markets. *Harvard Business Review, 83*(6), 63–76.

Kobrin, S. J. (1979). Political risk: A review and reconsideration. *Journal of International Business Studies, 10,* 67–80.

Kogut, B. (1989). The stability of joint ventures: Reciprocity and competitive rivalry. *Journal of Industrial Economics, 38,* 183–198.

Kogut, B. (1991). Joint ventures and the option to expand and acquire. *Management Science, 37,* 19–32.

Kogut, B., & Singh, H. (1988). The effect of national culture on the choice of entry mode. *Journal of International Business Studies, 19,* 411–432.

Kogut, B., & Zander, U. (1993). Knowledge of the firm and the evolutionary theory of the multinational corporation. *Journal of International Business Studies, 24,* 625–645.

Kostova, T. (1999). Transnational transfer of strategic organizational practices: A contextual perspective. *Academy of Management Review, 24,* 308–324.

Kostova, T., & Roth, K. (2002). Adoption of an organizational practice by subsidiaries of multinational corporations: Institutional and relational effects. *Academy of Management Journal 45,* 215–233.

Kumar, R., & Das, T. K. (2007). Interpartner legitimacy in the alliance development process. *Journal of Management Studies, 44,* 1425–1453.

Larsson, R., & Finkelstein, S. (1999). Integrating strategic, organizational, and human resource perspectives on mergers and acquisitions: A case survey of synergy realization. *Organization Science, 10,* 1–26.

Lee, J. Y., & Mansfield, E. (1996). Intellectual property protection and U.S. foreign direct investment. *Review of Economics and Statistics, 78*(2), 181–186.

Levinthal, D., & March, J. G. (1993). The myopia of learning. *Strategic Management Journal, 14*(Winter Special Issue), 95–112.

Luo, Y. (2002). Capability exploitation and building in a foreign market: Implications for multinational enterprises. *Organization Science, 13,* 48–63.

Luo, Y., & Peng, M. W. (1999). Learning to compete in a transition economy: Experience, environment, and performance. *Journal of International Business Studies, 30,* 269–296.

March, J. G. (1991). Exploration and exploitation in organizational learning. *Organization Science, 2*(1), 1–13.

Martínez, J. I., & Jarillo, J. (1989). The evolution of research on coordination mechanisms in multinational corporations. *Journal of International Business Studies, 20,* 489–514.

Matthews, J. A. (2006). Dragon multinationals: New players in 21st century globalization. *Asia Pacific Journal of Management, 23,* 5–27.

Meyer, K. E. (2001). Institutions, transaction costs and entry mode choice in Eastern Europe. *Journal of International Business Studies, 32,* 357–367.

Morosini, P., Shane, S., & Singh, H. (1998). National cultural distance and cross-border acquisition performance. *Journal of International Business Studies, 29,* 137–158.

Murtha, T. P., Lenway, S. A., & Bagozzi, R. P. (1998). Global mind-sets and cognitive shift in a complex multinational corporation. *Strategic Management Journal, 19,* 97–114.

North, D. C. (1990). *Institutions, institutional change, and economic performance.* New York, NY: Cambridge University Press.

Park, S. -H., & Ungson, G. (1997). The effect of national culture, organizational complementarity, and economic motivation on joint venture dissolution. *Academy of Management Journal, 40,* 279–307.

Perlmutter, H. V. (1969). The tortuous evolution of the multinational corporation. *Columbia Journal of World Business, 4*(1), 9–18.

Reich, R., & Mankin, E. (1986, March/April). Joint ventures with Japan give away our future. *Harvard Business Review,* 78–86.

Reuer, J., & Ariño, A. (2007). Strategic alliances contracts: Dimensions and determinants of contractual complexity. *Strategic Management Journal, 28,* 313–330.

Ring, P., & Van de Ven, A. (1992). Structuring cooperative interorganizational relationships. *Strategic Management Journal, 13,* 483–498.

Scott, R. W. (2001). *Institutions and organizations* (2nd ed.). Thousand Oaks, CA: SAGE.

Siegel, J. I., & Chang, J. J. (2008). *Samsung Electronics (Case # 9-705-508).* Boston, MA: Harvard Business School.

Staw, B. M. (1981). The escalation of commitment to a course of action. *Academy of Management Review, 6,* 577–587.

Steensma, H. K., Tihanyi, L., Lyles, M. A., & Dhanaraj, C. (2005). The evolving value of foreign partnerships in transitioning economies. *Academy of Management Journal, 48,* 213–2325.

Steensma, H. K., Barden, J. Q., Dhanaraj, C., Lyles, M. A., & Tihanyi, L. (2008). The evolution and internalization of international joint ventures in a transitioning economy. *Journal of International Business Studies, 39,* 491–507.

Teece, D. (1986). Profiting from technological innovation. *Research Policy, 15,* 285–305.

Tihanyi, L., Griffith, D. A., & Russell, C. J. (2005). The effect of cultural distance on entry mode choice, international diversification, and MNE performance: A meta-analysis. *Journal of International Business Studies, 36,* 270–283.

Very, P., Lubatkin, M., Calori, R., & Veiga, J. (1997). Relative standing and the performance of recently acquired European firms. *Strategic Management Journal, 18*(8), 593–614.

Walsh, J. P. (1988). Top management turnover following mergers and acquisitions. *Strategic Management Journal, 9(2),* 173–183.

Williamson, O. (1991). Comparative economic organization: The analysis of discrete structural alternatives. *Administrative Science Quarterly, 36,* 269–298.

Yiu, D., & Makino, S. (2002). The choice between joint venture and wholly-owned subsidiary: An institutional perspective. *Organization Science, 13*(6), 667–683.

Zaheer, A., McEvily, B., & Perrone, V. (1998). Does trust matter? Exploring the effects of interorganizational and interpersonal trust on performance. *Organization Science, 9,* 141–159.

Zaheer, S. (1995). Overcoming the liability of foreignness. *Academy of Management Journal, 38*(2), 341–363.

Zaheer, S., Schomaker, M., & Genç, M. (2003). Identity versus culture in mergers of equals. *European Management Journal, 21*(2), 185–191.

CHAPTER 2

SMARTER MOVER ADVANTAGE

A Longitudinal Analysis of International Joint Ventures in China's Auto Market

Qingjiu Tao, John E. Prescott, and Sean Tsuhsiang Hsu

Integrating the resource-based view and entry order effect research, we study two key international joint venture decisions, entry timing and initial resource commitment and their impact on intrafirm performance variation through a firm's life course and inter-firm performance variation overtime. Life course data for 113 international joint ventures in the Chinese auto industry (1983–2003) form a longitudinal dataset. Employing hierarchical linear modeling (HLM) allows us to isolate the economic consequences and developmental trend of the main and interaction effects of entry timing and initial resource commitment on joint venture performance. Our results indicate that early entry is a significant factor in initial performance, but not significant for long-term success. Early movers with high initial resource commitment are more likely to succeed in the long run but take time to achieve profitability. Late entrants with high initial resource commitments have positive performance. Methodologically, it is one of the first attempts to introduce HLM to international joint venture research where the important

Strategic Alliances in a Globalizing World, pp. 27–52

issue of parameter variation across firms or over time has not been effectively addressed. The results illustrate that longitudinal analysis is a more reliable and powerful tool in uncovering complex, dynamic relationships in entry order research. Our study also contributes to managerial practice by recognizing the interrelatedness of two key strategic decisions facing managers during time of international expansion.

INTRODUCTION

In emerging market economies such as China, international joint ventures have been the major market entry mode for multinational corporations. According to the resource-based view (RBV) of the firm, the rationale for alliance formation is the value creation potential of pooling unique, heterogeneous resources from two or more firms to achieve competitive advantages not possible through individual efforts (Das & Teng, 2000; Nielsen, 2003). In order to succeed in an emerging market, managers make strategic decisions on when to form a joint venture and the amount of initial resource commitment.[1] How managers address these two nested questions form the basis for entry decisions, have long-term performance consequences and are the focus of this chapter. Within the international joint venture context, firms forming ventures at different times, with different initial resource commitments can be conceptualized as an evolutionary process (Steensma, Barden, Dhanaraj, Lyles, & Tihanyi, 2008). By treating these two strategic decisions as interrelated and examining the entire life course history of international joint ventures we can better reveal the underlying causes/mechanisms related to their success and failure. We are specifically interested in the performance fluctuation of a joint venture since its founding and the persistence of performance differences among firms in the Chinese auto industry. Our context is unique and a controlled setting in the sense that the Chinese government mandated that interorganizational relationships in the auto industry must involve joint ventures with a Chinese partner. Our approach is consistent with the resource-based view's concern of why firms differ and how they achieve and sustain competitive advantages (Rumelt, Schendel, & Teece, 1994).

Timing of foreign direct investment plays a critical role in multinational corporations' international market entry strategy (Frynas, Mellahi, & Pigman, 2006; Luo & Peng, 1998). Over the years, numerous researchers have examined the relationship between timing of international market entry and its performance consequences (Buckley & Casson, 1981; Frynas et al., 2006; Isobe, Makino, & Montgomery, 2000;

Lieberman & Montgomery, 1998; Luo, 1998; Luo & Peng, 1999; Mascarenhas, 1992). However, the first-mover advantage (FMA) literature has provided a fuzzy picture about the existence and the magnitude of pioneering effects (Golder & Tellis, 1993; Kerin, Varadarajan, & Peterson, 1992; Lieberman & Montgomery, 1988; Suarez & Lanzolla, 2007). The majority of the literature has used cross-sectional data sets and short time periods to measure the success and failure of players in the market. This approach is not only subject to survivor bias but is also subject to observation time bias. Additionally, the nature of sustainable competitive advantage calls for longitudinal designs for the empirical testing of the timing-performance relationship (Eisenmann, 2006).

The extant literature in joint venture formation and timing of market entry has yet to address how the joint impact of initial market entry timing and initial resources commitment influence a joint venture's performance over its life course. In this chapter, we explore the following questions: How does market entry timing and initial resource commitments help explain interfirm performance differences and intrafirm performance trends in an emerging market environment? Equally important, what are the interaction effects of these two key nested strategic decisions on the performance of joint ventures over their life course?

THEORETICAL BACKGROUND

Research on Entry Order Effects (First Mover Advantages)

First-mover advantage can be defined as the ability of pioneering firms to earn positive economic profits (Lieberman & Montgomery, 1988; Suarez & Lanzolla, 2007). Previous studies on first-mover advantages have produced equivocal results both in their theoretical explanations as well as empirical documentation (see Suarez & Lanzolla, 2007 for a recent review). Two leading perspectives have been offered to explain first-mover advantage: economic and behavioral.

According to an economic perspective, when an industry has high economies of scale, high customer switching costs, steep experience curves, or network effects competitors try to establish early foot holds and develop a dominant market share position (Eisenmann, 2006). Under these conditions, firms that move early gain advantage over those that move later. Hence, the pioneering firms establish a significant barrier to entry. The barrier to entry implies that additional and significant resources must be expended by a nonpioneering firm to compete effectively in the marketplace relative to first movers (Kerin et al., 1992). The most often mentioned entry barriers are scale effects, experience effects, learning effects, asymmetric information about the product quality and risk-averse buyers, difference in marginal effects of advertising, reputation effects, technological leadership, preemption of scare resources, and buyer switching costs ((Eisenmann, 2006; Karakaya & Stahl, 1989). IJVs in general and the auto industry in particular are excellent contexts to study FMA because they exhibit many of the entry barriers hypothesized to contribute to sustained performance.

The lead-time that first movers earn brings monopolistic profit (Wooster, 2006). Game theorists have shown analytically the conditions under which a firm purposefully decides to be a first mover or later entrant (Gal-Or, 1987). However, these economic arguments supportive of first-mover advantages have rarely considered product-market, international or political contingencies that may moderate the proposed advantages of pioneering effects (Frynas et al., 2006).

According to the behavioral and marketing perspectives (Suarez & Lanzolla, 2007), at the product or brand level, being first in the marketplace results in a higher degree of consumer awareness and ongoing repurchase behavior which minimizes consumer perceived risk and information costs. Once this pattern is established, consumers may be reluctant to switch brands when other less know brands enter the market. Similar arguments derived from the psychology literature suggest that the first product introduced receives a disproportionate attention in consumers' minds. Late entrants must have a truly superior product, address an untapped market or else advertise more extensively than incumbents in order to be noticed by the consumer (Christensen, Anthony, & Roth, 2004; Lieberman & Montgomery, 1988).

In terms of the role of learning in consumer preference formation, when consumers know little about the product a first mover may be able to influence how attributes are valued and define the ideal attribute combination,. In effect, through its marketing efforts, the first mover may be able to establish the perceptual structure of the market to its advantage (Carpenter & Nakamoto, 1990).

However, behavioral and marketing perspectives fail to represent reality adequately in certain aspects. The implicit assumptions behind these perspectives are that: first movers can offer a high quality product, choose the correct positioning and pursue the most desirable competitive strategy. On the other hand, follower brands are assumed to create a me-too brand (Kerin et al., 1992). These assumptions ignore the possibility that a later entrant has the organizational skills and capabilities to attract the first mover's customers and customers newly entering the market by offering a product of perceived superior value.

While the above mentioned theoretical perspectives for the effects of FMA are appealing, the empirical evidence is less clear. For example, Kerin et al. (1992) examined 13 empirical studies on the first-mover advantage (FMA) issue. They found that these studies did not provide strong support for the effect of the pioneering effect. Many of these studies were found to be flawed in their methods in terms of "survivor bias" and timing measurement. Extending this line of reasoning, Lieberman and Montgomery (1998) summarized empirical work in the FMA stream and drew a number of general conclusions: (1) Entry order effects exist, especially with respect to market share, but they are better specified as interactions than as direct effects; (2) The magnitude of first-mover advantage varies greatly across product categories and geographic markets; (3) FMA dissipate over time but are enhanced by longer lead-time before competitive entry; and (4) Entry order effects, although significant and robust, are weaker than "marketing mix" effects related to price and advertising. Thus, late entrants can catch up to and surpass pioneers. More recently, Suarez and Lanzolla (2007) in a review of the FMA literature theorize how the pace of market and technological evolution interact to facilitate or hinder FMA.

The reviews of FMA research suggest that the resource based view (RBV) and FMA are related conceptual frameworks that can benefit from closer linkage. For example, the findings of FMA studies on initial resource commitments or resource accumulation can add to the RBV which seeks to explain sustained competitive advantage. Similarly, the FMA research stream can be strengthened if positioned within the broad theoretical perspective of RBV since FMA can be conceptualized as a resource. Researchers have also called for more international and cross-cultural studies to determine if the drivers of first-mover success and failure differ across countries (Frynas et al., 2006; Parkhe, 1993).

In summary, though research on first-mover advantage has provided valuable insights into the mechanisms underlying hypothesized effects, they have not succeeded in achieving compelling evidence that pioneering effect exist and persist over time. Additionally, most empirical studies have been conducted in mature market economies; fewer studies have been in the context of emerging market economies where there are opportunities for MNCs to explore first-mover advantages as well as late mover effects (Steensma et al., 2008; Wooster, 2006). Finally, a key weakness in much of the literature is the use of cross-sectional data sets that cannot avoid survivor bias and observation timing bias. We argue that though the theoretical importance of entry timing is suggested to be positively associated with organizational performance, the mixed empirical findings have somewhat limited the concepts strategic value for managers. One of the key questions we address is the timing of performance measurement. We suggest that performance should be measured over the life course of IJVs. Performance measurement should be examined during the early stage of market entry when there are only a few players as well as during later stages of the entry when the market has begun to mature. A life course measurement of IJV performance addresses both survivor and timing bias. That is, if we select two different time periods in the same market, we may find different results for the timing-performance relationship based on either of the biases. Thus, both the nature of resource-based advantages and the theoretical conceptualization of first mover advantages call for a longitudinal design. In Table 2.1, we highlight the limitation and deficiencies in the existing literature in explaining long-term performance variation within individual and across different IJVs as well as how we address them.

The Resource-Based View of Joint Venture Formation, Entry Timing, and Initial Resource Commitment

The resource-based theory views companies as unique collections of physical and intangible assets and capabilities (Barney, 1991). No two companies are alike because no two companies have the same set of experiences, acquired the same assets and skills or built the same organization cultures. These assets and capabilities determine how effectively and efficiently a company performs its functional activities (Collis & Montgomery, 1995). Following this logic, a company will be positioned to succeed in a market if it has the best and most appropriate stocks of resources and capabilities.

Table 2.1. Comparison of Most Extant Research and Current Approach

Streams of Literature	*Limitations and Deficiencies*	*How This Study Will Address These Limitations*
Entry Order Effects	Cross-sectional Data Set	Longitudinal Design
	Survivor Bias	Life Course History
	Lack of Consideration of Key Nested Factors	Interaction Effects
	Needs More Sophisticated Design and Analytical Tools	RBV as Theory Base HLM
	Market share as the main measure	Add Profit as a new measure
Initial Resource Commitment	Lack of Dynamic Change	Longitudinal Analysis
RBV and Joint Venture	Lack of Strong Empirical Base	Combination of RBV and Entry Order Research

A resource-based view of joint ventures suggests that the formation of a joint venture is about creating the most value out of one's existing resources by combining them with other firm resources, provided, of course, that this combination results in optimal returns (Das & Teng, 2000). Competitive advantage can be ultimately attributed to the ownership of valuable resources that enable the company to perform activities better or cheaper than competitors. Competitive advantage will therefore be based on developing a distinct set of resources and deploying them in a well-conceived strategy. Joint venture formation can be seen as one strategic move to secure a desirable position. Das and Teng argue that strategic alliances are essentially the result of resource integration among firms. The very objective of forming alliances is to join forces with partners in order to pursue market opportunities that are otherwise beyond reach. Each of the partners involved in forming the joint venture brings a set of unique resources to the joint venture. It is the combined resources that give the joint venture a competitive advantage over it competitors. The collective strength of the joint venture's overall resource endowments and capabilities contribute to ultimate joint venture performance (Beamish, 1987; Lu & Beamish, 2006). In this chapter we focus on one way for assessing the collective strength of a joint venture; its initial timing of entry and initial resource commitment.

To understand the path to success or failure, we draw mainly on the resource-based view of the firm and evolutionary perspective (Aldrich, 1999). The RBV suggests that performance differences are the result of imperfect strategic factor market and/or various path-dependent, historical processes of learning and asset accumulation (Barney, 1991; Dierickx & Cool, 1989). Before an IJV is formed, managers in the parent firms decide when the IJV should be established and how much resources (initial investment) are needed by the new joint venture.

Given that RBV is ultimately a theory about how to extract rent from resources (Peng, 2001), in an emerging market environment, those firm who can acquire a favorable initial resource position should be able to earn a early success, however, the sustainability of the early mover advantage should depend on joint effects of both the initial resource commitment and the timing of entry.

The Direct Effect of Timing

Timing or order of entry is a critical decision in international expansion; this is especially true in the context of emerging market economies (Luo & Peng, 1998). Many researchers have suggested that foreign investors should seek to obtain a first mover advantage since competition in the market will intensify over time (Luo, 1998; Shenkar, 1990; Wooster, 2006). When entering an emerging market, early movers can exercise technological leadership, have preemptive investment opportunities and set up higher entry barrier for late entrants.

On the other hand, another stream of research supports the wait-and-see approach, arguing that followers can benefit from early mover's efforts in learning and environment stabilization. Therefore, late movers are in a better position to be successful in the market (Luo, 1998). Given the long-lasting theoretical debate between the two camps, we need to go back to the empirical evidences and look for some answer or ways to address the problem. While the literature provides a somewhat mixed perspective, there is a significant amount of research that suggest that early entrants achieve positive benefits although how long and under what circumstances the benefits persist are topics that need extensive research (Kerin et al., 1992; Lieberman & Montgomery, 1998; Suarez & Lanzolla; 2007). Interestingly, both perspectives can be accurate.

The resource base view suggests that early movers are more likely to acquire rare, valuable and difficult to imitate resources in the market (Lieberman & Montgomery, 1998). In China's auto industry, early movers like Beijing Jeep and Shanghai VW received strong support from central and local governments in establishing supplier network, hard currency access, and so forth. These preferential treatments were not as readily available to later movers such as Honda and Toyota. Based on the literature and anecdotal we hypothesize the following:

Hypothesis 1a: Early timing will lead to positive initial performance for an IJV, ceteris paribus.

Hypothesis 1b: Early timing will lead to a positive performance trend over the life course of the IJV, ceteris paribus.

The Direct Effect of Initial Resource Commitment

According to resource-based view, resource commitment and deployment determine the sustainability of a firm's competitive advantages (Prahalad & Hamel, 1990). In this chapter, we define resource commitment as the size of resources (initial investment) that the foreign partners bring to the joint venture. If we assume the joint venture formation is a mutual selection process among potential partners, it is logical to expect that foreign firms with higher initial resource commitments can select or be selected by the most competent local partners. Initial investment in a joint venture, though measured in monetary value, includes capital, technology, management know-how, international marketing network, and so forth, from the foreign company (Eisenmann, 2006; Hitt, Dacin, Levitas, Arregle, & Borza, 2000). Combined with the complementary resources from the local partner, which usually includes capital, production facility, local market knowledge, and so forth, a joint venture creates its initial resource profile to start the operation.

Large-scale entry with more resources signals commitment to a market, it can also overcome entry barriers associated with absolute cost or scale economies (Mascarenhas, 1997). This is especially true in a manufacturing industry such as automobile. As an industry evolves toward maturity, demand becomes price-sensitive and as production becomes more efficient, small firms are more likely to fail when competing against large firms (Olleros, 1986).

It has been well-established that large-scale entry in domestic market leads to higher performance (Hobson & Morrison, 1983; MacMillan & Day, 1987). Dunne, Roberts, and Samuelson (1989) found that small entrants in U.S. based manufacturing industries had higher failure rates. However, several arguments suggest that large-scale entry may not be the best strategy in an international market. International markets are typically smaller, less familiar and more uncertain; this is especially true when it comes to an emerging market environment such as China. Mascarenhas (1997) found that larger initial resource commitments do not result in higher market shares or market survival in international markets. First entrants typically commit fewer resources, suggesting that firms with limited resources can pursue this strategy. However, the author did not specify the entry mode of those firms. It is not clear whether such results hold for those entering the market through joint venture (which is the dominant mode in emerging markets) rather than wholly owned foreign enterprise. A strong local partner with substantial resources can significantly lower the risk to the joint venture. In this regard, Wooster (2006) found that entry through less risky modes such as joint ventures were associated with high positive returns. In the Internet start-up context, Eisenmann (2006) found that early movers spent more on upfront marketing than late entrants. In China's auto market, foreign partners cannot own more than 50% of the joint venture equity. Based on the evidence, we think that high initial resource commitment from a foreign partner will lead to partnering with a strong local partner and thus a stronger initial resource profile for the joint venture.

Hypothesis 2a: Higher initial resource commitment will lead to higher initial IJV performance, ceteris paribus.

Hypothesis 2b: Higher initial resource commitment will lead to a positive performance trend for IJVs, ceteris paribus.

The Interaction Effects of Timing and Initial Resource Commitment

Timing and initial resource commitments are two strategic factors in market entry decision and they are usually considered at the same time and are thus interdependent to some degree (Mascarenhas, 1997). If we combine the argument from the direct effects of timing and initial resource commitment, we would conclude that early movers with high initial resource commitment will be more likely to receive preferential treatment from central and local government, have a stronger resource profile to start with and have more potential to earn superior profitability and market share throughout their life course (see Figure 2.1.).

Figure 2.1 shows four different types of IJV entry modes. Each IJV entry mode is associated with a performance trend over its life course. The committed early mode is characterized by first mover IJVs with high levels of initial resource commitment. These ventures should have the highest level of performance based on the arguments for the individual effects of entry timing and resource commitment. Conversely, tentative late ventures have the worst performance because they arrive late to the market and have low initial resource commitments. We predict that committed late movers will have above average performance while tentative early movers will perform at levels below committed late movers. In our framework, we give primacy to initial resource commitment over entry

		Initial Resource Commitment	
		High	Low
Timing of Entry	Early	***Best Performer*** **Committed Early**	***Average*** **Tentative Early**
	Late	***Good*** **Committed Late**	***Worst*** **Tentative Late**

Figure 2.1. The effect of entry timing and initial resource commitment on firm performance trends.

time. Our rationale is based in RBV logic where the development of a strong resource profile can overcome the liabilities of late entry.

Hypothesis 3a: Early movers with high initial resource commitment (committed early) will outperform all other strategies in initial performance, ceteris paribus.

Hypothesis 3b: Early movers with high initial resource commitment (committed early) will lead to a positive performance trend, ceteris paribus.

Hypothesis 3c: Early movers with high initial resource commitment (committed early) will outperform all other strategies in the long run, ceteris paribus.

Hypothesis 3d: Late movers with high initial resource commitment (committed late) will outperform tentative early mover in the long run, ceteris paribus.

METHOD

International Joint Ventures in the Chinese Auto Industry

As stated by Hitt, Bierman, Shimizu, and Kochlar (2001), the challenge in testing the resource-based view is identifying the most critical resources for the question at hand. It is helpful to focus on a single industry in which critical resources are evident and measurable. China's auto industry has become one of the most attractive industries to foreign investors after 20 years of development (Peng, 2000) and the contracted foreign capital in this industry has surpassed U.S.$5 billion. By the end of 2000, the auto industry in China had established over 600 joint ventures with foreign investors from more than 20 countries and regions since it first utilized foreign capital in 1983. We selected international joint ventures in China's automobile industry as the population, and focused on the major assemblers since they are a homogenous group which has made on average the largest investments in the industry. Our sample size is 113.

Research Design

Our theoretical model calls for a longitudinal design where the same subjects (IJVs) are followed at successive points in time. The subjects (IJVs) are measured repeatedly on a number of variables relevant to the phenomenon of interest. This type of design is suitable for investigating matters of intraindividual (the initial resource commitment-performance path of an IJV) as well as interindividual change (the different performance paths among IJVs in the industry). Therefore, it is appropriate to explore the evolution of IJV performance given entry timing and initial resource commitment. For each joint venture, its evolution of performance is captured by its initial performance and its growth trend.

Data Collection

To understand the dynamics of international joint venture evolution, we studied extant literature in the areas of strategic alliances and firm evolution and supplemented this knowledge with fieldwork in a few international joint ventures (Shanghai GM, Delphi Shanghai, Shanghai Yanfeng) as well as archival date on China's auto industry from 1981 to 2002 A substantial number of other sources were used to verify and understand the industry context and firm behavior, including case studies, trade journals, newspapers and interviews with experts in the auto industry.

Several secondary data sources were used to obtain data and cross verify the reliability of the data including Online database for China's auto industry (1997–2002; Directory of FDI in China (1984–1996); Chinese Auto Industry Year Book (1983, 1985, 1987, 1989–2001); Directory of FDI in China's auto industry (1996, 2000–2001 version); Internal documents on automobile manufacturers (1982, 1983–1984, 1986–1988, 1989, 1991, 1995, 1996, 1999); and trade journals, newspapers, books, and CATRC (1999).

The data collection effort started in 1999 and has been ongoing. Three trips covered Shanghai, Beijing, Tianjin, and Shenyang in 2000, 2001 and 2002. The editors of the yearbooks and databases were directly contacted to ensure the accurate interpretation of the parameters.

Measures of Research Constructs

Timing of Joint Venture Formation

Two thousand two minus the year of joint venture formation is our measure of age. Since we are examining performance trends, entry date is a reflection of age and therefore allows us to model performance trends for age cohorts. There are two commonly used approaches for measuring competitive market entry, categorical and continuous. The categorical approach assesses entry order in terms of strategy types, such as first (early) mover, second mover and late movers (Luo, 1998). This approach is often used for analyzing an oligopolistic industry or a market segment. The continuous approach sees entry as a degree of earlier/later; it measures timing by using the time difference in entry date and a specific date (it can be the date when the first mover came in). We use the continuous approach for our direct hypotheses and the categorical approach for our interaction hypotheses because it fits our theoretical and methodological approach as well as our context.

Initial Resource Commitment

Initial investment (in dollar value) from the foreign partner is our operationalizations of initial resource commitment. The initial investment from the foreign partner usually includes capital investment as well as technological and management expertise; the latter two were typically factored in the total investment figure during the negotiation stage. This measure has also been viewed as size of entry as used by Mascarenhas (1997).

Performances of International Joint Ventures

In entry order research, market share has been widely used as a measure to show the existence of a first mover advantage effects (Kerin et al., 1992). We use annual sales as a proxy for market share. Lieberman and Montgomery (1998) among others have called for using profitability measures to test entry order effect. Based on data availability, we use net income per employee of the IJV as a measure of performance. These two measures have been widely used in the strategy as well as the international joint venture literature (Geringer & Hebert, 1991).

Control Variables

Entry Mode

The international market entry literature suggests that entry mode can influence the extent of the resource commitment and the degree of the project's local dependence (Beamish & Banks, 1987; Luo, 1998; Wooster, 2006). Since joint venture is the dominant form of FDI in China's auto industry and all the firms in our sample are joint ventures, Entry mode has been controlled.

Equity Ratio

Equity ratio of the foreign partner is treated as a control variable because it represents a firm's resource commitment level to the joint venture and may influence its relative power; the extent of control over the IJV operation (Luo, 1997; Shan, 1991).

Size of the Joint Venture

(Number of employees.) Consistent with previous studies (Gomes & Ramaswamy, 1999; Luo, 1997) firm size is employed as a control variable. Firm size is measure by number of employees in the joint venture each year-end. It is used to control for potential effect of scale economies.

Data Structure

The data set can be viewed as an accelerated longitudinal design (cohort-sequential design). It covers all the main international joint ventures (assemblers) in China's auto industry. The time span is from 1983 (the year when the first IJV was established) to 2002 which covers the foreign direct investments in the auto industry from when joint venture opportunities were allowed in China. For each observation (firm year), we have a series of industry data, firm level data including IJV characteristics and IJV performance.

Since IJVs are formed in different years, we have 19 cohorts of IJVs from 1981 to 2003. Within each cohort, the number of IJVs is different. This data structure is best viewed in terms of observations nested within each IJV.

Hierarchical Linear Modeling

Given the nature of our hypotheses and the data set, hierarchical linear modeling (HLM) is an appropriate analytical tool. HLM can explicitly recognize and investigate systematic individual change patterns over time, it can provide for the estimation of both static and longitudinal performance parameters (i.e., intercept and slope), and it enables analysis of both within- and between-firm performance change patterns. Especially noteworthy is the possibility for both the number of observations per individual (IJV), and the spacing of these observations in time (year of entry), to vary (Raudenbush & Bryk, 2002).

HLM allows for the investigation of both within-and between group effects on an individual-level dependent variable through an empirical Bayesian estimation process in which two different models are estimated iteratively. A within group or "level 1" analysis is used to estimate two separate parameters describing the relationship between the predictors and the focal dependent variable within each group (i.e., within-group intercepts and slope). These intercept and slope parameters obtained from the level-1 analysis serve as the dependent variables in equations used for a between-group or "level-2" analysis. A group-level or contextual effect is suggested by the presence of a significant parameter estimate (gamma coefficient, γ) for level-2 predictors of the level-1 intercepts. This provides the operational test for our hypothesis. Further, a significant gamma associated with a level-2 predictor in an equation modeling variance in the slope estimates indicates that the variable moderates the relationship between level-1 independent and dependent variables. This provides the operational test for our hypotheses.

Almost all longitudinal investigations conducted by organizational scientists are hierarchical in nature. The nested nature of these data would include multiple observations within a group and a sample of multiple groups. Thus, one would have a within unit level 1 model, and a between unit level-2 model. From a theoretical perspective, one is essentially investigating between group differences and within group change (Hofmann, 1997). While several researchers have discussed and demonstrated the hierarchical, nested nature of longitudinal data (Hofmann, Jacobs, & Baratta, 1993), the use of HLM or other multilevel methods in the management field is still somewhat limited. To our knowledge, this study will be one of the first systematic applications of HLM in the strategic alliance and market entry domain.

There are two performance measures, net income per employees and sales. In test one, profitability is used as the dependent variable. In test two, sales volume is used as the dependent variable. Initially we included Age squared (timing of entry) to test a possible quadratic growth curve; it turns out to be not significant in both tests, so we removed it in the final tests. In order to identify different paths of success, we treated the variables timing and initial resource commitment as discrete/class variables, so that we could divide the whole sample into four groups that represent four distinctive pathways or strategies at the time of market entry. The four groups are Committed Early, Committed Late, Tentative Early, and Tentative LATE (see Figure 2.1).

Given the two measures for performance, we conducted eight separate tests for the two-way interaction effects on initial performance and performance growth trend. Two-level HLM was used to obtain the initial performance (intercept) and performance growth trend (slope).

A summary of the model specified (in equation format) is presented below:

Level-1 Model

Y = B0 + B1*(AGE)+ R

Level-2 Model

B0 = G00 + G01*(TIMING) + G02*(investment) + G03*(T x I) + G04*(EQUITY) +U0

B1 = G10 + G11*(TIMING) + G12*(investment) + G13*(T x I) + G14*(EQUITY) +U1

Note: The outcome variable Y is Market Share or Profitability by the end of the year
AGE is the age of the IJV at the time of evaluation
TIMING is timing
Investment is initial investment in millions (1990 constant RMB)
T x I is the interaction term of timing and initial investment
EQUITY is the equity ratio of foreign partner
B0 is the market share at the end of first year (age 0)
B1 is the slope of the market share growth line
G01 tests the effect of timing on initial performance
G02 tests the effect of Initial resource commitment on initial performance
G03 tests the interaction effect of timing and initial resource commitment on initial performance
G11 tests the effect of timing on performance growth trend
G12 tests the effect of Initial resource commitment on performance growth trend
G13 tests the interaction effect of timing and initial resource commitment on performance growth trend

Profitability as the Dependent Variable

Descriptive Statistics and Model Explanation

Table 2.2 presents the number of observations, means, standard deviation and minimum, maximum value of level-1 variables. Table 2.3 presents the same descriptive statistics for level-2 variables. All the numbers are in constant 1990 RMB.

As shown in Table 2.4, Hypothesis 1a predicts a direct positive effect of timing on initial performance. The effect coefficient G01 is positive and significant, thus H1a receive strong support, which suggests early movers are more likely to obtain higher initial profit. Hypothesis 1b predicts a positive impact of timing on performance growth trend. The effect coefficient G11 is significant. However, the direction of the impact is negative. Thus, H1b is not supported. Therefore, the direct effect of early entry is positively related to initial profitability while its long term trend is not.

Hypothesis 2a predicts a direct positive effect of initial resource commitment on initial performance. The effect coefficient G02 is positive and significant, thus H2a receive full support, which suggests that even if a firms is a later comer to the market, a strong investment entry is more likely to bring initial profit. Hypothesis 2b predicts a positive impact of initial resource commitment on performance growth trend. The effect coefficient G12 is insignificant. Thus, H2b is not supported, which suggests that high initial resource commitment is not sufficient for a positive growth trend.

Hypothesis 3a predicts a positive interaction effect of timing and initial resource commitment on initial performance. The effect coefficient G03 is negative and significant, thus H3a was not supported in the expected

Table 2.2. Level-1 Descriptive Statistics for Variables (Assemblers)

Variable Name	*Number of Observations*	*Mean*	*Standard Deviation*	*Minimum*	*Maximum*
Age	692	5.04	3.54	0	18
Sales	692	119205.84	317908.73	23922.82	3173557.10
Net income	692	16577.80	61447.59	–85167.61	731599.70

Table 2.3. Level-2 Descriptive Statistics for Variables (Assemblers)

Variable Name	*Number of Observations*	*Mean*	*Standard Deviation*	*Minimum*	*Maximum*
Timing	119	8.49	3.48	2.00	19.00
Initial Resource Commitment	119	42.78	139.28	.04	901.84
Timing x Initial Resource Commitment	119	393.80	1260.86	.21	10822.08
Equity Ratio	119	43.95	18.5	5.00	95.00

Table 2.4. Results of HLM Analysis for Assemblers With Net Income per Employee as the Dependent Variable

Fixed Effect	*Coefficient*	*Standard Error*	*T-ratio*	*d.f.*	*p-value*
For Intercept, B0					
Intercept, G00	2808.34	3590.37	.782	114	.436
Timing, G01	2979.33	1085.07	2.746	114	.007**
Investment, G02	269.62	48.56	5.553	114	<.001***
T x I, G03	–43.14	5.47	–7.886	114	<.001***
Equity, G04	15.33	186.44	.082	114	.935
For AGE slope, B1					
Intercept, G10	1736.85	697.31	2.491	682	.013
Timing, G11	–401.49	149.29	–2.689	682	.008**
Investment, G12	3.56	12.01	.296	682	.767
T x I, G13	5.12	.93	5.487	682	<.001***
Equity, G14	–16.34	28.14	–.580	682	.561

Notes: $^{***}p < .001$; $^{**}p < .01$; $^{*}p < .05$

direction. Hypothesis 3b predicts positive interaction effects of timing and initial resources commitment on performance growth trend. The effect coefficient G13 is positive and significant, thus H3b receive strong support. Early entry coupled with a large initial investment suppresses profits in the short term but have a positive performance trend.

Sales as Dependent Variable

Table 2.5 shows the results for sales, a proxy for market share. The results for sales as a dependent variable parallel those with net income per employee as the dependent variable. The direct effects are positive while their performance trends are either significantly negative or insignificant. The interaction of timing and initial investment reveals a trade-off between a negative short term impact on sales and a positive performance trend.

Identifying the Paths to Success

The two-way interaction effects of both initial and performance trends of timing and initial investment on profit and sales test hypotheses H3a

Table 2.5. Result of HLM analysis for Assemblers With Sales as the Dependent Variable

Fixed Effect	*Coefficient*	*Standard Error*	*T-ratio*	*df*	*p-value*
For Intercept, B0					
Intercept, G00	24848.19	18197.89	1.365	114	.175
Timing, G01	13235.58	5575.85	2.374	114	.019 *
Investment, G02	1459.27	251.68	5.798	114	<.001 ***
T x I, G03	−209.32	28.40	−7.371	114	<.001 ***
Equity, G04	−92.49	957.22	−.097	114	.924
For AGE slope, B1					
Intercept, G10	12636.37	3332.14	3.792	682	<.001 ***
Timing, G11	−1941.26	724.07	−2.681	682	.008 **
Investment, G12	−22.50	58.05	−.388	682	.698
T x I, G13	27.48	4.52	6.073	682	<.001 ***
Equity, G14	−65.98	135.81	−.486	682	.627

Notes: $^{***}p < .001$; $^{**}p < .01$; $^{*}p < .05$

through H3d. To create the four groups depicted in Figure 2.1, we operationalized first movers and initial investment in the following way. Firms entering the market between 1983 and 1992 were classified as early movers and we used the midpoint year 1988. Firms that entered between 1992 and 2002 were classified as late movers and we used the midpoint year 1992. We used the median initial investment as the split point for high versus low investment. The analytical test results are available upon request. We plotted the results in Figure 2.2 and Figure 2.3, to provide a visual demonstration of the different paths.

Hypothesis 3a predicts that early movers with high initial investment (committed early) will outperform the other pathways in initial performance. The hypothesis was not supported. Using net income per

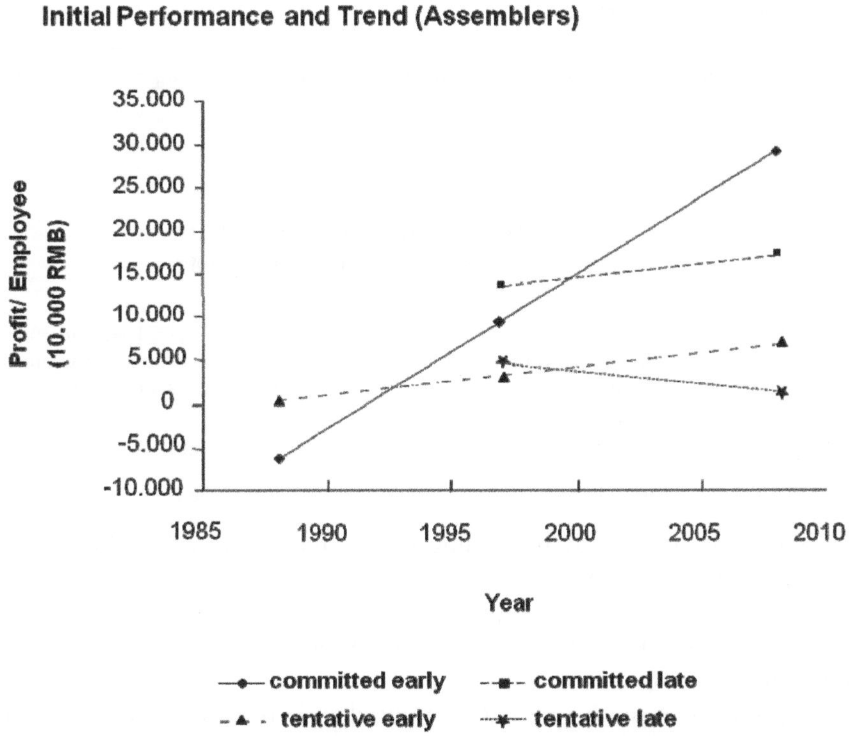

Note: For Early Movers, we assume they started in 1988, the mean between 1983 and 1992 We used 1992 as the dividing point for early or late, due to the historic change at the time. For Later Mover, we assume they started in 1997, the mean between 1992 and 2002.

Figure 2.2. Two-way interaction effects on net income per employee (with assemblers)

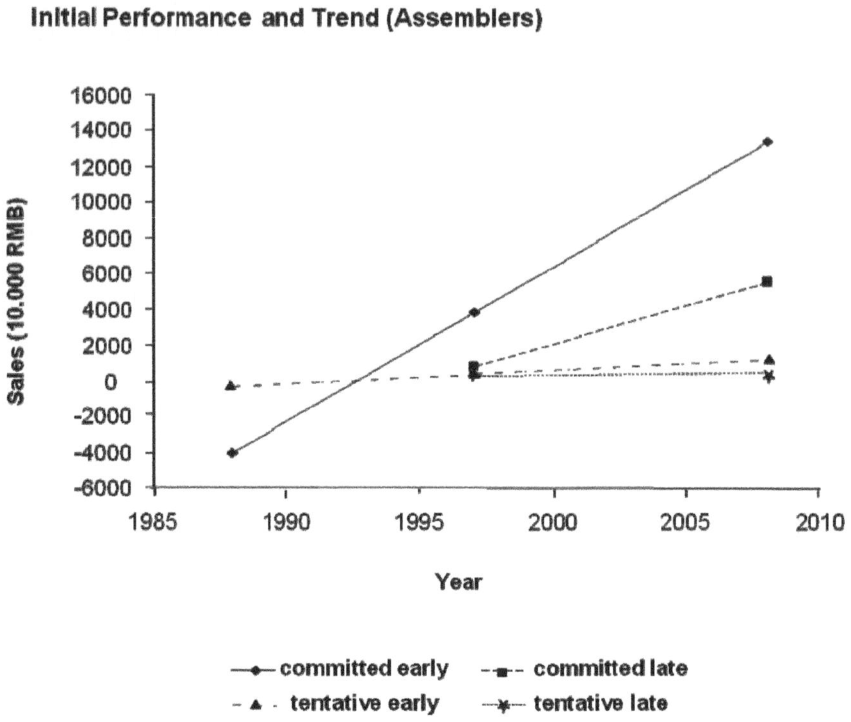

Note: For Early Movers, we assume they started in 1988, the mean between 1983 and 1992. We used 1992 as the dividing point for early or late, due to the historic change at the time. For Later Mover, we assume they started in 1997, the mean between 1992 and 2002.

Figure 2.3. Two-way interaction effects on sales (with assemblers).

employees as the dependent variable, committee late firms had the highest level of initial performance. Committed late firms also had the highest level of initial sales. Thus firms were able to enter the China auto market late and have positive initial performance as long as they had high levels of initial investment.

Hypothesis 3b predicted that committed early firms will exhibit a positive performance trend. Of the four approaches, committed early firms had the steepest performance trend for both profits and sales thus supporting the hypothesis. The most tenuous performance trends were with firms that were tentative either as first movers or late into the market. This results support our conjecture that for long term performance trends, initial investment trumps timing of entry.

Hypothesis 3c predicts committed early mover will outperform all other IJVs following different strategies. This hypothesis was supported for both the sales and net profit to employee dependent variables. Therefore moving early with high initial commitment is the best *long term* strategy for firms entering the Chinese automobile market.

Hypothesis 3d predicts committed late mover will outperform tentative early mover in the long run. This hypothesis was supported. For the profitability measure, the committed late movers and tentative early movers regression lines are parallel. However, the committed late regression line is significantly above the tentative early movers. In terms of sales, committed late and tentative early had similar starting points but committed late firms pulled away over time. This set of results is interesting because it points out alternative paths to success and explains why some late movers can outperform early movers.

DISCUSSION

We examined the direct and interaction effects of entry timing and initial resource commitment on international joint venture performance in the Chinese auto industry over its life course. Our context is unique in the sense that the only mode of entry into the Chinese auto market was through a joint venture. Thus, the setting can be considered a naturally occurring, quasi-experiment. A unique longitudinal database was developed and hierarchical linear modeling (HLM) was used to capture the evolutionary performance process of the joint ventures. Consistent with previous literature, we used sales (market share) as one of the performance measures and net income per employee as a profitability measure as called for by Lieberman and Montgomery (1998).

Our results showed that while early entry and high initial investment had positive effect on initial performance, they did not positively impact longer term performance trends. The interaction of early entry and high initial investment had a negative impact on initial performance but a positive performance trend over the ventures' life course. Of the four pathways, committed early firms had low initial performance but the most positive performance trend. Committed late ventures had the highest initial performance and a positive performance trend but not as high as committed early ventures. A key aspect of these findings is that it reveals multiple paths to success.

From a theory development standpoint, our study contributes to the integration of entry order effects and resource-base view. Investigating the performance trend evolution of joint ventures contributes to identifying empirical regularities and reconciling irregularities in the timing-performance relationship within the entry order effect literature (Suarez & Lanzolla, 2007). Additionally, our research contributes to the development of a resource-based theory of joint ventures. As Lieberman and Montgomery (1998) pointed out, the resource-based view has often been criticized for its lack of an empirical base, especially, of studies that consider how resources and capabilities contribute to the evolution of performance over time. Our study is one step in better understanding the interplay between initial resource commitment, entry timing and their impact on initial performance as well as performance trends over time.

Methodologically, individual growth modeling (HLM in this case) presents exciting opportunities in addressing performance trend questions with which researchers in the resource based and market entry areas are concerned. These methods allow for the analysis of longitudinal data and thus facilitate the process of uncovering multiple pathways along which successful performance trends may occur. A pathway approach is essential for researchers studying firm strategic behavior throughout its life course. The method outlined in this study allows for the incorporation of any number of predictors of development, including important contextual predictors such as industry environment, thus provide researcher with the tools to study the range of outcomes that may be associated with a particular set of predictors (multifinality) and to explore how similar outcomes may result from a variety of contexts (equifinality).

From the viewpoint of a strategist who seeks to find the best strategy to succeed in international market entry and establish a sustainable competitive advantage, this study has actionable implications. It is clear that moving fast or committing a high level of initial resources will not necessarily help a venture's initial success. However, early movers with high initial resource commitment on average will succeed in the long run. If a firm misses opportunities for early market entry their ventures can still be success if they enter late with high levels of initial resource commitment.

While this study has contributed several insights regarding the importance of using longitudinal data sets and the HML methodology in strategy and international market entry research, we identify a couple of interesting research tasks worth pursuing. First, extending our approach to other industries or the automobile industry in other emerging markets such as the Czech Republic, Mexico or Brazil where significant FDI activities can be found would be useful in understanding the generalizability of our results. Second, developing more comprehensive measures of a joint venture's resource profile (position) and studying its evolution is an intriguing area. Third, local firms in Chinese auto market have experienced co-evolutionary pressures during the past 2 decades. A longitudinal study on strategic behavior in a rapidly changing institutional environment and their performance/survival consequences can help address some of the fundamental questions in the strategy field: Why do firm differ? How do firms behave during co-evolution? What determines the international success or failure of joint ventures? (Peng, 2000).

Our study has a number of limitations worth noting. First, we use a one industry/market setting in one emerging market; generalizations to other contexts may not be warranted. China's auto industry has experienced a remarkable development in the last 2 decades and its institutional environment is very different from developed economies. However, the overall evolution from a centralized economy to a more decentralized economy is a common phenomenon in many emerging markets especially in the former planned economies, such as the Czech Republic, Poland, and Hungary.

Second, while we had 19 cohorts in our data set, it is limited in the sense that many firms were late entrants and therefore had fewer years of observations. The waves of data collected are still limited. More complex growth models increase data requirements—a quadratic model requires at least four waves, cubic models at least five. Parameter estimation will improve if additional waves of data are added to the sample. Third, we were able to collect a limited set of joint venture characteristics due to data availability. It would be useful to have additional controls to eliminate alternative hypotheses. Fourth, the inclusion of ongoing resource commitments over the life course of the ventures would provide additional insights into the concept of capability building and its impact on performance.

Examining the initial resource commitment, entry timing decisions and their performance implications for international joint ventures across their life course provides a rich theoretical and empirical foundation for beginning to resolve the mixed findings in this stream of research. We hope that in some small way, we encourage other researchers to explore similar types of questions in the international joint venture stream of research.

NOTE

1. A third set of decisions regarding the amount and timing of resource commitment over time is not part of this study but worthy of study.

REFERENCES

Aldrich, H. E. (1999). *Organizations evolving*. London, England: SAGE.

Barney, J. (1991). Firm resources and the theory of competitive advantage. *Journal of Management, 17*, 99–120.

Beamish, P. W. (1987). Joint venture in LDCs: Partner selection and performance. *Management International Review, 27*, 23–37.

Beamish, P. W., & Banks, J. C. (1987). Equity joint ventures and the theory of the multinational enterprise. *Journal of International Business Studies, 18*, 1–16.

Buckley, P. J., & Casson, M. (1981). The optimal timing of a foreign direct investment. *Economic Journal, 91*, 75–87.

Carpenter, G., & Nakamoto, K. (1990). Competitive strategies for late entry into a market with a dominant brand. *Management Science, 16*, 1268–1278.

CATRC. (1999). *Chinese automotive industry yearbook*. Tianjin, China: China Automotive Technology Research Center.

Christensen, C., Anthony, S., & Roth, E. (2004). *Seeing what's next*. Boston, MA: Harvard Business School Press.

Collis, D. J., & Montgomery, C. A. (1995, July–August). Competing on resources: Strategy in 1990s. *Harvard Business Review*, 118–128.

Das, T. K., & Teng, B. (2000). A resource-based theory of strategic alliances. *Journal of Management, 26*, 31–61.

Dierickx, I., & Cool, K. (1989). Asset stock accumulation and sustainability of competitive advantage. *Management Science, 35*, 1504–1511.

Dunne, T., Roberts, M. J., & Samuelson, L. (1989). The growth and failure of U.S. manufacturing plants. *Quarterly Journal of Economics, 104*, 671–698.

Eisenmann, T. R. (2006). Internet companies' growth strategies: Determinants of investment intensity and long-term performance. *Strategic Management Journal, 27*, 1183–1204.

Frynas, J. G., Mellahi, K., & Pigman, G. A. (2006). First mover advantages in international business and firm-specific political resources. *Strategic Management Journal, 27*, 321–345.

Gal-Or, E. (1987). First mover disadvantages with private information. *Review of Economic Studies, 28*, 279–292.

Geringer, J. M., & Hebert, L. (1991). Measuring performance of international joint ventures. *Journal of International Business Studies, 22*, 249–263.

Golder, P. N., & Tellis, G. J. (1993). Pioneer advantage: marketing logic or marketing legend? *Journal of Marketing Research, 30*, 158–170.

Gomes, L., & Ramaswamy, K. (1999). An empirical examination of the form of the relationship between multinationality and performance. *Journal of International Business Studies, 30*, 173–187.

Hitt, M. A., Bierman, L., Shimizu, K., & Kochlar, R. (2001). Direct and moderating effects of human capital on strategy and performance in professional service firms: A resource-based perspective. *Academy of Management Journal, 44*, 13–28.

Hitt, M. A., Dacin, M. T., Levita, E., Arregle, J., & Borza, A. (2000). Partner selection in emerging and develop market contexts: Resource-based and organizational learning perspectives. *Academy of Management Journal, 43*, 449–467.

Hobson, E. L., & Morrison, R. M. (1983). How do corporate start-up ventures fare? *Frontiers of entrepreneurship research*. Wellesley, MA: Babson College.

Hofmann, D. A. (1997). An overview of the logic and rationale of hierarchical linear models. *Journal of Management, 23*, 723–744.

Hofmann, D. H., Jacobs, R., & Baratta, J. E. (1993). Dynamic criteria and the measurement of change. *Journal of Applied Psychology, 78*, 194–204.

Isobe, T., Makino, S., & Montgomery, D. B. (2000). Resource commitment, entry timing, and market performance of foreign direct investment in emerging economies: The case of Japanese international joint ventures in China. *Academy of Management Journal, 43*, 468–484.

Karakaya, F., & Stahl, M. J. (1989). Barriers to entry and market entry decisions in consumer and industrial goods markets. *Journal of Marketing, 53*(2), 80–91.

Kerin, R. A., Varadarajan, P. R., & Peterson R. A. (1992). First-Mover advantage: A synthesis, conceptual framework, and research propositions." *Journal of Marketing, 56*, 33–52.

Lieberman, M. B., & Montgomery, D. B. (1988). First-mover advantages. *Strategic Management Journal, 9*, 41–58.

Lieberman, M. B., & Montgomery, D. B. (1998). First-mover (dis)advantages: Retrospective and link with the resource-based view. *Strategic Management Journal, 19*, 1111–1125.

Lu, J. W., & Beamish, P. W. (2006). Partnering strategies and performance of SME's international joint ventures. *Journal of Business Venturing, 21*, 461–486.

Luo, Y. (1997). Partner selection and venturing success: The case of joint ventures with firms in the People's Republic of China. *Organization Science, 8*, 648–662.

Luo, Y. (1998). Timing of investment and international expansion performance in China. *Journal of International Business Studies, 29*, 391–408.

Luo, Y., & Peng, M. W. (1998). First mover advantages in investing in transitional economies. *Thunderbird International Business Review, 40*, 141–163.

Luo, Y., & Peng, M. W. (1999). Learning to compete in a transition economy: Experience, environment, and performance. *Journal of International Business Studies, 30*, 269–295.

MacMillan, I. C., & Day, D. L. (1987). Corporate ventures into industrial markets: Dynamics of aggressive entry. *Journal of Business Venturing. 2*, 29–39.

Mascarenhas, B. (1992). Order of entry and performance in international markets. *Strategic Management Journal, 13*, 499–510.

Mascarenhas, B. (1997). The order and size of entry into international markets. *Journal of Business Venturing, 12*, 287–299.

Nielsen, B. (2003). An empirical investigation of the drivers of international strategic alliance formation. *European Management Journal, 21*, 301–323.

Olleros, F. J. (1986). The burnout of pioneers? *Journal of Product Innovation Management, 1*, 5–18.

Parkhe, A. (1993). Partner nationality and the structure-performance relationship in strategic alliances. *Management Science, 4*, 301–324.

Peng, M. W. (2000). Controlling the foreign agent: How governments deal with multinationals in a transition economy. *Management International Review, 40*, 141–166.

Peng, M. W. (2001). The resource-based view and international business. *Journal of Management* (Special Issue), *27*, 803–829.

Prahalad, C. K., & Hamel, G. (1990, May–June). The core competence of the corporation. *Harvard Business Review*, 79–91.

Raudenbush, S. W., & Bryk, A. S. (2002). *Hierarchical linear models: Applications and data analysis methods*. Thousand Oaks, CA: SAGE.

Rumelt, R. P., Schendel, D. E., & Teece, D. J. (1994). *Fundamental issues in strategy.* Boston, MA: Harvard Business School Press.

Shan, W. (1991). Environmental risks and joint venture sharing arrangements. *Journal of International Business Studies, 22*, 555–578.

Shenkar, O. (1990). International joint ventures' problems in China: Risks and remedies. *Long Range Planning, 23*(3), 82–90.

Steensma, H. K., Barden, J. Q., Dhanaraj, C. Q., Lyles, M., & Tihanyi, L. (2008). The evolution and internalization of international joint ventures in a transitioning economy. *Journal of International Business Studies, 39*, 491–507.

Suarez, F. F., & Lanzolla, G. (2007). The role of environmental dyanmics in building a first mover advantage theory. *Academy of Management Review, 32*, 377–392.

Wooster, R. B. (2006). US companies in transition economies: Wealth effects from expansion between 1987 and 1999. *Journal of International Business Studies, 37*, 179–195

CHAPTER 3

A SHIFT IN THE WIND?

Strategic Alliances Versus Wholly Owned Units in Global Industries

Ravi Madhavan

Among scholars who study strategic alliances, it is almost an article of faith that strategic alliances are central elements in the pursuit of global competitive advantage. However, Desai, Foley, and Hines (2004) offer a countervailing view, arguing that there has been a marked decline in the use of international joint ventures over the last 20 years. This is an intriguing finding, and one that I seek to further examine in this chapter. My goal is primarily to replicate Desai et al.'s core finding of the decline of alliances using other data sources (i.e., data on joint ventures and mergers and acquisitions from SDC Platinum rather than from Bureau of Economic Analysis survey data) while also tentatively exploring environmental and strategic drivers that may influence such shifts in managerial choice. By examining the evolving balance between shared ownership and full ownership in global industries, this chapter assesses the continuing relevance of strategic alliances, in the process suggesting ways to update their theoretical basis in a manner consistent with the shifting role suggested by the empirical patterns.

Strategic Alliances in a Globalizing World, pp. 53–66

INTRODUCTION

In July 2009, the Boeing Company, then struggling with continuing production difficulties and ensuing delays in its 787 Dreamliner aircraft project, announced that it was acquiring the South Carolina manufacturing plant of a key supplier, Vought Aircraft Industries, for $1 billion. The *New York Times* news story reporting this development began as follows (Drew, 2009a):

> The Boeing Company celebrated its new 787 Dreamliner as not only a state-of-the-art plane, but as a model of how to streamline its production process by relying on outsourcing.
>
> But on Tuesday, the company took a step away from that vision after it agreed to acquire the manufacturing plant of a troubled supplier, Vought Aircraft Industries, for $1 billion.
>
> Boeing has already had to contend with other supply and production problems on its delayed 787 Dreamliner, a model considered crucial to the company's future. It recently postponed its first test flight and has faced bottlenecks at Vought and other suppliers.
>
> Part of the trouble has come from Boeing's creation of a complex supply chain. It was meant to help the company escape rising labor costs, but has made it harder to control the production process.

Boeing's decision to internalize the production of parts of the 787's rear fuselage, which the Vought Aircraft Industries had been responsible for, and the subsequent debate about the decision (e.g., Drew, 2009b), illustrate the fundamental tension between the flexibility inherent in alliances and the need for control represented by full ownership. For example, the same *New York Times* story went on to quote two analyst comments that illustrated different aspects of the decision (Drew, 2009a):

> Ms. Wood [a Morgan Stanley analyst] said in her note that Boeing's decision to bring the work in-house would give it greater control over a "historically problematic process."
>
> But Robert Spingarn, an analyst at Credit Suisse, said recently that the acquisition would increase Boeing's fixed costs.

Risk-sharing has always been a key element in alliances. Indeed, Boeing's initial approach to the Dreamliner supply chain had been focused on risk-sharing. Here's the *New York Times* (Drew, 2009b) again:

> With the Dreamliner, Boeing aimed to expand its longtime outsourcing efforts, which had mainly focused on manufacturing parts, to a risk-sharing program in which the suppliers would also be Boeing's partners.

> "The idea was to get the risk off their books and get other people to do the heavy lifting for them," Mr. Aboulafia [an aviation analyst] said. "But the flaw was that led to a kind of 'engineering light' approach, and the problems on the 787 can be traced to that."
>
> For instance, Boeing contracted out the design and construction of the wings—one of the most exacting parts of the aircraft—for the first time ever. It also let other companies wrestle with the complicated task of baking and shaping the plastic composites.
>
> And instead of being paid when they shipped parts, the partners agreed to wait and recover their capital—and receive a share of the profits—once Boeing delivered the planes to the airlines.
>
> But Boeing officials now say that this left the whole process vulnerable, should any part of the chain face delays. Start-up problems and shortages of simple parts like nuts and bolts, along with a labor strike at Boeing last year, all caused delays and created a domino effect that intensified the pressure on the most poorly capitalized suppliers.
>
> "I think there were places where we went too far," said Scott Carson, who led the commercial division. He plans to retire at year-end and was replaced in the division post on Tuesday by Mr. Albaugh. "Clearly, we made some poor judgment calls in terms of what people's capabilities were."

As an example of strategy decision making, Boeing's choices—both to depend centrally on alliance partners and subsequently to reverse that stance—offer an instructive example for alliance scholars, among whom it is almost an article of faith that strategic alliances are central elements in the pursuit of global competitive advantage. Yet, as globalization proceeds apace, is it possible that the tradeoff between flexibility and control, between alliance intensity and ownership intensity, needs to be reexamined? This is the motivating question behind this chapter. One last excerpt from the press coverage of Boeing's decision (Drew, 2009b), reflecting both the cost of misreading the tradeoff and the need for a sophisticated approach to it, sets the stage for this chapter's exploratory data analysis of the shifting balance between alliances and ownership:

> The reverberating effects of Boeing's outsourcing missteps have taken a huge toll. The Dreamliner—the first passenger plane to be made mainly with light plastic composites—is now more than two years late and still awaits its first test flight tests.
>
> Boeing acknowledges that the problems have sorely tested the patience of suppliers and customers, and damaged its credibility. Already, 60 orders have been canceled, partly because of the delay.
>
> The company's chief, W. James McNerney Jr., concedes that Boeing lost control of the process by farming out more design and production work than ever and not keeping close tabs on suppliers. He says the company is retaking control.

> "You ultimately get to the question: Is it worth it?" Mr. McNerney says. "And my answer is yes. And that is why you take the risks. But could we have done it smarter? Yes."

BACKGROUND AND RESEARCH QUESTION

In 2004, Mihir Desai and his colleagues published a study in the *Journal of Financial Economics* on U.S. multinational corporations' international joint ventures (Desai, Foley, & Hines, 2004). Although little noted by alliance scholars, this study made two key empirical observations that are of great import to the alliance field, as well as most germane to the focus of this volume, *Strategic Alliances in a Globalizing World*. First, Desai et al. (2004) reported a marked decline in the use of joint ventures over the previous 20 years. Their study relied on data from the Bureau of Economic Analysis (BEA) annual survey of U.S. foreign direct investment from 1982 to 1997. Over this time frame, the prevalence of minority-owned affiliates (i.e., joint ventures) declined from 17.9% of affiliates to 10.6%; in contrast, the prevalence of wholly owned affiliates increased from 72.3% of affiliates to 80.4% (Desai et al., 2004, p. 329). Minority-owned and wholly owned affiliates were very similar in median sales, assets and employment.

Second, the study concluded that firms are more likely to choose whole ownership when they coordinate integrated production activities across different locations, transfer technology, and/ or take advantage of worldwide tax planning. Building on this empirical observation, Desai et al. (2004) suggest that there is a growing gap between the costs of running foreign operations as joint ventures and the costs of running them as wholly owned units. They interpret the above three drivers of whole ownership as the primary sources of the rising coordination costs of shared ownership—tax inefficiencies, intellectual property transfer issues, and goal conflict between partners.

Desai et al. (2004) end their abstract with the provocative statement: "The forces of globalization appear to have diminished, rather than accelerated, the use of shared ownership" (p. 323). From the standpoint of alliance scholars in strategy and related fields, this assertion poses an intriguing conundrum: How relevant are strategic alliances in the face of continued globalization? Clearly, while strategic alliances remain an important vehicle for achieving global competitiveness, an assessment of their relative importance may help to anchor alliance research more closely to the phenomenon. Alliances were especially important in the early stages of globalization, when the risks of cross-border expansion as well as local restraints on foreign ownership were great (e.g., Ohmae, 1989). However, is it true that their relative importance has diminished, as Desai et al. (2004) claim? This appears to be a question that will be of interest to alliance scholars.

Given the above motivation, I ask the following research question in this chapter: *What is the trend in alliance and M&A activity (jointly labeled transactions) among the world's most transaction-active firms?* In addressing this question, I complement the Desai et al. (2004) study in two ways. First, by including non-U.S. firms in the sample, I extend the empirical scope of the analysis. Second, I assess whether their findings can be replicated using a different data source. The analysis is exploratory and largely atheoretical (Miller, 2007), focused on identifying empirical patterns and assessing their implications for alliance research. In the next section, I describe my data. The subsequent section describes the results. The final section discusses the implications of the study.

DATA AND ANALYSIS

I drew my sample from two Thomson/SDC databases, M&A and Joint Ventures, both established data sources that are well accepted by the community of strategy scholars. My goal was to construct a sample of global firms that were continuously active in both alliance and M&A transactions. In other words, I wanted to isolate transactions made by firms that were not "occasional players." The sample construction proceeded in two stages. In the first stage, a research assistant compiled a joint dataset of 21652 alliance and M&A transactions, extracting from the respective databases transactions by firms that satisfied the criterion of making at least one transaction of either type in most years during the period 2001–2008. In the second stage, I randomly selected 51 firms such that each firm had at least 5 transactions during the 8-year period, as well as excluding firms, such as private equity operators, that engaged in purely financial transactions. This process resulted in a sample of 3924 transactions over 8 years. It is important to stress that the sampling procedure *intentionally* advantaged the most active firms—thus, the results will point to the alliance stances of the most active firms, and not merely to the overall occurrence patterns of each type of transaction.

For each transaction, I had data describing the identities of the firms, their nationality, primary SIC, business description and a synopsis of the transaction.

The analysis consisted of simple summary tables, cross-tabs, visual analyses and linear trend extrapolation. As indicated earlier, the goal was exploratory data analysis to identify empirical patterns, and not hypothesis testing.

RESULTS

Table 3.1 presents the alliance and M&A transactions by the sample firms. Of the total 3924 transactions, 226 were alliances and 3698 were M&A—5.8% and 94.2% respectively. Alliances were at their peak in 2001 (61), at their lowest in 2004 (8) and never regained the peak even after recovering somewhat in the years following the trough.

Figure 3.1 presents the trend in alliance and M&A activity visually. While cyclicality is evident in both transaction types, M&A swings appear to have greater amplitude as well as numbers in any given year. The quick-and-dirty trend extrapolation suggests a slight positive slope for the M&A curve and a slight negative slope for the alliance curve. Thus, the patterns in the sample appear to corroborate Desai et al. (2004) finding of a decline in the use of alliances.

Further visual analysis presented in Figure 3.2 supports the conclusion. Here, I calculated the average number of alliance and M&A transactions for each firm in the sample, and plotted the averages—along with a trend line. The average propensity to engage in M&A appears to be on the increase, while the average propensity to engage in alliances appears to be decreasing.

In Figure 3.3, I plotted the sample firms' M&A and alliance intensity. Since firms engage in both types of transactions, noting mere numbers of each transaction may not be the most informative. Rather, it may be instructive to ask how much emphasis the firm places on each transaction relative to the other one. This analysis suggests results that are consistent with that of the previous analyses—M&A intensity continues to far outstrip alliance intensity, running at about 0.9 versus 0.1 respectively.

Table 3.1. Alliance and M&A Transactions by Sample Firms During 2001–08

Year	*Number of Alliances*	*Number of M&A Transactions*	*Total Number of Transactions*
2001	61	560	621
2002	31	388	419
2003	11	377	388
2004	8	328	336
2005	23	458	481
2006	37	465	502
2007	24	613	637
2008	31	509	540
Grand Total	**226**	**3,698**	**3,924**

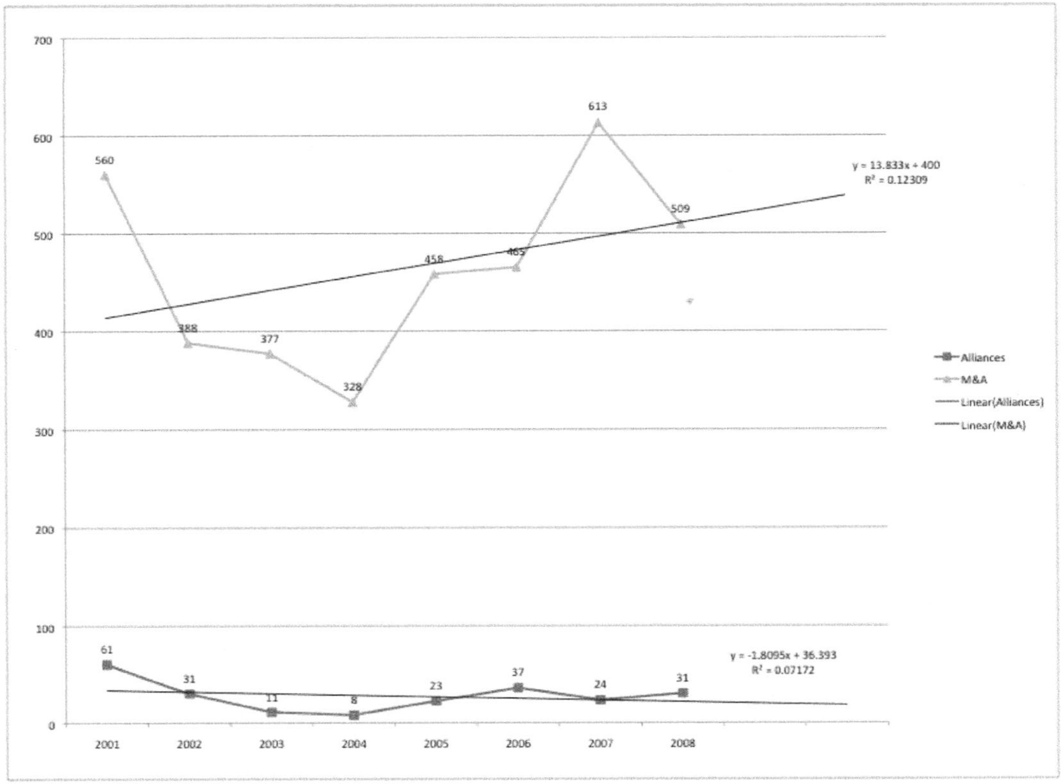

Figure 3.1. Trend in alliance & M&A Activity in sample.

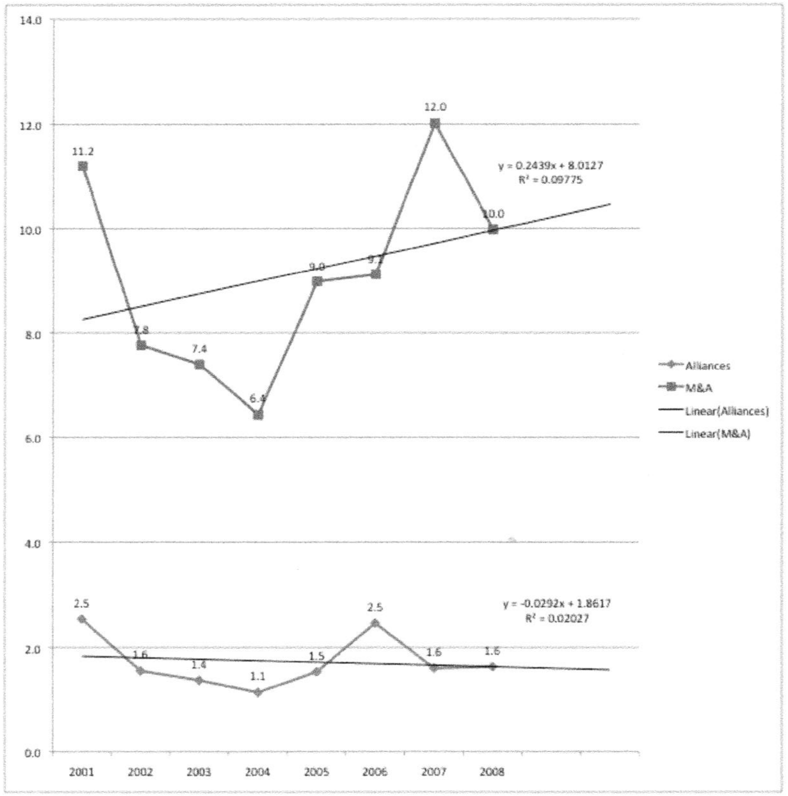

Figure 3.2. Trend in Sample Firm Averages of Alliance and M&A Transactions.

Alliance Intensity

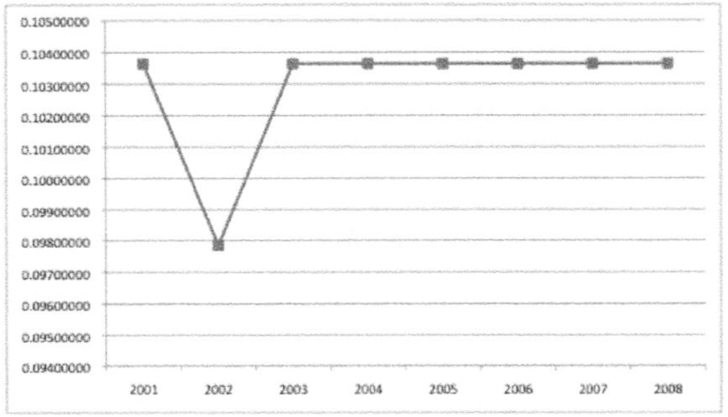

M&A Intensity

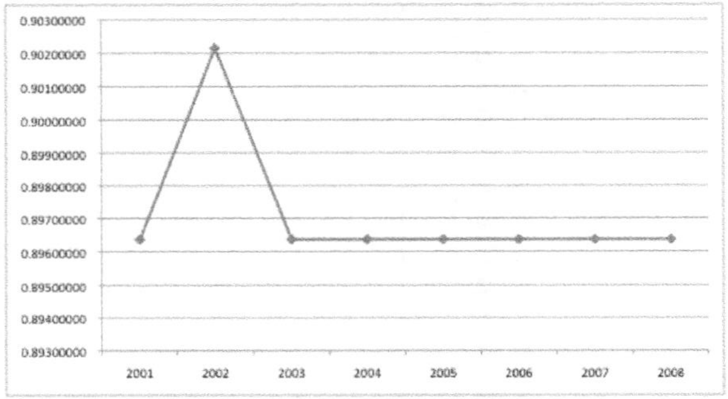

M&A Intensity = (No. of M&A transactions) / (No. of M&A transactions + No. of Alliance transactions).
Alliance Intensity = (No. of Alliance transactions) / (No. of M&A transactions + No. of Alliance transactions).

Figure 3.3. Trend in sample firms' M&A and alliance intensity.

Table 3.2 presents a subset of findings from a country-level analysis. Clearly, Japanese firms show a relatively high alliance intensity level—nearly 0.15 as against 0.03 for the United States. Even for Japanese companies, however, alliance activity levels appear to have declined over the sample period.

Table 3.2. Differences in Alliance Intensity Between the United States and Japan

Sample Firms From the United States			
		Transaction	
Year	*JV*	*M&A*	*Grand Total*
2001	6	85	91
2002	3	79	82
2003	1	62	63
2004	1	92	93
2005	1	92	93
2006	3	99	102
2007	3	125	128
2008	3	104	107
Grand Total	21	738	759
Overall Transaction Intensity	**0.027667984**	**0.972332016**	
Sample Firms From Japan			
		Transaction	
Year	*JV*	*MA*	*Grand Total*
2001	31	66	97
2002	14	46	60
2003	6	65	71
2004	3	51	54
2005	8	73	81
2006	16	72	88
2007	9	115	124
2008	13	87	100
Grand Total	100	575	675
Overall Transaction Intensity	**0.148148148**	**0.851851852**	

Finally, I also examined industry patterns in alliance and M&A activity. Across the roughly 250 four-digit SIC segments represented in the sample, the alliance intensity ranged from 0 to 1, with a mean level of 0.06. Table 3.3 presents the four industries with the highest alliance intensity—coal mining, metals service centers, motor vehicles and passenger car bodies, and bank holding companies.

The implications of these findings are discussed next.

DISCUSSION

In the exploratory data analysis presented here, I have attempted to identify *trends in alliance and M&A activity (jointly labeled transactions) among the world's most transaction-active firms*. Before discussing the implications of the findings, I must acknowledge certain limitations of the study. The sample is intentionally focused on the most active firms, and thus the findings may not be generalizable to all firms—for example, it could well be that firms making occasional forays into global transactions will choose alliances more often than is suggested here. Further, the sample, although randomly drawn, is small (51 firms engaging in 3,294 transactions over an 8-year period). Finally, no attempt has been made to explain the empirical patterns through hypothesis testing. Thus, the findings reported here should be viewed as tentative and aimed at generating questions for further research.

My point of departure for this chapter was the observation that the dynamic tension between alliances and M&A—as alternative vehicles for global expansion—needs to be continuously monitored. The anecdotal illustration featuring Boeing's Dreamliner project highlighted the tradeoff between risk-sharing partnerships and the need for control explicit in M&A. The empirical findings reported by Desai et al. (2004) as

Table 3.3. Industries With Highest Alliance Intensity

Industry	*Alliance Intensity*
Coal mining	0.33
Metals service centers	0.67
Motor vehicles, passenger car bodies	1.00
Bank holding companies	1.00

Excludes 4-digit SIC codes with less than 5 transactions.
Alliance Intensity = (No. of Alliance transactions)/ (No. of M&A transactions + No. of Alliance transactions).

well as their headline assertion that "The forces of globalization appear to have diminished, rather than accelerated, the use of shared ownership" (p. 323) thus pose a multi-faceted challenge for the alliances scholar. First, there is a need to determine whether there has indeed been a change in the relative importance of alliances. Second, if alliances have experienced a relative decline in their use, there is a need to better to understand why. Third, there is a need to refocus alliance research on the specific contexts in which they continue to be valuable tools. Finally, and more broadly, there is a need to rethink alliances not as standalone entities that may be worth studying simply because they exist, but rather as complementary vehicles that need to be understood as part of a menu of strategic choices. Below, I discuss each of these four challenges in turn.

The empirical patterns reported here have reinforced Desai et al. (2004) finding that alliances have declined in importance relative to wholly owned foreign affiliates. Thus, the provocative assertion that alliances may be becoming less numerous as globalization gathers pace appears to have some face validity, having survived independent analyses based on two entirely different datasets. However, the conclusion should be further stress-tested to a much greater degree. For example, the sample analyzed here could be expanded to point to more robust empirical conclusions. Apart from sample size, further sophistication can be added to the transaction attributes. For instance, given the paucity of financial data that normally characterizes alliance data from Thomson SDC, it was not possible to compare the size of the two types of transactions. Notwithstanding Desai et al.'s observation that minority-owned and wholly owned foreign units were comparable in size, could it be that alliances are used to a greater degree with larger or smaller transactions? (The logic could be risk-sharing for larger transactions and peripherality for smaller transactions.) Thus, the empirical pattern of the relative decline of alliances will benefit from further examination.

Assuming, for the moment, the face validity of such a relative decline, it is critical to understand better the drivers of such decline. What are the conditions under which the control afforded by M&A would be of greater value than the flexibility afforded by alliances? The extant literature offers several clues: maturing industries (e.g., Auster, 1992), reduction in technological uncertainty (e.g., Santoro & McGill, 2005), greater learning and confidence on the part of the transacting firm (cf. Das & Teng, 1998), high degree of interdependence (Dyer, Kale, & Singh, 2004), and so forth. What is the extent to which such drivers explain the shift in the data? If we could de-average the conclusions to narrow down on specific industry and firm situations, would we find that alliance-intensity varies based on those situations? For example, it could be that operational contexts such as global supply chains tend to privilege wholly owned units while more options-oriented contexts such as such as research and development (R&D) or or market development tend to privilege minority-owned units. These are definitely questions that future research should address.

A more sophisticated understanding of the drivers of a shift away from alliances would help alliance scholars hone their research to focus on those specific contexts that are tailor-made for alliances. For example, might one argue that alliances will be more important for entrepreneurial and small firms, for whom the tradeoff between flexibility and control is less weighted toward control? If so, a greater focus on the intersection between alliances and entrepreneurship would be warranted. Similarly, if R&D or market development projects are a more natural fit for alliances, it may behoove us to focus on their specific characteristics rather than on production joint ventures. Such a fine-tuning of approach would allow us not only to locate the best empirical settings for alliance research, but also to position the field to impact the applications for which it is best suited.

Another facet worth commenting upon is the difference in alliance intensities between firms from different countries. There is an established literature on the role of culture in international alliances (e.g., Kogut & Singh, 1988), which makes it clear that cultural predispositions and cultural distance do impact choice of entry mode. However, given the indication of significant and pronounced differences between firms from different countries—for example, Japan and the United States—it may be worth investing greater attention to why such differences persist despite globalization.

Finally, the shift in the balance between alliances and M&A might force us—as alliance scholars—to confront the invisible silos that divide alliance research from M&A research. In recent years, a number of studies have begun to address this challenge (e.g., Dyer, Kale, & Singh, 2004; Wang & Zajac, 2007; Yin & Shanley, 2008). If alliances and M&A are alternative means to accomplish the same goals of global coordination, it is critical that we not only begin to address them as part of a broader menu to strategy actions but also to actively monitor environmental changes that may trigger changes in their relative balance.

CONCLUSION

As alliance scholars, we tend to assume that strategic alliances are central elements in the pursuit of global competitive advantage. However, following Desai et al. (2004), I have offered a countervailing view in this chapter, documenting a decline in alliance intensity among the most transaction-active firms. Stemming from two different datasets, this is an intriguing finding with crucial implications for how we shape future research into strategic alliances. By examining the shifting balance between shared ownership and full ownership in global industries, I have attempted to empirically assess the continuing relevance of strategic alliances, as well as suggest ways to elaborate and update their theoretical basis in a manner consistent with their shifting role in global competition.

ACKNOWLEDGMENT

I thank Franky Supriyadi for his assistance with the data collection.

REFERENCES

Auster, E. R. (1992). The relationship of industry evolution to patterns of technological linkages, joint ventures, and direct investment between U.S. and Japan. *Management Science, 38*, 778–792.

Das, T. K., & Teng, B. (1998). Between trust and control: Developing confidence in partner cooperation in alliances. *Academy of Management Review, 23*, 491–512.

Desai, M. A., Foley, C. F., & Hines, J. R., Jr. (2004). The costs of shared ownership: Evidence from international joint ventures. *Journal of Financial Economics, 73*, 323–374.

Drew, C. (2009a, July 8). Boeing buys plant that makes crucial part of Dreamliner. *New York Times*. Retrieved from http://www.nytimes.com/2009/07/08/business/08boeing.html

Drew, C. (2009b, September 6.). A dream interrupted at Boeing. *New York Times*. Retrieved from http://www.nytimes.com/2009/09/06/business/06boeing.html

Dyer, J. H., Kale, P., & Singh, H. (2004). When to ally and when to acquire? *Harvard Business Review, 82*(7/8), 108–115.

Kogut, B., & Singh, H. (1988). The effect of national culture on the choice of entry mode. *Journal of International Business Studies, 19*, 411–432.

Miller, D. (2007). Paradigm prison, or in praise of atheoretic research. *Strategic Organization, 5*, 177–184.

Ohmae, K. (1989). The global logic of strategic alliances. *Harvard Business Review, 67*(2), 143–152.

Santoro, M. D., & McGill, J. P. (2005). The effect of uncertainty and asset co-specialization on governance in biotechnology alliances. *Strategic Management Journal, 26*, 1261–1269.

Yin, X., & Shanley, M. (2008). Industry determinants of the "merger versus alliance" decision. *Academy of Management Review, 33*, 473–491.

Wang, L., & Zajac, E. J. (2007). Alliance or acquisition? A dyadic perspective on interfirm resource combinations. *Strategic Management Journal, 28*, 1291–1317.

CHAPTER 4

CONTRACTUAL ALLIANCE GOVERNANCE

Impact of Different Contract Functions on Alliance Performance

Dries Faems, Rutger Alberink, Gjalt de Jong, Aard Groen, and Rosalinde Klein Woolthuis

Recent research on alliance governance has emphasized that contracts can have both a control and coordination function. In this chapter, we test the impact of these different contract functions on alliance performance. Conducting structural equation analyses on a sample of 270 Dutch technology alliances, we disentangle the relationship between different contract functions, partner cooperation and alliance success. Our data show that different contract roles have a different impact on partner cooperation within the alliance. In addition, we find strong indications that the presence/absence of prior trustful collaboration and the number of alliance partners moderate the relationship between contract functions and partner cooperation. Finally, our data provide evidence that contract functions indirectly influence alliance success via partner cooperation.

Strategic Alliances in a Globalizing World, pp. 67–92

INTRODUCTION

Alliances have become an increasingly popular strategy for organizations to complement and supplement their internal activities (Doz & Hamel, 1998; Hagedoorn, 2002; Kale & Singh, 2009). Although popular, their failure rates are high (Bleeke & Ernst, 1991), instigating numerous scholars to study the governance of alliances (Faems, Janssens, Madhok, & Van Looy, 2008). In this research stream, contracts or "agreements in writing between two or more parties, which are perceived as legally binding (Lyons & Mehta, 1997, p. 241)" have been identified as an important mechanism to effectively govern alliances.

Whereas alliance contract research has traditionally focused on the complexity of the contract (i.e., the amount of clauses in the contract), some scholars (e.g., Faems et al., 2008, Hagedoorn & Hesen, 2007; Klein Woolthuis, Hillebrand, & Nooteboom, 2005; Mayer & Teece, 2008) have recently started to also consider the content of the contract. In this way, these scholars managed to identify that contracts can both (1) allow for formal control of the partner's behavior; and (2) facilitate coordinated action However, research on the impact of such different contract roles on the performance of the alliance has remained absent (de Jong & Klein Woolthuis, 2008).

In this chapter, we therefore explore the impact of different contract functions on alliance performance. In order to do so, we rely on a sample of 270 Dutch technology alliances. Conducting structural equation analyses, we explore the relationships between contract functions, partner cooperation and alliance success. Our data provide strong indications that different contract functions can significantly influence partner cooperation during the alliance. For instance, we find that the more important the contractual control function, the lower the partner cooperation within the alliance. In addition, we find that the presence/absence of trustful prior collaboration and the number of alliance partners moderate the relationship between contract roles and partner cooperation. In particular, we find that the negative impact of the contractual control function on partner cooperation disappears when partners share a history of trustful collaboration. In addition, we observe that, in the setting of dyadic alliance, the contractual coordination function has a significant negative impact on partner cooperation. Finally, our data provide consistent evidence that contract roles indirectly influence alliance success via partner cooperation.

The remainder of this chapter is structured in four sections. First, we position our study in the existing alliance governance literature. Subsequently, we discuss the methodology that we applied to examine the impact of contract functions on alliance performance. Next, we present the main findings of our study. Finally, we discuss the main theoretical and managerial implication of our findings, discuss the main limitations of this study and identify several avenues for future research.

THEORETICAL BACKGROUND AND HYPOTHESES

Contractual Alliance Governance: Complexity Versus Content of the Contract

Whereas alliance governance research has long been dominated by a concern for the choice between equity or nonequity structures, scholars have also started focusing on the role of specific structural and relational governance mechanisms (Ariño & Reuer, 2005). In this literature stream, contracts have been recognized as an important structural governance mechanism. Alliance contract studies (e.g., Anderson & Dekker, 2005; Luo, 2002; Parkhe, 1993; Poppo & Zenger, 2002; Reuer, Ariño, & Mellewigt, 2006) have mainly focused on the complexity of the contract or the amount of clauses that are present in the contract. In particular these studies examined (1) the impact of several transactional and relational conditions on the amount of clauses that are present in the contract; (2) the impact of contract complexity on alliance performance, and (3) the relationship between contract complexity and trust or "a psychological state comprising the intention to accept vulnerability based on positive expectations of the intentions or behavior of another" (Rousseau, Sitkin, Burt, & Camerer, 1998, p. 395). However, these studies often provided inconsistent results. For instance, whereas some scholars (e.g., Luo, 2002; Poppo & Zenger, 2002) provided evidence for a complementary relationship between contract complexity and trust others (e.g., Lyons & Mehta, 1997; Malhotra & Murnighan, 2002) pointed to the existence of a substitutive relationship between these structural and relational governance mechanisms.

Several scholars (e.g., Faems et al., 2008, Hagedoorn & Hesen, 2007; Klein Woolthuis, Hillebrand, & Nooteboom, 2005; Mayer & Teece, 2008) have therefore started exploring not only the complexity of the contracts, but also the actual content of the clauses that are defined in alliance contract. Based on this content-based assessment, these scholars came to the conclusion that contracts might play different roles in the governance of alliances. Mellewigt, Madhok, and Weibel (2007) identify two different contract roles. First, in line with insights from transaction cost theory (e.g., Williamson, 1985), they emphasize that alliance contracts might have a control role, reducing the risk that one of the partners will abuse the alliance for opportunistic reasons. Second, in line with organizational theory (e.g., Galbraith, 1977; Thompson, 1967), they stress that the contract might also contain clauses that facilitate coordinated action between the partners. Other scholars have come to similar conclusions. Klein Woolthuis et al. (2005) argue that contracts might have a safeguarding or coordination function in alliances. (Klein Woolthuis et al. [2005] identify a third contract role. They stress that contracts may also serve as a tangible expression of partners' trust in each other and their intention to be loyal partners. In other words, the contract might also function as a signal of commitment.) Examining 88 strategic alliances, Reuer and Ariño (2007) empirically demonstrate that contractual clauses in alliance contracts can have both enforcement and coordination functions.

Impact of Contract Roles on Alliance Performance: A Conceptual Framework

Whereas scholars have provided valuable insights into the different functions that contracts may have in governing alliances, they remain silent on how these contract roles influence alliance performance. Below, we develop a conceptual framework in which we (1) link the different contract functions to partner cooperation and alliance success and (2) hypothesize on the potential moderating effects of history of trustful collaboration and number of alliance partners (see Figure 4.1).

Impact of Contractual Control Function on Partner Cooperation

One key difference between single-firm strategies and interfirm alliances is the uncertainty attending the cooperation among partners. When independent firms collaborate together, there is the risk of the partner not cooperating in good faith in addition to the usual risk of unsatisfactory business performance (Das & Teng, 2001, p. 253). Applying a transaction cost framework, scholars have referred to this kind of behavioral uncertainty in terms of opportunistic behavior or "seeking self interest with guile" (Williamson, 1985). Opportunistic behavior in alliances is exemplified by "cheating, shirking, distorting information, misleading partners, providing substandard products/services, and appropriating partners' critical resources" (Das & Teng, 1998, p. 492).

In line with transaction cost theory, numerous alliance governance scholars have argued that alliance partners can negotiate safeguarding clauses, inflicting penalties for the omission of cooperative behaviors or commission of violative behaviors (Parkhe, 1993). As a result, the cost of self-interest activities subsequently increases, curbing partners' willing-

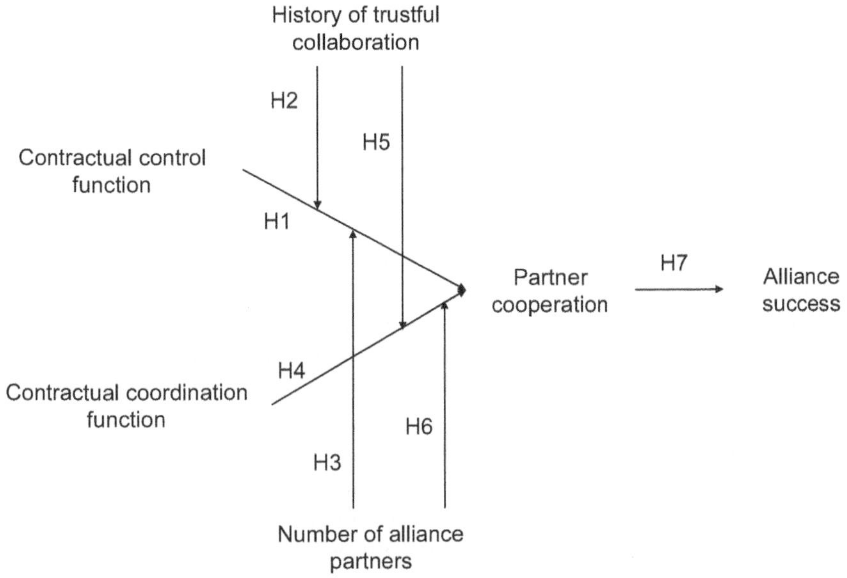

Figure 4.1. Conceptual framework.

ness to act opportunistically (Dyer & Singh, 1998). In other words, safeguarding clauses allow for formal control or the utilization of formal rules, procedures, and policies to monitor and punish undesirable behavior and/or outcomes (Anderson & Dekker, 2005; Das & Teng, 2001), reducing the likelihood of opportunistic behavior. First indications are also present that, when the contract has a strong control function, knowledge transfer between the partners will be more open and transparent. Examining three R&D alliances, Faems, Janssens, and Van Looy (2007), for instance, observed that, in cases were explicit contractual clauses were present that controlled the exchange of knowledge, partners were much more willing to disclose sensitive knowledge to the other partner.

In sum, we expect that, the more alliance partners rely on contracts as a mechanism to control for opportunistic behavior, the lower the probability that opportunistic behavior will occur and the higher the willingness to transfer knowledge between the partners. We therefore formulate the following hypothesis:

> **Hypothesis 1:** The more important the control function of alliance contracts, the higher the partner cooperation within the alliance.

Several scholars have argued that the relevance of the contractual control function might be dependent on alliance partners' history of prior collaboration. When partners share a history of successful prior collaboration, they are likely to have build up "resilient trust" or a psychological state between collaborating partners, characterized by shared norms, values and beliefs that emphasize faith in the moral integrity or goodwill of others (Ring, 1997). Looking from a social exchange perspective (e.g., Blau, 1964), several scholars (e.g., Das & Teng, 1998, 2001; Dyer & Singh, 1998; Inkpen & Currall, 2004; Jones & George, 1998; Ring & Van de Ven, 1994) argued that the presence of resilient trust influences how partners work together in alliances. First, under conditions of resilient trust, "shared valued underlying trust provide individuals with the assurance that knowledge and information will be used for the greater good and that one need not exercise power to protect one's own interests" (Jones & George, 1998, p. 542). In other words, when resilient trust is present, the perception of opportunistic hazards is likely to be reduced. In the alliance literature, these dynamics have been referred to in terms of "social control" (Das & Teng, 2001; Inkpen & Currall, 2004). Opposite to formal control, emphasizing rules, procedures and policies, social control tries to minimize divergence of preferences among participants by relying on the development of shared values, beliefs, and goals among members (Eisenhardt, 1985; Ouchi, 1979). In such circumstances, partners' incentives to behave opportunistically are reduced (Das & Teng, 2001; Dyer & Singh, 1998).

In sum, in case of prior trustful collaboration, alliance partners do not need formal control because they can rely on social control to mitigate opportunistic behavior and stimulate open knowledge exchange. We therefore expect that the contractual control function is especially relevant for stimulating partner cooperation in settings where a history of trustful prior collaboration is absent:

> **Hypothesis 2:** The positive impact of the contractual control function on partner cooperation is stronger when alliance partners do not share a history of trustful collaboration.

In the alliance literature, a distinction is made between dyadic alliances, in which only two organizations collaborate, and multilateral alliances, in which the collaboration involves more than two partners. Moreover, some scholars (e.g., Garcia-Canal, Valdés-Llaneza, & Arino, 2003; Gong, Shenkar, Luo, & Nyaw, 2007) provide first indications that the impact of the contractual control function on the quality of interaction might differ in dyadic and multilateral alliances. Both Garcia-Canal et al. (2003) and Gong et al. (2007) provide empirical evidence that, in multilateral alliances, contract complexity has a significant positive impact on alliance performance, whereas such a relationship is not present in the setting of dyadic alliances. To explain these findings, these scholars argue that, the more partners are present in an alliance, the more difficult it becomes to monitor the actions of all different parties and to align the partners' goals. In such a setting, partners' incentives to engage in opportunistic behavior are likely to increase (Das & Teng, 2002), which increases the relevance of using the contract as a formal control mechanism. We therefore hypothesize:

> **Hypothesis 3:** The positive impact of the contractual control function on partner cooperation is stronger in multilateral alliances.

Impact of Contractual Coordination Function on Partner Cooperation

Whereas transaction scholars focus on the behavioral uncertainty of alliances, other scholars, applying insights from organization theory (e.g., Lawrence & Lorsch, 1967; Thompson, 1967), emphasize the difficulty of achieving coordinated action in alliances. Two main reasons have been mentioned to explain the difficulties of coordination in alliance. First, alliances can not make an appeal to all hierarchical structures and systems that are available within organizations to achieve coordinated action (Gulati & Singh, 1998). Second, differences in national context as well as differences in corporate cultures further complicate the coordination between collaborating partners (Parkhe, 1991).

At the same time, the alliance contract has been identified as a viable mechanism to improve coordination. In particular, through extensively defining performance control systems, action planning systems, and standard operating procedures in the formal contract, the division of labor and the interactions between partners become more predictable and joint decisions can be made more by rules than by exception (Klein Woolthuis et al., 2005; Mellewigt et al., 2007; Reuer & Ariño, 2007). In other words, a contract allows for standardized coordination (Mintzberg, 1979), facilitating cooperation between the involved partners:

> **Hypothesis 4:** The more important the coordination function of alliance contracts, the higher the partner cooperation within the alliance.

Based on a longitudinal study of contracting in the personal computer industry, Mayer and Argyres (2004, p. 394) concluded that contracts may also function as "repositories for knowledge about how to govern collaborations." In particular, they argue that when collaborative partners share a history of previous collaboration, they are likely to adjust the content of the contract based on their mutual learning experiences in their previous collaborative transactions. In addition, Faems et al. (2008) empirically illustrate that this contract learning effect is particularly important for coordination clauses in the contract. Based on these observations, we expect that, when partners share a history of trustful collaboration, they will be able to define in the contract more fine-grained coordination clauses, which will reinforce the positive impact of contractual coordination function on partner cooperation:

> **Hypothesis 5:** The positive impact of the contractual coordination function on partner cooperation is stronger when alliance partners share a history of trustful collaboration.

Focusing on the distinction between dyadic and multilateral alliances, several scholars (Das & Teng, 2002; Garcia-Canal et al., 2003; Gong et al., 2007) argue that multilateral alliances do not only imply a higher risk of opportunistic behavior, but also entail a higher risk of problematic coordination. After all, the more alliance partners, the more likely substantial differences will be present in terms of organizational culture, structure and strategic vision, which complicate achieving coordinated action. At the same time, it is argued that, in dyadic alliances, partners do not need standardized coordination, but can rather rely on coordination by mutual adjustment (Mintzberg, 1979). In sum, the relevance of the contractual coordination function seems to be higher in multilateral alliances compared to dyadic alliances. We therefore hypothesize:

> **Hypothesis 6:** *The positive impact of the contractual coordination function on partner cooperation is stronger in multilateral alliances.*

Impact of Partner Cooperation on Alliance Success

According to existing alliance research (e.g., Dyer & Singh, 1998; Madhok & Tallman, 1998; Zajac & Olsen, 1993), the extent of partner cooperation has a strong impact on alliance success or the degree to which partners manage to realize or even exceed the initial expectations. In particular, it is argued that the more cooperative behaviors (e.g., open exchange of knowledge between partners, joint sensemaking, joint problem solving) are present and the more noncooperative behaviors (e.g., shirking, stealing knowledge, hiding information) are absent, the higher the ability of partners to come to synergistic value creation within the alliance. We therefore expect that:

> **Hypothesis 7:** Higher partner cooperation increases alliance success.

METHODOLOGY

Research Design and Sample

To test our hypotheses, we use a sample of Dutch firms that participated in technology alliances. The sample was constructed with the help of Senter Novem, an agency of the Dutch ministry of Economic affairs. The main goal of Senter Novem is to support the development and innovation activities of Dutch firms on both domestic and international markets. Among other things, Senter Novem manages a funding scheme (i.e., WBSO [Wet Bevordering Speur- en Ontwikkelingswerk]) that allows firms, knowledge institutes, and individuals to receive tax compensation for a technological innovation projects. The research sample for this studies consists of firms that (1) made use of this particular funding scheme for technological innovation project, (2) indicated that they formally collaborated with other partners for this particular innovation project, and (3) indicated that this particular innovation project was recently finished or was in the final stage of being finished. The initial sample consisted of 648 firms that had filed for tax compensation for a particular technological innovation project in 1999. Three hundred and ninety one organizations eventually responded to the survey. Because of missing values on the variables that we constructed, the size of our sample was further restricted. In total, the sample of this study consists of 270 collaborative innovation projects. Table 4.1 gives some additional information about the survey response rate.

An external research organization was made responsible for the data collection phase. This research organization made use of telephone surveys to collect the needed information. The responding firms were active in the areas of: biotechnology, new materials, information technology, maritime technologies, chemicals, and environmental technologies.

Measures

Contract Roles

Whereas previous alliance contract research has focused on measuring the complexity of the contract through counting the number of contractual clauses or evaluating the presence/absence of a set of predefined contractual clauses, we wanted to measure to which extent respondents used the contract as a control and/or coordination mechanism. In order to do so, we asked respondents to indicate on a five point Likert scale (i.e., 1 = strongly disagree; 5 = strongly agree), (1) whether the contract functioned as a guarantee against opportunistic behavior of the other part-

Table 4.1. Overview of Sampling Procedure

Initial Sample	**648 firms**
Unable to come in contact with project leader	24 firms
Double address in database	18 firms
Project leader has quitted the company	6 firms
Not a cooperative project	28 firms
Total base for response	**572 firms**
Unable to locate project leader during data collection phase	115 firms
Respondent only wants to answer in written form	6 firms
Respondent does not want to cooperate for various reasons	60 firms
Total response rate	**391 firms (68.5%)**
Missing values on constructs	121 firms
Final sample	**270 firms**

ner(s), and (2) whether the contract functioned as a plan of action in order to streamline the collaboration. The scores on these items were used to measure the importance of the contractual control function and the contractual coordination function.

Partner Cooperation

In line with Luo (2002) and Gong et al. (2007), we measured partner cooperation through evaluating the absence or presence of specific cooperative situations. In particular, we asked respondents to rate on a 5 point Likert scale (1 = strongly disagree, 5 = strongly agree) the degree to which three cooperative situations and two noncooperative situations characterized the relationship among partners (see Table 4.2). Subsequently, we conducted an explorative factor analysis, indicating that all items loaded on one single factor (see Table 4.2). In line with our expectations, the cooperative situations loaded positively on this factor, whereas the noncooperative situations loaded negatively on this factor. Next, we relied on the standardized factor score for each case to construct the variable "partner cooperation."

Alliance Success

Alliance scholars (e.g., Ariño, 2003; Geringer & Hebert, 1991) have provided evidence that subjective measures of alliance success highly correlate with objective measures of success. Following previous alliance

Table 4.2. Exploratory Factor Analysis on Partner Cooperation

	Factor Loadings
We and our partner always talked openly and informally about our ideas, feelings, and wishes	0.522
We and our partner always gave each other all information that is relevant for the project	0.874
We and our partner could openly criticize each other when this contributes to the execution of the project	0.601
Our partner tried to get more advantages from the project than could be justified based on her efforts	–0.684
Our partner kept important information hidden for us	–0.788

Table 4.3. Exploratory Factor Analysis on Alliance Success

	Factor Loadings
the project has become a technological success	0.715
the project has lead to lower development costs than if we would have done the project alone or if we would have done the project with another partner	0.640
the result of the collaboration has exceeded my expectations	0.748

research (e.g., Geringer & Hebert, 1991; Gong et al., 2007) we adopt a multidimensional approach to measure alliance success. We asked respondents to rate on a 5 point Likert scale (1 = totally disagree, 5 = totally agree) the following three aspects: (1) the project has become a technological success; (2) the project has lead to lower development costs than if we would have done the project alone or if we would have done the project with another partner; (3) the result of the collaboration has exceeded my expectations. Subsequently, we conducted an explorative factor analysis, indicating that all items loaded on one single factor (see Table 4.3 above). Next, we relied on the standardized factor score for each case to construct the variable "alliance success."

History of Trustful Collaboration

Previous alliance research (e.g., Garcia-Canal et al., 2003; Gulati, 1995; Mellewigt et al., 2007) has relied on the presence of prior collaboration as an indicator of resilient trust. However, these studies ignore that prior collaboration might have been unsuccessful, which might even trigger negative trust dynamics (Faems et al., 2008). In this study, we therefore rely on a more fine-grained measure of prior collaboration. In particular, we asked respondents whether a friendly connection already existed before the project. Based on this question, we constructed a dummy variable, representing the absence (value = 0) or presence (value =1) of "prior trustful collaboration." In our sample 176 (65.2%) of the observed alliances had a history of trustful collaboration.

Number of Alliance Partners

In the survey, respondents had to indicate the amount of partners that were involved in the alliance. Based on this information, we constructed a dummy variable "number of alliance partners," representing the difference between dyadic alliances (value = 0) and multilateral alliances (value = 1). In our sample 96 (35.6%) alliances were of a dyadic nature whereas 174 (64.4%) were of a multilateral nature.

Contract Complexity

Although we focus in this study on the different functions of the contract, we also wanted to control for contract complexity. In line with previous alliance contract research (e.g., Parkhe, 1993; Poppo & Zenger, 2002; Reuer & Ariño, 2007), we therefore provided respondents with a list of 13 specific contractual clauses and asked them to indicate whether these contractual clauses were present in the contract. Based on this information, we constructed the variable contract complexity, representing the sum of these 13 items.

Alliance Objectives

Firms can rely on collaboration with external partners for both explorative and exploitative innovation projects (Faems, Van Looy, & Debackere, 2005; Lavie & Rosenkopf, 2006; Rothaermel & Deeds, 2004). Explorative innovation projects refer to projects in which the focus is on fundamental research in order to generate new technological capabilities. Exploitative innovation projects are defined as projects in which the focus is on applied research in order to leverage existing technological capabilities. In the alliance literature (e.g., Bijlsma-Frankema & Costa, 2005; Faems, Janssens, Bouwen, & Van Looy, 2006; Koza & Lewin, 1998) first indications have been provided that explorative and exploitative collaborations are characterized by different interaction patterns and have different success rates. We therefore wanted to control for the objective of the collaboration in our analyses. In the survey, we asked respondents to indicate whether the collaborative innovation project was (1) very fundamental; (2) rather fundamental; (3) in the middle between fundamental and applied research; (4) rather applied;

(5) very applied. Based on this information, we constructed the variable "Exploitative orientation."

RESULTS

Descriptive Statistics and Analyses

Table 4.4 gives an overview of the most important descriptive statistics. This table shows the presence of a significant positive correlation between the contractual control function and the contractual coordination function. This indicates that alliance partners can simultaneously apply the contract as a mechanism to safeguard against opportunistic behavior and, at the same time, rely on it as a tool to facilitate coordinated action.

To test the hypotheses, we used structural equation modeling (SEM) with manifest variables. Compared to ordinary linear regression models, this technique has two advantages (Sels, De Winne, Maes, Delmotte, Faems, & Forrier, 2006). First, the method enables to define and test hypothesized relationships between variables. The output indicates whether the model is supported by the data as a whole and gives a significance test for the various individual relationships. Second, a variable in a SEM model can either be dependent or independent. This allows testing the indirect influence, if any, of certain variables.

We relied on the Calis procedure in the SAS software package to conduct our SEM analyses. First, we analyzed the relationship between contract functions, partner cooperation and alliance success on the full sample. In this model, we did not take into account the potential moderating impact of history of trustful collaboration and number of alliance partners. Instead, we integrated these latter variables as control variables in addition to contract complexity and exploitative orientation. Subsequently, we did split the full sample based on the variable "history of trustful collaboration" in order to test the moderating impact of it. After splitting the sample we ran one SEM analysis for the cases that lacked a history of trustful collaboration and one analysis for the cases that were characterized by the presence of prior trustful collaboration. A similar procedure was conducted to test the moderating impact of the number of alliance partners. In all models, we programmed the existence of a significant correlation between the contractual control function and the contractual coordination function. The goodness-of-fit overview (see Table 4.5) indicates that the different analyzed models were adequately supported by the data.

Below we interpret and explain the effects. First, we look at the effect of the contractual control function on partner cooperation. Second, we assess the impact of the contractual coordination function on partner cooperation. Third, we evaluate the indirect effect of these contract functions on

Table 4.4. Descriptive Statistics and Correlations

Variable	*Mean*	*S*	*Partner Cooperation*	*Alliance Success*	*Contractual Coordination Function*	*Contractual Control Function*	*Exploitation Orientation*
Partner cooperation	0.00	1.00	1				
Alliance success	0.00	1.00	0.217***	1			
Contractual coordination function	3.34	1.66	–0.027	0.033	1		
Contractual control function	2.03	1.46	–0.150*	–0.077	0.145*	1	
Exploitation orientation	3.56	1.23	–0.057	0.075	–0.022	–0.118	1
Contract complexity	9.17	2.81	–0.034	0.065	0.048*	0.213**	–0.290

Note: * Correlation is significant at the 0.05 level; ** Correlation is significant at the 0.01 level.

alliance success via partner cooperation. Fourth, we discuss the impact of our control variables. For the different models, the standardized path coefficients are listed in Table 4.6, Table 4.7, Table 4.8, Table 4.9, and Table 4.10. The results are also represented in Figure 4.2 and Figure 4.3. The control variables have been omitted in these graphical representations in order not to overload the figures.

Impact of Contractual Control Function on Partner Cooperation

In our first hypothesis, we expected a positive impact of the importance of the control function of the contract on partner cooperation. Our find-

Table 4.5. Goodness-of-Fit Measures

	Model 1: Full Sample (n =270)	*Model 2: No History of Trustful Collaboration (n = 94)*	*Model 3: History of Trustful Collaboration (n = 186)*	*Model 4: Dyadic Alliances (n = 96)*	*Model 5: Multilateral Alliances (n = 184)*
Bentler's Comparative Fit index	1.00	1.00	1.00	1.00	1.00
Bentler and Bonett's Non-normed index	1.26	1.00	0.99	1.09	1.27
Bentler and Bonett's Normed Fit index	0.99	0.98	0.97	0.98	0.98
Chi-Square test (p-value)	0.68	0.37	0.36	0.48	0.60

Table 4.6. Standardized Path Coefficients Model 1: Full Sample

Path From/To	*(3)*	*(4)*
(1) Contractual control function	–0.14*	
(2) Contractual coordination function	–0.01	
(3) Partner cooperation		0.22***
(4) Alliance success		
Control Variables		
(6) Exploitation orientation	–0.08	0.10
(7) Contract complexity	–0.03	0.10
(8) History of trustful collaboration	0.05	0.02
(9) Multilateral collaboration	0.04	0.14*

$^{\dagger}p < 0.10$; $^{*}p < 0.05$; $^{**}p < 0.01$; $^{***}p < 0.001$

Table 4.7. Standardized Path Coefficients Model 2: No History of Trustful Collaboration

Path From/To	*(3)*	*(4)*
(1) Contractual control function	–0.20**	
(2) Contractual coordination function	–0.01	
(3) Partner cooperation		0.20**
(4) Alliance success		
Control Variables		
(6) Exploitation orientation	–0.11	0.01
(7) Contract complexity	–0.16*	0.07
(8) History of trustful collaboration		
(9) Multilateral collaboration	–0.02	0.22**

$^{\dagger}p < 0.10$; $*p < 0.05$; $**p < 0.01$; $***p < 0.001$

Table 4.8. Standardized Path Coefficients Model 3: History of Trustful Collaboration

Path From/To	*(3)*	*(4)*
(1) Contractual control function	–0.09	
(2) Contractual coordination function	–0.03	
(3) Partner cooperation		0.23***
(4) Alliance success		
Control Variables		
(6) Exploitation orientation	–0.05	0.16*
(7) Contract complexity	0.07	0.10
(8) History of trustful collaboration		
(9) Multilateral collaboration	0.08	0.10

$^{\dagger}p < 0.10$; $*p < 0.05$; $**p < 0.01$; $***p < 0.001$

Table 4.9. Standardized Path Coefficients Model 4: Dyadic Alliances

Path From/To	*(3)*	*(4)*
(1) Contractual control function	–0.11	
(2) Contractual coordination function	–0.19**	
(3) Partner cooperation		0.26***
(4) Alliance success		
Control Variables		
(6) Exploitation orientation	–0.03	0.21**
(7) Contract complexity	0.04	0.06
(8) History of trustful collaboration	0.00	0.08
(9) Multilateral collaboration		

$^{\dagger}p < 0.10$; $^{*}p < 0.05$; $^{**}p < 0.01$; $^{***}p < 0.001$

Table 4.10. Standardized Path Coefficients Model 5: Multilateral Alliances

Path From/To	*(3)*	*(4)*
(1) Contractual control function	–0.17*	
(2) Contractual coordination function	0.09	
(3) Partner cooperation		0.20**
(4) Alliance success		
Control Variables		
(6) Exploitation orientation	–0.10	0.03
(7) Contract complexity	–0.04	0.11
(8) History of trustful collaboration	0.09	–0.02
(9) Multilateral collaboration		

$^{\dagger}p < 0.10$; $^{*}p < 0.05$; $^{**}p < 0.01$; $^{***}p < 0.001$

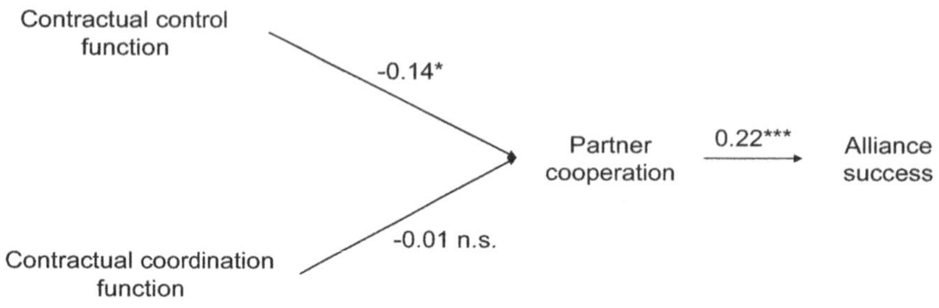

†$p < 0.10$; *$p < 0.05$; **$p < 0.01$; ***$p < 0.001$

Figure 4.2. Result for full sample.

ings in model 1 (see Table 4.6 and Figure 4.2), however, suggest the existence of a significant negative effect of the contractual control function on partner cooperation. This means that, the more the contract was used as a mechanisms to control the behavior of the partners, the less (more) likely (non)-cooperative behaviors were to emerge within the alliance.

In hypothesis 2, we also expected a moderation effect of the presence of prior trustful collaboration. Model 2 and Model 3 (see Table 4.7, Table 4.8, and Figure 4.3) provide strong indications that prior trustful collaboration indeed moderates the relationship between the contractual control function and partner cooperation. In particular, we observe that the significant negative impact of the contractual control function on partner cooperation disappears when a history of prior collaboration is present.

Finally, we also find that the number of alliance partners has a moderating impact on the relationship between contractual control function and partner cooperation. However, whereas we expected in hypothesis 3 that the contractual control function has a more positive impact on partner cooperation in the setting of a multilateral alliance, Model 5 (see Table 4.10 and Figure 4.3) points to a significant negative impact of the contractual control function on partner cooperation in this particular setting, At the same time, Model 4 (see Table 4.9 and Figure 4.3) indicates that the contractual control function has no impact on partner cooperation in dyadic alliances.

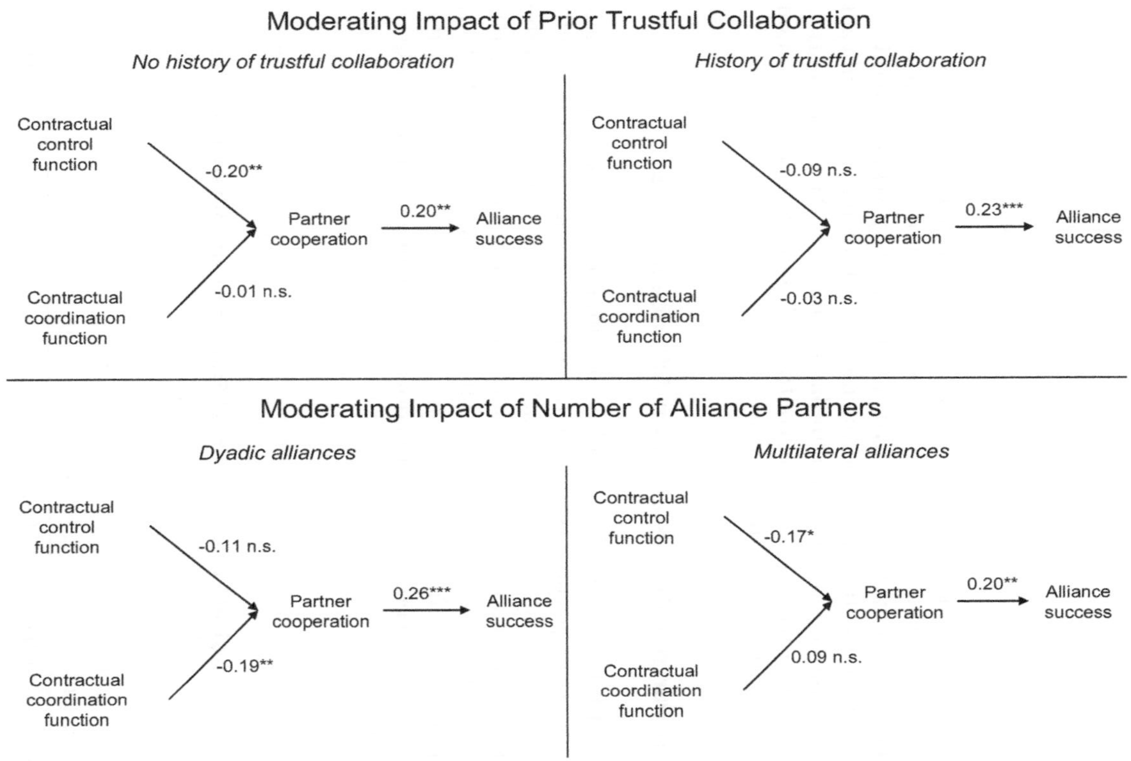

$^{\dagger}p < 0.10$; $^{*}p < 0.05$; $^{**}p < 0.01$; $^{***}p < 0.001$

Figure 4.3. Results for split samples.

Impact of Contractual Coordination Function on Partner Cooperation

In contrast to our hypothesis 4, we do not find a significant impact of the contractual coordination function on partner cooperation for the full sample (see Table 4.6 and Figure 4.2). In addition, we do not find that the relationship between the contractual coordination function and partner cooperation is moderated by the presence or absence of prior trustful collaboration (see Table 4.7, Table 4.8, and Figure 4.3). At the same time, we find strong indications that the number of alliance partners moderates the relationship between contractual coordination function and partner cooperation (see Table 4.9, Table 4.10, and Figure 4.3). Whereas model 5 indicates that the contractual coordination function has no significant impact on partner cooperation in multilateral alliances, Model 4 points to a significant negative impact of the contractual coordination function on partner cooperation in dyadic alliances.

Impact of Partner Cooperation on Alliance Success

In line with hypothesis 7, we find in all different models a significant positive impact of partner cooperation on alliance success. This significant effect also implies the existence of some indirect effects between the contractual control/coordination function and alliance success in different models. An overview of these indirect effects can be found in Table 4.11. This overview of the indirect effects shows that the actual impact of the contractual control/coordination functions on alliance success is close to zero or negative.

Table 4.11. Indirect of Contractual Functions on Alliance Success

	Model 1: Full Sample (n =270)	*Model 2: No History of Trustful Collaboration (n = 94)*	*Model 3: History of Trustful Collaboration (n = 186)*	*Model 4: Dyadic Alliances (n = 96)*	*Model 5: Multilateral Alliances (n = 184)*
Contractual control function	–0.03	–0.04	–0.02	–0.03	–0.03
Contractual coordination function	0.00	0.00	–0.01	–0.05	0.02

Impact of Control Variables

In the different models, we controlled for contract complexity, exploitation orientation, presence of prior trustful collaboration and number of alliances partners. For the full sample, we observe that multilateral alliance have a significant higher alliance success rate than dyadic alliances (see Table 4.6). If we only consider the alliances in which a history of trustful collaboration is lacking, this positive effect of multilateral alliances on alliance success becomes even more pronounced (see Table 4.7). At the same time, we do not find a significant effect of the number of alliance partners on alliance success for alliance that are characterized by a history of trustful collaboration (see Table 4.8).

In the full sample, we do not find an effect of exploitation orientation on alliance success (see Table 4.6). However, we also observe that exploitation orientation has a positive impact on alliances success for (1) alliances that are characterized by a history of trustful collaboration (see Table 4.8) and (2) dyadic alliances (Table 4.9). In other words, we find that the impact of the exploitation orientation on alliance success depends on the presence/absence of prior trustful collaboration and the number of alliance partners.

Previous studies (e.g., Luo, 2002; Poppo & Zenger, 2002) have examined the impact of contract complexity on alliance success. However, our study indicates that, when we also consider the actual functions of the contract, the explanatory value of contract complexity becomes rather low. We only find a significant negative effect of contract complexity of partner cooperation for alliances in which partners lack a history of trustful collaboration. In the other models, no significant impact of contract complexity on partner cooperation or alliance success was observed.

DISCUSSION AND CONCLUSION

In this section, we first discuss our main findings. Subsequently, we present their main managerial implications. Finally, we point to the main limitations of this study and suggest interesting avenues for future research.

Contractual Control Function and Partner Cooperation

Previous research has provided evidence that, in settings were the risk of opportunistic behavior is high (e.g., high asset specificity, high uncertainty), alliance partners are likely to negotiate more complex contracts (Parkhe, 1993) and are likely to pay more attention to control clauses in such contracts (Reuer & Ariño, 2007). Based on these findings and in line with transaction cost theory, these scholars pointed to contracts as an important control mechanism in alliance settings.

In this study, we actually tested the impact of this contractual control function on partner cooperation. In contrast to our expectations, we found that the more important the contractual control function, the less (more) likely (non)-cooperative behaviors are to emerge in alliances. This unexpected result can be explained in different ways. A first explanation might be that when partners pay a lot of attention to negotiating control clauses, they actually signal to each other that they expect the manifestation of opportunistic or noncooperative behavior. Subsequently, it might be that partners will act in line with these initial expectations, engaging in opportunistic actions. In other words, negotiation of control clauses might function as a self-fulfilling prophecy were the announcement of the risk of opportunistic behavior will indeed become true.

A second potential explanation is that, when partners emphasize the control function of the contract, they actually create a foundation of distrust. In such a setting, it might be that alliance partners are more likely to link the emergence setbacks during the alliance to the endogenous behavior of the other partner (i.e., opportunistic action) instead of attributing such negative events to exogenous conditions. Our observation that the negative impact of the contractual control function on alliance contracts disappears when partners share a history of prior trustful collaboration seems to support this latter reasoning.

Contractual Coordination Function and Partner Cooperation

Adopting insights from organization theory, several scholars (e.g., Mellewigt et al., 2007; Reuer & Ariño, 2007) have stressed that contracts can not only used as a formal control mechanisms, but can also be used as a mechanism to facilitate coordinated action. Our analyses, however, suggest that the actual impact of the contractual coordination function on partner cooperation is quite limited. This result might suggest that contractual coordination clauses mainly have an informational purpose (i.e., they inform partners about how they will perform the tasks), but do not really have a facilitating impact (i.e., they do not really stimulate more cooperative behavior).

In addition, we observe a significant negative effect of the contractual coordination function on partner cooperation in the particular setting of dyadic alliances. This latter finding might be explained by the fact that the standardized coordination, which is imposed on the alliance via contractual coordination clauses, might actually obstruct the emergence of coordination by mutual adjustment that is easily established in dyadic alliances.

Managerial Implications

In the alliance governance literature, numerous scholars have argued that, when managers are able to adjust the complexity of the contract to the transactional and relational conditions in which the alliance is embedded, the contract can have a positive impact on the success of the alliance. Based on our findings, we rather caution managers for the potential negative impact of contracts on the success of alliances. In particular, we emphasize that negotiating a strong contractual control function is likely to have a negative impact on alliance performance especially when no history of trustful collaboration is present. In addition, we warn for the use of contracts as mechanisms for achieving standardized coordination in the setting of dyadic alliances.

Limitations and Future Research

Although the goodness-of-fit of the tested models turns out to be very satisfactory, there is a lot of potential to improve the explanatory power of the models. For instance, we only could find significant effects of the contractual functions on partner cooperation, whereas all the control variables did not have a significant impact on this variable. These results suggest that there are other transactional and/or relational characteristics that determine the level of (non)-cooperative behaviors during the alliance. A more fine-grained assessment of the determinants of partner cooperation in alliances therefore seems to be necessary.

Our research was situated in a very particular setting. More specifically, we focused on subsidized technological innovation projects in which different firms were involved. This particular setting might limit the generalizability of our findings. Additional survey research on the impact of contractual functions on performance in other interfirm settings therefore seems to be necessary.

A final limitation of our study was that we could only survey one partner of the alliance. However, it might be that different partners have different opinions about the function of the contract, the nature of partner cooperation and the success of the alliance. We therefore encourage future research on alliance governance that incorporates the opinions of all involved partners.

Despite these limitations, this study has triggered first insights in how different contractual functions influence alliance performance. We hope that our findings might help alliance managers in optimizing their contractual governance strategies. In addition, we hope that our insights might motivate other scholars to further examine the governance of interfirm relationship in a wide variety of organizational settings.

REFERENCES

Anderson, S. W., & Dekker, H. C. (2005). Management control for market transactions: The relation between transaction characteristics, incomplete contract design, and subsequent performance. *Management Science, 51*, 1734–1752.

Ariño, A. (2003). Measures of strategic alliance performance: An analysis of construct validity. *Journal of International Business Studies, 34*, 66-79.

Ariño, A., & Reuer, J. J. (2005). Alliance contractual design. In O. Shenkar & J. J. Reuer (Eds.), *Handbook of strategic alliances* (pp. 149–167). Thousand Oaks, CA: SAGE.

Bijlsma-Frankema, K., & Costa, A. C. (2005). Understanding the trust-control nexus. *International Sociology, 30*, 259–282.

Blau, P. (1964). *Exchange and power in social life.* New York: Wiley.

Bleeke, J., & Ernst, D. (1991, November–December). The way to win in cross-border alliances. *Harvard Business Review,* 127–135.

Das, T. K., & Teng, B. (1998). Between trust and control: Developing confidence in partner cooperation in alliances. *Academy of Management Review, 23*, 491-512.

Das, T. K., & Teng, B. (2001). Trust, control, and risk in strategic alliances: An integrated framework. *Organization Studies, 22,* 251–283.

Das, T. K., & Teng, B. (2002). Alliance constellations: A social exchange perspective, *Academy of Management Review, 27*, 445–456.

De Jong, G., & Klein Woolthuis, R. J. A. (2008). Contract research and high-tech alliances: Vistas for future studies. *Scandinavian Journal of Management, 24*, 284–289.

Doz, Y., & Hamel, G. (1998). *Alliance advantage: The art of creating value through partnering.* Boston, MA: Harvard Business School Press.

Dyer, J. H., & Singh, H. (1998). The relational view: Cooperative strategy and sources of interorganizational competitive advantage. *Academy of Management Review, 23*, 660–679.

Eisenhardt, K. M. (1985). Control: Organizational and economic approaches. *Management Science, 31*, 134–149.

Faems, D., Janssens, M., Bouwen, R., & Van Looy, B. (2006). Governing explorative R&D alliances: Searching for effective strategies. *Management Revue, 17*, 9–29.

Faems, D., Janssens, M., Madhok, A., & Van Looy, B. (2008). Towards an integrative perspective on alliance governance: Connecting contract design, contract application and trust dynamics. *Academy of Management Journal, 51*, 1053–1078.

Faems, D., Janssens, M., & Van Looy, B. (2007). The initiation and evolution of interfirm knowledge transfer in R&D relationships. *Organization Studies, 28*, 1699–1728.

Faems, D., Van Looy, B., & Debackere, K. (2005). Interorganizational collaboration and innovation: Toward a portfolio approach. *Journal of Product Innovation Management, 22*, 238–250.

Galbraith, J. R. (1977). *Organization design.* Reading, MA: Addison-Wesley.

Garcia-Canal, E., Valdés-Llaneza, A., & Ariño, A. (2003). Effectiveness of dyadic and multi-party joint ventures. *Organization Studies, 24*, 743–770.

Geringer, J. M., & Herbert, L. (1991). Measuring performance of international joint ventures. *Journal of International Business Studies, 22*, 249–264.

Gong, Y., Shenkar, O., Luo, Y., & Nyaw, M-K. (2007). Do multiple parents help or hinder international joint venture performance? The mediating roles of contract completeness and partner cooperation. *Strategic Management Journal, 28*, 1021–1034.

Gulati, R. (1995). Does familiarity breed trust? The implications of repeated ties for contractual choice in alliances. *Academy of Management Review, 38*, 85–112.

Gulati, R., & Singh, H. (1998). The architecture of cooperation: Managing coordination costs and appropriation concerns in strategic alliances. *Administrative Science Quarterly, 43*, 781–814.

Hagedoorn, J. (2002). Inter-firm R&D partnerships: An overview of major trends and patterns since 1960. *Research Policy, 31*, 477–492.

Hagedoorn, J., & Hesen, G. (2007). Contract law and the governance of inter-firm technology partnerships: An analysis of different modes of partnering and their contractual implications. *Journal of Management Studies, 44*, 342–366.

Inkpen, A. C., & Currall, S. C. (2004). The coevolution of trust, control, and learning in joint ventures. *Organization Science, 15*, 586–599.

Jones, G. R., & George, J. M. (1998). The experience and evolution of trust: Implications for cooperation and teamwork. *Academy of Management Review, 23*, 531–546.

Kale, P., & Singh, H. (2009). Managing strategic alliances: What do we know now, and where do we go from here? *Academy of Management Perspectives, 23*(3), 45–62.

Klein Woolthuis, R., Hillebrand, B., & Nooteboom, B. (2005). Trust, contract and relationship development. *Organization Studies, 26*, 813–840.

Koza, M. P., & Lewin, A.Y. (1998). The co-evolution of strategic alliances. *Organization Science, 9*, 255–264.

Lavie, D., & Rosenkopf, L. (2006). Balancing exploration and exploitation in alliance formation. *Academy of Management Journal, 49*, 797–819.

Lawrence, P. R., & Lorsch, J. W. (1967). *Organization and environment.* Boston, MA: Harvard Business School Press.

Luo, Y. (2002). Contract, cooperation, and performance in international joint ventures, *Strategic Management Journal, 23*, 903–919.

Lyons, B., & Mehta, J. (1997). Contracts, opportunism and trust: Self-interest and social orientation. *Cambridge Journal of Economics, 21*, 239–257.

Madhok, A., & Tallman, S. B. (1998). Resources, transactions and rents: Managing value through interfirm collaborative relationships. *Organization Science, 9*, 326–339.

Malhotra, D. & Murnighan, J. K. (2002). The effects of contracts on interpersonal trust. *Administrative Science Quarterly, 47*, 534–559.

Mayer, K. J., & Argyres, N. S. (2004). Learning to contract: Evidence from the personal computer industry. *Organization Science, 15*, 394–410.

Mayer, K. J., & Teece, D. J. (2008). Unpacking strategic alliances: The structure and purpose of alliance versus supplier relationships. *Journal of Economic Behavior & Organization, 66*, 106–127.

Mellewigt, T., Madhok, A., & Weibel, A. (2007). Trust and formal contracts in interorganizational relationships—substitutes *and* complements. *Managerial and Decision Economics, 28*, 833–847.

Mintzberg, H. (1979). *The structuring of organizations: A synthesis of the research.* Englewood Cliffs, NJ: Prentice-Hall.

Ouchi, W. G. (1979). A conceptual framework for the design of organizational control mechanisms. *Management Science, 25*, 833–848.

Parkhe, A. (1991). Interfirm diversity, organizational learning, and longevity in global strategic alliances. *Journal of International Business Studies, 22*, 579–601.

Parkhe, A. (1993). Strategic alliances structuring: a game theoretic and transaction cost examination of interfirm cooperation. *Academy of Management Journal, 36*, 794–829.

Poppo, L., & Zenger, T. (2002). Do formal contracts and relational governance function as substitutes or complements? *Strategic Management Journal, 23*, 707–725.

Reuer, J. J., & Ariño, A. (2007). Strategic alliance contracts: Dimensions and determinants of contractual complexity. *Strategic Management Journal, 28*, 313–330.

Reuer, J. J., Ariño, A., & Mellewigt, T. (2006). Entrepreneurial alliances as contractual forms. *Journal of Business Venturing, 21*, 306–325.

Ring, P. S. (1997). Processes facilitating reliance on trust in inter-organizational networks. In M. Ebers (Ed.), *The formation of inter-organizational networks.* Oxford, England: Oxford University Press.

Ring, P. S., & Van de Ven, A. H. (1994). Developmental processes of cooperative interorganizational relationships. *Academy of Management Review, 19*, 90–118.

Rothaermel, F. T., & Deeds, D. L. (2004). Exploration and exploitation alliances in biotechnology: A system of new product development. *Strategic Management Journal, 25*, 201–221.

Rousseau, D. M., Sitkin, S. B., Burt, R. S., & Camerer, C. (1998). Not so different after all: A cross-discipline view of trust. *Academy of Management Review, 23*, 393–404.

Sels, L., De Winne, S., Maes, J., Delmotte, J., Faems, D., & Forrier, A. (2006). Unraveling the HRM-performance link: Value-creating and cost-increasing effects of small business HRM. *Journal of Management Studies, 43*, 319–342.

Thompson, J. D. (1967). *Organizations in action.* New York, NY: Mc-Graw-Hill.

Williamson, O. E. (1985). *The economic institutions of capitalism.* New York, NY: Free Press.

Zajac, E. J., & Olsen, C. P. (1993). From transaction cost to transactional value analysis: Implications for the study of interorganizational strategies. *Journal of Management Studies, 30*, 131–145.

CHAPTER 5

GOVERNANCE STRUCTURE CHOICE IN STRATEGIC ALLIANCES

The Roles of Alliance Objectives, Alliance Management Experience, and International Partners

Bing-Sheng Teng and T. K. Das

Strategic alliances have a variety of governance structures that can be broadly classified as joint ventures, minority equity alliances, and contractual alliances. In this chapter we empirically examine the roles of four key determinants of governance structure choice, namely, joint R&D and joint marketing objectives, alliance management experience, and international partners. We develop several hypotheses regarding governance structure choice and test them with data from 765 alliances. We used a multinomial logistic regression (logit) model for statistical analysis, with five control variables. All hypotheses are supported, so that the roles of alliance objectives, alliance management experience, and international partners are demonstrated as significant determinants of governance structure choice in alliances. Limitations stem from the data being from a single source, one that

Strategic Alliances in a Globalizing World, pp. 93–115

also relies upon press announcements that may be biased toward larger alliances. Alliance managers should find it useful to assess the relative presence of the four determinants of structural choice studied in this investigation in order to make an informed selection of the appropriate governance structure. The chapter contributes to our knowledge of the key determinants of governance structure choice in strategic alliances by examining empirically, with a large sample of alliances from various industries, the significant roles of four factors, namely, joint R&D and joint marketing objectives, alliance management experience, and international partners.

INTRODUCTION

Strategic alliances serve the strategic objectives of partner firms (Doz & Hamel, 1998). Due to factors such as globalization and emerging technologies, it is increasingly difficult to obtain sustainable competitive advantage in rapidly changing markets (D'Aveni, 1994). Any one firm by itself often does not possess all the necessary resources and capabilities to compete effectively. Strategic alliances offer an alternative to such firms, whereby they could join forces with other firms in the pursuit of opportunities that would otherwise be beyond the firm's current capabilities. In essence, alliances allow partner firms to creatively combine resources in the establishment of joint competitive advantage.

Strategic alliances come in a variety of structures, including such popular arrangements as joint ventures, minority equity alliances, enhanced buyer-supplier partnerships, joint production, joint bidding, and code-sharing in the airline industry. Alliance structure is a critical determinant of alliance performance (Parkhe, 1993a). Yoshino and Rangan (1995) report that virtually all managers they interviewed believed that an alliance's success depended on its structure. Killing (1988) and Teece (1992) believe structural decisions are among the most important decisions alliance partners make. The reason is that structural decisions impact almost all aspects of the alliance, including operational process, control mechanisms, and even exit possibilities (Das & Teng, 1996).

Researchers have been studying alliance structures for some time, particularly from the perspective of transaction cost economics (Oxley, 1997; Pisano, 1989). In this view, alliance structural choice reflects the need to deal with behavioral uncertainty such as opportunism and reduce transaction costs between the partners. Equity arrangement can be used to align the partners' interests when the risk of opportunism is significant (Gulati, 1995). Further, Gulati and Singh (1998) find that both coordination costs and appropriation concerns influence alliance structural choices.

Other theories that have been used to understand alliance structures include game theory (Parkhe, 1993b), risk perception (Das & Teng, 1996, 2001), agency theory (Reuer & Miller, 1997), network theory (Rowley, Behrens, & Krackhardt, 2000), and resource-based view of the firm (Das & Teng, 2000). For instance, Parkhe (1993b) finds that alliances perform better when payoff patterns are structured to punish cheating in alliances, as they often represent a prisoner's dilemma situation. Das and Teng (1996, 2001) reason that alliance partners' perception of relational risk and performance risk significantly influences their structural decisions. Thomas and Trevino (1993) demonstrate through several cases that alliance structuring is a process of information processing.

In this study we empirically test several key factors that may influence governance structure choices: alliance objectives (including joint R&D and joint marketing), alliance management experience, and international partners. While two of the factors (namely, joint R&D and international partners) were examined in a previous study (Gulati & Singh, 1998), we aim to provide additional evidence regarding their effects. We also include in our study two more factors, namely, joint marketing and alliance management experience. While much research has been done on R&D alliances (Carson, Madhok, Varman, & John, 2003; Hoang & Rothaermel, 2005), joint marketing as an important alliance type has not received adequate attention in the literature (Bucklin & Sengupta, 1993). Alliance management experience is included in this study on account of its close relationship with alliance performance (Lane, Salk, & Lyles, 2001; Sampson, 2005). Whereas previous studies have often used the total number of prior alliances between two partners as an indicator for alliance management experience (Goerzen, 2007), our investigation includes all the prior alliances formed by the partners and is reflective of the notion of "collaborative know-how."

Our results regarding the roles of these four factors as determinants of governance structure are, we believe, valuable in their own right. This study not only confirms that joint R&D alliances and international partners tend to have more equity involvement, but also reveals the significant roles of joint marketing activities and alliance management experience. Thus, this study makes a contribution in identifying new determinants of alliance structures.

THREE TYPES OF ALLIANCES

While strategic alliances have a great variety of forms, many researchers agree that the basic forms of alliance include joint ventures, minority equity alliances, and contractual alliances (Das & Teng, 1998; Gulati &

Singh, 1998; Yoshino & Rangan, 1995). Joint ventures refer to separately incorporated entities jointly owned by partners. Minority equity alliances include an acquisition of equity shares by either one or more partner firms, while contractual alliances involve no equity transaction or creation of a new entity in the agreement.

Researchers have emphasized the role of equity arrangements in differentiating alliance structures (Hennart, 1988; Pisano, 1991). Most empirical studies have focused on the structural choice between equity-based alliances (including both joint ventures and minority equity alliances) and contractual alliances, primarily from a transaction cost perspective (Gulati, 1995; Osborn & Baughn, 1990). According to Gulati and Singh (1998), although joint ventures and minority equity alliances have the common characteristic of shared ownership, they ought to be separated along the dimension of hierarchical control. Alternatively, the three alliance types can be differentiated through the notion of equity involvement. According to Nooteboom (1999), interfirm relations differ in terms of the strength of the linkage between the firms, and equity involvement is concrete manifestation of that strength of inter-firm linkage.

Furthermore, equity arrangements are believed to help align the interests of partner firms (Gulati, 1995). When there is shared equity, partner firms realize that their interests are intertwined and hence opportunistic behavior tends to be discouraged. In addition, shared equity serves as a mutual hostage for partners to retaliate and punish an opportunistic party (Kogut, 1988). Since equity arrangements are not easily terminated, it is difficult for an opportunistic party to quickly exit the alliance after taking advantage of the other party. In sum, an equity arrangement can ease partners' concern over opportunism in alliances.

Shared equity often facilitates the coordination and control of the collaborative effort. Partner firms may accomplish their work separately as in a joint bidding agreement or they can have integrated processes and centralized control as in a joint venture. According to Larson (1992) the coordination of partner firms through "dense communications and administrative systems" can be called "operational integration" (p. 91). When partner firms work together in a joint venture, their behavior can be directly observed and measured. Centralized procedures and policies can also be developed, which provide a uniformed standard for all parties. Thus, joint ventures are preferred in more complex types of collaborations (Garcia-Canal, 1996).

Joint ventures are the most integrative form of alliances. A joint venture represents a new entity (i.e., equity creation) that combines partner firms in a selected area. Not only do firms have shared equities, but their operation is also combined in the selected area. Centralized control and collaboration are the hallmark of joint ventures.

Minority equity alliances, by comparison, have a modest level of structural integration. When one firm owns a meaningful portion of another firm, the two are partially integrated through ownership. However, the equity arrangement is partial because only a limited portion of equity is involved. As compared to joint ventures in which all equities for the new entity are shared, minority equity alliances feature limited equity exchange and thus represent a lower level of equity exchange. In addition, in contrast to joint ventures, minority equity alliances usually do not have integrated processes and centralized control. Without forming a new entity, partner firms carry out their cooperative activities separately.

Contractual alliances have the lowest degree of structural integration among the three alliance types. The partner firms do not have an integrated entity to carry out the joint activities, nor do they have any equity arrangements. Contractual alliances are operated merely based on the agreements for the partner firms to work together in a certain way, such as in pursuing joint research and joint marketing. Again, such tentative structures lack centralized control that come with a joint venture.

ALLIANCE OBJECTIVES

Joint R&D Alliances

To the extent that structure follows and implements strategy, the objectives of alliances have several implications for alliance structure. In this chapter, we deal with two alliance objectives—joint R&D and joint marketing—that are common in alliances (Glaister & Buckley, 1996; Hagedoorn, 1993). As to joint R&D, the key lies in the transfer of a critical resource—technological knowledge. In two contrasting ways, knowledge transfer and learning affect the choice of alliance structure. The reason is that both knowledge acquisition and protection are important. The challenge is to facilitate *legitimate* learning while simultaneously deterring *illegitimate* (or opportunistic) learning, in order to protect one's core competences (Das & Kumar, 2007; Kale, Dyer, & Singh, 2002; Larsson, Bengtsson, Henriksson, & Sparks, 1998).

Strong governance is desirable for effective joint R&D activities, since legitimate knowledge transfer and learning are essential for their success (Khanna, Gulati, & Nohria, 1998; Powell, Koput, & Smith-Doerr, 1996). When firms collectively conduct research, a certain level of common knowledge and process is a prerequisite. As such, joint R&D often requires the partners to work side-by-side in one R&D setting, because physical proximity and face-to-face meetings facilitate knowledge transfer and learning (Athanassiou & Nigh, 2000; Galbraith, 1990). Clearly, equity-based governance in alliances helps create a common setting in which learning can take place. In this sense, it is believed that joint ventures are the most effective form of alliance for learning and knowledge transfer purposes (Kogut, 1988). Empirical research confirms that more integrative alliance forms facilitate knowledge transfer between partners (Mellewigt & Das, 2007; Mowery, Oxley, & Silverman, 1998).

Furthermore, if knowledge acquisition is done without the consent of the knowledge owner, it is considered opportunistic. Thus, illegitimate knowledge transfer can be a serious threat. Firms in alliances often try to get ahead of their partners through learning races, which may result in the loss of firm-specific knowledge for some firms (Bleeke & Ernst, 1995; Hamel, 1991). If partner firms are direct or potential competitors, one may use what it secretly learned from the other to compete against it in the marketplace (Dussauge, Garrette, & Mitchell, 2000). Thus, partners employ various control mechanisms to deter opportunistic learning and protect their intellectual capital (Das, 2005; Inkpen, 1998). A key control mechanism is equity (Baughn, Denekamp, Stevens, & Osborn, 1997). As noted earlier, shared equity ownership aligns partners' interests, as a result of which partners are more likely to refrain from self-serving activities at others' expense. In addition, equity positions serve as a mutual hostage for partners so that they can be used to punish opportunistic parties. In sum, joint R&D activities require more equity-based governance structures because equity integration deters illegitimate knowledge transfer.

Hypothesis 1a: Alliances formed to conduct joint R&D will have more equity-based governance structures.

Joint Marketing Alliances

Joint marketing, that is, combining firms' marketing activities in a given market, is another popular objective in alliances (Bucklin & Sengupta, 1993). For example, telecom firms have formed a number of global alliances (e.g., Concert by British Telecom and AT&T) to jointly sell worldwide telecom services to multinational corporations. A key feature of joint marketing alliances is that partner firms usually combine their marketing efforts by offering a unified image in the given marketplace. Their brand names thus become integrated to a certain extent. For example, in the alliance between KLM and Northwest Airlines, the two firms combined their brand names and logos. Similarly, when Coca-Cola recruited Danone of France to jointly market its Minute Maid orange juice in Europe and Latin America, both firms' logos were used. Such an integrated market image is distinctive in joint marketing alliances.

The combination of brand names may complicate the allocation of "residuals" in joint marketing alliances. Such outcome allocation is important in alliances and is about developing a compensation structure that divides the payoffs of the alliance. This issue is particularly relevant when the alliance is to be terminated. In joint marketing alliances, outcome allocation tends to be more difficult since brand names and images of the partners are intermingled. As compared to physical, human, and financial resources, marketing resources such as reputation and brand image are more intangible and, once mixed, more difficult to separate and allocate proportionately between partners. Hence, *ex ante* contractual provisions tend to be insufficient in specifying the contingencies (Teece, 1992).

Thus, there is a high degree of residuals in joint marketing alliances that cannot be easily attributed and allocated to a given party. Partners need "a compensation structure under which they each bear some of the residuals from their exchange" (Chi & Roehl, 1997, p. 280). To that end, an equity-based governance structure provides a much-needed mechanism to apportion residuals. Shared equity can "provide a mechanism for distributing residuals when *ex ante* contractual agreements cannot be written to specify or enforce a division of returns" (Teece, 1992, p. 20). With shared equity, there is an understanding that residual allocation starts with equity positions, which reduces the concerns of partners prior to alliance formation.

The benefit for residual allocation is particularly significant in joint ventures, since there is separate equity creation in joint ventures and only partial equity arrangement in minority equity alliances. As Kogut (1988) put it, joint ventures help "both parties share in the residual value of the venture" (p. 321) since partners' equity positions in the joint venture serve as an undisputed basis for residual allocation. In contrast, in minority equity alliances partners will eventually need to negotiate for residual allocation. In sum, since there are considerable residuals in joint marketing alliances, equity arrangement is particularly needed.

Hypothesis 1b: Alliances formed to conduct joint marketing will have more equity-based governance structures.

ALLIANCE MANAGEMENT EXPERIENCE

A valuable resource in alliances is a firm's alliance management experience, which comprises a firm's overall experience in forming and managing strategic alliances (Hoang & Rothaermel, 2005; Sampson, 2007). Simonin (1997) argues that firms differ in their "collaborative know-how," or the capability in managing alliances. Through past alliances, partner firms accumulate valuable knowledge about alliance management (Hagedoorn & Duysters, 2002). Kale and Singh (2007) find that alliances offer great learning opportunities for firms to develop firm capabilities. Other research has found evidence that firms learn to manage alliances more effectively over time (Anand & Khanna, 2000; Barkema, Shenkar, Vermeulen, & Bell, 1997). Gulati (1999) reports that the greater a firm's alliance experience and capability, the more likely that it will form a new alliance in the future. Understandably, firms are interested in taking advantage of their collaborative know-how by forming additional alliances.

When firms develop collaborative know-how in alliances, the need for more equity-based governance structures tends to decrease. The argument here is that firms need more equity-based governance structures (such as joint ventures) to align the interests of partner firms when interfirm trust is insufficient (Gulati, 1995). Trust can be defined as "a type of expectation that alleviates the fear that one's exchange partner will act opportunistically" (Bradach & Eccles, 1989, p. 104). Trust is critical in strategic alliances as it is directly associated with the challenging issues of alliances—incomplete contracts and opportunism (Carson et al., 2003; Krishnan, Martin, & Noorderhaven, 2006). Since interfirm trust provides confidence (Das & Teng, 1998) that opportunistic behavior is unlikely, trust effectively reduces the need for contractual safeguards and thus lowers transaction costs (Dyer & Chu, 2003; Lui & Ngo, 2004).

Therefore, partner firms need more equity-based alliance structures if they do not have sufficient trust in each other (Das & Teng, 1998). Alliance novices are made more comfortable by equity-based governance structures. As we noted, shared equity helps align partners' interests and deter opportunistic behavior such as cheating and shirking (Pisano, 1991). For alliance novices, such a mechanism is much needed and provides confidence in partner cooperation. As the firm learns how to deal with partners in alliances, it will be able to rely less on equity arrangements and more on intangible factors such as reputation and interfirm trust. Thus, a high number of prior alliances between two firms has been found to encourage the use of less equity-based governance structures (Gulati, 1995).

Although equity-based structures such as joint ventures take more time and effort to forge as well as to terminate, they are particularly worthwhile for new players in the alliance field. As time goes on and the firm learns how to deal with alliances, more flexible arrangements will become more attractive. After all, contractual alliances, with a nonequity governance structure preserve much of the flexibility that will be valuable in case spin-offs are called for. Thus, the aggregated alliance experience of the partner firms predicts the alliance structure:

> **Hypothesis 2:** The greater the previous alliance management experience of the partner firms (between themselves or with any other firms), the less equity-based will be their alliance structures.

INTERNATIONAL PARTNERS

Partner nationality is found to moderate the relationship between alliance structure and alliance performance (Parkhe, 1993a), and also affects the relative importance of various strategic motivations in alliances (Glaister & Buckley, 1996). International alliances are exposed to an additional risk called international risk, which has its roots in national differences in terms of cultures, regulations, technological standards, and business practices (Brouthers, 1995).

Partners of different nations tend to have a low degree of resource similarity, or a high level of resource heterogeneity. The kinds of human, technological, physical, and organizational resources held by firms of different nations are more likely to be dissimilar, and therefore lack compatibility. It has been found that partner firms in international alliances have different needs and offer different resources and capabilities (Hitt, Dacin, Levitas, Arregle, & Borza, 2000).

We suggest that resource heterogeneity requires more deliberate resource integration efforts in alliances, and an equity-based governance structure is an important step in that direction. Equity involvement helps create a formal structure within which centralized control could take place. For instance, if two firms employ vastly different technologies, an integration of the two technologies is a must for any co-production alliance. An equity-based governance structure brings the parties together in one entity, often with one physical setting that facilitates better utilization of resources. Research suggests that face-to-face meetings are more effective than distant communication for knowledge transfer (Athanassiou & Nigh, 2000). Thus, more equity involvement would reduce resource heterogeneity between firms.

When two firms are from two different institutional environments, they usually follow different norms of business operation (Kostova, 1999). Consequently, there tends to be a lack of understanding and trust between international partners, as compared to domestic partners (Gulati, 1995). For instance, intellectual property protection regimes vary significantly across nations and can be a source of concern in international alliances (Oxley, 1997). Since equity arrangements deter opportunistic behavior, they are preferred when interfirm trust is insufficient. Empirically, Gulati and Singh (1998) find some evidence that cross-region alliances (three regions including the United States, Japan, and Europe) are likely to have more equity-based alliances than domestic (or within-region) ones. Thus:

Hypothesis 3: International alliances will have more equity-based governance structures than domestic alliances.

METHODS

Data

The data for this study were drawn from an alliance database published by *Alliance Analyst* (1994–1997), a bi-weekly publication specializing in alliance-related issues. *Alliance Analyst* offers one of the most complete and publicly available alliance databases, as it covers a wide range of publications such as *New York Times Index* and *Wall Street Journal Index*. The collection of press announcements as a source of alliance data has been widely used by researchers to generate research databases of strategic alliances (e.g., Glaister & Buckley, 1996; Reuer & Miller, 1997). The *Alliance Analyst* database provides the following information: names of the partners and their nationalities, industry of the alliance, alliance type, alliance objectives, and a fairly detailed description of the alliance agreement.

We used five selection criteria to construct the data set used in this study. First, the time frame covered was between September 1994 and May 1997 (the publication ceased a short time thereafter). We started with the date that *Alliance Analyst* was launched, that is, September 1994. During the initial 3-year period, 1994–1997, there were significant strategic alliance activities (*Alliance Analyst*, 1994–1997). Second, only those alliances that were actually formed during that period were included. Numerous announcements of intentions to form strategic alliances were not used because many of them did not materialize. Modifications of existing alliances were not included either.

Third, only two-party (or dyadic) alliances with at least one U.S. partner were included in the data set. Although most of our argument applies to multipartner alliances, a focus on dyadic alliances simplifies the empirical tests. Limiting the data to alliances with at least one U.S. partner is based on the concern that *Alliance Analyst* is probably more comprehensive with alliances involving U.S. firms.

Fourth, while strategic alliances between not-for-profit organizations are booming, this study focuses on alliances between for-profit companies. Some of the arguments here may not be applicable to other types of organizations, such as government agencies and universities.

Fifth, we included eight common types of strategic alliances: joint ventures, equity alliances, joint production, joint marketing and promotion, joint R&D, enhanced supplier partnerships, sponsored R&D, and licensing agreements. Arm's length agreements such as subcontracting and regular supplier agreements were not included. Whereas the first two types—joint ventures and equity alliances—are clear in our three-part typology discussed earlier, the other six types of alliances were classified as either equity-based or contractual-based, depending on whether or not there was any equity arrangement in the deal.

These five criteria led to a data set of 765 alliances. Like the *Alliance Analyst* database, our data set includes eleven major industrial groups: airline and aerospace (3.0%), automotive (4.8%), business services (1.4%), consumer product/retail/food and beverage (36.9%), computers and communication (7.3%), energy and natural resources (6.8%), entertainment and leisure (5.0%), financial services (13.3%), healthcare/chemical (17.3%), industrial machinery and equipment (3.5%), and transport (0.6%). As compared to similar studies on alliances (Gulati & Singh, 1998; Parkhe, 1993b), this study covers more industries and thus is possibly more representative of the alliance population.

Variables

The dependent variable in this study is alliance structure choice, which measures the level of equity arrangement in the alliance. Since joint ventures have the highest degree of equity involvement, they are coded 3. Minority equity alliances are coded 2 due to its moderate level of equity arrangement. Finally, contractual alliances involve no use of equity and are thus coded 1.

There are four independent variables. *Joint R&D* and *joint marketing* are two important objectives in alliances. The *Alliance Analyst* database provides information regarding these two objectives based on public announcements made by the alliance partners. Since the objectives of an alliance are known, it is coded 1 if it has a joint R&D component and 0 if not. The same rule applied to the *joint marketing* variable. The variable *alliance management experience* is about the total alliance experience the two partner firms had prior to the formation of the particular alliance. Thus, it is measured as the total number of previous alliances that the two partner firms had formed since September 1994, between themselves or with any other firm. As noted earlier, previous studies often focused on the impact of partner-specific alliance experience (Goerzen, 2007). By comparison, our measure reflects the overall alliance management experience of partner firms. The variable *international partners* is about whether the partner firms are of the same nation, and is coded 1 for international alliances and 0 for domestic ones.

There are five control variables in this study, all of which are used to account for external trends regarding alliances. The first two variables, *percent minority equity* and *percent joint ventures*, measure the percentage of alliances in the 1994–1997 period that were minority equity alliances and joint ventures, respectively. To some extent, these two variables account for the external environment which may favor one type of alliance over another, as well as the institutional view that firms mimic popular strategies of other firms (Gulati & Singh, 1998). In addition, the temporal trend is controlled by including three dummy variables for each year (*Y95*, *Y96*, *Y97*) in the 1994–1997 period, with the default year being 1994.

Statistical Model

Logistic regression can be used to test structural choices between equity alliances and nonequity alliances. However, since our dependent variable has trichotomous responses (i.e., three categories) and the independent variables include both categorical and continuous ones, the appropriate statistical approach is a multinomial logistic regression (logit) model. An ordinal model would be inappropriate since the three choices are nominal in nature. A multinomial logit model allows us to test a single choice among three alliance structures: joint ventures, minority equity alliances, and contractual alliances. The general specification of the model used was as follows:

$$\text{In } (p_j/p_o) = a + b_j x_j$$

Where p_j is the probability of an event taking place for the jth case. In models 1–2 the two possible events are (1) a minority equity alliance and (2) a joint venture. P_0 is the probability of the default condition, taken here to be either a contractual alliance (models 1–2) or a joint venture (model 3). X_j is the vector of independent variables. The CATMOD procedure of the SAS program was used to run the logit model.

RESULTS

Table 5.1 reports the basic descriptive statistics and correlations for all variables included in this study. It shows that the average number of prior alliances was 2.8, and that 47% of the alliances were international. While 55% had a joint R&D component, 71% had a joint marketing component in the alliance. During the period, 14% and 40.5% were formed as minority equity alliances and joint ventures, respectively, which leaves 45.5% as contractual alliances. The correlations show that multicollinearity is not a serious problem for the data.

Table 5.2 provides results for the multinomial logistic regression analysis on alliance structure choice. Since the choice is among three alliance governance structures (e.g., joint ventures, minority equity alliances, and contractual alliances), in models 1–2 we used contractual alliances as the base category and contrasted it against the other two. The differences between joint ventures and minority equity alliances were further examined through another regression (model 3) in which joint ventures were set as the base category. The coefficients in the models show the effects of the variables for each alliance type relative to their effects for the base category.

To examine the robustness of the results, we gradually entered variables in the models. Model 1 included the control variables only. The results show that the institutional and temporal trends had a significant impact on alliance structural choices. For example, joint ventures were less likely in years 1995 and 1996 as compared to year 1994. Overall, the model is highly significant, as is evident in the goodness-of-fit results (chi-square of likelihood ratio = 63.20). The p-value (.58) is much higher than .05, indicating a good fit with the data.

In model 2 we added the four independent variables. The model is highly significant, based on the high goodness-of-fit number. Besides, there is significant improvement from model 1 to model 2 (chi-square of likelihood ratio increased from 63.20 to 771.00 and p-value from .58 to .99), indicating that the four independent variables indeed contribute to the explanatory power of the model. Model 3 and model 2 have the same independent and control variables, except that they have joint ventures and contractual alliances as the base category for the dependent variable, respectively. In other words, model 2 compares its base category of contractual alliances against minority equity alliances and joint ventures. Model 3 compares the base category of joint ventures against the other two forms. Thus, the coefficients for joint ventures in model 2 and those for contractual alliances in model 3 have the same values but opposite signs, since both compare joint ventures with contractual alliances. For example, a positive and significant coefficient under joint venture in model 2 (such as joint R&D) suggests that joint R&D alliances are more likely to be joint ventures than contractual ones (the base category). Throughout models 1–3, the effects of the control variables are quite consistent.

Table 5.1. Descriptive Statistics and Correlations[a]

Variables	*Mean*	*S.D.*	*Low*	*High*	*1*	*2*	*3*	*4*	*5*	*6*	*7*	*8*	*9*	*10*
1. Alliance Structure Choice	1.95	.93	1	3	–									
2. Joint R&D	.55	.50	0	1	.14	–								
3. Joint Marketing	.71	.45	0	1	.19	.01	–							
4. Alliance Management Experience	2.80	5.54	0	46	–.21	.09	.01	–						
5. International Partners	.47	.50	0	1	.24	–.07	–.05	–.15	–					
6. Percent Minority Equity	14.00	5.75	0	40	–.06	.03	–.09	.03	.03	–				
7. Percent Joint Ventures	40.52	16.06	0	75	.32	–.04	.04	–.18	.10	–.38	–			
8. Y95	.50	.50	0	1	–.08	.01	–.01	–.14	.05	.04	.01	–		
9. Y96	.23	.42	0	1	–.03	.10	–.01	.32	-.09	–.02	–.01	–.55	–	
10. Y97	.08	.27	0	1	.01	.08	.03	.07	-.05	–.10	.03	–.29	–.16	–

[a] $N = 765$. Correlations with absolute value >.07 are significant at the 5% level, >.09 significant at the 1% level.

Table 5.2. Multinomial Logistic Regression of Tendency to Form Different Types of Alliances

	Model 1		*Model 2*		*Model 3*	
Variables	*Minority Equity*	*Joint Venture*	*Minority Equity*	*Joint Venture*	*Contrac-tual*	*Minority Equity*
Intercept	−4.48***	−3.01***	−3.85***	−3.23***	3.22***	−.62
	(.67)	(.43)	(.72)	(.51)	(.51)	(.72)
Joint R&D			.24*	.55***	-.55***	-.31*
			(.12)	(.10)	(.10)	(.13)
Joint Marketing			−.0.1	.67***	−.67***	−.67***
			(.12)	(.11)	(.11)	(.13)
Alliance Management Experience			−.09**	−.07**	.07**	−.02
			(.03)	(.02)	(.02)	(.04)
International Partners			.06	.58***	−.58***	−.53***
			(.12)	(.09)	(.09)	(.12)
Percent Minority Equity	.11***	.02	.11***	.02	−.02	.09***
	(.02)	(.02)	(.03)	(.02)	(.02)	(.03)
Percent Joint Ventures	.03***	.05***	.03**	.05***	−.05***	−.02**
	(.01)	(.01)	(.01)	(.01)	(.01)	(.01)
Y95	−.11	−.44***	−.09	−.52***	.52***	.43**
	(.15)	(.11)	(.16)	(.12)	(.12)	(.16)
Y96	−.34	−.38**	−.18	−.31*	.31*	.13
	(.19)	(.13)	(.20)	(.15)	(.15)	(.20)
Y97	−.22	−.29	−.12	−.36	.36	.24
	(.27)	(.18)	(.27)	(.20)	(.20)	(.28)
Chi-square of Likelihood Ratio	63.20		771.00		771.00	
p-value	.58		.99		.99	

$N = 765$; all two-tailed tests; * $p < .05$, ** $p < .01$, *** $p < .001$

Coefficients are effects of covariates for each alliance type relative to their effects for the base category, which is contractual alliances for models 1–2 and joint ventures for model 3, respectively. Standard errors are in parentheses.

Hypothesis 1a proposes that the alliance objective of joint R&D would encourage more equity-based governance structures. This hypothesis is consistently supported by the results in models 2 and 3. With a joint R&D component in alliances, joint ventures were found to be more likely than minority equity alliances ($p < .05$ in model 3), which in turn were more likely than contractual alliances ($p < .05$ in model 2). Accordingly, the difference between joint ventures and contractual alliances is even more significant ($p < .001$ in model 2).

Hypothesis 1b predicts that the alliance objective of joint marketing would lead to more equity-based governance structures. Consistent with this hypothesis, the positive coefficient in model 2 suggests that joint ventures are more likely than contractual alliances when there is a joint marketing component ($p < .001$). The negative coefficient in model 3 further confirms that, with joint marketing, joint ventures are more likely than minority equity alliances ($p < .001$). However, no significant difference was found between minority equity alliances and contractual alliances in model 2. Thus, hypothesis 1b is mostly supported.

Hypothesis 2 suggests that firms with more alliance management experience tend to form less equity-based alliances. Significant and negative coefficients in model 2 confirm that more alliance experience makes minority equity alliances and joint ventures less likely ($p < .01$). However, no significant difference was found between minority equity alliances and joint ventures in model 3. Overall, hypothesis 2 is largely supported.

Hypothesis 3 predicts that international alliances tend to have more equity-based governance structures. The positive coefficients in model 2 suggest that, consistent with hypothesis 3, joint ventures are more likely than contractual alliances in international alliances ($p < .001$). Yielding additional support, model 3 shows that minority equity alliances are less likely than joint ventures in international alliances ($p < .001$). No significant difference was found between minority equity alliances and contractual alliances. Thus, hypothesis 3 is mostly supported.

Overall, there is strong and consistent support for our hypotheses. In sum, the level of equity in the governance structures will be high when (1) there is a joint R&D objective or a joint marketing objective, (2) the partners have limited alliance management experience, and (3) the partners are from different nations.

DISCUSSION

This study aims at understanding alliance structural choices in terms of the three key factors, namely, alliance objectives, alliance management experience, and international partners. The empirical results are strongly supportive of our hypotheses and thus lead to several conclusions. First, the results support the idea that the bifurcated approach toward alliance structure (i.e., equity vs. nonequity alliances) needs to be refined. Previously, researchers often used the bifurcated approach to understand alliance structures for purposes of simplicity and for highlighting the role of equity arrangement (Das & Teng, 2000; Gulati, 1995; Osborn & Baughn, 1990). However, as Gulati and Singh (1998) argued, within equity alliances, joint ventures and minority equity alliances could be significantly different. Our results support their position and suggest that the three categories used in this study are warranted. Of the four independent variables, only one (i.e., alliance management experience) fails to show a significant difference between joint ventures and minority equity alliances (see model 3).

Second, we found that alliance objectives, alliance management experience, and international partners are important determinants of alliance governance structure. In a previous study, Gulati and Singh (1998) examined the effects of joint R&D and international alliances on alliance structure. They found that alliances with an "expected technological component" (i.e., joint R&D) preferred more equity involvement. Based on partner nationality, their study showed some evidence that cross-regional partners tended to use more equity involvement. This tendency was most significant with European firms, partially significant with Japanese firms, but nonsignificant with U.S. firms. In our current study, we confirm that joint R&D alliances indeed have more equity involvement. Regarding partner nationality, our dummy variable is based on a cross-national classification rather than the cross-regional classification used by Gulati and Singh. Our study generally confirms that international alliances have more equity involvement. The results are highly significant between joint ventures and the other two forms but not significant between minority equity alliances and contractual alliances. Importantly, Gulati and Singh use contractual alliances as the base category in all regressions, so that they do not examine the difference between joint ventures and minority equity alliances. By comparison, our analyses cover all possible comparisons among the three kinds of alliance structures.

We also tested two additional factors, namely, the alliance objective of joint marketing and alliance management experience. Previous studies often used the total number of prior alliances between two specific partners as an indicator of interfirm trust. In contrast, our measure includes all prior alliances formed by the firms (with any partner) and is thus better reflective of the notion of "collaborative know-how" (Simonin, 1997). Our confirmative result indicates that firms' overall experience with alliances matter substantially in the choice of the alliance structure. In addition, we have included another important and under-tested alliance objective—joint marketing—which turns out to be highly significant as well. Thus, this study makes a contribution in identifying additional determinants of alliance structures.

Our findings are subject to the following limitations, which point to directions for future research. First, since all data for this study came from a single source, there is some potential for common method bias. Second, our data were based on a published source that relies upon press announcements of alliances. Although this approach has been popular among alliance researchers, there is a potential bias toward larger alliances in the selection process. Smaller alliances tend to be reported less and thus are less likely to be included in the database. Obviously, the solution lies in developing a comprehensive alliance database that would allow studies with a focus on specific industries or strategic groups. Third, since this study used a large multi-national sample, we were not able to collect firm-specific information for some common control variables such as firm size, performance, and standard industrial classification (SIC) codes. Future research using a survey method may be needed to gather information regarding these additional control variables.

The findings of this study hold important implications for alliance managers. First, we find that joint R&D alliances need more equity-based governance structures. The implication is that knowledge acquisition and protection are both important in R&D alliances. Joint ventures not only provide a setting for legitimate knowledge transfer to take place, the equity arrangement also serves as a control mechanism against illegitimate knowledge acquisition. Thus, alliance managers should pay special attention to ensure the appropriate balance between knowledge acquisition and knowledge protection. Control mechanisms other than alliance structure (such as close monitoring and tight knowledge regulation) should be considered as well.

Second, joint marketing alliances also have more equity-based structures. Many alliance managers face a difficult task of determining outcome allocation early on in order to avoid possible disputes later, especially as an alliance can be vulnerable to termination. When an alliance involves considerable intangible assets, such as brand image and reputation (as in a joint marketing alliance), such ex ante allocation could be challenging. Thus, managers ought to use alliance structures to help deal with the residual allocation issue.

Third, alliance management experience leads to a less emphasis on equity involvement. This finding suggests that many firms carefully evaluate their collaborative know-how prior to alliance formation. The cognitive process seems to aim at a balance between flexibility and stability. While equity structures promote stability and confidence in cooperation, their level of flexibility is lower. Thus, they are usually preferred when firms lack alliance experience. In contrast, experienced firms may find the equity structures to be unnecessarily rigid and thus prefer more flexible arrangements. This appears to be a rational approach that managers could explicitly develop in choosing alliance structures.

Finally, the fact that international alliances have more equity involvement highlights the importance of resource management in alliances. The conventional wisdom views structural choices of international alliances through a risk perspective, which suggests that international alliances should have flexible structures since they are more risky due to cultural and regulatory factors. Our result shows that managers do not follow such logic. Equity structures are used instead, presumably to better deal with high resource heterogeneity in international alliances. Indeed, resource management should be a critical consideration in structuring alliances (Das & Teng, 2000). For instance, managers could choose desirable alliance structures by systematically examining the types of resource contributed by each partner.

In conclusion, this empirical investigation advances our understanding of governance structure choices in strategic alliances. The four determinants of higher equity involvement include a joint R&D objective, a joint marketing objective, limited alliance management experience, and international partners.

ACKNOWLEDGMENT

This chapter was earlier published as Teng, B., & Das, T. K. (2008). Governance structure choice in strategic alliances: The roles of alliance objectives, alliance management experience, and international partners. *Management Decision, 46*, 725–742.

REFERENCES

Alliance Analyst. (1994–1997). Philadelphia, PA: Newcap Communications.

Anand, B. N., & Khanna, T. (2000). Do firms learn to create value? The case of alliances. *Strategic Management Journal, 21*, 295–315.

Athanassiou, N., & Nigh, D. (2000). Internationalization, tacit knowledge and the top management teams of MNCs. *Journal of International Business Studies, 31*, 471–487.

Barkema, H. G., Shenkar, O., Vermeulen, F., & Bell, J. H. J. (1997). Working abroad, working with others: How firms learn to operate international joint ventures. *Academy of Management Journal, 40*, 426–442.

Baughn, C. C., Denekamp, J. G., Stevens, J. H., & Osborn, R. N. (1997). Protecting intellectual capital in international alliances. *Journal of World Business, 32*(2), 103–117.

Bleeke, J., & Ernst, D. (1995). Is your strategic alliance really a sale? *Harvard Business Review, 73*(1), 97–105.

Bradach, J. L., & Eccles, R. G. (1989). Price, authority, and trust: From ideal types to plural forms. *Annual Review of Sociology, 15*, 97–118.

Brouthers, K. D. (1995). The influence of international risk on entry mode strategy in the computer software industry. *Management International Review, 35*(1), 7–28.

Bucklin, L. P., & Sengupta, S. (1993). Organizing successful co-marketing alliances. *Journal of Marketing, 57*(2), 32–46.

Carson, S. J., Madhok, A., Varman, R., & John, G. (2003). Information processing moderators of effectiveness of trust-based governance in inter-firm R&D collaboration. *Organization Science, 14*, 45–56.

Chi, T., & Roehl, T. W. (1997). The structuring of interfirm exchanges in business know-how: Evidence from international collaborative ventures. *Managerial and Decision Economics, 18*, 279–294.

Das, T. K. (2005). Deceitful behaviors of alliance partners: potential and prevention. *Management Decision, 43*, 706–719.

Das, T. K., & Kumar, R. (2007). Learning dynamics in the alliance development process. *Management Decision, 45*, 684–707.

Das, T. K., & Teng, B. (1996). Risk types and inter-firm alliance structures. *Journal of Management Studies, 33*, 827–843.

Das, T. K., & Teng, B. (1998). Between trust and control: Developing confidence in partner cooperation in alliances. *Academy of Management Review, 23*, 491–512.

Das, T. K., & Teng, B. (2000). A resource-based theory of strategic alliances. *Journal of Management, 26*, 31–61.

Das, T. K., & Teng, B. (2001). A risk perception model of alliance structuring. *Journal of International Management, 7*, 1–29.

D'Aveni, R. A. (1994). *Hypercompetition: Managing the dynamics of strategic maneuvering*. New York: Free Press.

Doz, Y. L., & Hamel, G. (1998). *Alliance advantage: The art of creating value through partnering*. Boston, MA: Harvard Business School Press.

Dussauge, P., Garrette, B., & Mitchell, W. (2000). Learning from competing partners: Outcomes and durations of scale and link alliances in Europe, North America and Asia. *Strategic Management Journal, 21*, 99–126.

Dyer, J. H., & Chu, W. (2003). The role of trustworthiness in reducing transaction costs and improving performance: Empirical evidence from the United States, Japan, and Korea. *Organization Science, 14*, 57–68.

Galbraith, C. S. (1990). Transferring core manufacturing technologies in high technology firms. *California Management Review, 32*(4), 56–70.

Garcia-Canal, E. (1996). Contractual form in domestic and international strategic alliances. *Organization Studies, 17*, 773–794.

Glaister, K. W., & Buckley, P. J. (1996). Strategic motives for international alliance formation. *Journal of Management Studies, 33*, 301–332.

Goerzen, A. (2007). Alliance networks and firm performance: The impact of repeated partnerships. *Strategic Management Journal, 28*, 487–509.

Gulati, R. (1995). Does familiarity breed trust? The implication of repeated ties for contractual choice in alliances. *Academy of Management Journal, 38*, 85–112.

Gulati, R. (1999). Network location and learning: The influence of network resources and firm capabilities on alliance formation. *Strategic Management Journal, 20*, 397–420.

Gulati, R., & Singh, H. (1998). The architecture of cooperation: Managing coordination costs and appropriation concerns in strategic alliances. *Administrative Science Quarterly, 43*, 781–814.

Hagedoorn, J. (1993). Understanding the rationale of strategic technology partnering: Interorganizational modes of cooperation and sectoral differences. *Strategic Management Journal, 14*, 371–385.

Hagedoorn, J., & Duysters, G. (2002). Learning in dynamic inter-firm networks: The efficacy of multiple contacts. *Organization Studies, 23*, 525–548.

Hamel, G. (1991). Competition for competence and inter-partner learning within international strategic alliances. *Strategic Management Journal, 12*(Summer), 83–103.

Hennart, J.-F. (1988). A transaction costs theory of equity joint ventures. *Strategic Management Journal, 9*, 361-374.

Hitt, M. A., Dacin, M. T., Levitas, E., Arregle, J.-L. & Borza, A. (2000). Partner selection in emerging and developing market contexts: Resource-based and organizational learning perspectives. *Academy of Management Journal, 43*, 449–467.

Hoang, H., & Rothaermel, F. T. (2005). The effect of general and partner-specific alliance experience on joint R&D project performance. *Academy of Management Journal, 48*, 332–345.

Inkpen, A. (1998). Learning and knowledge acquisition through international strategic alliances. *Academy of Management Executive, 12*, 69–80.

Kale, P., Dyer, J. H., & Singh, H. (2002). Alliance capability, stock market response, and long-term alliance success: The role of the alliance function. *Strategic Management Journal, 23*, 747–767.

Kale, P., & Singh, H. (2007). Building firm capabilities through learning: The role of the alliance learning process in alliance capability and firm-level alliance success. *Strategic Management Journal, 28*, 981–1000.

Khanna, T., Gulati, R., & Nohria, N. (1998). The dynamics of learning alliances: Competition, cooperation, and relative scope. *Strategic Management Journal, 19*, 193–210.

Killing, J. P. (1988). Understanding alliances: The role of task and organizational complexity. In F. J. Contractor & P. Lorange (Eds.), *Cooperative strategies in international business* (pp. 55–68). Lexington, MA: Lexington Books.

Kogut, B. (1988). Joint ventures: Theoretical and empirical perspectives. *Strategic Management Journal, 9*, 319–332.

Kostova, T. (1999). Transnational transfer of strategic organizational practices: A contextual perspective. *Academy of Management* Review, *24*, 308–324.

Krishnan, R., Martin, X., & Noorderhaven, N. G. (2006). When does trust matter to alliance performance. *Academy of Management Journal, 49*, 894–917.

Lane, P. J., Salk, J. E., & Lyles, M. A. (2001). Absorptive capacity, learning and performance in international joint ventures. *Strategic Management Journal, 19*, 1139–1161.

Larson, A. (1992). Network dyads in entrepreneurial settings: A study of the governance of exchange relationships. *Administrative Science Quarterly, 37*, 76–104.

Larsson, R., Bengtsson, L., Henriksson, K., & Sparks, J. (1998). The interorganizational learning dilemma: Collective knowledge development in strategic alliances. *Organization Science, 9*, 285–305.

Lui, S. S., & Ngo, H. (2004). The role of trust and contractual safeguards on cooperation in non-equity alliances. *Journal of Management, 30*, 471–485.

Mellewigt, T., & Das, T. K. (2007). *Alliance structure choice: Resource type or resource heterogeneity?* Paper presented at the annual meeting of the Academy of Management, Philadelphia, PA.

Mowery, D. C., Oxley, J. E., & Silverman, B. S. (1998). Technological overlap and interfirm cooperation: Implications for the resource-based view of the firm. *Research Policy, 27*, 507–523.

Nooteboom, B. (1999). Innovation and inter-firm linkages: New implications for policy. *Research Policy, 28*, 793–805.

Osborn, R. N., & Baughn, C. C. (1990). Forms of interorganizational governance for multinational alliances. *Academy of Management Journal, 33*, 503–519.

Oxley, J. E. (1997). Appropriability hazards and governance in strategic alliances: A transaction cost approach. *Journal of Law, Economics, and Organization, 13*, 387–409.

Parkhe, A. (1993a). Partner nationality and the structure-performance relationship in strategic alliances. *Organization Science, 4*, 301–324.

Parkhe, A. (1993b). Strategic alliance structuring: A game theory and transaction cost examination of interfirm cooperation. *Academy of Management Journal, 36*, 794–829.

Pisano, G. P. (1989). Using equity participation to support exchange: Evidence from the biotechnology industry. *Journal of Law, Economics, and Organization, 5*, 109–126.

Pisano, G. P. (1991). The governance of innovation: Vertical integration and collaborative arrangements in the biotechnology industry. *Research Policy, 20*, 237–249.

Powell, W. W., Koput, K. W., & Smith-Doerr, L. (1996). Interorganizational collaboration and the locus of innovation: Networks of learning in biotechnology. *Administrative Science Quarterly, 41*, 116–145.

Reuer, J. J., & Miller, K. D. (1997). Agency costs and the performance implications of international joint venture internalization. *Strategic Management Journal, 18*, 425–438.

Rowley, T., & Behrens, D., & Krackhardt, D. (2000). Redundant governance structures: An analysis of structural and relational embeddedness in the steel and semiconductor industries. *Strategic Management Journal, 21*, 369–386.

Sampson, R. C. (2005). Experience effects and collaborative returns in R&D alliances. *Strategic Management Journal, 26,* 1009–1031.

Sampson, R. C. (2007). R&D alliances and firm performance: The impact of technological diversity and alliance organization on innovation. *Academy of Management Journal, 50,* 364–386.

Simonin, B. L. (1997). The importance of collaborative know-how: An empirical test of the learning organization. *Academy of Management Journal, 40,* 1150–1174.

Teece, D. J. (1992). Competition, cooperation, and innovation: Organizational arrangements for regimes of rapid technological progress, *Journal of Economic Behavior and Organization, 18,* 1–25.

Thomas, J. B., & Trevino, L. K. (1993). Information processing in strategic alliance building: A multiple-case approach. *Journal of Management Studies, 30,* 779–814.

Yoshino, M. Y., & Rangan, U. S. (1995). *Strategic alliances: An entrepreneurial approach to globalization*. Boston, MA: Harvard Business School Press.

CHAPTER 6

TURNING EXPERIENCE INTO ALLIANCE CAPABILITY

Alliance Evaluation in Rolls-Royce

Ard-Pieter de Man, Mike Nevin, and Nadine Roijakkers

Over the past years researchers have paid attention to alliance capability building as a success factor in alliance management. Research identified alliance tools that increase alliance success rates (Draulans, De Man, & Volberda, 2003; Dyer, Kale, & Singh, 2001; Heimeriks & Duysters, 2007) and showed the role of experience in alliance learning (Anand & Khanna, 2000). However, the question as to how experience can be turned into explicit learning is largely unanswered. This chapter connects the "experience" literature with the "tools" literature by researching how alliance tools can help to turn experience into explicit learning and thus contribute to the building up of an alliance capability. Specifically, we highlight the role of alliance evaluation techniques that are common in practice. A detailed case study into the way Rolls-Royce learned from an evaluation tool will show also that alliance evaluation clearly helps companies to accumulate lessons learned and to capture them. It has some impact on integrating those lessons in alliance policies, but a limited impact on the diffusion of alliance learning. An additional finding from the case is that there may be a number of barriers to alliance capability building, which have not yet been studied in extant literature.

Strategic Alliances in a Globalizing World, pp. 117–138

ALLIANCE CAPABILITY, EXPERIENCE, AND LEARNING ABOUT ALLIANCES

Alliance capability is defined as the mechanisms or routines that are purposefully designed to accumulate, store, integrate, and diffuse relevant organizational knowledge acquired through individual and organizational experience with alliances (Kale, Dyer, & Singh, 2002). There are several important elements in this definition that require attention. One element is the role of experience with alliances. It is well known that companies with more experience with alliances tend to be more successful than companies with limited alliance experience (Anand & Khanna, 2000; Powell, Koput, & Smith-Doerr, 1996). Learning-by-doing is a first step for building an alliance capability, but it is not sufficient. Companies also need to focus on mechanisms or routines that formalize lessons learned and transfer alliance best practices inside companies (Spekman & Isabella, 2000). The effect of such dedicated alliance management has been proven in some large-scale empirical studies. Alliance training, alliance evaluation, and having an alliance specialist in a company was shown to raise alliance success rates, especially after learning-by-doing had reached its limits (Draulans, De Man, & Volberda,.2003; Heimeriks & Duysters, 2007). Similarly, the presence of an alliance department in a company, which acts as a repository for learning and stimulates the exchange of alliance best practice, significantly increases alliance success (Kale et al., 2002). However, in the empirical literature alliance experience and alliance management mechanisms are treated as separate phenomena. Even though Kale et al.'s (2002) definition links mechanisms to experience, empirical studies into this link are absent. We present a case study of one such mechanism (alliance evaluation) and explore to what extent this mechanism helps companies to translate experience into alliance capability.

Alliance management mechanisms need to perform four functions in order to contribute to alliance capability building. They must help to accumulate, store, integrate, and diffuse knowledge gained from experience (Kale et al., 2002). "Accumulate" refers to searching and finding alliance management practices that seem to have worked well and searching and finding alliance management practices that are inadequate and require improvement. "Store" refers to registering these practices in company reports, on websites or presentations. "Integrate" refers to incorporating the practices in the alliance tools, processes, and alliance training programs a company has. "Diffuse" refers to spreading these tools, processes, training programs to other alliances or departments in the company or to alliance partners.

In the literature alliance evaluation has been identified as one of the most important tools contributing to alliance success and to company success in alliances. The Association of Strategic Alliance Professionals' Second State of Alliance Management Study (De Man & Duysters, 2007) showed that the use of alliance evaluation techniques was the most important differentiator between companies with high alliance success rates and those with low alliance success rates. Companies with alliance success rates of 60% or higher paid significantly more attention to measuring and evaluating their alliances than companies with success rates of 40% or lower. So far, however, it remains unclear how alliance evaluation translates into higher success rates on a company level rather than on an alliance level. Do companies only improve the alliances they evaluate once or does alliance evaluation help to build a capability that can be applied to numerous alliances?

It is clear why evaluation is important for improving the success of individual alliances. Alliances are often used in a dynamic context (Duysters & De Man, 2003). They may be affected by external conditions, like new competitors, technologies or regulatory change. Alliances are also subject to numerous internal tensions (Das & Teng, 2000). Tensions may come from trying to find the right balance between cooperation and competition or differences in the time horizon of the partners. Consequently, alliances will often have to be adapted to changing situations (Reuer, Zollo, & Singh, 2002). To monitor whether an alliance is still on track, individual (one partner evaluates for himself) and joint (partners evaluate an alliance together) evaluation are important. It shows where modifications in an alliance are necessary to meet changing conditions. Evaluation thus facilitates single loop learning (Argyris & Schon, 1978): it helps companies to determine where and how to modify their alliance.

Single loop learning, however, is not sufficient to build an alliance capability. That also requires double loop learning (Argyris & Schon, 1978): taking the lessons learned in individual alliances and embed them in the organization. In an ideal situation alliance evaluation should affect alliance capability building in a number of ways. It may help to accumulate lessons learned by methodically reviewing alliance success factors and identifying which have not been met and which have been met. Next, the lessons are stored in company presentations and reports. Companies may use the lessons learned described in those presentations and reports to incorporate them in new alliance tools, processes, and training programs. Finally, the new alliance tools, processes, and training programs may be made available inside the company via websites, presentations, training sessions, etc. and thus reach a wider audience.

Finding out whether the process described above occurs in practice requires a detailed case analysis. It is necessary to trace what happens with individual bits of alliance knowledge that emanate from an alliance evaluation. We will provide such a case analysis below. First, however, the next section will show the relevance of this question for practice. It will show that alliance evaluation is a widely spread practice. Therefore it is empirically relevant to study whether the investments made in alliance evaluation deliver value in terms of double loop learning.

OVERVIEW OF ALLIANCE EVALUATION TECHNIQUES

In practice three types of alliance evaluation have been identified (De Man, Duysters, & Neyens, 2009). The first type is individual evaluation. Individual evaluation means that each alliance partner evaluates for himself whether a specific alliance is running well for that company, whether it meets the company's strategic goals, and whether its organization and governance run well. This type of evaluation is usually based on metrics (Hoffman, 2001) that companies have defined previously, often combined in an alliance scorecard. This type of evaluation has two functions. First, it aims at ensuring that a particular alliance still fits with the company strategy. Second, it reviews whether the company is able to appropriate sufficient value from the alliance.

Joint evaluation refers to a diagnosis of an alliance in which all partners of an alliance are involved. An example is Eli Lilly's voice of the alliance tool (Futrell, Slugay, & Stephens, 2001) and Alliance Best Practice's alliance diagnostic (for more information, see www.alliancebestpractice.com). These tools contain a number of standardized questions about a broad set of alliance success factors like alliance strategy, alliance governance, cultural differences, planning, decision-making process, and trust. For each of these success factors questions are asked that respondents can rate on a scale. The questionnaire is sent out to a number of people participating in the alliance such as the alliance manager, a board member or a member of an alliance team. By gathering the responses and depicting them graphically in, for example, a spider web diagram, the alliance partners can essentially identify two types of areas for improvement. The first area is where both partners score low. Low scores indicate that a success factor is not met. Second, areas where the partner scores diverge may also cause a problem for the alliance. This indicates that the partners do not see the alliance in the same way. Divergent opinions may lead to issues arising in an alliance. Based on this analysis, the alliance partners can develop an action plan to improve their collaboration. This type of alliance evaluation aims at maintaining the fit between partners (Douma, Bilderbeek, Idenburg, & Looise, 2000) and at maintaining the fit between the alliance and the environment it operates in.

The third form of evaluation is cross-alliance evaluation. In this form of evaluation one company compares a number of its own alliances on specific aspects. For example, a company may compare its alliances on their governance structures to identify new lessons learned or best practices that can be used in other alliances. This type of evaluation stimulates learning between alliance managers of the company. It also helps to identify company specific problems or mistakes. For example, a finding may be that a company does not pay sufficient attention to the soft side of partnering or is not consistent in defining alliance exit strategies.

Data from the First State of Alliance Management Study (De Man & Duysters, 2002) and the Third State of Alliance Management Study (De Man et al., 2009) show that alliance evaluation is a widely spread practice. In addition, it has become increasingly popular over the past years. Table 6.1 shows that individual evaluation is the most widely used tool, with the vast majority of companies using it. Cross-alliance evaluation is used by fewer than half of the companies in 2009, but still the number of companies performing such evaluations has more than doubled since 2002. Individual and joint evaluations have become standard best practices; cross-alliance evaluation is rapidly becoming standard as well.

Further details from the State of Alliance Management Studies show that there are no major differences in the use of alliance evaluation techniques across sectors. The IT sector is slightly ahead of other sectors and financial service firms have a lower implementation rate, but the differences are minimal. Likewise, alliance evaluation is not only relevant for large companies, but for small and medium-sized firms as well. Table 6.2 shows that in 2009 companies of all sizes were using alliance evaluation techniques. Concluding, alliance evaluation has become a widely used alliance management technique. Hence it is relevant to research whether they help to build alliance capability, and if so, how.

Table 6.1. Percentage of Companies Using Alliance Evaluation Techniques in 2002 and 2009

	2002	*2009*
Individual evaluation	65%	84%
Joint evaluation	42%	76%
Cross-alliance evaluation	20%	49%

Table 6.2. Percentage of Small, Medium-Sized, and Large Companies Using Alliance Evaluation in 2009

	Small Firms (1–500 Employees)	*Medium-Sized Firms (501–1,000 Employees)*	*Large Firms (Over 1,000 Employees)*
Individual evaluation	81%	61%	89%
Joint evaluation	73%	82%	76%
Cross-alliance evaluation	45%	42%	52%

METHOD

To discover whether evaluation leads to capability building, we executed an embedded, single case study. We study one multipartner alliance in-depth: the Global Physical Logistics alliance (from here onwards referred to as the GPL alliance) initiated by Rolls-Royce involving three other partners. The focus lies on the use of a joint evaluation tool in this alliance. The joint evaluation tool used is the Alliance Diagnostic developed by Alliance Best Practice. As this tool contains 52 questions on alliances, it should present many opportunities for learning. By studying a multi-partner alliance we can trace whether all partners learn from alliance evaluation to the same extent. The GPL case has one additional benefit. The partners in the alliance have no previous alliances. This makes it much easier to follow the learning process in the partners: we can trace learning processes from this alliance, without having to research whether any lessons learned might have come from previous alliances.

For the case study we triangulated our data gathering. The method followed was a combination of action research, interviews, and the study of company documents. One of the authors was involved in diagnosing the alliance under review in 2004. Five years later, in 2009, the research team returned to the alliance to study the alliance again. In 2009 seven interviews were held with representatives from the partners and company documents were studied to see whether the partners had learned from the evaluation process. In 2009 structured interviews were held with people involved in the alliance evaluation process in 2004 and with alliance managers that joined the alliance later to establish whether lessons learned were transferred to them. Table 6.3 lists the positions, affiliations, and dates of the interviews. After gathering the material, it was analyzed to find instances of accumulating, storing, integrating, and diffusing lessons learned. The case study and the analysis were next sent to the alliance companies for validation.

Table 6.3. Overview of Professionals, Involved in the Alliance, Interviewed

Function	*Company*	*Date of the Interview*
GPL director	Rolls-Royce	3 August 2009
Purchasing executive-Services	Rolls-Royce	29 July 2009
Head of GPL development	Rolls-Royce	24 July 2009
Global purchasing executive-Facilities & Logistics	Rolls-Royce	21 August 2009
Director airfreight	KN	18 August 2009
Head of business development	CEVA	31 July 2009
Business development director	CEVA	31 July 2009

ALLIANCE EVALUATION IN ROLLS-ROYCE

Company Background

Rolls-Royce, a world-leading provider of power systems and services for use on land, at sea and in the air, has established a strong position in global markets—civil aerospace, defense aerospace, marine, and energy. The company has a broad customer base comprising more than 600 airlines, 4,000 corporate and utility aircraft and helicopter operators, 160 armed forces, more than 2,000 marine customers, including 70 navies, and energy customers in nearly 120 countries, with an installed base of 54,000 gas turbines. Rolls-Royce employs over 38,000 skilled people in offices, manufacturing and service facilities in 50 countries.

Our case focuses on the Global Physical Logistics department within Rolls-Royce. This department handles the logistics for direct materials (i.e., materials that end up in original equipment manufacturers' (OEM) products), spare parts, and finished OEM products. To maintain its leading position in the engine making business, Rolls-Royce is committed to establish and maintain world-class supply chains for all its products and services. In order to achieve this, the company cooperates closely with its preferred suppliers through the GPL alliance. The GPL alliance came into existence in 2004 and initially included, besides Rolls-Royce, TNT Logistics (currently named CEVA Logistics), KLM Cargo Aerospace Logistics in a joint bid with Kuehne + Nagel Ltd (KN), and Daher Sawley Ltd. In 2009 the GPL alliance consists of Rolls-Royce, CEVA, KN, and Daher. KLM and KN switched positions in 2006 with KN becoming the contractual supplier and KLM the second tier.

Alliance Background

The reason for setting up the GPL alliance was Rolls-Royce's aim to achieve operational excellence. The business model that Rolls-Royce had been predominantly working with so far was focused mainly on buying materials "delivery included" and selling them "ex-works." In order to gain supply chain control, Rolls-Royce decided to move away from this existing business model towards a new supply chain model where the company collects the most critical goods from its main suppliers. This business model is also used extensively in the automotive industry. Also, in its Total Care (TM) contracts, Rolls-Royce plc is accountable for the quality, cost and performance of the logistics operation that delivers the maintenance materials to the point of use, and this increases the importance of optimized and dependable logistics operations to the overall customer service experience. The need for a logistics function within Rolls-Royce thus became increasingly pressing.

Early 2000, however, there was no formal logistics group in Rolls-Royce. Instead, the supply chain was managed by a stand-alone purchasing group, which mainly focused on costs. A new logistics group was thus set up that started to consider several options for further implementing the logistics function within Rolls-Royce. The company could have decided to manage the execution of this logistics function by itself through a large network of local service providers. Alternatively, it could have followed its competitors by employing a single lead logistics partner (fourth party logistics or 4PL) to manage that network on its behalf. However, Rolls-Royce found itself unable to resource the management of a large (diverse) subcontractor network. Furthermore, the company was unable to find a single logistics company that possessed all the capabilities it needed on a global scale. In addition, Rolls-Royce was not particularly keen of the added costs and commercial hazards of working with a single 4PL. Therefore, the new logistics group started to create a new collaboration based model and began negotiations with several logistics partners to be part of a new alliance.

The goal of this alliance was to serve an increasingly global market with customer expectations increasing in terms of delivery assurance, speed, responsiveness, and cost. As no one company had all the required capabilities, Rolls-Royce selected partners that were able to deliver capabilities in three areas: road transport, international freight forwarding, and packaging (the decision to also outsource warehousing was taken by Rolls-Royce at a later stage in time). After a careful partner selection process where several other partners were also considered, Rolls-Royce selected three core partners for the alliance: CEVA, KLM with KN as its second tier, and

Daher (see Table 6.4 for background descriptions of each of these partners). Rolls-Royce looked for partners with overlapping, yet complementary capabilities. The overlap was deemed necessary in case that, for whatever reason, one of the partners would have to leave the alliance. In that case, the other partners should be able to fill the gap left behind by that partner temporarily, but for a sufficiently long time to find a new partner to plug the gap.

For the partners the new way of working was quite different than before. Normally the partners would coordinate bilaterally with Rolls-Royce for delivering their services. As Rolls-Royce believed that better

Table 6.4. Description of the Partners Involved in the GPL Alliance

CEVA
CEVA Logistics is a leading global supply chain management company. Providing end-to-end design, implementation and operational solutions in contract logistics and freight management to large and medium-sized national and multinational companies. CEVA employs circa 50,000 people and runs an extensive global network with facilities in over 100 countries. For the year ending 31 December 2008, the Group reported revenues of €6.3bn. CEVA Logistics has been the most important transport provider to Rolls-Royce since 2000. During the course of the GPL alliance CEVA has increasingly taken on outsourced warehousing activities.
KLM Cargo Aerospace Logistics
From its home base at Schiphol Airport, The Netherlands, KLM Cargo serves more than 300 destinations worldwide. With a fleet that includes 17 Boeing 747–400 combi aircraft and 3 Boeing 747-400 Extended Range Freighters, KLM Cargo's freight traffic was 4,400 million ton kilometers in 2008. KLM Cargo has 2,700 employees worldwide. KLM Cargo joined the GPL alliance in 2004 through a joint bid with Kuehne + Nagel Ltd. Rolls-Royce awarded the partnership a contract to manage inbound and outbound international freight forwarding for sites in the United Kingdom, United States, Germany, and Canada.
Kuehne + Nagel
Kuehne + Nagel is a global logistics provider. It was founded in 1890 and has over 55,000 employees at 900 locations in more than 100 countries. KN particularly holds strong market positions in seafreight, airfreight, and contract logistics, with a clear focus on providing IT-based Supply Chain Management services. Although KN initially acted as a second tier supplier to KLM in the GPL alliance, in 2006 the company took over from KLM and gained contractual supplier status with Rolls-Royce.
Daher Sawley Ltd
Sawley Packaging Ltd, owned by Rolls-Royce, focused on the supply of packaging services and manufacture of packaging containers primarily to Rolls-Royce, though in later years also to a diverse set of other customers. In September 2003 the company was acquired by the French Daher Group to become the focus of the group's UK operations. The company's name was changed to Daher Aerospace Ltd. It is located in Derby and employs over 120 people, generating revenues in excess of €15 million. Daher provides supply chain management and integrated logistics services; containers and shelters; ground support equipment; parts for civil and military fixed and rotary wing aircraft.

coordination between partners would deliver major benefits in terms of cost saving and speed, the partners were now asked to coordinate among each other as well. As downtime of planes was very expensive, pre-planning and scheduling of maintenance activities could deliver substantial cost savings. The more integrated the collaboration with the various partners would be, the faster engines could be repaired or maintained and the lower the costs.

This of course increased the partners' costs. Their incentive to participate was that they would be better positioned to potentially get more business from Rolls-Royce. Based on studies of other industries where similar endeavors had been undertaken Rolls-Royce had identified a strong business case of supply chain savings of nearly 20% per year. In addition to cost savings Rolls-Royce also wanted better quality and higher speed. Supply chain response time was to be reduced significantly. Since the inception of the alliance, Rolls-Royce and its partners have consistently realized significant cost savings and service improvements. For example, CEVA's inbound collection service for gas turbine materials in the United Kingdom is on time in over 99.87% of the cases every year. Furthermore, KN has achieved significant cost reductions while the rest of the market has gone up in price.

Partners do not have a preferred status: they need to be competitive with non-partners. However, they have two benefits from the alliance. The first is that they have more intimate knowledge of Rolls-Royce's requirements and therefore they are better able to pitch for Rolls-Royce business. Second, the alliance has put in place a joint risk-reward scheme that improves the partner's margins.

The Initial Alliance Evaluation: 2004

After having selected the partners and agreeing on the contracts, the alliance started. There were, however, many questions with respect to: how to set up the alliance; whether the groundwork for the alliance was complete; whether all success factors had been incorporated in the alliance design. Rolls-Royce then decided to evaluate their alliance. They selected a method of joint alliance evaluation, called the Alliance Best Practice Diagnostic.

The Alliance Best Practice Diagnostic consists of 52 questions about alliance success factors, derived from alliance literature. Respondents can rate answers to these questions on a 1–100 scale. Table 6.5 gives an overview of these success factors. Alliance Best Practice interviewed managers in Rolls-Royce and in the partners about the alliance. For each partner, three respondents were interviewed, each having a different function in the alliance. The data gathered were first reported back on a bilateral level; that is, they diagnosed the relationship between Rolls-Royce and an individual partner. Next, the data were used to analyze the entire GPL alliance. The conclusions of the exercise were reported in a group meeting of the partners, held in August 2004.

The results of the evaluation were presented in PowerPoint format. At the core of the presentation are three slides: one slide listing things that went well, one slide listing areas for improvement, and one slide listing lessons learned. Below we quote from this presentation literally (Alliance Best Practice, 2004).

Table 6.5. Success Factors Incorporated in the Alliance Best Practice Alliance Diagnostic Tool

Diagnostic				
Commercial Success Factors	*Technical Success Factors*	*Strategic Success Factors*	*Cultural Success Factors*	*Operational Success Factors*
• Breakthrough Value Proposition (BVP) • Due Diligence • Optimum Legal / Business Structure • Alliance Audit • Key metrics • Alliance reward system • Commercial cost • Commercial benefit • Process for negotiation • Expected Cost value ratio	• Valuation of technical assets • Partner company market position • Host company market position • Market fit of proposed solution • Product fit with partners offerings • Identified mutual needs in the relationship • Process for team problem solving • Shared Control • Partner accountability	• Shared objectives • Relationship Scope • Tactical and strategic risk • Risk sharing • Exit strategies • Senior Exec support • B2B Strategic alignment • Fit with strategic business path • Other relationships with same partner • Common strategic ground rules • Common vision	• Trust • Collaborative corporate mindset • Collaboration skills • Dedicated alliance manager • Alliance centre of excellence • Decision-making process • Other cultural issues • B2B Cultural alignment	• Alliance process • Speed of progress so far • Distance from revenue • Formal business plan • Communication • Quality review • Memorandum of Understanding and Principles • Change management • Operational metrics • B2B Operational alignment • Exponential breakthroughs • Internal alignment • Project plan • Issue escalation

The report listed that among others the following things went well:

Senior executive support—Without exception all the interviewees recognized the high level of support granted to the project and the critical importance of that support. This factor alone was seen as the single most important factor in the progress made to date and in the chances of continued progress in the future.

Existence of dedicated alliance manager support—It was clear that all sides recognized the critical need of such a role and almost without exception this was seen to be working well. Responsibility was clear on all sides and identified individuals had a clearly understood role to play.

Next, the report listed among others the following areas for improvement:

The need for a more formal process—All interviewees conceded that the absence of processes and formal procedures had delayed the project. Many people interviewed felt that the project could not withstand such delays in the future and maintain its credibility.

Internal communication and validation of the model within Rolls-Royce—There is evidence that the model is not universally understood within Rolls-Royce. This in turn has led to resistance on the part of key functions and has damaged and delayed partner relationships.

The third element that was highlighted is the lessons learned so far. These included:

Personal energy and vision is not enough—Personal drive and determination (from a number of the key players in the model) has carried the project thus far. However, if the project is to have organizational credibility both within and without Rolls-Royce, the time has now come to use a more formal structure to drive the alliance relationship.

Passing the contractual negotiations to a formal purchasing function—All the potential partner suppliers (both successful and unsuccessful) had reservations about transferring the sole responsibility at the negotiation stage to purchasing. This is not to say that purchasing should not commercially lead the negotiation process; they should. However, as it was considered by the partner suppliers that the purchasing function was not entirely congruent with what the GPL model was seeking to achieve, purchasing were perceived to have applied a more traditional vendor/supplier model to the negotiations. (Note: The presentation quoted describes partners' sentiments at a relatively early stage of the alliance (2004). By no means are these value judgments related to the current state of knowledge regarding the GPL model within the purchasing function at Rolls-Royce.)

In short, the evaluation process indicated areas for improvement for the alliance. In a workshop it was established that the need for a formal alliance process was most pressing. This led to the development of a governance model as a direct result of the evaluation process.

In the new governance model the alliance was structured around three levels: the executive level, the alliance management level, and the project management level. Each partner was to appoint one person at each of these levels to be the alliance representative. On the executive level an alliance board was formed, chaired by Rolls-Royce. The board meets every six months and approves and commits activities and resources. The alliance management group meets monthly to monitor the progress of the activities and to identify further possibilities for the alliance to propose to the board. The operational project management group meets at least monthly, but sooner when required. The project teams are responsible for implementation of alliance projects.

Postevaluation Capability Building: 2004 and Beyond

Since its inception in 2004 the GPL alliance has changed somewhat in terms of the group of companies participating in the alliance. While KN was a second tier supplier to KLM at the start of the alliance, the company took over from KLM as a preferred supplier in the alliance in 2006. The role of CEVA in the cooperation has changed significantly during the course of the alliance. The company has taken on board an increasing number of outsourced warehousing activities. Despite the recession, Rolls-Royce's order book continues to be strong and the alliance has generated substantial revenues over the years. The alliance is acting for all major trading and customer facing units (i.e., Civil, Defense, Energy, and Marine) active in Rolls-Royce's business. The GPL partners, although having to compete with outside suppliers, generate considerable business from their cooperation with Rolls-Royce as they know better what the company needs than their competitors.

Below we describe how Rolls-Royce engaged in double loop learning since the initial alliance evaluation in 2004, focusing on the four elements of learning: accumulation, storage, integration, and diffusion. The initial alliance evaluation was carried out at the level of each bilateral relationship within the cooperation as well as at the level of the alliance as a whole. As a result lessons (what went well and what went not so well) were drawn for improving the whole of the GPL alliance and for each of the relations Rolls-Royce engaged in with individual partners. The results pointed at the need for the GPL alliance to be based on a formal governance model, the need for GPL representatives to better communicate the value of the alliance and gain commitment for it within Rolls-Royce, and the need for Rolls-Royce to start building an alliance capability. As such, important lessons with respect to formalization and communication were *accumulated* from the joint evaluation. The PowerPoint generated by Alliance Best Practice shows these lessons. As the GPL director at Rolls-Royce points out:

> The evaluation gave us structure and a common language to address our problems. They also gave us confidence to continue. We could see that others had done something similar before (e.g., Bank of America, British Telecom, and most importantly Boeing). This meant that the tension went down and we were able to concentrate on the issues.

Partners in the GPL alliance picked up these lessons and made an effort to *store* important information regarding the alliance and lessons learned from it in reports and company presentations. Each of the partners received a report storing the results of both the evaluation on the alliance level and the bilateral evaluation to use as a communication device within their parent company. These presentations were used by GPL representatives to communicate information about the cooperation within Rolls-Royce and its partners. The person heading up business development at CEVA states: "We have extensive documentation that [the GPL director at Rolls-Royce; authors] has developed based on the frameworks supplied by Alliance Best Practice.... As time went on and his team produced more presentations, ... executives became happier to accept the framework."

Not only were important results from the evaluation stored in reports and company presentations, the findings were also *integrated* in alliance governance and training. Firstly, the lessons learned with respect to formalization led to the instigation of a new governance model ensuring strong alliance management, interpartner communication, and performance reviews at three distinct levels: strategic, managerial, and operational. Furthermore, the new governance model ensures stakeholder management at the top managerial levels within each of the partners. According to CEVA's head of business development "it [governance model, authors] drove people's behavior to work in a collaborative way." Secondly, the results were used to set up training programs within Rolls-Royce. First and foremost the training materials are used to create a shared mindset within the group of professionals working for the alliance. All incoming professionals receive the same briefing so that they share a common background in the alliance goals, vision, and history. In the words of the GPL director at Rolls-Royce:

> We changed our personnel ... which meant that we had to educate some people on what we are trying to achieve and what some key concepts meant. To do this we had to start writing stuff down so that we could explain it in the same way in a consistent manner to multiple people.

Materials are also used to facilitate recurring road shows to Rolls-Royce sites, information sessions for incoming graduates, and annual leadership meetings hosted for Rolls-Royce employees and partners. All sessions are targeted at educating people and convincing them of the general value of engaging in the GPL alliance. The head of business development at CEVA in his interview talks about the value in sharing this type of knowledge: "We in CEVA have used [the GPL director at Rolls-Royce, authors] often to present to our own executive teams and also on occasions to present to other potential customers the value of deeper relationship management." Thirdly, the new model also entailed setting up a small "alliance management office" within Rolls-Royce to facilitate the day-to-day functioning and the longer-term development of the cooperation. The person heading up Airfreight at KN explains the practical workings of this alliance office: "We provide an alliance manager to Rolls-Royce. He works for [the person heading up development, authors]. The KN alliance manager is a senior supply chain technician. The team is three Full Time Equivalents (FTE's) provided from all three core partners."

A final result of the joint evaluation is the spread or *diffusion* of knowledge regarding the alliance within Rolls-Royce, the partners to the GPL alliance, and beyond. Within Rolls-Royce all trading units are currently benefiting from the GPL alliance. Furthermore, the lessons learned from the multi-partner cooperation are not only used by Rolls-Royce's larger set of suppliers but have also started to spread to other organizations and prospective partners. Rolls-Royce's GPL partners CEVA and KN use the alliance governance model as a reference case to inform their clients and to set up new alliances. In this respect, the Purchasing executive-Services at Rolls-Royce mentions that "the [governance; authors] model has won a number of logistics awards and is now used as a reference site in Rolls-Royce.... I have used it in [other areas; authors] and I think generally the principles have gone down well." The head of business development at CEVA states that "Rolls-Royce was heralded as a case study in relationship management and we have used the concepts with other clients." Hence, new alliances benefit from the governance model developed as a result of the joint evaluation process in the GPL alliance.

Despite the obvious benefits that were reaped from the joint evaluation in terms of learning, there are a number of specific factors that may have resulted in Rolls-Royce not realizing the full learning potential present in the evaluation results. First of all, as none of the partners involved in the alliance had previous experience with alliances, it is difficult to build up an alliance capability. There is no knowledge base on which to build and hence it is more difficult to realize the full potential for learning from an alliance evaluation process (Lane & Lubatkin, 1998). The GPL director at Rolls-Royce describes this lack of experience in the following manner: "The variation in knowledge in individual companies was very large at the beginning and in particular there was a huge divergence of ability to understand [partnering; authors] even within individual companies." As a result, even though all involved believed the evaluation was very valuable, the evaluation was never repeated. A recurring evaluation could have shown progress made and the results could have guided the further diffusion of alliance knowledge within Rolls-Royce and partners. Building an alliance capability from scratch appears to be a difficult, slow, and somewhat haphazard process.

Second, existing views on collaboration with suppliers do not fit with a partnering approach. It is difficult to change the prevailing mindset and that makes it difficult to implement all lessons learned. Or in the words of CEVA's head of business development: "Originally both Rolls-Royce and we ourselves had naïve supplier views." In this respect, a purchasing executive at Rolls-Royce describes the results of an evaluation conducted at the time: "the suppliers did not value the way that Rolls-Royce worked with them." Although knowledge of collaboration is surely spreading through Rolls-Royce and the attitude towards cooperation is significantly changing with new people entering senior management positions, it is a process that takes time. The strong background in cost-based purchasing and the accompanying focus on control hampers the swift spread of alliance knowledge and the development of alliance capabilities within Rolls-Royce as a whole. As a result the GPL alliance still has many characteristics of a supplier network rather than a collaborative network of equal partners. Particularly, the tooling used to manage the alliance is very much grounded in supply chain management rather than alliance management. For example the QCR (quality, cost, and response) index is used as a key performance indicator. This index is a standard tool in the supply chain management world. The GPL director at Rolls-Royce confirms that "we are using standard Rolls-Royce purchasing and logistics processes adapted to our needs.... We have no GPL specific processes identified." Therefore rather than using individual alliance mechanisms, combinations of mechanisms may be required to build up an alliance capability.

Third, the change management issues in Rolls-Royce are also present in the logistics sector at large. The sector is mainly purchasing driven instead of partner driven. In general, companies operating in this industry are very suspicious of their competitors/partners and find it hard to share information with them even though this may benefit their cooperative relation as a whole. The Global purchasing executive-Facilities & Logistics of Rolls-Royce hints at this general industry attitude as he thinks back to the very start of the GPL alliance:

> It took a long time before partners would dedicate resources to the alliance in the absence of any guarantees of extra work. There was an initial suspicion from the partners that they did not know what Rolls-Royce was up to so consequently they were not prepared to commit more than token resources to the project."

However, the problem did not only persist at the level of the partners but was also present in Rolls-Royce. The GPL director at Rolls-Royce proclaims that "one of our biggest barriers is openness with partners. There are people in Rolls-Royce who are less comfortable with sharing information with partners. This stops the partners from doing as good a job as they could do." This again underlines the difficulty of changing existing practices and engaging in double loop learning.

ANALYSIS AND DISCUSSION

Table 6.6 presents an overview of instances of alliance capability building in the partners of the GPL alliance. It lists the examples of accumulating, storing, integrating, and diffusing lessons learned from the alliance evaluation.

This leads us to the next conclusions. First, all elements of learning are present and hence alliance evaluation contributes to alliance capability building. Lessons drawn from the alliance evaluation were accumulated, stored, integrated, and diffused. The joint evaluation of the alliance has led to single loop learning: the alliance has improved. A new governance model was developed and other changes in the alliance have been made based on the outcome of the evaluation process. In addition, double loop learning took place. Examples of double loop learning include the fact that Rolls-Royce applies lessons from the GPL alliance to indirect suppliers and that CEVA uses the governance structure as a benchmark for other relationships. Finally, another indication that alliance capability building is taking place is that lessons are not only confined to the heads of individuals and subsequently lost when these people leave. Instead, new people are trained in alliance thinking.

A second observation is a qualification of the first one. Alliance evaluation may not cover each element of the process of accumulating, storing, integrating, and diffusing lessons to the same extent. It appears to be particularly strong in accumulating and storing lessons. As the alliance evalu-

Table 6.6. Alliance Capability Building Based on Alliance Evaluation in the GPL Alliance

Element	*Example in Rolls-Royce*
Accumulate	• Evaluation highlighted what went well, areas for improvement, lessons learned • Specific attention required for formalization of the alliance and alliance capability building in Rolls-Royce • Lessons taken from bilateral relationships (Rolls-Royce and each individual partner) and on the alliance level
Store	• Accumulated lessons learned were stored in a PowerPoint presentation describing merit and commercial value of the alliance • The results were presented to the alliance partners; each partner received a report
Integrate	• Results from the diagnostic were integrated in a new governance model • Internal company presentations (roadshows, training of incoming graduates, and annual leadership meetings) are held to convince and educate people involved inside Rolls-Royce; people replacing others involved in the alliance receive the same training so that they have a similar background • Initial group in Rolls-Royce developed towards a miniature version of an alliance department (all partners assign an alliance manager to be part of this group)
Diffuse	• First internally: all trading units of Rolls-Royce are involved • Second, to other relationships: Rolls-Royce indirect suppliers now also use lessons from the alliance • Third, CEVA uses governance model as a reference model for their new alliances • Fourth, KN uses governance model to inform their clients • Fifth, external presentation to other organizations and prospective Rolls-Royce partners

ation process in this case ended with the development of an improvement program, it also made a start with integration of the lessons learned. However, the development of the new governance structure that integrated the lessons learned was not technically a part of the evaluation process. Instead, it was a follow up project. Evaluation had the least impact on the diffusion phase. Even though the lessons learned through the evaluation were to some extent diffused to other individuals and organizations, this was not part of the alliance evaluation itself. Instead, this depended on the management and the alliance group that came into being. Hence, alliance evaluation may ensure the capture and storage of lessons learned, but it may be less helpful in integrating and diffusing those lessons. To achieve the latter two elements, further mechanisms (like an alliance committee or alliance office) may be required.

Third, learning is limited in two ways. The first is that not all elements that were discussed in the evaluation process were picked up. Most of the learning is incorporated in the governance model, but other elements received little or no attention. The second limitation is that not all partners learned to the same extent. CEVA and Rolls-Royce appear to have been most active with conscious learning. This study suggests three reasons why learning may be limited: the absence of a knowledge base to build on, internal barriers in the partners, and barriers related to the culture present within the logistics sector. The first point is the traditional chicken and egg problem of capability building. When no capability exists and prior knowledge and experience is absent, the only way to start building a capability is to just start. The partner's capacity to absorb alliance knowledge was limited in the beginning and needed to be built up step by step. The other two elements raise an intriguing point. The literature on alliance capability so far has only focused on elements that stimulate the build-up of an alliance capability. There is no literature on barriers to building alliance capability. The elements mentioned in the GPL case are barriers that have been highlighted in the change management literature as well (Boonstra, 2004). It may be interesting to research whether the change management literature can provide insights into alliance capability building processes.

Fourth, double-loop learning may be direct and indirect. An instance of direct double-loop learning occurs when lessons from the evaluation are incorporated in company training. Indirect learning occurs when lessons from the evaluation are incorporated in the governance structure. People who use this structure may not always be aware that this practice derives from an alliance evaluation process. It is invisible, but still an important value generated by alliance evaluation.

THEORETICAL IMPLICATIONS AND FURTHER RESEARCH

As research into the role and effectiveness of the widespread alliance practice of evaluation is still in its infancy, there are many issues that need to be addressed. Based on this study we identify the following areas as being promising for further research. First, the strong relationship between experience and success may exist because alliance management mechanisms transfer experience into capability. Kale and Singh (2007) suggested this could take place because an alliance department facilitated learning. This case shows that other management tools and processes may have this effect as well. Further research may therefore be directed at studying other tools and processes. In particular it may be valuable to research how combinations of tools increase effective learning. Alliance evaluation is strong in the "accumulate" and "store" phases of the alliance capability building process. Perhaps the combination with an alliance department may be necessary to benefit more from alliance evaluation, because such a department may support the "integrate" and "diffuse" phases.

Second some instances of factors that inhibit alliance learning are found. The literature so far has mainly looked at elements stimulating learning and capability building. Further theorizing may be directed at factors that hold back learning and capability building. Is the fact that not all possibilities for learning from the evaluation process were exploited an indication that managers find some elements of learning more valuable than others? If so, what determines whether they believe something is valuable? The case also showed some barriers to change. Internal processes in Rolls-Royce and sector culture have been seen by some respondents as slowing down the learning process. The literature on change management may help to understand why this happens and what types of interventions are necessary to overcome those barriers. This may work in two directions: change management literature may help to shed more light on the difficulties of alliance capability building and how to overcome them. On the other hand, the field of change management may be advanced to include inter-organizational change. Most research into change management is of an intracompany nature. Can the research results be applied on an interorganizational level as well? Do alliances have different sources of resistance to change than organizations internally? Are there any interventions that work across organizational boundaries? Or should new techniques for organizational change be developed that apply specifically to alliances and incorporate more than one organization? On an industry level it may be interesting to see whether certain business systems are more amenable to alliances than others. What characteristics should business systems have to be receptive to alliance learning? How can companies deal with obstacles to capability building that are of a systemic nature?

Third, the case shows that joint evaluation of alliance is important. Individual evaluation and cross-alliance evaluation have not been studied yet, but are heavily used in practice. What do they add over and above joint evaluation? Is cross-alliance evaluation more suitable to diffuse lessons across alliances? Is there a correct order in which to apply evaluation techniques to maximize learning, for example first individual, than joint and finally cross-alliance evaluation? Or should the methods be used simultaneously or independently from each other?

Finally, empirically most work on alliance capability building has been large scale and focused on one point in time. This case study shows that it is possible to trace learning over a longer time period. More fine grained studies may shed more light on the process of learning. The current case studied learning at two points in time, 5-years apart. Perhaps better insights might have been generated when the case was tracked continuously over that time period. There is a need for longitudinal case studies to answer many of the questions surrounding the build-up of alliance capability.

ACKNOWLEDGMENT

The authors are grateful to Rolls-Royce, CEVA Logistics, Kuehne + Nagel Ltd, and Daher Sawley Ltd for their contribution to this study. Naturally, the conclusions expressed in this chapter are entirely our own.

REFERENCES

Alliance Best Practice (2004, August 25). *Rolls-Royce plc: Unpublished PowerPoint lecture presented to the Starfish group*. Birmingham, England: Author.

Anand, B. N., & Khanna, T. (2000). Do firms learn to create value? The case of alliances. *Strategic Management Journal, 21*, 295–315.

Argyris, C., & Schon D. A. (1978). *Organizational learning*. Reading, MA: Addison-Wesley.

Boonstra, J. J. (Ed.) (2004). *Dynamics of organizational change and learning*. Chichester, England: Wiley.

Das, T. K., & Teng, B. (2000). Instabilities of strategic alliances: An internal tensions perspective. *Organization Science, 11*, 77–101.

De Man, A. P., & Duysters, G. M. (2002). *The first state of alliance management study*. Needham, MA: Association of Strategic Alliance Professionals.

De Man, A. P., & Duysters, G. M. (2007). *The second state of alliance management study*. Needham, MA: Association of Strategic Alliance Professionals.

De Man, A. P., Duysters G. M., & Neyens, I. (2009). *The third state of alliance management study*. Needham, MA: Association of Strategic Alliance Professionals.

Douma, M., Bilderbeek, J., Idenburg, P., & Looise, J. K. (2000). Strategic alliances: managing the dynamics of fit. *Long Range Planning, 33*, 579–598.

Draulans, J., De Man, A. P., & Volberda, H. W. (2003). Building alliance capability: management techniques for superior alliance performance. *Long Range Planning, 36*, 151–166.

Duysters, G. M., & De Man, A. P. (2003). Transitory alliances: an instrument for surviving turbulent industries? *R&D Management, 33*, 49–58.

Dyer, J. H., Kale, P., & Singh, H. (2001). How to make strategic alliances work. *Sloan Management Review, 3*, 37–43.

Futrell, D., Slugay, M., & Stephens, C. H. (2001). Becoming a premier partner: Measuring, managing and changing partnering capabilities at Eli Lilly and Company. *Journal of Commercial Biotechnology, 8*, 5–13.

Heimeriks, K. H., & Duysters, G. M. (2007). Alliance capability as mediator between experience and alliance performance: An empirical investigation into the alliance capability development process. *Journal of Management Studies, 44*, 25–49.

Hoffman, D. (2001). *Alliance metrics*. Unpublished paper, Leverage Point Consulting, Raleigh, NC.

Kale, P., Dyer, J. H., & Singh, H. (2002). Alliance capability, stock market response, and long-term alliance success: The role of the alliance function. *Strategic Management Journal, 23*, 747–767.

Kale, P., & Singh, H. (2007). Building firm capabilities through learning: The role of the alliance learning process in alliance capability and firm-level alliance success. *Strategic Management Journal, 28*, 981–1000.

Lane, P. J., & Lubatkin, M. (1998). Relative absorptive capacity and interorganizational learning. *Strategic Management Journal, 19*, 461–477.

Powell, W. W., Koput, K. W., & Smith-Doerr L. (1996). Interorganizational collaboration and the locus of control of innovation: Networks of learning in biotechnology. *Administrative Science Quarterly, 41*, 116–145.

Reuer, J. J., Zollo, M., & Singh, H. (2002). Post-formation dynamics in strategic alliances. *Strategic Management Journal, 23*, 135–151.

Spekman, R. E., & Isabella, L. (2000). *Alliance competence*. New York, NY: Wiley.

CHAPTER 7

THE FORMATION OF INTERNATIONAL STRATEGIC ALLIANCES BY BORN GLOBAL FIRMS

A Theory-Grounded Review

Robert Gannon and Noushi Rahman

Although much has been written about firms that are international at the time of or soon after inception, there has been little research investigating the factors that enable firms to engage in international strategic alliances during their start-up phase. This study attempts to advance our understanding of the international strategic alliance formation of born global firms, utilizing knowledge based, top management team, and network perspectives. Our review of the pertinent literature is augmented by interviews and questionnaires completed by the top management teams of high technology start-ups. It is believed that the integration of these theories will lead to a better understanding of international strategic alliance formation by newly formed businesses. Propositions are developed to facilitate further research.

Strategic Alliances in a Globalizing World, pp. 139–157

INTRODUCTION

Since it first became a topic of academic interest in the 1990s (Bell, 1995; Coviello & Munro, 1995; Etemad, 1999; Jones, 1999), much has been written on firms that adopt an international strategy from inception. Our review suggests that incremental stage models (Johanson & Vahlne, 1977) do not fully explain the actions of small firms that internationalize soon after founding. While older, larger firms usually favor exporting and foreign direct investments, start-up firms that internationalize early utilize foreign-based resources owned by other firms throughout their value chain as a means of overcoming the "liability of newness" (Phiri, Jones, & Wheeler, 2004). Further, the conceptual framework of international new venture research has relied heavily on the small business literature, but this literature does not necessarily explain or integrate new venture issues (Coviello & Jones, 2004).

Additionally, the Born Global phenomena has become a topic of interest because recent growth in exports has been driven by small and medium sized businesses (SMEs) and small enterprises (Alon, 2004; Etemad, 1999; Etemad & Wright, 1999; McDougall & Oviatt, 2000; McDougall, Oviatt, & Shrader, 2003). High technology start-ups have been seen to engage in a variety of international activities (Bell, 1995; Bloodgood & Sapienza, 1996; Jones, 1999). Affordable communication and transportation, technological innovation, and trade liberalization have fueled the proliferation of Born Global Firms (BGFs). BGFs now have access to international customers, markets, suppliers and collaborators that were unavailable prior to these dramatic changes (Andersson & Wictor, 2003; Dicken, 2003; Etemad & Wright, 1999; Gilpin, 2001). In addition to exporting, international activities have been noted in various places along the value chain, such as R&D collaboration, international outsourcing of design and production, as well as licensing of innovations to foreign entities (Knight & Cavusgil, 1996, 2004).

The profit and survival potential of BGFs is constrained by their lack of resources and small size. Intrinsic to their success is leveraging knowledge and innovation in a manner that will allow them to compete with larger, established firms (Oviatt & McDougall, 1994). Therefore, the key to success may be to cultivate synergies with complementary firms and develop interfirm resources and processes (Dyer & Singh, 1998). Strategic alliance formation can be an efficient, low cost strategy used by start-up firms to gain access to necessary resources. Not only are the governance costs low (Williamson, 1991), but coordination costs of strategic alliances are low (Mauri, 1993) when compared to other types of interfirm collaboration such as merger, acquisition and joint venture. This allows a resource constrained start-up to potentially pursue multiple alliances at various points along its value chain to compensate for its lack of resources. BGFs pursue international strategic alliances for a variety of reasons such as international market entry (Mauri, 1993), access to inexpensive manufacturing resources, and to achieve scale economies (Oviatt & McDougall, 1994). Although Kessler, Allocca, and Rahman (2007) found that alliance partnerships had negative consequences for small and medium sized firms in a variety of industries. Deeds and Hill (1996) found that the number of alliance partners has a positive effect on the speed of new product development in biotechnology firms. Differences may stem from the age of the firm at the time alliance formation commenced.

The international experience of the CEO and top management team (TMT) of BGFs has been suggested as one reason why they pursue an international, rather than a domestic strategy (McDougall et al., 2003). Alliance formation and Born Global behavior have been studied from the transaction cost perspective (Oviatt & McDougall, 1994) and the network perspective (Bell, 1995; Coviello, 2006; Etemad, 1999). However, despite the current and anticipated impact of firms that are international on or near inception, few studies investigate the alliance formation behavior of entrepreneurial firms that opt for an international strategy at inception. Studies that focus on the alliance behavior of small firms are more general in their scope. They focus on the international alliance behavior of SMEs without differentiating between new and more established small businesses. To address this void, the purpose of this research is to explore the alliance behavior of BGFs from different theoretical perspectives. An attempt will be made to illustrate how these perspectives are interrelated, which, when considered together, will shed new light on the alliance formation of BGFs. BGF alliance formation will be investigated from the knowledge based, TMT and networking perspectives. This research utilizes the existing literature, as well as informal surveys and interviews with the TMT of high tech start-ups to inform its perspective. To collect data, sixty-three members of the TMTs of start-up firms were contacted. Eight individuals agreed to respond. The responses serve as the pilot data for a larger project on the strategic alliance formation behavior of BGFs. It is hoped that the propositions offered will stimulate further research into the reasons why so many BGFs engage in international alliance formation.

BORN GLOBAL FIRMS AND STRATEGIC ALLIANCES

BGFs are firms that adopt a global strategy right from the start or very shortly thereafter (Andersson & Wictor, 2003). Andersson and Wictor (p. 254) combine existing definitions by Oviatt and McDougall (1994) and Knight and Cavusgil (1996) to propose that BGFs be defined as: "A company that has achieved a foreign sales volume of at least 25% within three years of its inception and that seeks to derive significant competitive advantage from the use of resources and the sales of outputs in multiple countries" (Andersson & Wictor, p. 254). Scholars have coined different names for the process: "International New Venture" (Oviatt & McDougall, 1997); "Born Global" (Knight & Cavusgil, 1996); "Instant Exporter" (McAuley, 1999); and "Instant International" (Preece, Miles, & Baetz, 1999). For reasons of convenience, this chapter will refer to the various iterations above as "Born Global Firms" (BGFs).

However, a distinction should be made between firms which are considered to be Born-Global, and firms that experience internationalization later in their histories. For example, the participation of small and medium-sized enterprises (SMEs) and small businesses in innovation-centered cross-border relationships is defined as international entrepreneurship. International entrepreneurship is defined as "a combination of innovative, proactive and risk-seeking behavior that crosses national borders and is intended to create value in organizations" (McDougall & Oviatt, 2000, p. 903). However, an SME can engage in international entrepreneurship at any age or at any state of development. Therefore, the process of internationalization is seen as unique in BGFs because the managers of older SMEs may already have preconceived notions toward internationalization (Chen & Huang, 2004), while the managers of new firms may be more flexible in their behavior. Early internationalization is driven by the globalization of markets which involves international sourcing, production and marketing, as well as cross-border alliances for product development and distribution (Knight & Cavusgil, 2004; Rahman, 2008).

Along with these favorable environmental and technological changes, another fundamental change has taken place which allows smaller firms to compete on an international basis. In the past, survival and success was directly related to the tangible assets owned or controlled by a firm. These tangible assets and the corporations which owned them were the prime movers of innovation (Galbraith, 1967; Wright & Dana, 2003). Large corporations used their formidable assets to fund internal research and development efforts as a means of creating the economies of scale necessary to wring profit from their large investment in industrial plant and equipment. However, survival and success has increasingly come from sources outside of the large industrial corporation in the form of knowledge creation and innovation (Chesbrough, 2003; Wright & Dana, 2003).

The ability to exploit key firm advantages has become a function of the intangible knowledge assets that lead to innovation (Doz, Santos, & Williamson, 2001). This has allowed entrepreneurs to form start-up endeavors to leverage their knowledge and innovations into profitable enterprises. Research on entrepreneurship has shown that new ventures are often constrained by resource limitation and this becomes a formidable obstacle in transforming entrepreneurship into high-performance enterprises (Alon, 2004; Hitt, Ireland, Camp, & Sexton, 2001). Thus, entrepreneurs will seek support for their endeavors from their network (Nummela, 2004). Existing networks that are international in scope have a tendency to support and speed up the internationalization process of entrepreneurial start-ups. Further, networks provide firms with the information necessary to find appropriate, trustworthy alliance partners (Gulati, 1998).

Strategic alliances can be defined as "interfirm cooperative arrangements aimed at achieving the strategic objectives of the partners" (Das & Teng, 1998, p. 491). Similarly, strategic alliances have been defined as "an administrative arrangement to govern an *incomplete contract* between separate firms in which each partner has limited control" (Gomes-Casseres, 1997, p. 34). Alliance formation has been studied in light of resource dependence theory (Pfeffer & Nowak, 1976; Van de Ven, 1976), institutional theory (Hite, 2005; Human & Provan, 2000), transaction cost economics (Anderson & Gatignon, 1986; Coase, 1937; Steensma, Marino, Weaver, & Dickson, 2000), and the resource based view (Das & Teng, 2000; Eisenhardt & Schoonhoven, 1996; Sharma & Blomstermo, 2003). Also, network (Barney, 1991; Burt, 1992; Coviello, 2006; Granovetter, 1985; Gulati, 1998) and knowledge-based (Cowan & Jonard, 2009; Doz et al., 2001; Grant, 1996, 2001; Leonard & Sensiper, 1998; Nonaka, 1991, 1994) perspectives have broadened our understanding. Notwithstanding, application of these theories has typically centered on large, established firms or small firms that are already established (Gomes-Casseres, 1997). Table 7.1 summarizes selected studies that inform our analysis of strategic alliance formation by BGFs. In the following section, we examine how various theory-based concepts influence the alliance formation behavior of BGFs.

ALLIANCE FORMATION BY BORN GLOBAL FIRMS

Influence of Knowledge Assets and Innovation

Knowledge has attained the status of being the most important asset for creating and maintaining a competitive position (Leonard & Strauss, 1997; Nonaka, 1991, 1994; Teece, 2000; Wright, McMahan, & McWilliams, 1994; Zárraga & Bonache, 2003). Size has become less of a determinant in a firm's success. Innovating firms develop their own special

Table 7.1. Selected Studies on the BGF Characteristics and Strategic Alliance Formation

Studies	*Findings*
Bell (1995)	A firm's participation in a foreign market develops according to an established chain. Evidence is offered that a relationship with foreign suppliers led to export initiation by the firms studied. These relationships may have been critical in the decision to export.
Coviello (2006)	Builds on existing works that suggest that network theory and analysis are fundamental to international entrepreneurship. Study supports the idea that BGF network density decreases over time, but network breadth increases over time.
Coviello & Munro (1995)	Knowledge gained from external business partners was crucial to identifying countries for initial market penetration.
Das & Teng (1998)	Because of the threat of opportunistic behavior in strategic alliances, firms need to have confidence that partners will act cooperatively. The authors suggest that trust and control are supplementary concepts. Trust mitigates the need for control and control mitigates the need for trust in alliances. Various ways to build trust are also discussed.
Das & Teng (2000)	Examines the role of firm resources in strategic alliances. Offers a general resource-based theory of strategic alliances that includes rationale, formation, structural preferences and performance. Characteristics of resources such as imperfect mobility, imitability, and substitutability are key to value creation and alliance formation.
Deeds & Hill (1996)	Strategic alliances utilize their partner's strengths to penetrate new markets, sustain high performance levels and develop new products. Strategic alliances enhance a firm's chances for survival.
Dyer & Singh (1998)	Critical firm resources are embedded in interfirm resources and routines. The relationship between firms may be a critical unit of analysis for understanding rent generation and competitive advantage.
Eisenhardt & Schoonhoven (1996)	Alliances form when firms are in strategically vulnerable positions because of risky market conditions or risky projects. Additionally, alliances form when firms have strong, experienced management teams with a large network of contacts.
Gomes-Casseres (1997)	It is firm size relative to competitors which defines its competitive vulnerabilities. Firms that lack resources or that lag behind in technology vis-à-vis their competitors are more likely to engage in strategic alliance formation.
Gulati (1998)	Network ties allow firms to find trustworthy alliance partners. Unconnected firms are more likely to enter into an alliance if the potential partner is referred by a current network partner.

Hite (2003)	It is the actions of the entrepreneur, or entrepreneurs that conceive of and start the enterprise that needs to be researched. Successful emergence of an entrepreneurial start-up is contingent on the social and economic potential of the entrepreneur's network ties.
Jones (1999)	For high technology firms, expansion via the conventional, incremental export development route is not the only available or suggested method of international development. A five-tier classification scheme for international development is proposed.
Knight & Cavusgil (1996)	Born Global firms are entrepreneurial start-ups that possess knowledge based innovative cultures. Recent advances in information, communications, production and logistics technologies have created an environment where resource constrained start-ups can pursue global strategies.
McDougall, Oviatt & Schrader (2003)	BGFs have higher levels of international industry experience. BGF strategy was more aggressive than domestic start-ups. BGFs placed a greater emphasis on innovation, quality, service and marketing than their domestic counterparts.
Oviatt & McDougall (1994)	BGFs provide a significant challenge to stage theories of international development. Early internationalizing is analyzed via a four part framework that integrates international business, entrepreneurship, and strategic management theory.
Oviatt & McDougall (1997)	The intangible nature of knowledge resources make them more mobile. BGFs combine these knowledge assets into new innovations. The mobility of knowledge facilitates internationalization.
Shane (2000)	Technological innovations are unique resources that savvy entrepreneurs turn into a business advantage. The ability to recognize these innovations is conditioned by the entrepreneur's previous education and experience.
Sharma & Blomstermo (2003)	BGFs possess market knowledge, pre-inception, that is based on their existing knowledge and knowledge supplied by their network.

knowledge and capabilities that are vital to their organizational performance. New product/market development in young entrepreneurial firms is fluid and dynamic (Bell, 1995; Shane, 2000). This is quite the opposite of what would have been found in large industrial firms in the 1960s and 1970s (Galbraith, 1967). Flexibility has allowed entrepreneurs to seize opportunities to create, embellish and/or combine knowledge resources in ways that serve the needs of customers (Chesbrough, 2003).

BGFs are more likely than older firms to establish cross-border activity in key value chain and associated activities that require innovation and knowledge in an inward direction, an outward direction, or both (Coviello & Munro, 1995; Jones, 1999). Knight and Cavusgil (1996) discuss the role of innovation and knowledge in the rapid internationalizing of entrepreneurial firms. Their research also suggests that young firms with strong innovative cultures tend to internationalize earlier than young firms that lack a predisposition toward innovation. The same innovation culture facilitates the acquisition of knowledge, which leads to the entrepreneurial capabilities that drive organizational performance. Further, Sapienza, Autio, George and Zahra (2006) find that BGFs go through a process of "imprinting," and the earlier in its life that a BGF establishes itself internationally, the easier it finds the process of sensing dynamic opportunities. Knight and Cavusgil (1996) conclude that BGFs are entrepreneurial almost by definition, and they exhibit the qualities of aggressive innovation and proactive knowledge acquisition.

Because the need to acquire knowledge of foreign markets is critical for international entrepreneurship and for the survival and performance of BGFs, they will typically utilize their networks, rather than formal processes to obtain this knowledge. Indeed, informal knowledge of foreign markets is often discovered as early as the planning stages of the business (Phiri et al., 2004), and prior to firm inception (Davidsson & Honig, 2003). Sharma and Blomstermo (2003) state:

> Because Born Globals lack previous successes and fixed routines in entering foreign markets, Born Globals are innovative in combining their own resources with the resource of others through JVs and partnerships (or low control market entry modes). Partnerships may partially compensate for the resource disadvantage of Born Globals. (p. 748)

Bell (1995) discusses the importance of a BGFs informal network contacts when assessing the feasibility of internationalization. His study of small Scandinavian software firms indicated that contact with foreign suppliers to obtain hardware, software distribution rights and licenses to produce software led to the firm's export initiative. Informal foreign contacts supplied knowledge of local needs, import restrictions and other cultural and regulatory issues necessary for a BGF to internationalize.

Proposition 1: The degree of innovation and knowledge orientation of BGFs is positively correlated with the formation of international strategic alliances.

Proposition 2: The degree of knowledge and resource limitations of BGFs is positively correlated with the formation of international strategic alliances.

Influence of BGF's CEO and Top Management Team

A key contributor to the continued success or ultimate failure of a small business is the management activities pursued by its CEO or president

(Miller & Friesen, 1978; Mintzberg, 1973). These activities typically reveal the CEO's position with regard to information gathering, information processing and control systems (Merz & Sauber, 1995). In addition to the CEO, the founding TMT has been shown to have a significant effect on the growth of high technology new ventures, and the influence of the TMT on the performance of young firms is strong (Eisenhardt & Schoonhoven, 1990). Especially in small businesses, strategic choices have a behavioral component, and to some extent they reflect the idiosyncrasies of decision-makers (Hambrick & Mason, 1984).

Factors associated with the economic performance of small businesses are based on the "molding" of a firm's top executives, especially the CEO (Hambrick & Mason, 1984). A portion of the issues associated with the "liability of newness" experienced by start-up firms can be mitigated by the prior experiences of the TMT (Sapienza et al., 2006). Additionally, it has been shown that TMTs with short tenures have fresh, diverse information and are not constrained by industry norms and are more willing to take risks (Finkelstein & Hambrick, 1990; Hambrick & Mason, 1984). Because of the resource limitations encountered by entrepreneurial executives in BGFs, they must position their start-up business to take advantage of the relationship options open to them (Coviello & Munro, 1995; Sharma & Blomstermo, 2003). A crucial element in the success of BGFs is the ability of the TMT to recognize global opportunities and muster their network resources in pursuit of them (Andersson & Wictor, 2003). Sharma and Blomstermo (2003) conclude that BGFs with international knowledge have a higher degree of internationalization than older domestic firms that do not possess international experience. Similarly, Shane (2000) has found that it is the pre-inception network ties and knowledge of the firm's founder and TMT that have a marked impact on the firm's eventual development. The key factor in undertaking global marketing strategic alliances is the attitude of the owner of the business (Chen & Huang, 2004). The CEO of an early-stage biochemical company stated that his firm's TMT possessed extensive foreign experience. Their foreign experience included attendance at a foreign university, experience in managing foreign interests from both a domestic and a foreign location, as well as long-term residency in a foreign company. A high tech medical company responded similarly, and further stated that their CEO regularly attends foreign trade shows to highlight the firm's product offering, develop network connections and ascertain the fit between his firm's product and foreign market needs.

Proposition 3: International experience of the CEO and the top management team of BGFs is positively correlated with the formation of international strategic alliances.

Proposition 4: International education of the CEO and top management team of BGFs is positively correlated with the formation of international strategic alliances.

It is interesting to note that the executives interviewed responded that no one on their TMT was fluent in a foreign language. This contradicts recent research on executive attributes and export performance, where fluency in a foreign language was seen as significant in export performance of Turkish firms (Atabay, 2008). This may illustrate a significant difference between existing firms that are international and BGFs.

For entrepreneurs, networking is the use of personal relationships to obtain resources they do not control. The diversity of these resources allows the entrepreneur to draw on a much wider range of external assets to supplement the limited resources within the emerging entrepreneurial enterprise. These resources can, variously, be financing, advice, access to value chain resources, "insider" sales and other external assets that are crucial to the firm's development (Birley, 1985). Although aspects of the process of internationalization have been addressed by the literature, most of the studies have focused on larger enterprises. For example, stage models, such as the Uppsala model, have been utilized to explain the internationalization process (Bell, 1995; Etemad & Wright, 1999; Johanson & Vahlne, 1977; Spence, 2003). The Uppsala model is the most notorious of the stage models of internationalization. It assumes that a lack of knowledge necessitates an approach to internationalization that stresses gradual acquisition, integration and use of knowledge, along with an incremental commitment to foreign markets (Johanson & Vahlne, 1977, 1990).

It has become apparent, however, that the older stage models which were applicable to the analysis of large firms have little explanatory power when analyzing small firms and SMEs (Bell, 1995). As opposed to the stage theories of internationalization (Johanson & Vahlne, 1977), the network model provides a new way of viewing rapid internationalization of BGFs. The network view considers the entrepreneur as a "socioeconomic actor" with a unique personal background, private concerns and individualized economic interests. Therefore, the relationship of the entrepreneur to the environment cannot necessarily be viewed from the context of a larger, formal organization that solely emphasizes tasks, market prices, transaction costs, market contexts, and so forth (Larson & Starr, 1993). The network approach takes into consideration the relational embeddedness of network ties that provide critical opportunities and resources to the entrepreneurial firm that would be unavailable via more traditional transactions. Additionally, most of the literature on entrepreneurial behavior stresses the firm, but in actuality, it is the actions of the entrepreneur who conceptualizes the opportunity and commences the endeavor. In fact, it is the major managerial task of the entrepreneur to maximize the social and economic potential embedded in these relationally embedded network ties (Hite, 2003).

Network analysis has been a fruitful area of research for those investigating international entrepreneurship. Further, Oviatt and McDougall (1997) stress the importance of networks to BGFs, because new firms are dependent on their relationships with financiers, suppliers and customers. Knight and Cavusgil (1996) emphasize the importance of formal as well as informal networks for BGFs, as do Coviello and Munro (1995). Bell (1995) concludes that the pattern of internationalization for high tech start up firms is not amenable to analysis via linear models such as stage theories, because their behavior is frequently dynamic, interactive and decidedly nonlinear. In areas such as marketing infrastructure and marketing capabilities, where small high-tech companies are traditionally weak, Coviello and Munro (1995) found that establishing and utilizing relationships with other firms is an effective means for young firms to internationalize.

In their study, Phiri et al. (2004) concluded that international network contacts consisting of friends, related professionals, and industry specialists formed the first and most fundamental relationships in the internationalization decisions of the five medical firms studied. Similarly, investigations into the entrepreneurial behavior of James Dyson, one of Britain's best known and most successful entrepreneurs, illustrates that the ability of the entrepreneur to extend his network across national borders in search of scarce resources is critical to the internationalization of smaller, emerging firms.

It is the role of the CEO and TMT of a BGF to not only utilize resources within the firm, but to exploit external resources found in their already existing networks. Entrepreneurs need to participate in networks in order to attract or outsource necessary resources for the successful development of projects. One interviewee remarked that the existing international network of the CEO was directly responsible for the development of their strategic alliance network in Europe. Although the CEO had no direct contacts with appropriate firms or individuals, he leveraged his existing networks to find individuals in foreign firms that were amenable to alliance formation.

Proposition 5: The number of international network partners in the network of the CEO and top management team of BGFs are positively correlated with the formation of international strategic alliances.

Proposition 6: Recent international contacts of the CEO and top management team of BGFs are positively correlated with the formation of international strategic alliances.

Influence of BGF's Social Networks

Resource paucity and asset parsimony explain a preponderance of the strategic alliance formation by BGFs (Gulati, 1999; Oviatt & McDougall, 1994). The critical resources of the firm may not reside exclusively within its boundaries. Rather, these crucial resources may be embedded in interfirm resources, structure, and processes (Dyer & Singh, 1998). Additionally, these obstacles constrain a start up firm's ability to attain superior results (Hitt et al., 2001) and superior profits (Dyer & Singh, 1998). Strategic alliances increase a firm's rate of new product development and enhance the chances for firm survival (Deeds & Hill, 1996). Learning, provided by complementary alliances or alliances with competitors, can enhance a start up firm's chances for survival and success (Baum, Calabrese, & Silverman, 2000).

The issues confronting the BGF with regard to appropriate alliance formation and exploitation have to do with the connectedness of business relationships (Anderson, Haykansson, & Johanson, 1994). Members of BGF networks that were involved or anticipating involvement in international strategic alliances stated definitively that they found international alliances attractive, because they did not possess the resources internally to effectively market their innovation commercially, or to fully exploit all the applications for their product. Given the short product life cycle of most knowledge-based innovations (Etemad, 1999), the ability to quickly cultivate marketing channels and to exploit the possibilities of an innovation are critical to the survival and growth of BGFs.

Proposition 7: The number of international network partners of the CEO and top management team of BGFs is positively correlated with the formation of international strategic alliances.

DISCUSSION AND CONCLUSIONS

The above review has attempted to show that strategic alliance formation is an integral part of the survival and profitability of BGFs. Although many studies focus on the alliance formation behavior of international entrepreneurs, the emphasis has been on transaction cost economics and recource-based explanations. Therefore, we investigated BGF alliance formation from salient, underutilized perspectives. Although the knowledge based view, TMT theory and network theory are well represented in the international entrepreneurship literature, BGF behavior differs in significant ways from that of more established small firms. Second, we attempted to integrate these theories and apply them to BGF alliance behavior. Finally, we have proposed that CEO and TMT international experience, coupled with the depth and breadth of their informal international networks may provide fertile ground for future research into successful international alliance formation of BGFs, especially when investigating small knowledge intensive firms (SKIFs) and high tech start-ups.

Knowledge-based theories concern themselves with the entrepreneurial aspects of BGFs, because combining knowledge in unique ways and innovating is at the heart of the entrepreneurial endeavor. However, the knowledge that drives innovation is not enough. Typically, BGFs lack the resources (financial, technical, etc.) to transform an idea into a commercially viable product or service. Further, their lack of resources will compel start-up enterprises to favor alternative governance structures (Oviatt & McDougall, 1994) and shun more formal agreements that necessitate equity involvement and the long-term commitments that are characteristic of formal cooperative arrangements. Therefore, as a BGF progresses through its start-up phase, it will prefer alliances, because they require little commitment, but may yield large rewards. BGFs with the skill and acumen to develop productive strategic alliances will be in a better position to succeed.

A start-up firm must be able to react to its environment by reconfiguring and integrating its internal and external resources (Teece, Pisano, & Shuen, 1997). Contrary to Knight and Cavusgil's (2004) findings that BGFs follow an intended strategy, Coviello (2006) believes that there is a balance between strategy and unintended occurrences which influence the actions of BGFs. Strategic alliances can be seen as building blocks that can be initiated, reconfigured, and/or terminated by the BGF based on its need to react to internal and external threats and opportunities. In addition to technological skills, much of a start-up firm's success is contingent on the skills of a firm's managers (Finkelstein & Hambrick, 1990). We believe that the international knowledge and experience of the CEO and TMT of a BGF, along with their network of relationships, will impact the formation of international strategic alliances.

Further, why would a domestic firm seek international strategic alliances rather than domestic strategic alliances? Doz et al. (2001) observed that innovative expertise is found in global geographic clusters. Technology allows for international communication and international cooperation at a very low cost to a resource-poor start up venture. When knowledge is not easily available at home, a start-up firm can parsimoniously discover and cultivate pockets of knowledge internationally, mobilize its resources in concert with another firm, and operationalize the complementary technologies to generate and sustain a unique competitive strategy.

However, many successful start-up endeavors never seek or develop international strategic alliances. The CEO and the TMT of a start-up firm wield significant power and influence on the firm's direction and strategy attainment. Therefore, it logically follows that the establishment of international strategic alliances would be contingent upon the international predisposition of the CEO and TMT of a start-up endeavor. Additionally, we believe that international experience, such as foreign university attendance and/or residing abroad, are salient indicators that the CEO and/or TMT will be comfortable in finding and establishing international strategic alliances. Therefore, international experience, whether professional or personal, needs to be augmented by the CEO and TMT's network ties.

Preliminary anecdotal evidence targeting the senior management of high tech start-up firms was gathered for this chapter. Data was collected via interviews and e-mailed surveys. International strategic alliances were created by firms where the CEO and/or TMT had numerous and frequent informal contacts with international network partners. These contacts came from past work relationships, frequent international travel, and attendance at international trade shows. Conversely, our research indicates that international strategic alliances were absent or failed to become productive when the CEO and TMT had no informal international network partners, even among SKIFs and high tech start-ups.

Case study research has been the preferred form of inquiry for studying BGFs. However, descriptive research typically leads to conclusions that are specific to certain industries or industry segments. Research methodologies that allow for more generalized conclusions regarding the behavior of BGFs should be utilized. Survey methodologies would allow for a larger, more diverse sample, which might prove valuable in devising a more comprehensive model of BGF alliance formation. Sample data can be generated via Internet searches directed at business incubators, venture capitalist websites and regional and local technology councils.

The survey participants in this study do not constitute a scientific sample, because the sample size was small, and some participants were identified by the authors. There was no attempt made to analyze the exact nature of the participant's network relations, nor was there a distinction made between differing affects of formal and informal network ties on alliance formation. This would require rigorous network analysis that is beyond the scope of this chapter. Additionally, there may be other important TMT characteristics that could be included in future research that were not considered, such as TMT member age, education level and profession. Finally, intervening variables such as a foreign born CEO or foreign born members of the TMT are not taken into consideration. It is believed that foreign origin would predispose senior executives to seek alliances with firms from their home country.

TMT international experience provides a foundation for conducting business abroad. Experience mitigates cultural, economic and governance issues that will be encountered during the search for appropriate partners. The TMT of a BGF that has an understanding of these issues is in a better position to identify favorable alliance partners and to create a productive alliance relationship. This is because international experience and network connections of a BGF's CEO and TMT broaden the range of potential network partners, which may optimize search behavior. International strategic alliances can aid BGFs by supplying resources from geographic clusters that specialize in the needed resources. The ability of the CEO and TMT to utilize their international network connections to ferret out the most appropriate partners will aid in establishing and sustaining an effective strategy and adapting to environmental opportunities and threats. Additionally, understanding how international alliances are different from domestic alliances, and having the foundation to deal with these differences, will make the international alliances formed more effective and productive.

REFERENCES

Alon, I. (2004). International market selection for a small enterprise: A case study in international entrepreneurship. *SAM Advanced Management Journal, 69*(1), 25–33.

Anderson, E., & Gatignon, H. (1986). Modes of foreign entry: A transaction cost analysis and propositions. *Journal of International Business Studies, 17*, 1–26.

Anderson, J. C., Haykansson, H., & Johanson, J. (1994). Dyadic business relationships within a business network context. *Journal of Marketing, 58*(4), 1–15.

Andersson, S., & Wictor, I. (2003). Innovative internationalization in new firms: Born Globals—The Swedish case. *Journal of International Entrepreneurship, 1*, 249–276.

Atabay, I. (2008). The effect of the business manager's attributes on export performance. *The Social Sciences, 3*, 494–497.

Barney, J. (1991). Firm resources and sustained competitive advantage. *Journal of Management, 17*, 99–120.

Baum, J. A. C., Calabrese, T., & Silverman, B. S. (2000). Don't go it alone: Alliance network composition and startups' performance in Canadian biotechnology. *Strategic Management Journal, 21*, 267–294.

Bell, J. (1995). The internationalization of small computer software firms: A further challenge to "Stage" theories. *European Journal of Marketing, 29*(8), 60–75.

Birley, S. (1985). The role of networking in the entrepreneurial process. *Journal of Business Venturing, 1*, 107–117.

Bloodgood, J. M., & Sapienza, H. J. (1996). The internationalization of new high-potential U.S. ventures: Antecedents and outcomes. *Entrepreneurship: Theory & Practice, 20*(4), 61–76.

Burt, R. S. (1992). *Structural holes: The social structure of competition*. Cambridge, MA: Harvard University Press.

Chen, H. L., & Huang, Y. (2004). The establishment of global marketing strategic alliances by small and medium enterprises. *Small Business Economics, 22*, 365–377.

Chesbrough, H. W. (2003). A better way to innovate. *Harvard Business Review, 81*(7), 12–14.

Coase, R. H. (1937). The nature of the firm. *Economica, 4*, 386–405.

Coviello, N. E. (2006). The network dynamics of international new ventures. *Journal of International Business Studies, 37*, 713–731.

Coviello, N. E., & Jones, M. V. (2004). Methodological issues in international entrepreneurship research. *Journal of Business Venturing, 19*, 485–508.

Coviello, N. E., & Munro, H. J. (1995). Growing the entrepreneurial firm: Networking for international market development. *European Journal of Marketing, 29*(7), 49–61.

Cowan, R., & Jonard, N. (2009). Knowledge portfolios and the organization of innovation networks. *Academy of Management Review, 34*, 320–342.

Das, T. K., & Teng, B. (1998). Between trust and control: Developing confidence in partner cooperation in alliances. *Academy of Management Review, 23*, 491–512.

Das, T. K., & Teng, B. (2000). A resource-based theory of strategic alliances. *Journal of Management, 26*, 31–62.

Davidsson, P., Honig, B. (2003). The role of social and human capital among nascent entrepreneurs. *Journal of Business Venturing, 18*, 301–331.

Deeds, D. L., & Hill, C. W. L. (1996). Strategic alliances and the rate of new product development: An empirical study of entrepreneurial biotechnology firms. *Journal of Business Venturing, 11*, 41–55.

Dicken, P. (2003). *Global shift: Reshaping the global economic map in the 21st century*. New York: Guilford Press.

Doz, I., Santos, J., & Williamson, P. (2001). *From global to metanational: How companies win in the knowledge economy*. Boston, MA: Harvard Business School Press.

Dyer, J. H., & Singh, H. (1998). The relational view: Cooperative strategy and sources of interorganizational competitive advantage. *Academy of Management Review, 23*, 660–679.

Eisenhardt, K. M., & Schoonhoven, C. B. (1990). Organizational growth: Linking founding team, strategy, environment, and growth among U.S. semiconductor ventures, 1978–1988. *Administrative Science Quarterly, 35*, 504–529.

Eisenhardt, K. M., & Schoonhoven, C. B. (1996). Resource-based view of strategic alliance formation: Strategic and social effects in entrepreneurial firms. *Organization Science, 7*, 136–150.

Etemad, H. (1999). Globalisation and the small and medium sized enterprise: Search for potent strategies. *Global Focus, 11*(3), 85–104.

Etemad, H., & Wright, R. W. (1999). Internationalization of SMEs: Management responses to a changing environment. *Journal of International Marketing, 7*(4), 4–10.

Finkelstein, S., & Hambrick, D. C. (1990). Top-management-team tenure and organizational outcomes: The moderating role of managerial discretion. *Administrative Science Quarterly, 35*, 484–503.

Galbraith, J. K. (1967). *The new industrial state*. Boston, MA: Houghton, Mifflin & Co.

Gilpin, R. (2001). *Global political economy: Understanding the international economic order.* Princeton, NJ: Princeton University Press.

Gomes-Casseres, B. (1997). Alliance strategies of small firms. *Small Business Economics, 9*(1), 33–44.

Granovetter, M. (1985). Economic action and social structure: The problem of embeddedness. *American Journal of Sociology, 91*, 481–510.

Grant, R. M. (1996). Toward a knowledge-based theory of the firm. *Strategic Management Journal, 17*(Winter Special Issue), 109–122.

Grant, R. M. (2001). Knowledge and organization. In I. Nonaka & D. J. Teece (Eds.), *Managing industrial knowledge: Creation, transfer and utilization* (pp. 145–169). Thousand Oaks, CA: SAGE.

Gulati, R. (1998). Alliances and networks. *Strategic Management Journal, 19*, 293–317.

Gulati, R. (1999). Network location and learning: The influence of network resources and firm capabilities on alliance formation. *Strategic Management Journal, 20*, 397–420.

Hambrick, D. C., & Mason, P. A. (1984). Upper echelons: The organization as a reflection of its top managers. *Academy of Management Review, 9*, 193–206.

Hite, J. M. (2003). Patterns of multidimensionality among embedded network ties: A typology of relational embeddedness in emerging entrepreneurial firms. *Strategic Organization, 1*, 9–49.

Hite, J. M. (2005). Evolutionary processes and paths of relationally embedded network ties in emerging entrepreneurial firms. *Entrepreneurship: Theory & Practice, 29*(1), 113–144.

Hitt, M. A., Ireland, R. D., Camp, S. M., & Sexton, D. L. (2001). Guest editors' introduction to the special issue on "Strategic entrepreneurship: entrepreneurial strategies for wealth creation." *Strategic Management Journal, 22*, 479–491.

Human, S. E., & Provan, K. G. (2000). Legitimacy building in the evolution of small-firm multilateral networks: A comparative study of success and demise. *Administrative Science Quarterly, 45*, 327–365.

Johanson, J., & Vahlne, J. E. (1977). The internationalization process of the firm: A model of knowledge development and increasing foreign market commitments. *Journal of International Business Studies, 8*, 23–32.

Johanson, J., & Vahlne, J. E. (1990). The mechanism of internationalism. *International Marketing Review, 7*, 11–24.

Jones, M. V. (1999). The internationalization of small high-technology firms. *Journal of International Marketing, 7*, 15–41.

Kessler, E. H., Allocca, M. A., & Rahman, N. (2007). External knowledge accession and innovation speed in the small and medium sized enterprise (SME). *Small Enterprise Research: The Journal of SEAANZ, 15*(1), 1–21.

Knight, G., & Cavusgil, S. (1996). The born global firm: A challenge to traditional internationalization theory. *Advances in International Marketing, 7*, 11–26.

Knight, G., & Cavusgil, S. (2004). Innovation, organizational capabilities, and the born-global firm. *Journal of International Business Studies, 35*, 124–141.

Larson, A., & Starr, J. A. (1993). A network model of organization formation. *Entrepreneurship: Theory & Practice, 17*(2), 5–15.

Leonard, D., & Sensiper, S. (1998). The role of tacit knowledge in group innovation. *California Management Review, 40*(3), 112–132.

Leonard, D., & Strauss, S. (1997). Putting your company's whole brain to work. *Harvard Business Review, 75*(4), 110–121.

Mauri, A. J. (1993). The influence of technology on strategic alliances: An application of the Utterback and Abernathy model of process and product innovation. *Academy of Management Best Paper Proceedings*, 137–141.

McAuley, A. (1999). Entrepreneurial instant exporters in the Scottish arts and crafts sector. *Journal of International Marketing, 7*(4), 67–82.

McDougall, P. P., & Oviatt, B. M. (2000). International entrepreneurship: The intersection of two research paths. *Academy of Management Journal, 43*, 902–906.

McDougall, P. P., Oviatt, B. M., & Shrader, R. C. (2003). A comparison of international and domestic new ventures. *Journal of International Entrepreneurship, 1*(1), 59–82.

Merz, G. R., & Sauber, M. H. (1995). Profiles of managerial activities in small firms. *Strategic Management Journal, 16*, 551–564.

Miller, D., & Friesen, P. H. (1978). Strategy making and the environment: The third link. *Strategic Management Journal, 4*, 221–235.

Mintzberg, H. (1973). Strategy making in three modes. *California Management Review, 16*(2), 44–53.

Nonaka, I. (1991). The knowledge-creating company. *Harvard Business Review, 69*(6), 96–104.

Nonaka, I. (1994). A dynamic theory of organizational knowledge creation. *Organization Science, 5*, 14–37.

Nummela, N. (2004). Is the globe becoming smaller or is the small becoming global? Globalization and internationalizing SMEs. In M. V. Jones & P. Dimitratos (Eds.), *Emerging paradigms in international entrepreneurship* (pp. 125–151). Northampton, MA: Edward Elgar.

Oviatt, B. M., & McDougall, P. P. (1994). Toward a theory of international new ventures. *Journal of International Business Studies, 25*, 45–64.

Oviatt, B. M., & McDougall, P. P. (1997). Challenges for international process theory: The case of international new ventures. *Journal of International Business Studies, 37*(Special Issue 2), 85–99.

Pfeffer, J., & Nowak, P. (1976). Joint ventures and interorganizational interdependence. *Administrative Science Quarterly, 21*, 398–418.

Phiri, T., Jones, M. V., & Wheeler, C. (2004). Returning to the field in internationalization: An exploratory study of contemporary small firms in the advanced medical products industry. In M. V. Jones & P. Dimitratos (Eds.), *Emerging paradigms in international entrepreneurship* (pp. 249–275). Northampton, MA: Edward Elgar.

Preece, S. B., Miles, G., & Baetz, M. C. (1999). Explaining the international intensity and global diversity of early-stage technology-based firms. *Journal of Business Venturing, 14*, 259–281.

Rahman, N. (2008). Resource and risk trade-offs in *guanxi*-based IJVs in China. *Asia Pacific Business Review, 14*, 233–252.

Sapienza, H. J., Autio, E., George, G., & Zahra, S. A. (2006). A capabilities perspective on the effects of early internationalization on firm survival and growth. *Academy of Management Review, 31*, 914–933.

Shane, S. (2000). Prior knowledge and the discovery of entrepreneurial opportunities. *Organizational Science, 11*, 448–469.

Sharma, D. D., & Blomstermo, A. (2003). The internationalization process of Born Globals: A network view. *International Business Review, 12*, 739–754.

Spence, M. (2003). International strategy formation in small Canadian high-technology companies. *Journal of International Entrepreneurship, 1*, 277–296.

Steensma, H. K., Marino, L., Weaver, K. M., & Dickson, P. H. (2000). The influence of national culture on the formation of technology alliances by entrepreneurial firms. *Academy of Management Journal, 43*, 951–973.

Teece, D. J. (2000). *Managing intellectual capital*. New York: Oxford University Press.

Teece, D. J., Pisano, G., & Shuen, A. (1997). Dynamic capabilities and strategic management. *Strategic Management Journal, 18*, 509–533.

Van de Ven, A. H. (1976). On the nature, formation, and maintenance of relations among organizations. *Academy of Management Review, 1*, 24–36.

Williamson, O. E. (1991). Comparative economic organization: The analysis of discrete structural alternatives. *Administrative Science Quarterly, 36*, 269–296.

Wright, P. M., McMahan, G. C., & McWilliams, A. (1994). Human resources and sustained competitive advantage: A resource-based perspective. *International Journal of Human Resource Management, 5*, 301–326.

Wright, R. W., & Dana, L. P. (2003). Changing paradigms of international entrepreneurship strategy. *Journal of International Entrepreneurship, 1*(1), 132–152.

Zárraga, C., & Bonache, J. (2003). Assessing the team environment for knowledge sharing: An empirical analysis. *International Journal of Human Resource Management, 14*, 1227–1246.

CHAPTER 8

THE CONTAINMENT OF OPPORTUNISM IN THE POST FORMATION PERIOD OF INTERORGANIZATIONAL RELATIONSHIPS

Kerstin Neumann and Reinhard Bachmann

This chapter analyzes the post formation period of interorganizational relationships (IORs) on the basis of the assumption that opportunism—particularly between competitors—remains a key problem after the formation and structuring of the IOR. As opportunism negatively influences the performance of the IOR, it will be shown that it is important to understand the factors which foster the willingness to cooperate. The chapter combines transaction cost economics and resource-based theory perspectives to explain ex post cooperative behavior of the partners. In so doing, it integrates both governance and resource related issues for a more comprehensive view of the post formation period. It is proposed that there are four factors that largely determine whether ex post opportunism will be successfully suppressed in an ongoing relationship: (1) the complexity of the ex ante formal contract, (2) the efforts made by the partners to establish and encourage trust, (3) the degree of sustained resource complementarity, and

Strategic Alliances in a Globalizing World, pp. 159–184

(4) the level of interdependencies. These factors are shown to be intertwined and to have effects in fostering sustained cooperative behavior and success of the partnership. This theoretical concept will be supported by empirical data gathered in the context of a case study of an IOR between two European airlines.

INTRODUCTION

Many contributions to the literature identify the initial implementation of a detailed governance structure that includes the partner selection process as a vital condition for the success of an interorganizational relationship (IOR). Since the possibility of opportunism between partners can never be ruled out, a detailed governance structure, containing both formal and relational mechanisms, is needed to safeguard IOR performance. However, IOR conditions are not static. Rather, they can significantly change over time. Also, governance solutions are intrinsically incomplete. Hence, we suggest that the ex ante governance implementation can only be one of a number of elements incorporated into the management of interfirm cooperation (Reuer, Zollo, & Singh, 2002), and that ex post arrangements are necessary to avoid inefficiency in an ongoing partnership.

In recent years, only a few researchers have begun investigating the post formation period of IORs more closely. Initially, such studies looked at instability in IORs from a bargaining power perspective (Inkpen & Beamish, 1997; Pearce, 1997). During the 1990s, progress in understanding alliance dynamic came predominantly from deductive theoretical approaches and dynamic statistical models of joint venture termination. Factors affecting the likelihood of termination were identified at different levels (Reuer et al., 2002), for example, environmental factors like industry demand shocks (Kogut, 1991) or transaction level elements such as opportunism (Park & Russo, 1996). Furthermore, several process models have been developed to explain interorganizational evolution (e.g., Ring & Van de Ven, 1994; Zajac & Olsen, 1993; for a systematic discussion of this strand of the IOR literature see, for example, De Rond & Bouchikhi, 2004). More recently, researchers have also started to investigate the incidence and antecedents of post formation governance changes in IORs (Bensaou & Venkatraman, 1995; Reuer & Ariño, 2002; Reuer et al., 2002). The latter research indicates that corrective interventions are often made simply to ensure the survival of the alliance, sometimes by mutual agreement and in response to changing contingencies (Reuer & Ariño, 2002). Such changes might be seen as a normal and a necessary response to environmental and internal developments of the IOR to ensure its stability in the longer term.

This chapter analyses the post formation period of strategic partnerships on the basis of the assumption that opportunism is not only necessary to contain in the initial stages of an IOR but also at later stages of its life-cycle. However, there are currently only few studies focusing on the problem of opportunism in the post formation period of IORs (e.g., Das, 2005; Das & Rahman, 2010; Jap & Anderson, 2003; Park & Russo, 1996). Some of the contributions to this literature suggest that the competitive situation between such partners creates a fundamental potential for opportunism and puts the survival and success of such relationships at high risk (Bucklin & Sengupta, 1993; Park & Russo, 1996). Bucklin and Sengupta, for example, emphasize that in IORs between competitors "the potential for serious conflict is always present as partners often compete with each other in other product lines and, on occasion, in those directly covered by the ... agreement" (p. 33). Similarly, Van de Ven and Walker (1984) argue that the likelihood of territorial disputes, conflicts and competition may increase over time in an ongoing IOR. Despite the high levels of motivation that abound when the IOR is formed as a result of the value expected to be generated from an IOR with a competitor, and despite the best attempts of the partners to implement sound governance structures to reduce potential opportunism, "competitive factors that motivate the alliance can be only imperfectly redressed and can cause future problems and instability. In a broad sense, failure occurs when excessive rivalry eclipses cooperative tendencies" (Park & Ungson, 2001, p. 37). Examples of opportunistic behavior might include withholding or misrepresenting important information, providing false information and cheating (Park & Ungson, 2001), reneging explicit or implicit commitments, shirking (Jap & Anderson, 2003), or trying to reallocate collaborative rents opportunistically by exploiting the partner's dependence on specific investments (Inkpen & Beamish, 1997).

In fact, in many cases, authors report high failure rates for IORs or dissatisfaction among partners with IOR performance (e.g., Ireland, Hitt, & Vaidyanath, 2002; Park & Ungson, 2001; Parkhe, 1993; Young-Ybarra & Wiersema, 1999). This suggests that even when synergies exist or are anticipated in the pooling of complementary resources, success in IORs can still be elusive in the longer term (Ireland et al., 2002; Madhok & Tallman, 1998). Khanna, Gulati, and Nohria (1998) argue that "an important reason for the disappointment of some firms with alliances is their poor understanding of the strategic dynamics within such partnerships" (p. 194).

In the next section, we will present our theoretical argument emphasizing the importance of the formal contract complexity, ex post trust building efforts, sustained resource complementarity and sustained interdependence as key factors that decide the chances of successful long-term cooperation in IORs. We will then move on to present an instructive case study of a high performance strategic alliance from the airline industry. In the conclusion we will summarize our findings and evaluate their relevance for theory building and future empirical research.

ENHANCING COOPERATIVE BEHAVIOR AND PREVENTING EX POST OPPORTUNISM IN INTERORGANIZATIONAL RELATIONSHIPS

Organizational theorists (e.g., Eisenhardt, 1985; Ouchi, 1979) and economic literature (e.g., Baker, Gibbons, & Murphy, 2002) consider formal and informal (i.e. relational) mechanisms to be part of the governance structure of IORs. While the key formal mechanism is often seen in the legal contract, the latter constitutively hinge on issues related to trust building (Bachmann & Zaheer, 2008). From our point of view, the investigation of the effects of governance characteristics in the post formation period of IORs is most beneficial when formal and relational or trust-based governance mechanisms are discussed in such a way that their intrinsic interrelatedness is highlighted.

The bulk of the IOR literature broadly agrees on the need of implementing governance mechanisms in IORs to manage potential opportunism (e.g., Dekker, 2004; Stump & Heide, 1996). However, what also matters in this context are resource-related complementarities and the density of the relationship (i.e., the level of interdependencies). The key questions that we want to answer in this chapter is whether and how formal governance structures and informal governance mechanisms as well as complementarities and interdependencies can together contribute to the continued success of cooperative relationships and suppress ex post opportunism when the IOR is already established.

Formal Contract Complexity

In theory, the formal contract for an IOR specifies decisions relevant for allocating responsibilities, controlling, required outcomes and rewards, individual resource commitments and the level and nature of the risks involved (Ring & Van de Ven, 1994). By agreeing on a detailed contract, the parties try to establish a comprehensive agreement which specifies all mechanisms that are expected to govern the decision-making processes in the relationship (Pearce, 1997), that is, the formal governance structure. Formal governance mechanisms consist of outcome and behavior control (Eisenhardt, 1985; Ouchi, 1979; specifically for IOR contexts, see e.g., Dekker, 2004; Neumann, 2010; Stump & Heide, 1996).

The more complex the formal agreement, the more ex post uncertainty about the future behavior of the partner is supposed to be reduced, although the ex ante complete resolution of uncertainty is neither possible nor efficient (Williamson, 1975). A more detailed contract will sometimes even enhance the "scope of opportunity for unforeseen developments that necessitate adjustment or refinement (e.g., renegotiation) of the contract" (Pearce, 1997, p. 207). Generally, however, by negotiating more elaborate formal safeguards, firms can avoid much of the risks associated with ex post renegotiations. Strong forms of contractual safeguards increase transparency and clarify rights and duties of each party (Reuer & Ariño, 2002). Baker, Gibbons, and Murphy (1994) point out that a failure to specify certain formal contractual elements enhances incentives for opportunistically seeking short-term profits and, thus, lowers the expectations of cooperative behavior. Broadly speaking, it can be assumed that the more specified the formal agreement, the better the alignment of goals and behavior and the lower the risk of opportunistic behavior (Das, 2005). Thus it should also hold that the higher the potential of ex post opportunism in IORs, the more complex the formal contract is likely to be, although complex contract negotiations and the subsequent implementation of highly complex contracts result in considerable ex ante costs and may postpone the realization of the IOR's intended value (Pearce, 1997).

Trust Building Efforts

Mayer, Davis, and Schoorman (1995) define trust as

> the willingness of a party to be vulnerable to the actions of another party based on the expectation that the other will perform a particular action important to the trustor, irrespective of the ability to monitor or control the other party. (p. 712)

Vulnerability implies that there is something to be lost, hence trust is based on a trustor's willingness to take a risk. At the same time, trust also implies the expectation that something can be gained from a trustor's point of view, even if that is not or very vaguely specifiable. This is a necessary assumption if actors are not to be viewed as irrational.

Although different conclusions have been drawn on the effect of trust in IOR, empirical evidence clearly indicates a positive influence on performance (Zaheer & Harris, 2006). Sarkar, Echambadi, Cavusgil, and

Aulakh (2001) point out that "cooperative behavior springs from the development of relational capital between partners, which is critical in transforming the potential value of an alliance into actualized collaborative economic rents" (p. 359). Ring and Van de Ven (1994) argue that trust between exchange partners is needed to counter the different problems stemming from opportunism. Therefore, since ex post opportunism may arise after the formation of the IOR, trust building processes between the partner organizations are essential and can effectively help to suppress opportunism.

A fundamental question in this context is how interorganizational trust is created and develops over time in IORs (Ring & Van de Ven, 1994; Zaheer & Harris, 2006). A certain level of interorganizational trust must always already be in place before the partners begin negotiating the cooperation contract (Zaheer & Harris, 2006). Potential partners will only enter into an IOR if they are fairly confident of their partner's subsequent willingness to behave trustworthily and cooperatively (Das & Teng, 1998; for recent empirical evidence on the impact of trust on the decision to cooperate, see Hoffmann, Neumann, & Speckbacher, 2010). For example, they might ex ante be familiar with each other from previous relationships (Gulati, 1995), have a strong general reputation in the market, share a specific cultural background (Das & Rahman, 2010; Zucker, 1986), and/or inhabit a highly regulated institutional business environment which minimizes incentives for opportunistic profit maximizing (Bachmann, 2001; Lane & Bachmann, 1997).

Once cooperative activities have started, the interpersonal relationships established between individual members of the partner firms, resulting from their repeated interaction with each other, are likely to encourage the development of interorganizational trust (Zaheer & Harris, 2006; also Neumann, 2010). Several empirical studies investigate the importance of interpersonal trust in this context (e.g., Currall & Judge, 1995; Dyer & Chu, 2000; Moorman, Deshpande, & Zaltman, 1993; Zaheer, McEvily, & Perrone, 1998). However, Zaheer and Harris (2006) point out that while interorganizational and interpersonal trust are indeed related (as argued, e.g., also by Zaheer et al., 1998), they are still two different phenomena. Nonetheless, the emergence of trust between organizations can often be seen as related or linked to trust between individual members of those organizations. A key issue here is the development of interpersonal trust between boundary spanners (Currall & Judge, 1995; Seabright, Levinthal, & Fichman, 1992). Knowing and trusting their counterpart in the partner organization makes it more difficult for a person to make opportunistic decisions which may harm the partner firm and, hence, that particular individual. Also interpersonal trust among senior executives is seen to have a very positive influence on interfirm relationships (Zaheer, Lofstrom, & George, 2002).

For established relationships, economic models of relational governance (e.g., Baker et al., 2002; Klein, 1996) emphasize the importance of simple, repeated exchanges in enhancing cooperative behavior. The reason for this is thought to lie in the fact that the long-term gains from the cooperation with the partner are expected to exceed any short-term gains (Poppo & Zenger, 2002). Hence, trust in this context could appear as calculative (see also Coleman, 1990). Conversely (and closely linked to the discussion of interpersonal trust in IORs), Ring and Van de Ven (1994) suggest a dynamic process view on the emergence of trust and argue that trust in cooperative arrangements between firms "is produced through interpersonal interactions that lead to social-psychological bonds of mutual norms, sentiments, and friendships" (p. 93). In this view, the importance of expectations and values commonly developed over time are emphasized with regard to developing trust in the IOR.

Sustaining a High Degree of Complementarity

So far we have explained factors suppressing opportunism in IORs from a governance perspective. While such formal and relational governance mechanisms are necessary they are, however, usually not sufficient for confining the risk of opportunism. A focus solely on governance-related factors ignores the value enhancing perspective on the cooperation which is a key incentive for the IOR. Therefore, drawing on resource-based arguments, we suggest that sustaining resource or partner complementarity is usually required in addition to the governance-related factors and that they are equally important with regard to reducing opportunism in IORs. Such complementarity not only plays a vital role in the partner selection process (e.g., Barney & Hesterly, 1996; Chung, Singh, & Lee, 2000; Park, 1996), but also serves to encourage cooperative behavior among partners after the establishment of the IOR and to "keep the partnership going," as it is the complementarity which creates value for both partners. This is particularly true for cooperation between competitors where, in addition to governance-related issues, specifically strong incentives for cooperative behavior are required (Parkhe, 1993). Resource complementarity exists to the extent to which each cooperation partner brings unique and valuable resources into the IOR (Barney, 1991; Sarkar et al., 2001) so that synergies emerge because these resources have more value when combined in an IOR than when they stand alone (Inkpen, 2001).

It is often argued, particularly from a resource-based perspective, that the primary incentive for engaging in interfirm cooperation is to exploit resource complementarity (e.g., Barney & Hesterly, 1996; Inkpen, 2001). Only an intelligent combination of complementary resources or activities generates rents and thus, a competitive advantage (Argyres & Zenger, 2007; also, e.g., Amit & Shoemaker, 1993). Putting this into economic terms, resources or activities are mutually complementary if the input of one of the partners increases the marginal profitability of the other, creating a close relationship between these resources or activities (Milgrom & Roberts, 1992, p. 108). From this perspective, high resource complementarity of the IOR partners may perhaps not be the sole reason for a successful cooperation but can also serve as a powerful incentive mechanism in reducing the threat of opportunism and keeping this risk low in an established IOR. If the partners continually own complementary resources which they make available to the other partner this complementarity produces strategic symmetry and a reciprocal commitment on the part of the two partners of the relationship. It "creates an environment that facilitates the achievement of joint goals and objectives" (Sarkar et al., 2001, p. 359; also Parkhe, 1993). Thus, we suggest that the ongoing complementary matching of resources secures the partners' positions over competitors outside the cooperative agreement; it enables them to "initiate and perform competitively on projects that they could not have done alone" (Sarkar et al., 2001, p. 361).

Sustaining a High Degree of Interdependencies

The concept of interdependence, going back on early works of systems theorists, like Ashby (1956) and Thompson (1967), describes the degree of complexity in decomposing tasks and the extent to which it will require ongoing mutual adjustment and modification to complete joint tasks (Gulati & Singh, 1998). Interdependence is therefore closely related to the resource- based argument of complementarities, as it is the pooling of resources and capabilities which decides the level of interdependence. The extent of the interdependence between two IOR partners depends on the tasks the cooperation agreement covers and the subsequent forms of division of labor and communication. Therefore, the level of interdependence in IORs may reach from a low level with little need for adjustments over time to a broad extent of interdependence resulting from complex and overlapping joint tasks which are closely and mutually performed. In the latter case, ongoing and subsequent adjustments of the partners' joint activities are required. Increasing information flows play a vital role, too (Tomkins, 2001).

As interdependence involves coordination costs, scholars have applied this concept primarily to issues of organizational design where the degree of interdependence is more or less equivalent to the degree of coordination costs. Hence, the performance of an IOR might, as some scholars argue, even be negatively influenced by a high interdependence (Gulati & Singh, 1998), making, at the end, a merger the most straightforward solution to reduce high coordination costs between two cooperating firms. In contrast to our view, Park and Russo (1996, p. 879) argue that interfirm cooperation with a high degree of interdependence are more likely to fail than IORs with a low degree of interdependence. Particularly the following reason has been considered in this context: As high interdependent cooperative activities require deep and close information sharing and decision making processes, there is a good opportunity for appropriating strategic skills and knowledge from the partner (see also Teece, 1986). However, the latter notion seems more the exception than the rule. It seems reasonable that those processes are characterized by repeated interactions among individuals. This is, as already mentioned, important for interpersonal trust building and, thus, will usually help reducing opportunistic tendencies. Furthermore, when looking at the emergence of ex post cooperative behavior, it appears to be equally important to take into account that interdependence can be helpful in suppressing ex post opportunism in another way. Highly interdependent IOR activities imply that the partner organizations are linked very closely to each other, and hence, are very dependent on a mutual basis. In such IORs it seems reasonable that an IOR failure, resulting from opportunistic tendencies of the partners, might cause considerable costs for both partners. This effect can be very conducive to sustaining a cooperative behavior, rather than increasing risk and caution between both parties.

Interplay of Factors

Any investigation of the post formation period in IORs from a perspective of suppressing ex post opportunism and encouraging cooperative behavior would be incomplete if it did not also examine the possible interactions between the factors explained in theoretical terms. For example, the interplay between formal and relational governance mechanisms is complex and changes over time. In the early and more vulnerable stages of a partnership a high degree of contractual complexity can often contribute to success by helping develop a trusting relationship. Formal, highly complex contracts signal long-term commitment and reinforce expectations of cooperative behavior in the future (Arrighetti, Bachmann, & Deakin, 1997; Neumann, 2010). At later stages of the IOR, frequent trust-based interactions, especially when negotiations of the formal contracts are necessary and when the partners need to bring the IOR to life. Thus, both formal and informal governance mechanisms need to be interlinked effectively, in particular when there is a high risk of opportunism.

Generally, it can be said that the longer an IOR continues successfully, the more emphasis will be on interpersonal (and subsequently interorganizational) trust (e.g., Ring & Van de Ven, 1994; Tomkins, 2001). If the partners realize they can trust each other at the interpersonal level they, in the longer term, usually perceive a lower need for formal safeguards and, even in times of high uncertainty and/or competitive pressure, a climate of give-and-take can flourish. The need to monitor the other party and to exercise control in the cooperative activities can be reduced considerably. Furthermore, partners develop routines and procedures which render the need for formal regulations and obligations. In doing so, they save transaction costs and increase managerial flexibility (Ring & Van de Ven, 1994). Nevertheless, it is the magnitude of opportunistic hazards that will significantly influence the reliance on formal governance mechanisms (Dekker, 2004), suggesting that IOR partners will always rely to some extent on formal safeguards which need not necessarily conflict with the growing importance of informal arrangements. Along these lines of argument, Ring and Van de Ven (1994) state "that even though the parties may be confident of each other's trustworthiness, they also may be uncertain whether to rely exclusively upon it" (p. 93). This is even more important for IORs between competitors.

In IORs the function of formal and relational governance mechanisms over time is also affected by the degree of complementarity and interdependence of the cooperative activities. In general, complementarity creates interdependence. Thus, high complementary and interdependent activities require certain control and coordination efforts based on suitable formal and relational mechanisms. Furthermore, in IORs between competitors the complementary resources the partners pool are to a large extent strategic resources (often requiring specific investments) which can be highly attractive for the other party to appropriate. Thus, although we have proposed that a high degree of complementarity is likely to create cooperative behavior over time, it in turn might also produce opportunistic tendencies. Therefore, both formal and relational governance are needed to capitalize on complementary resources.

Interdependencies generally raise the costs of "exit" strategies (Hirschman, 1970) and help to reduce ex post opportunism. This factor, in our view, will thus also play an important role in the structuring and dynamics of an ongoing IOR and be heavily interwoven with governance mechanisms and resource complementarities. For example, multilevel interdependencies can enhance the importance of informal governance mechanisms and thus raise the chance of renegotiating contracts ("voice," in Hirschman's terminology) if need be and reduce ex-post opportunism.

AN EXPLANATORY CASE STUDY

Research Design and Methodology

This section presents and discusses findings from a case study on an IOR between two European airlines (see also Neumann, 2010). All data were collected between May 2005 and May 2006. Both airlines were members of a world-wide airline alliance and had established a strong bilateral strategic partnership within this alliance over a period of 6 years. (Since in the airline business the term "network" is used to refer to the traffic network, the term "alliance" is used here (instead of the economic term "network") to describe airline alliances with several members.) Multilateral alliances in the airlines industry are usually, as in the case of airlines A and B, a bundle of bilateral relationships, although central alliance structures exist.

Our empirical study is structured on the basis of the theoretical propositions developed in the previous section. Consequently, the collected data on this IOR represent the factors and relationships between these factors discussed in the theoretical part of this chapter. The case study was generally designed as an explanatory case study (Yin, 1994), a methodological approach which has been successfully applied in other research on IORs (e.g., Dekker, 2004; Van der Meer-Kooistra & Vosselman, 2000). An explanatory approach allows theoretical interpretations of empirical observations and does not only rely on an inductive research philosophy (Otley & Berry, 1994). With this approach, shortcomings in the theoretical propositions can be identified should the empirical evidence suggest a need for modification (Dekker, 2004) and empirical observations can be classified and interpreted in a consistent manner. The case research method is generally suitable for the explanation and description of complex phenomena in its real-life context with little available empirical evidence (Yin, 1994; see also Dekker, 2004; Van der Meer-Kooistra & Vosselman, 2000).

The data were gathered by interviews and the analysis of written documents. The latter included the cooperation contract (including additional, more detailed written agreements) and other documents, for example, quarterly and annual reports, internal strategy reports, and so forth. The analysis of contractual documents was conducted in order to obtain a comprehensive picture of the formal governance structure and the goals and context of the cooperation. The other documents provided general corporate level and alliance level information, and information on the post formation period. The analysis of documents in addition to sourcing data from interviewing provided for a broad overview of the situation of the firms and their industry, allowing a deep analysis and interpretation of the results. According to Yin (1994), the use of multiple sources of evidence ("triangulation") provides more reliable and convincing results than a single-source-based data collection.

For this study, managers from both firms, airlines A and B, were interviewed. The interviewees were second and third tier executives, depending on the organizational structures of their organizations. They had all participated in governance design (heads of "*Public Affairs,*" "*International Relations & Alliances*" and "*Corporate Policy*") or were involved in the strategic management and operating of the cooperation activities on a day-to-day basis from the beginning (heads of "*Network Scheduling & Fleet Planning,*" "*Network Development Western Europe,*" "*Sales Western Europe,*" "*Alliances & Market Strategy Europe,*" "*Sales Europe*" and "*Product Management*"). Some of our respondents were interviewed more than once. In total, 11 semistructured interviews were conducted, each lasting between 80 and 120 minutes. The interviews were recorded on tape and transcribed. For verification purposes, all transcripts were forwarded to the interviewees to avoid misinterpretations before the analysis of the data was completed (Yan & Gray, 1994).

The Case

This section provides descriptive information on the case, the scope of the relationship as covered by the contract and the general context of the IOR at the time of the data collection. In the following section we will then interpret our data in that we apply the conceptual framework which we have developed in the theoretical part of this chapter.

In October 1999, airlines A and B formally agreed to establish a close bilateral relationship. The partners started their cooperation activities on a day-to-day basis in March 2000, that is, with the summer flight schedule for that year. The two airlines involved are similar regarding their business model as both are so-called network carriers. Given their roots as the former national carriers of their home countries, they operate a traffic network with major hubs, a wide variety of destinations and many flight frequencies. This business concept differs essentially from the more recently developed so-called low fare model which is generally based on point-to-point traffic.

The business model of network carriers requires per se cooperation with other airlines as customers should be able to book through-going flights from any one point in the world to another. For this reason network carriers are typically members of worldwide operating multilateral airlines alliances, for example, Star Alliance, One World, or Skyteam. Although having a similar business model, airlines A and B, which are both part of the same global alliance, differ in their business strategies. Airline A, at the time of data gathering still partly state-owned, operates a geographic niche strategy concentrating in particular on the traffic between its home market and the Far East, the Middle East, and Central and Eastern Europe. It has focused on a first mover strategy and is therefore constantly searching for new destinations in its major markets. Airline B, far larger than airline A, is one of the world's leading airlines and its global strategy includes the markets in which airline A operates as a niche carrier. Hence, the partners complement each other in many ways, but they are also competitors in various fields not covered by the cooperation contract.

By cooperating in certain areas, airlines A and B expected to attract more customers (and thus, to achieve higher revenues) by providing a better product with regard to frequencies, destinations and services than a single firm could offer. Furthermore, the aim of the cooperation was to considerably save costs by pooling resources, such as aircrafts (on certain routes), technical systems, marketing activities, and so forth.

Airlines A and B were specifically keen to cooperate in the traffic between their home markets (the so-called country-to-country traffic), because operating this important traffic together would reduce production costs on both sides. Optimizing the traffic network between both countries by operating the traffic together makes connecting flights better coordinated and allows the optimization of the number of flights between two destinations. In addition, resources of each partner, like aircrafts and crews, formerly needed for operating the country-to-country traffic, can be used now to enhance frequencies in the country-to-country traffic or diverted to other routes to generate revenues where capacities were missing in the past, also outside this particular traffic network. With the cooperation between airlines A and B, flights between their home countries are operated in a code share basis, i.e. every flight is identified with the flight number and airline prefix of both airlines, irrespective of who operates it. All revenues and costs incurring in the joint traffic have been agreed to be split between the two partners.

The partners agreed to run operational and commercial IT systems (e.g., ticketing and reservation) as well as the customer loyalty program, that is, the frequent flyer program (FFP), jointly. With regard to these systems, airline A agreed to migrate to the systems in use at airline B. Thus, airline A replaced its operational and support systems, transferred its data, and retrained its staff. The fact that airline B gave this migration project of airline A highest priority in its own organization was intended to ensure a smooth transition. Airline B also agreed to carry half the switching costs and grant airline A preferred status regarding technical support and system upgrades.

Furthermore, it was agreed to combine forces for joint marketing and sales activities in both home countries as well as in other markets. This also helped to reduce redundancies and to make the cooperation visible to costumers and staff. Finally, they expressed their intention to cooperate in the future in the traffic to and from Central and Eastern Europe in a similar way they had agreed on in country-to-country traffic. Loose cooperation on occasion, which was also covered by the contract, includes activities in airport facilities and services, cargo, handling and engineering support.

The IOR between airlines A and B is based on a very complex formal governance structure which consists of a variety of formal control mechanisms and institutional arrangements. With the cooperation contract a board structure to coordinate and monitor cooperation activities was agreed. It includes two bodies responsible for strategic and operational decisions respectively, namely the alliance board (at the board of directors level) and the alliance steering committee (at senior management level). Additionally, a third body that was only concerned with the country-to-country traffic, the traffic committee, was established. Both partners send the same number of representatives to each body, and the decisions of the bodies require unanimity. The responsibilities of each of these bodies are set out in great detail in the cooperation contract. The alliance board develops the IOR strategy, is responsible for general strategic decisions and it assumes an authoritative role. The alliance steering committee is responsible for supervising the day-to-day operations of the IOR. The contract specifies in depth that this board has to monitor the joint services with regard to the advantages achieved for both parties. Also, it belongs to the steering committee's task to specify and control quality standards as well as to work on continuing improvements in the IOR to gain further synergies and establish working groups whenever necessary. The traffic committee is responsible for the operations and the development of the air traffic between both partners' home countries and it has to monitor in detail all results achieved in this particular field of the cooperation.

Since 1999, the year when airlines A and B entered into their cooperation, global conditions in the airline industry changed dramatically for various reasons. First, political deregulation in the European Union enhanced competitive pressure. New airlines, so-called low fare carriers, successfully established an essentially different business model which focuses on point-to-point travel and not on traffic networks. That meant that various traffic routes within the traffic networks of A and B, irrespective of whether they were covered by the cooperation agreement or not, were put under massive competitive pressure from new competitors. As a result, A and B had to fundamentally restructure their ticket pricing as well as their routes and, subsequently, were even forced to introduce further cost saving measures and to enhance loading factors for their aircrafts. Due to its smaller size and traffic network, airline A came much more under pressure than airline B. In this context it is important to note that market deregulation in the European Union made it also easier for airlines to merge with other airlines from different countries. Therefore, not only very close cooperative IORs are very important but also more merger and acquisition activities were considered and can be expected in the future. Another external factor which fundamentally shocked the industry was the 9/11 terror attack. This caused a temporary but significant reduction in passenger numbers, and, more importantly, forced airlines to make large additional investments to improve security systems.

In the period between the cooperation agreement and our data collection, that is, between 1999 and 2006, the cooperation partners' strategic situations also changed due to internal developments. For example, airline A made high specific investments related to the FFP and other IT systems, which notably reduced A's options of switching to an alternative partner if they had wished to do so. Although airline B made some specific investments in the migration of A's systems, a fundamental hold-up danger for A was created. B's more powerful position in terms of tangible and intangible resources strengthened their bargaining position.

Against this background it seems reasonable to assume that the higher levels of competitive pressure caused by increased market uncertainty might enhance the risk of opportunistic behavior within and outside the cooperation agreement. This risk could now be greater than what the partners had expected at the beginning of their relationship. Asymmetric bargaining power usually represents a considerable opportunity to change the initial agreements at the expense of the weaker partner making it, especially from B's point of view, tempting to use their powerful position opportunistically. However, it emerged that after more than six years of the cooperation, the two parties both remained satisfied and committed with their cooperation. Both cooperation partners are convinced that it is mutually beneficial to continue the partnership. Nevertheless, the activities within the cooperative relationship differ to some extent from the content of the cooperation contract signed in 1999. Specifically, the envisaged joint activities in the Central and Eastern European markets and fully harmonized joint marketing activities in markets outside of the two partners' home countries have not been realized and await further efforts to be made by the two firms.

The Analysis

The Formal Governance Structure of the Relationship

The contract and its complexity fulfilled various functions from the point of view of our interviewees. In many ways the contract was seen as the central safeguarding mechanism in the relationship. All our respondents saw it as a necessary means to lay the ground for a productive cooperative relationship between two firms which, in principle, were and remained competitors. This closely corresponds to our theoretical argument that, especially in IORs between competitors, opportunism is a crucial management problem (see also Park & Russo, 1996), and detailed formal governance structures are needed for safeguarding reasons. One of our respondents, the senior manager responsible for B's 'Sales Europe', phrased it as follows: "Opportunistic behavior is there ... and this is the reason why we have so many formal reassurances. We are competitors." Another respondent, the senior manager responsible for "Network Development Western Europe" at airline A, insisted "I always need the contract, I need guarantees ... whoever says something different has never been in the real world." Especially airline A, as the smaller partner, found the formal contract very important as a means to protect themselves. The respondent representing airline B's 'Sales Europe' said explicitly: "We know that this [the contract] is particularly important for airline A ... if you think of the different sizes of our firms."

Many of our interviewees saw it as vital that the contract specified the role of the standing committees in the partnership. "The complexity of the committees ... governance ... it is important to have guarantees ... it becomes more transparent that way and more reliable," the senior manager responsible for "Sales Western Europe" at airline A mentioned. Another respondent, the senior manager responsible for "Corporate Policy" at B, found, referring to the role of committees that were described in the contract at length, that "if in doubt you need automatically activated control mechanisms ... you always need them."

As our theoretical considerations suggested, the function of the contract was seen as persisting as the relationship continued. Both parties argued that they needed a reliable basis on which they can fall back at any point in time. One of our respondents (senior manager responsible for "Sales Europe" at B) said that occasionally misinterpretations of the agreement emerge and that these can be resolved by reference to the contract: "It still happens that somebody says: guys, may I remind you of the contract ... look here, I quote from paragraph 1, section 2 ...." Another interviewee hinted to the fact that the contract will not always specify every detail of the relationship but it remains key to the relationship. "As said, the formal assurance mechanisms ... they are certainly not always activated but they do exist" (senior manager responsible for "Product Management" at A).

Trust Building Efforts in the Partnership

Looking at the role of trust in the partnership it is particularly important to see that members of A felt relatively vulnerable as a result of B's powerful position. However, both parties were convinced from the outset that the IOR would only be successful if opportunistic behavior was not only effectively constrained by means of formal governance but also by means of informal mechanisms. Thus they invested considerable effort in developing trust in the partnership. Most of our respondents did not see a contradiction between complex contractual safeguards and trust. Rather, the contrary seems to be the case: "Formal things are important for developing trust" (senior manager responsible for "Sales Europe" at B). Our case study largely confirms the argument made by those IOR scholars who insist that formal and informal mechanisms often complement each other (see e.g., Arrighetti et al., 1997; Poppo & Zenger, 2002). By contrast, another stream of literature assumes that there should be a substitute relationship (see, e.g., Dyer & Singh, 1998) in that complex formal structures will destroy trust by signaling a deep doubt about the partner's benevolence. This notion could not be confirmed in the light of our empirical research.

At the beginning of the partnership, A and B used small task groups made up of staff from both firms to enhance trust between the partners and reduce the likelihood of misunderstandings in the day-to-day activities of the cooperation. All our respondents felt that much active facework was needed to foster the development of trust. Without doubt, frequent face-to-face contacts played a major role and openness and transparency seems to be the key vehicle for establishing trust in the relationship. "That must fit ... especially with regard to openness" (senior manager responsible for "Alliances & Market Strategy Europe" at B). Another respondent said "Sharing information, making your data available to the partner ... by that you create trust" (senior manger responsible for "Sales Europe" at B). Again, this underscores the importance of formal governance mechanisms for creating trust.

Despite the importance of personal relationships, our respondents remained always conscious about their functional roles in the organization. The senior manager responsible for "Sales Europe" at the larger partner, for example, said: "My counterpart [sic!] at A and I traveled a lot, particularly at the beginning, and so did our colleagues." A manager from A, which is the smaller partner, said "When you know and like your counterpart [sic!], it is really difficult to cheat, because you know it will hurt him (senior manager responsible for 'Sales Western Europe' at A)."

While interpersonal trust plays a key role at all levels it was also believed that trust at senior management level is a conditio sine qua non. With reference to trust development one of our respondents (responsible for "Network Development Western Europe" at A) said: "If it [trust] is missing up there then this is really bad." Another interviewee (responsible for "Alliances & Market Strategy Europe" at B) said: "The member of the board of directors must like each other ... the organization as such, I mean the lower people sometimes do not like each other that much." Despite the last part of this quotation all our respondents felt that missing trust at the lower levels can be highly problematic. As one respondent (head of "Sales Europe" at B) said, "We made a lot of efforts to convince our staff down in the markets that the cooperation with A is a good thing, and so did our colleagues at A." And the senior manager responsible for "Sales Western Europe" at A mentioned: "We did a good job in developing personal relationships at the more operational management levels, e.g., by organizing events, etc. This helps a lot." Our findings confirm both the importance of interpersonal trust for running a successful relationship (as mentioned also by, e.g., Zaheer et al., 1998) and that it is important to develop interpersonal trust at different levels of the organizational hierarchy.

It was also very interesting that trust was generally not seen as an overly fragile mechanism. Especially the tight interrelatedness of trust and formal control mechanisms was viewed as a stable basis for a successful and long-term oriented partnership. "You need a clear strategic explanation why you run a partnership and you need a strong formal governance ... but the success ultimately depends on the people" said one interviewee (senior manager responsible for "Sales Europe" at B), and revealed that where trust has been established "you can later also occasionally shout at each other without ruining the whole relationship."

The Role of Resource Complementarity Between the Partners

As the partners' general goal was to gain synergies by efficiently pooling complementary resources, the partner selection processes were dominated by such considerations on both sides. Each airline regarded the resource base of the other partner as the main reason for the establishment of the IOR. In the initial phases of the partnership between A and B complementarities were especially expected in the traffic networks between their home countries and the intended joint operation of IT and FFP systems. These complementarities remained essential also in the following phases of the IOR and are heavily interlinked with formal and informal governance factors. Thus, our empirical data support the view that a main reason for the decision to engage into an IOR is the search for complementarities (e.g., Barney & Hesterly, 1996).

The continued relevance of complementarities was, for example, emphasized by one of our respondents with the following words:

> In general, we are sufficiently complementary and in country-to-country traffic we are completely complementary. Therefore, the cooperation helps to stabilize and enlarge the traffic network. It also helps to reduce costs because we do not need to operate all flights ourselves

(senior manager responsible for "Network Development Western Europe" at A). Interestingly, complementarities became more important at later stages of the relationship than it was at the time of formation of the IOR. The reason for this was mainly due to the fact that the emergence of new competitors, especially from the low fare sector, dramatically changed the competitive situation in the country-to-country traffic so that neither A nor B would have been able to compete with the new competitors individually as effectively as they could do jointly. Hence, the case supports our theoretical assumption that partners need high complementarities which function as a strong incentive for establishing and sustaining a relationship with a competitor. As the expected value generated from the complementarities aligns the interest of the partners, ex post opportunisms can be contained effectively (Sarkar et al., 2001).

The IOR between A and B illustrates that while the focus on complementarity of the partners is an important factor that enhances cooperative behavior, it might potentially also lead to fragility and instability when complementarities become less obvious. One respondent at B said: "It's all about making money. It's all about creating a win-win situation. And thus, it is only reasonable to cooperate in those fields where we perform better together than alone. Everything else simply doesn't work. This is not a honeymoon" (senior manager responsible for "Alliances & Market Strategy Europe" at B). Similarly, a respondent at A (senior manager responsible for "Network Development Western Europe") noted: "Both the partners must be sure there is a win-win situation. It is the only way to cooperate with a competitor." The IOR is permanently controlled by each party to ensure that the cooperation remains mutually beneficial. This is, for example, indicated by the following statement made by a manager responsible for "Sales Western Europe" at A: "We must always check the value of the cooperation, we cannot close our eyes. And we must control it."

Although A and B established a successful partnership there remained significant areas where complementarity do not fully exist, as for example in the development of new markets in Eastern and Central Europe. Thus, serious tensions could never be excluded: "This is the risk with cooperation. If one party takes something away from the other or seems to do so, then things can start to get a bit rough ... then the ride can start to get a bit bumpy" (senior manager responsible for "Network Development Western Europe" at A). Hence, it was not surprising that at one point the IOR was renegotiated to exclude this particular traffic from the agreement. This resulted in a relatively noncooperative presence in the markets in Central and Eastern Europe and also did occasionally have some negative effects on the "cooperative atmosphere" between the partners, as was confirmed by several of our respondents on both sides. This shows that developing complementarities over time often goes hand in hand with the impression to forgo strategic opportunities in favor of the partner making the exploitation of complementarities rather difficult.

Interdependence Between Both Partners

Similar to resource complementarities, interdependencies can be very conducive to reducing the risk of ex post opportunism in strategic partnerships. One of our respondents said: "We have a deep relationship ... we had from the beginning an integrated picture of the cooperation. Then it does work" (senior manger responsible for 'Alliances & Market Strategy Europe' at B). As mentioned earlier, our interviewees pointed to the fact that all hierarchical levels eventually need to be integrated if the partnership was to be successful. As we have considered in the theoretical part of this chapter, exit costs increase considerably where multi-level interdependencies exist and that this was of considerable importance for both partners in our case. One of our respondents said: "We are linked so deeply to each other. That is all so unbelievably complicated, if you want to leave the partnership.... The reservation system, the FFP, etc." (senior manager responsible for 'Network Scheduling & Fleet Planning' at A).

Especially in connection with formal governance mechanisms a high level of interdependencies was seen as a way to keep the partnership going and to focus both partners' attention on common interests rather then issues of competition and lock-in effects. A respondent representing the larger partner (senior manager responsible for "Alliances & Market Strategy Europe" at B) said: "Well, there are also mechanisms that help me to deal with competition and pointed to the joint FFP and other systems that interlinked both parties in many different areas." By contrast, another respondent (senior manager responsible for "Sales Europe" at B) gave an example of another bilateral relationship his firm had within their multilateral alliance where the cooperation did not reach a very high level as the joint use of FFP and other systems was rejected by the approached partner. However, the high interdependent activities of the partners are to some extent subject to concerns on appropriation of sensitive information from the other party. Like in the case of resource complementarities strong forms of interdependence may have their dark sides. "Sometimes, even after such a long time, some of our staff complain on giving all the data to B. But how should we manage it otherwise?" (senior manager responsible for "Product Management" at A). Our empirical data support to a certain degree the view that the information sharing processes required in high interdependent activities are risky (e.g., Park & Russo, 1996). However, this is clearly compensated by the positive effects of interdependence on cooperative behavior we have also emphasized in the theoretical section.

CONCLUSIONS

Applying an explanatory approach, this study enhances our understanding of the post formation period of IORs. This is a phase of the relationship in which the possibility of ex post opportunism, especially in the case of IORs between competitors, can be a crucial problem. Our research targets this issue at the theoretical as well as the empirical level.

Our case study of a strategic alliance in the airline industry widely supports our theoretical propositions that governance-related factors, particularly highly complex formal contracts and the development of interorganizational trust, as well as resource-related factors, that is, sustained partner complementarity and highly interdependent activities, can successfully suppress ex post opportunism and, thus, improve the survival chances and performance of the IOR. Our case illustrates that a substantial degree of partner complementarity is key to the nature and dynamics of a cooperative relationship between partners who in principle remain competitors. This is consistent with many previous studies on strategic IORs. It enhances the economic efficiency and qualitative effectiveness of the tasks performed jointly and increases mutual benefits of the IOR. As partner complementarity is a precondition for achieving synergies, it has a direct effect on the success of the IOR. This can be interpreted as an effect enhancing cooperative behavior irrespective of whether there is the risk of opportunism or not. But it has also an indirect effect because resource complementarity enhances the reciprocal commitment of the partners just as much as interdependencies do, and thus serves as a powerful mechanism that helps to suppress ex post opportunism and align partners' interests (Sarkar et al., 2001).

Our empirical data also support the theoretical assumption that complex formal governance mechanisms specified in a detailed formal contract are still needed in the post formation period of an IOR as opportunism between two partners who are at the same time competitors can never be ruled out. Closely related to formal governance mechanisms is the development of trust in the relationship. Our empirical case suggests that the ability and willingness of the partners to develop interpersonal and interorganizational trust serve as important factors in encouraging cooperative behavior over time. The development of trust is fostered by strong interpersonal links between boundary spanners and top managers as well as complex formal governance structures (Arrighetti et al., 1997; Neumann, 2010).

Our research also reveals that interorganizational trust should not only be interpreted as a factor that enhances cooperative behavior by suppressing opportunism but also as a factor that enhances cooperative behavior by increasing transaction value (Hoffmann et al., 2010). As our case shows, interorganizational trust is gained by combining the economic opportunism constraining perspective with a more sociological interpretation of trust which highlights the importance of trust as a socially embedded coordination mechanism (e.g., Lane & Bachmann, 2000; Ring, 1996; Sydow, 2000), highly intertwined not only with formal governance mechanisms but also the complementarity and interdependencies between both sides of the IOR.

The general situation of the airline industry, the specific business model of network carriers and case specific circumstances, such as the fact that one partner (A) at time of data gathering is still partly state-owned, are doubtless factors which may, of course, also have a strong influence on the nature and dynamics of the IOR. They set preconditions for the way the governance and resource-based factors come to the fore and are intertwined with each other.

REFERENCES

Amit, R., & Schoemaker, P. J. H. (1993). Strategic assets and organizational rent. *Strategic Management Journal, 14*, 33–46.

Argyres, N., & Zenger, T. (2007, August). *Are capability-based theories of firm boundaries really distinct from transaction cost theory?* Paper presented at the Annual Meeting of the Academy of Management, Philadelphia, PA.

Arrighetti, A., Bachmann, R., & Deakin, S. (1997). Contract law, social norms and inter-firm cooperation. *Cambridge Journal of Economics, 21*, 171–195.

Ashby, W. R. (1956). *Introduction to cybernetics.* London: Chapman and Hall.

Bachmann, R. (2001). Trust, power and control in trans-organizational relations. *Organization Studies, 22*, 337–365.

Bachmann, R., & Zaheer, A. (2008). Trust in inter-organizational relations. In S. Cropper, M. Ebers, C. Huxham, & P. S. Ring (Eds.), *Oxford handbook of inter-organizational relations* (pp. 533–554). Oxford, England: Oxford University Press.

Baker G., Gibbons, R., & Murphy, K. J. (1994). Subjective performance measures in optimal incentive contracts. *Quarterly Journal of Economics, 109,* 1125–1156.

Baker G., Gibbons, R., & Murphy, K. J. (2002). Relational contracts and the theory of the firm. *Quarterly Journal of Economics, 117,* 39–84.

Barney, J. B. (1991). Firm resources and sustained competitive advantage. *Journal of Management, 17,* 99–120.

Barney, J. B., & Hesterly, W. (1996). Organizational economics: Understanding the relationship between organizations and economic analysis. In S. R. Clegg (Ed.), *Handbook of organization studies* (pp. 115–147). London: SAGE.

Bensaou, M., & Venkatraman, N. (1995). Configurations of interorganizational relationships: A comparison between U.S. and Japanese automakers. *Management Science, 41,* 1471–1492.

Bucklin, L. P., & Sengupta, S. (1993). Organizing successful co-marketing alliances. *Journal of Marketing, 57,* 32–46.

Chung, S., Singh, H., & Lee, K. (2000). Complementarity, status similarity and social capital as drivers of alliance formation. *Strategic Management Journal, 21,* 1–22.

Coleman, J. S. (1990). *Foundations of social theory.* Cambridge, MA: Harvard University Press.

Currall, S. C., & Judge, T. A. (1995). Measuring trust between organizational boundary role persons. *Organizational Behavior and Human Decision Processes, 64,* 151–170.

Das, T. K. (2005). Deceitful behaviors of alliance partners: Potential and prevention. *Management Decision, 43,* 706–719.

Das, T. K., & Rahman, N. (2010). Determinants of partner opportunism in strategic alliances: A conceptual framework. *Journal of Business and Psychology, 25,* 55–74.

Das, T. K., & Teng, B. (1998). Between trust and control: Developing confidence in partner cooperation in alliances. *Academy of Management Review, 23,* 491–512.

Dekker, H. C. (2004). Control of inter-organizational relationships: evidence on appropriation concerns and coordination requirements. *Accounting, Organizations and Society, 29,* 27–49.

De Rond, M., & Bouchikhi, H. (2004). On the dialectics of strategic alliances. *Organization Science, 15,* 56–69.

Dyer, J. H., & Chu, W. (2000). The determinants of trust in supplier-automaker relationships in the U.S., Japan, and Korea. *Journal of International Business Studies, 31,* 259–285.

Dyer, J., & Singh, H. (1998). The relational view: Cooperative strategy and sources of interorganizational competitive advantage. *Academy of Management Review, 23,* 660–679.

Eisenhardt, K. M. (1985). Control: Organizational and economic approaches. *Management Science, 31,* 134–149.

Gulati, R. (1995). Does familiarity breed trust? The implications of repeated ties for contractual choice in alliances. *Academy of Management Journal, 38,* 85–112.

Gulati, R., & Singh, H. (1998). The architecture of cooperation: managing coordination costs and appropriation concerns in strategic alliances. *Administrative Science Quarterly, 43,* 781–814.

Hirschman, A. O. (1970). *Exit, voice, and loyalty: Responses to decline in firms, organizations, and states.* Cambridge, MA: Harvard University Press.

Hoffmann, W. H., Neumann, K., & Speckbacher, G. (2010). The effect of interorganizational trust on make-or-cooperate decisions: Disentangling opportunism-dependent and opportunism-independent effects of trust. *European Management Review, 7,* 101–115.

Inkpen, A. (2001). Strategic alliances. In A. M. Rugman, & T. L. Brewer (Eds.), *Oxford handbook of international business* (pp. 402–427). Oxford, England: Oxford University Press.

Inkpen, A., & Beamish, P. W. (1997). Knowledge, bargaining power, and the instability of international joint ventures. *Academy of Management Review, 22,* 177–202.

Ireland, R. D., Hitt, M. A., & Vaidyanath, D. (2002). Alliance management as a source of competitive advantage. *Journal of Management, 28,* 413–446.

Jap, S. D., & Anderson, E. (2003). Safeguarding interorganizationl performance and continuity under ex post opportunism. *Management Science, 49,* 1684–1701.

Khanna, T., Gulati, R., & Nohria, N. (1998). The dynamics of learning alliances: competition, cooperation, and relative scope. *Strategic Management Journal, 19,* 193–210.

Klein, B. (1996). Why hold-ups occur: The self-enforcing range of contractual relationships. *Economic Inquiry, 34,* 444–463.

Kogut, B. (1991). Joint ventures and the option to expand and acquire. *Management Science, 37,* 19–33.

Lane, C., & Bachmann, R. (1997). Cooperation in inter-firm relations in Britain and Germany: The role of social institutions. *British Journal of Sociology, 48,* 226–254.

Lane, C., & Bachmann, R. (2000). (Eds.) *Trust within and between organizations: Conceptual issues and empirical applications.* Oxford, England: Oxford University Press.

Madhok, A., & Tallman, S. B. (1998). Resources, transactions, and rents: Managing value through interfirm collaborative relationships. *Organizations Science, 9,* 1–14.

Mayer, R. C., Davis, J. H., & Schoormann, F. D. (1995). An integrative model of organizational trust. *Academy of Management Review, 20,* 709–734.

Milgrom, P., & Roberts, J. (1992). *Economics, organization and management.* Englewood Cliffs, NJ: Prentice-Hall.

Moorman, C., Deshpande, R., & Zaltman, G. (1993). Factors affecting trust in market research relationships. *Journal of Marketing, 57,* 81–101.

Neumann, K. (2010). Ex ante governance decisions in inter-organizational relationships: A case study in the airline industry. *Management Accounting Research, 21,* 220–237.

Otley, D. T., & Berry, A. J. (1994). Case study research in management accounting and control. *Management Accounting Research, 5,* 45–65.

Ouchi, W. G. (1979). A conceptual framework for the design of organizational control mechanisms. *Management Science, 25,* 833–848.

Park, S. H. (1996). Managing an interorganizational network: a framework of the institutional mechanism for network control. *Organization Studies, 17,* 795–824.

Park, S. H., & Russo, M. V. (1996). When competition eclipses cooperation: An event history analysis of joint venture failure. *Management Science, 42,* 875–890.

Park, S. H., & Ungson, G. R. (2001). Interfirm rivalry and managerial complexity: A conceptual framework for alliance failure. *Organization Science, 12,* 37–53.

Parkhe, A. (1993). Strategic alliance structuring: A game theory and transaction cost examination of interfirm cooperation. *Academy of Management Journal, 36,* 794–829.

Pearce, R. J. (1997). Toward understanding joint venture performance and survival: A bargaining and influence approach to transaction cost theory. *Academy of Management Review, 22,* 203–225.

Poppo, L., & Zenger, T. (2002). Do formal contracts and relational governance function as substitutes or complements? *Strategic Management Journal, 23,* 707–725.

Reuer, J. J., & Ariño, A. (2002). Contractual renegotiations in strategic alliances. *Journal of Management, 28,* 47–68.

Reuer, J. J., Zollo, M., & Singh, H. (2002). Post-formation dynamics in strategic alliances. *Strategic Management Journal, 23,* 135–151.

Ring, P. S. (1996). Fragile and resilient trust and their roles in economic exchange. *Business & Society, 35,* 148–175.

Ring, P. S., & Van de Ven, A. H. (1994). Developmental processes of cooperative interorganizational relationships. *Academy of Management Review, 19,* 90–118.

Sarkar, M. B., Echambadi, R., Cavusgil, S. T., & Aulakh, P. S. (2001). The influence of complementarity, compatibility, and relationship capital on alliance performance. *Journal of the Academy of Marketing Science, 29,* 358–373.

Seabright, M. A., Levinthal, D. A., & Fichman, M. (1992). Role of individual attachments in the dissolution of interorganizational relationships. *Academy of Management Journal, 35,* 122–160.

Stump, R. L., & Heide, J. B. (1996). Controlling supplier opportunism in industrial relationships. *Journal of Marketing Research, 33,* 431–441.

Sydow, J. (2000). Understanding the constitution of interorganizational trust. In C. Lane & R. Bachmann (Eds.), *Trust within and between organizations: Conceptual issues and empirical applications* (pp. 31–63). Oxford, England: Oxford University Press.

Teece, D. J. (1986). Profiting from technological innovation: Implications for integration, collaboration, licensing, and public policy. *Research Policy, 15,* 285–305.

Thompson, J. D. (1967). *Organizations in action: Social science bases of administration.* New York: McGraw-Hill.

Tomkins, C. (2001). Interdependencies, trust and information in relationships, alliances and networks. *Accounting, Organizations and Society, 26,* 161–191.

Van de Ven, A. H., & Walker, G. (1984). The dynamics of interorganizational coordination. *Administrative Science Quarterly, 29,* 589–621.

Van der Meer-Kooistra, J., & Vosselman, E. G. J. (2000). Management control of interfirm transactional relationships: The case of industrial renovation and maintenance. *Accounting, Organizations and Society, 25,* 51–77.

Williamson, O. E. (1975). *Markets and hierarchies: Analysis and antitrust implications.* New York: Free Press.

Yan, A., & Gray, B. (1994). Bargaining power, management control, and performance in united states-china joint ventures: A comparative case study. *Academy of Management Journal, 37,* 1478–1517.

Yin, R. K. (1994). *Case study research: Design and methods.* London, England: SAGE.

Young-Ybarra, C., & Wiersema, M. (1999). Strategic flexibility in information technology alliances: The influence of transaction cost economics and social exchange theory. *Organizations Science, 10,* 439–459.

Zaheer, A., & Harris, J. (2006). Interorganizational trust. In O. Shenkar & J. J. Reuer (Eds.), *Handbook of strategic alliances* (pp. 169–197). Thousand Oaks, CA: SAGE.

Zaheer, A., Lofstrom, S., & George, V. P. (2002). Interpersonal and interorganizational trust in alliances. In F. J. Contractor & P. Lorange (Eds.), *Cooperative strategies and alliances* (pp. 347–380). London, England: Pergamon.

Zaheer, A., McEvily, B., & Perrone, V. (1998). Does trust matter? Exploring the effects of interorganizational and interpersonal trust on performance. *Organization Science, 9,* 141–159.

Zajac, E. J., & Olsen, C. P. (1993). From transaction cost to transaction value analysis: Implications for the study of interorganizational strategies. *Journal of Management Studies, 30,* 131–145.

Zucker, L. G. (1986). Production of trust: Institutional sources of economic structure, 1840–1920. *Research in Organizational Behavior, 8,* 53–111.

CHAPTER 9

RELATIONSHIP MANAGEMENT IN INTERNATIONAL STRATEGIC ALLIANCES AND NETWORKS

Poul Houman Andersen

This chapter discusses relationship management in international strategic alliances and networks, building on and synthesizing parts of the relationship management literature. The chapter provides a model linking three generic relationship management tasks with three levels of management, identifying nine focus areas for relationship management efforts. Rather than distinguishing between the management of external and internal resources, the integration of external and internal resources is the focus, meaning that all managerial tasks have both internal and external consequences for the organization. Empirical examples and cases are included to illustrate or contextualize certain points.

Strategic Alliances in a Globalizing World, pp. 185–217

INTRODUCTION

For a researcher interested in the management of strategic alliances and networks in international firms, entering into the LEGO System meeting facilities in Billund, Denmark, is an interesting experience. The headquarters of the multinational manufacturer of toys is placed in a small town in the western outskirts of rural Denmark. The building complex for the administration is dominated by a conference center, where the meeting facilities are. It consists of one large room that is further divided into ten smaller meeting rooms by glass walls—five on each side of a large corridor, which holds tables and coffee vending machines. When you walk down the corridor of meeting rooms, you notice several of the LEGO top managers are there. On the right hand side, meetings are taking place between the operation and supply managers and a German strategic supplier of packaging machinery, trying to come up with a durable solution for LEGO's bottleneck problems, involving a 100 million dollar investment aiming at increasing the agility of LEGO by reducing time-to-market. Further down on the left hand side, meetings are taking place with creative managers from LEGO and representatives from a leading film company, discussing the LEGO merchandizing strategy for the next Harry Potter movie. In the meeting room opposite you see two researchers from MIT discussing how LEGO developers can embrace recent advances in robot technology for advancing Mindstorms, their robot-building product range. In the room next to them, everything is dark, but a note on the door explains that this meeting room cannot be booked as it is reserved for a virtual meeting with Asian partners starting at 5 A.M.

Increasing globalization and increasingly complex and unstable forms for organizing business activities across national and organizational boundaries are challenging fundamental management assumptions. Traditionally, managerial tasks have reflected the conventions of the industrial age, emphasizing systematic approaches to planning, steering, and control to ensure smooth operation conditions and reduce the costs of coordination and direct supervision in the organization (Miles, Snow, Mathews, Miles, & Coleman, 1997; Piore & Sabel, 1984; Thompson, 1967). This has also been reflected in the administrative heritage of multinational corporations (Bartlett & Ghoshal, 1998; Hamel & Prahalad, 1994). However, advances of information and communication technology have radically changed the opportunities to coordinate and configure activities beyond the scope of the single firm, reshaping managerial realities. Best practices in management and organization are no longer guided by the ability to ensure realization of scale and scope within the confines of a single firm, but must also extend their managerial reach to include the suppliers, buyers, and other business partners constituting the firm's portfolio of alliances and other business relationships. The ability to cope with variability and to learn and act quickly in collaboration with the organization's constituents is central to the new management repertoire in an age of globalization and organizational complexity.

The underlying dynamic of this change is the expanding role of knowledge as crucial for creating value. As a focus on core competencies is necessary to keep pace with this escalating development, companies increasingly specialize, leaving complementary value creating activities to trusted and competent actors in the network. Castells (1996) describes the dawn of the network economy, in which managerial and organizational abilities to orchestrate resources and activities across organizational and national boundaries are critical for survival. This notion was well captured by Boeing managers, who described their aircraft as "six million spare parts flying in close combination." The typical Boeing aircraft contains components supplied by partners in more than 60 countries (Greenwald & Pascual, 1998). Likewise, the rapid development of both Microsoft's X-Box (in order to ensure a position in the game console industry) and General Electric's wind division (in order to ensure a position in the wind turbine industry) exemplify the experience of successful firms in which the pursuit of emerging global business opportunities depends on management skills to activate a global network of alliances and partnerships in combination with internal resources.

Several authors have already discussed the critical role of orchestrating and managing relationships with other organizations. In particular, as the role of collaboration in enhancing knowledge creation and innovation increases in importance, the linkage between collaboration and the need for management that builds on exchange rather than on control will increase in importance (Miles, Snow, & Miles, 2000). Consequently, managerial priorities are shifting: from being focused within the limits of ownership control, they now emphasize creating and maintaining optimum conditions for configuring and controlling a network of relationships with external actors. Relational capital, in the sense of the firm's position in the network, is considered the new crucial resource (Gulati & Kletter, 2005). Coevolving with this is the need to rethink management in terms of relationships and networks.

Globalization only increases the need for this change. When various cultures and norms must be integrated in a concerted whole, it is crucial to understand and act in accordance with the diverging expectations and heuristics of alliance partners rooted in different culturally bound belief systems. Managers must fundamentally rethink the management task to meet these challenges. This chapter seeks to integrate and extend previous research to design relationship management as an emerging managerial discipline. Rather than distinguishing between the management of external and internal resources, the integration of external and internal resources is the emphasis, meaning that all managerial tasks have both internal and external consequences for the organization.

MANAGEMENT CONDITIONS IN THE NETWORKED ENTERPRISE

The management of relationships and networks differs fundamentally from traditional management, as it unfolds in a negotiated context beyond the scope of ownership control. Although some resources and activities are indeed under management control, the distinguishing feature is that task execution cannot be dictated via managerial authority, as value creation using internally controlled activities and resources depends on the coalignment of activities and resources controlled by actors outside organizational boundaries. The network of relationships thus becomes the locus of managerial influence. In this sense, a network of alliances and partnerships is an organizational form, which can be influenced by individual actors and may have the requisite variety to enable actors to configure and coordinate activities on a broader scale than is possible in the organizational context. For management, however, since networks cannot be subsumed to hierarchical control, the chief task shifts to creating access and to mobilizing, coordinating, and developing resources and activities vested in other organizations, with the principal aim of strengthening the positioning and business opportunities of one's own firm (Das & Teng, 2000). Designing collaborative architectures, creating inducements for collaboration, and employees' collaborative and networking skills within and beyond organizational boundaries are becoming important management challenges.

However, it is still unclear what these new forms of networked enterprises really mean for management practice and what consequences they might have for an organization seeking to implement relationship management. Although research contributions are surfacing from management scholars, there is clearly a need to develop a consistent conceptual framework that can be used to describe the content of relationship management. This chapter seeks to provide a systematic assessment of the content of this management task by presenting an integrative framework of relationship management.

THE DISCIPLINE OF MANAGEMENT: DEFINITION AND FUNDAMENTAL CHALLENGES

Despite considerable research effort, management remains a nebulous concept that defies formal definition, and a clear-cut definition has yet to be formulated (Shenhar & Reiner, 1996; Squires, 2001). In the business literature, management is often likened to authority, understood as the power vested in a managerial body and legitimized through a formal hierarchy. Chandler (1977) expresses it in the following way: "Modern business is easily defined ... it has two distinguishing characteristics: it contains many distinct operating units and is managed by a hierarchy of salaried employees" (p. 79). Most definitions of management therefore emphasize control as the locus of management (Shenhar & Reiner, 1996). This link between management and legitimate authority, however, is too narrow to capture how authority in the form of legitimate power relates to relationship management, as it is clearly linked to the formal organization of a firm, stipulating responsibilities, rights, and roles. However, a defining characteristic of relationship management is that it unfolds outside the nexus of ownership control, focusing on management ability to configure and organize network resources and activities; this calls for a definition of managerial authority based on the notion of executing exchange, while maintaining some sort of authority to direct exchange activities.

Weber (1968) defined legitimized authority much more broadly as the probability that a directive or command with a specific content will be followed by a given group of people. Weber distinguishes between three forms of authority: legal (or formal), traditional, and charismatic authority. Formal authority has already been discussed, while traditional authority relates to social order as the legitimizing principle; for example, authority may be conferred through inheritance, as in a family-owned firm, in which management responsibility passes from one generation to the next. Finally, charismatic authority relates to the legitimate power given to particular actors based on their persuasive or rhetorical capabilities, providing them with the power to define a situation and issue directions for others to follow. This latter notion of authority is interesting in the present context, as it does not assume the presence of institutional order (e.g., rights enforced by law) nor organizational order (e.g., in the organizational hierarchy) for resources and activities to be directed. In a negotiated context, relationship managers frame reality and use the expectations of others who recognize the manager as trustworthy. This is the fundamental mechanism that provides access to resources and activities controlled by other actors in the network. A definition of management consistent with the notion of charismatic authority is offered by Barnard (1938). He defines management as the process by which managers seek to obtain results through convincing others to collaborate. In his view, managerial authority rests more strongly on the other's acceptance of the managerial ego's leadership, rather than on the powers vested in him or her by virtue of position in the organizational hierarchy. Definitions of management involving transcendence of organizational legitimacy are difficult to find.

Some see relationship management as the effort to subsume other organizations to a focal or "lead" firm's authority (Zheng, Johnsen, Harland, & Lamming, 2001).

Although the context of the above management ideas is no longer internal, their perspective on management is very much the same as that found in theoretical approaches taking the organization as their unit of analysis. Decision-making power and with it managerial authority are seen as inhering in the lead firm, on which suppliers are more dependent rather than vice versa. Hence, a hierarchy among organizational units is assumed. This form of hierarchy is increasingly being challenged by the business premises of the knowledge economy, in which long-term competitive advantage, and with it stable positions in the value chain, have ceased to exist. In this system, legitimacy is not conferred by value-chain position alone. From being contingent on organizational structure, managerial legitimacy, positions, and roles are now negotiable; the willingness to allow organizations to configure and coordinate activities of other firms depends on whether management in these other firms see direct advantages in choosing this over the alternatives. Paraphrasing Chandler's famous dictum, there is no visible hand, steering the network in one direction; rather, there are many visible hands, negotiating and seeking to create situations that create relational and positional benefits for the individual actor (Ritter, Wilkinson, & Johnston, 2004).

The principal aim of relationship management in international alliances and networks is to create acceptance or legitimacy on the part of actors controlling critical activities and resources beyond the ownership control of the firm. Likewise, Möller and Halinen (1999) describe relationship management as: "A firm's ability to mobilize and coordinate the resources and activities of other actors" (p. 414).

Both definitions need further specification in order to embrace the full range of management tasks relating to relationship management. Managers play a crucial role as decision-makers directing resources in an effort to achieve recognized aims, rather than simply being mediators and facilitators in an otherwise self-organizing scheme of business networks. We will therefore define *relationship management* as *the task of envisioning and configuring networks, to create access to actors and to mobilize, coordinate, and develop actors' activities and resources, with the aim of creating value through collaboration*. This definition is consistent both with the fundamental assumptions of social exchange theory, suggesting that economic exchange is inseparable from social exchange and evolves in relationships, and with the social capital literature, which depicts relationships as a resource for social action. Social exchange theory suggests that authority is legitimated by honoring one's obligations to other actors. Peter Blau (1964), in developing his famous concept of the norm of reciprocity, states: "An individual who supplies rewarding services to another obligates him. To discharge this obligation, the second must furnish benefits to the first in turn" (pp. 90–91). Likewise, the literature on social capital identifies that obligations arise from feelings of gratitude or from those rights institutionally enforced by membership in a specific group that can encourage and sanction specific forms of behavior. The latter is described as credentials, which entitle actors to credit in various senses of the word (Bourdieu, 1986, p. 249).

TOWARD A MODEL OF RELATIONSHIP MANAGEMENT

The definition of relationship management provided in the previous section takes as its departure point actor positions in the network. This means that a network is mapped from the focal actor's network horizon, illustrating the direct ties the actor has with other actors and how they are linked to the wider network of which the actor is part. Hence, a network position indicates both a strategic field for influencing resources and activities outside the ownership and the extent to which other actors depend on and seek to influence the focal actor. This position is fundamental to understanding the maneuverability of an actor relative to actors in other positions. The overall aim of relationship management is to strengthen the position of the actor in a context of heterogeneous resources that may represent different values on the buyer and seller sides. Three principal relationship management activities are accordingly defined:

- activities aiming at initiating and establishing new relationships
- activities aiming at activating and coordinating activities and resources
- activities aiming at changing the current network configuration

The primary purpose of activities aiming at initiating and establishing new relationships is to gain access to resources and activities that are unavailable in the present portfolio of strategic alliances and network relationships. Establishing a strategic partnership or alliance between two or more companies to gain access to technology and other forms of knowledge illustrates this type of activity. When General Electric developed its wind division, it formed strategic partnerships with several leading global suppliers of critical components, such as blades and brakes. As a wind turbine is a complex technology comprising interrelated subsystems, GE's wind division is dependent on exchanging knowledge with external partners in order to align internal development of new turbine designs. Although General Electric is one of the world's most resourceful enterprises, with a vast array of energy technologies available internally, it was dependent on external partners to access relevant knowledge in this specialized field.

The general purpose of activities aiming at activating and coordinating activities and resources is to create value through coordination and transformation activities both inside and outside managerial control. This relates to stabilizing and routinizing value-creating activities that cross organizational and national boundaries.

The third principal activity relates to changing the current network configuration. This may include changing how, and by whom, resources are used or activities are executed in the network, for example, customers and suppliers collaborating on inventory management or reshuffling activities among actors to create more efficient activity flows or better resource use. This may also include activities intended to terminate existing relationships in order to improve effectiveness. One example concerns downstream relationships with international intermediaries, in which tasks are centralized or decentralized to achieve more market leverage (Kragh & Andersen, 2009).

The content of the relationship management task can also be systematized in accordance with the level of abstraction or reach of the managerial decisions to be made. These levels simultaneously describe the actors' range of control over activities and over the opportunities to direct activities. Three levels of managerial reach can be outlined: (1) the internal activities of the organization, (2) the dyadic relationship level, and (3) the network level. The dividing line separating the internal and external activities of a firm has been discussed to some extent, whereas the distinction between relationships on the dyadic level and networks as such from a relationship management perspective needs further explanation. The critical difference is that, on the relationship level, we are chiefly concerned with the past, current, and future activities specific to relationships with a single other actor and how to manage the evolution of these relationships effectively. From a network perspective, we take a broader view: we are concerned with relationship interconnection and network positions and how these may provide an overall framework for the prospects of the single relationship (Håkansson & Snehota, 1995). Hence, this perspective envisions a single relationship as an asset, which may be combined with other assets to create value, but does not directly involve how this relationship should be initiated, managed, or reconfigured.

In addition, the three levels together also represent a nested hierarchy, in the sense that managerial initiatives taken on the network level constrain and focus decisions made on the relationship and organizational levels. This is not meant to suggest that strategies are plans that are followed and then executed in a linear fashion. Strategies may well represent the outcome of intended planning and emergent opportunities, usually being a mixture of the two (Mintzberg & McHugh, 1985). However, in terms of enacting strategies as a relationship management endeavor, it is here assumed that decisions made regarding network positioning, allocation, and configuration serve to direct decisions made on the relationship and organizational levels. As such, they are sense-making procedures enacted to create a collective belief system, or consensus (Das & Kumar, 2010; Weick, 1995).

The components of a relationship management model based on these dimensions are outlined in Figure 9.1. Although the relationship management tasks are separated for analytical purposes, many of their features are highly interrelated, as indicated by the arrows connecting them.

Based on these dimensions, relationship management must address nine critical challenges:

1a: What is our position in the network of partners and what opportunities does this give us to achieve legitimacy and create value?

1b: How do we select partners and how are relationships initiated in our organization?

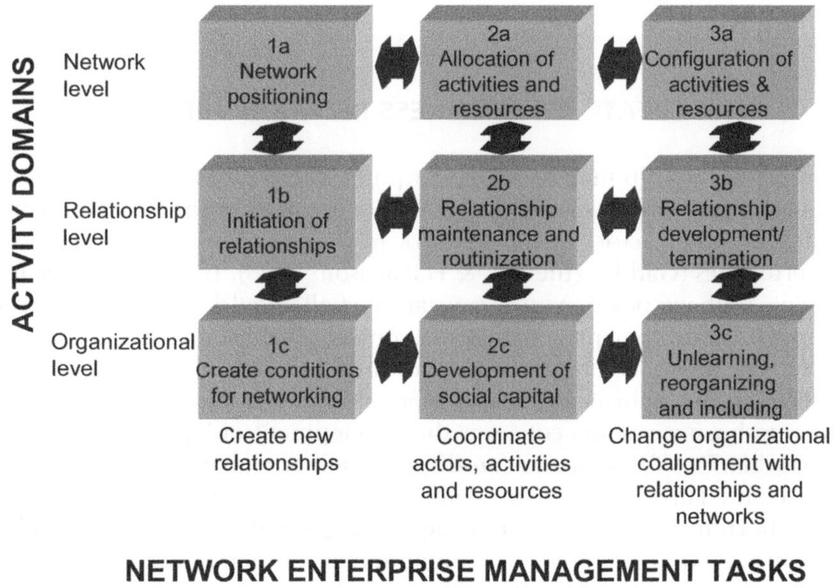

Figure 9.1. Management Tasks and activity domains: an overview

1c: How do we support our employees' opportunities to create linkages to central actors inside and outside our organization?
2a: How do we balance interests and mobilize relationships in our focal network?
2b: What is our policy with respect to developing relationships with suppliers and customers? Do we have a relationship management program?
2c: How do we maintain and explore personal relationships developed by our employees? How do we maintain productive relationships with former employees?
3a: How and when do we audit the present configuration of activities in the network to strengthen our current network position and value-creation ability?
3b: How do we best adjust our relationship management activities on the dyadic level to our portfolio of activities on the network level?
3c: How do we revitalize or terminate relationships that are no longer of value to us?

We will use the larger part of the chapter to explore these challenges in more detail and link them to specific tools and heuristics aiding managerial choice, and briefly return to the interrelationships among them in the last section.

CREATE NEW BUSINESS RELATIONSHIPS

From a relationship management viewpoint, the creation of new business relationships concerns gaining access to activities and resources controlled by other actors in the network in order to renew one's business opportunities (Gadde, Huemer, & Håkansson, 2003). In a dynamic economy, incumbent positions are constantly challenged by the strategizing efforts of both other players and newcomers (Andersen, 2008; Mathews, 2006). Therefore, creating new relationships is a central strategic activity in the constant reformulation and renewal of network activities. Creating access to business actors concerns the development of legitimacy (Kumar & Das, 2007), so that actors can dispose their resources and activities as they see fit. This is also why mechanisms for creating and destroying trust are important aspects of relationship management. The success of relationship creation requires at a minimum that other actors not distrust one's intentions. Congruent with the notion of charismatic authority, actors must hold reasonable expectations that providing this access will lead to value creation for both parties; otherwise, they would prefer their resources and activities to be deployed elsewhere.

1a: Network Positioning in Relation to Other Actors

The most abstract perspective in the relationship management framework presented emphasizes seeing and communicating the opportunities and limitations presented by the present network horizon of the company. In a network, therefore, new opportunities for repositioning evolve continuously—not least in a global economy. Identifying these opportunities is a crucial task of relationship management. Ojasalo (2004) identifies two tasks in relation to this outlook function: (1) identifying key opportunities that can be exploited and that will create value for the firm and (2) identifying key actors—existing or new—who should be involved in pursuing these opportunities. Both tasks call for intercultural competencies, as tasks and opportunities differ across national and cultural boundaries.

From a network perspective on relationship management, a central issue regarding the creation of new business relationships is defining possible positional advantages relative to existing activities (Andersen, 2008). Formulating the strategic objectives on the network level of a potential collaboration with a partner influences actors other than just the focal firm (Holmen & Pedersen, 2003). As pointed out by Burt (1992), the central optimization challenge in a network context is, with limited resources, to access the widest range of diverse but complementary resources. In some cases, this formulation process is a rather explicit and ex ante part of forming a new relationship; for example, in the case of developing a building and construction project, in which the roles of others may be clearly specified (Andersen, Cook, & Marceau, 2004). In other cases, this process has an emergent character, in which business opportunities and inducements for involving more actors gradually crystallize.

Developing an overview of a business actor's position in its focal network has been discussed as the creation of a network image (Ford, 2003), which helps business actors analyze whether resources and activities are being allocated optimally relative to current business opportunities. A network image, or map, may help strategists identify direct links and couplings to the wider network of actors and lead to the identification of market opportunities. However, although there are various approaches to doing so, the procedures for network mapping are still underdeveloped. These methods for aiding relationship management decision making mainly focus on network positioning and the addition of new relationships from an innovation viewpoint: how unbundling and re-bundling existing activities and resources may lead to the creation of entirely new forms of value. Besides looking at the compatibility of new relationships and strategic innovation advantages, there is a need to evaluate positioning advantages arising from adding or subtracting relationships similar to those in which the firm may already be involved. As this is closer to traditional portfolio management thinking, other models have been developed for evaluating the value of existing customer relationship portfolios and informing portfolio decisions, acknowledging the role of scale economics with respect to customer capabilities and problem-solving behavior (Johnson & Selnes, 2004).

1b: Initiation of Relationships

Moving to the relationship level, the key issue concerns how partners—chiefly customers and suppliers—are selected and relationships are created. From a relationship management perspective, the creation of business relationships calls for systematic assessment and procedures, while also allowing for adaptation to the unique characteristics of business partners. Developing and implementing best practices of relationship creation throughout the organization in order to take advantage of some form of scope economies in the process and exploit more explicitly what has been learned from previous relationship creation efforts are key tasks of relationship managers, as pointed out by Storbacka (1997) in a study of how commercial banks establish business activities. Having said this, it is also important to understand that relationships may differ in terms of intensity and significance, so there is no one-size-fits-all model of relationship creation (Pels, 1999). In particular, in an international business context, universalistic expectations with respect to the formation and management of business relationships are problematic and often lead to termination (Andersen, Christensen, & Damgaard, 2009).

The ability to enact schemes to initiate and support new relationships when necessary is an important aspect of relationship management. Not all potential contacts are equally attractive given the positioning aims of the firm, and the opportunities, partner objectives, partner scope, and potential pitfalls must carefully be evaluated as a part of making appropriate decisions as to whether and how a relationship should be initiated. For example, Lei, Slocum, and Pitts (1997) outline an approach to assessing the strategic value of potential strategic alliance partners.

At the same time, following up leads calls for the investment of considerable resources, so that all possible leads cannot be followed up simultaneously. Being able to select and deselect opportunities to initiate relationships and partnerships and to allocate responsibility for this is an important relationship management skill (Ehret, 2004). This entails evaluating the potential value of a single relationship, including its potential costs and benefits. From this perspective, Ulaga and Eggert (2006) suggest a framework including three sources of value creation as drivers of benefits and costs. These drivers relate to (1) the *core offering*, such as product costs, quality, and delivery performance, (2) the *acquisition process*, linking to service support and the potential for reaping (mutual) rationalization benefits, and (3) *customer operations*, involving the provision and demand for know-how in the form of advice or new technology.

1c: Creating the Boundary Conditions for Personal Networking

The term "relationship" implies that business relationships are social in nature (Hallén & Sandström, 1991). They are formed by actors and involve elements of personal trust. Therefore, employee ability to form personal ties and use these in pursuing projects and ideas for the employer constitutes a vital resource for the networking firm, for example, in the case of new product development or in acquiring international market intelligence (Andersen, 2006). The managerial challenge for the firm in relation to initiating new relationships and partnerships is, while motivating employees to explore opportunities to initiate network relationships, also to create and communicate properly the resource conditions and responsibilities relating to this task. In relation to this, it is important that employees who have opportunities to form these relationships understand their boundary-crossing options; that is, they must understand how much autonomy they have to explore the opportunities to establish relationships and engage the firm in new partnerships, and have a sense of whether their actions fit the overall positioning aim of the firm (Weick, 1995).

Establishing relationships and partnerships critical to the firm has formerly rested primarily in the hands of specialized key account or key supply managers, and the critical challenge of defining the appropriate conditions for these actors to develop relationships while attending to organizational goals has been discussed in the literature on boundary crossers (Workman, Homburg, & Jensen, 2003). The focus is therefore on the norms and expectations communicated by relationship management regarding the advancement of personal networking and knowledge sharing both inside and outside organizational perimeters. This perspective extends beyond that of boundary crossers, suggesting that networking with actors external to the organization is not compartmentalized in the procurement or marketing function (Gummesson, 1991).

Managerial support of personal networking activities enhances loyalty among key employees and supports knowledge sharing within the organization. Properly managed social networks encourage employees to keep learning outside the organization's boundaries and to apply their knowledge to challenge existing corporate wisdom (Burt, 2005).

One example of managerial support for personal networking in international strategic alliances and networks concerns when collaborations are influenced by personal conflict (Andersen & Kumar, 2006). Misunderstandings emerging from culturally divergent mental maps may lead to emotional conflicts and lead business relationships into critical phases or even to termination (Andersen & Ellegaard, 2010).

However, it is clear that these activities imply careful balancing on the part of relationship management. Drawing the line between personal networking activities promoting the interests of the company and networking activities promoting only the interests of the person involved may be difficult. This is the classic problem of shirking behavior in teams, as identified by Demsetz (1992). Relationship managers must implement networking policies that both favor the coalignment of personal and corporate interests and to some extent monitor the outcome of such activities. Others have suggested inducement schedules that promote solidarity among team members to ensure some degree of peer pressure. However, these problems are not easily solved, and applying a scheme without some form of direct managerial involvement and trust is more likely to destroy than promote such activities, as demonstrated in other knowledge-based environments (Mintzberg & McHugh, 1985).

Fostering the conditions for systematic networking is a relationship management task that requires the motivation of organizational members and implementing principles for how they should approach, develop, and maintain personal relationships formed in connection with work activities. Despite its importance, this crucial issue suffers from a lack of research attention. One contribution suggests that management should employ five organizational skills for initiating and developing relationships, that is, positioning, hunting, coaching, leading, and farming as specific subtasks to be addressed in the process (Masciarelli, 1998)

COORDINATING ACTORS, ACTIVITIES, AND RESOURCES

The ability of relationship managers to effectively coordinate actors, activities, and resources concerns their principal role of creating stable conditions for ongoing value-generating activities to unfold. Whereas the creation of new business relationships builds the foundations for value creation, the ability to manifest these activities within an organizing framework, allowing them to be carried out as efficiently as possible, is required for value to be realized. Since some of the resources needed to carry out activities are available only in a negotiated context, creating incentives for aligning external and internal actors, activities and resources is the fundamental organizing challenge faced by relationship management. If relationship management is unable to create value through activity coordination, resource owners and activity holders quickly lose confidence and withdraw their support. Hence, the coordination of actors, activities, and resources in relationships is an activity that affects the network, relationships, and organizational levels.

2a: Allocation of Resources and Activities

No firm is an island, but is dependent on resources provided by external partners for strategic leverage (Håkansson & Snehota, 1989). The allocation of resources and activities inside and outside a firm fundamentally defines its business model, including its function and role in the value-creation process, in which all actors in a given business network are involved. A basic challenge concerning the management of resources and activities concerns deciding which component activities of the value-creating process the organization wishes to command by means of ownership and which are best left to others and accessed through business relationships, as discussed repeatedly in the strategy literature on core competencies (Prahalad & Hamel, 1990) and in the resource-based view of the firm (Barney & Hesterly, 2006; Das & Teng, 2000). These questions directly concern the role of firm legitimacy in captaining the resources of other actors, while balancing their interests against its own. Relationships are often long-term in nature and, through a stronger commitment to one specific actor, the firm is adding rigidity and reducing flexibility. On the other hand, since command over critical resources and activities directly affects value-creation opportunities, proximity to other actors enhances learning opportunities, as cognitive distance is reduced (Nooteboom, 2000).

Strategic focus on long-term commitment to single relationships or on short-term commitments constitute two approaches to mobilizing resources and activities in the network and call for very different approaches to relationship management (Miles & Snow, 1992). Flexible networks are dynamic, assembled for a given period and then dismantled. Stable networks comprising long-term relationships call for mutual investment in relationship-specific assets that are not easily deployed outside the relationships in which they were developed, but entail treating relationships as long-term assets of mutual dependence. Both strategies may be viable. However, there is a tendency for dynamic networks to be more viable in cases of innovative disruption, which call for product innovation, whereas in mature technologies, which call for process innovation, long-standing relationships are more likely to be efficient. Moreover, while these strategies do not affect the fundamental challenges of relationship management outlined here, they certainly affect the priorities and organizational skills required for successful relationship management.

It is important for relationship managers to understand how interdependencies among activities and resources on the network level influence the internal effectiveness of the organization. Firm allocation and coordination are strongly contingent on ties developed in the broader network context. On the network level, these may include the intertwined forces of the social, regulative, cognitive, normative, and technical ties of a focal company (Håkansson & Snehota, 1995; Scott, 1995). By social ties on a network level we refer to the overall standing of a company in a network context, that is, its image as a reliable (or unreliable) partner. *Regulatory ties* concern binding laws as well as law-like customs and rules affecting the focal firms' ability to create value or be regarded as a legitimate actor. *Cognitive ties* concern socially constructed facts, what is believed to be viable and objectively true among other business actors, and *normative ties* concern the expected business practices, customs, and norms to be followed. Finally, *technical ties* concern the trajectory traced by a specific technological solution spreading in the network. The central task of relationship management with respect to allocation of resources on the network level is to create effective and efficient forms of allocation, which may create sustainable value-creation positions for all parties involved. At the same time, management must be aware of potential tradeoffs between existing and future opportunities. Ties are binding, particularly in situations in which fundamental technological changes are operative. One example of this is found in the hard disc drive industry (Christensen, 1993). In this case, intensive collaboration led partners to engage in mutually binding long-term contracts. As new actors with new technologies entered the scene, the computer producer was not able to respond to the strategic challenge right away but only after considerable delay, due to its commitment with the hard disc supplier.

From a relationship management perspective, resources must be deployed to support the collaborative context of the firm. Rather than increasing cost pressures on suppliers, firms should collaborate with them to enhance their competencies and drive costs down through improving supplier quality (Handfield, Ragatz, Petersen, & Monczka, 2000; Wagner & Johnson, 2004). Decision-making frameworks supporting the ability of relationship managers to optimize and rationalize on a network level are still lacking. However, there have been some theoretical contributions supporting managers in this effort. One concerns the role of the technical ties of a company, addressing the potentials and pitfalls of seeking to loosen or tighten relationships through the promotion, enforcement, or adaptation of component interfaces. Here, the role of appropriation regimes in technical systems has been addressed by Chesbrough and Teece (2002).

There are several metrics for making informed judgments regarding the allocation of resources and activities on the network level, in terms of both dynamic relationship portfolio models (Johnson & Selnes, 2004) and models addressing cash flows in relationships.

2b: Stabilizing and Routinizing Relationships

Moving to the relationship level (Miles & Snow, 1992), the stabilization and routinization of relationships relate to the ongoing adaptation of tasks and roles and to the development of a set of mutually acknowledged relationship norms (Spekman, Salmond, & Lambe, 1997). The ability to balance and ensure some degree of repetition in exchange is crucial for the creation of value in organizations (Weick, 1991).

From a relationship management perspective, it is important to ensure that all actors understand that all contacts with members of a partner firm contribute to the overall perception of the firm and add to the members of the partner organization's shared understandings of and attitudes toward the firm. Actions taken in the past and critical events shape the understanding of reality according to which contemporary and future activities are understood. It is important that relationship managers establish the necessary mechanisms to monitor the interactions between the organization and its key partners. However, few organizations systematically collect such information or act on it (Holmlund, 2004). Other organizations focus on building communities in order to promote relationship stability, hosting and facilitating arenas in which the complementary interests of suppliers, customers, and other constituents (e.g., shareholders) can debate. The Internet provides facilities for enhancing and realizing such activities; for example, Coloplast, a Danish producer of medical supplies, uses web-based brand communities to support relationships with nurses—key people in the buying center for hospital supplies (Andersen, 2005).

Some of the central issues in stabilizing and routinizing business relationships have been addressed in the literature on norms in business relationships. Relationship-specific norms can be compared to a set of game rules accepted by all. This is a precondition for aligning activities efficiently in the relationship. Shared and mutually accepted norms reduce the risk of communication failures, supporting the process of mutual specialization and the creation of efficient problem-solving heuristics across organizational boundaries (Spekman et al., 1997). Collaboration expectations are often expressed as a matter of establishing mutual trust. Trust reduces the need for mutual control and thereby the cost of monitoring activities (Das & Teng, 1998). However, the existence of trust is not a prerequisite for collaboration to prevail. Mutual or at least complementary expectations with respect to profits accruing from increased revenues or reduced costs can be sanctioned by mechanisms external to the organizations involved.

In addition to ensuring that interaction in relationships is monitored in some way, more formal procedures for ensuring and maintaining communication channels linking intraorganizational departments and crossing interorganizational boundaries are called for. Managerial frameworks for implementing such systems are being developed in the literature on customer relationship management (Parvatiyar & Sheth, 2001) and on supplier relationship management (Cox, Lonsdale, Watson, & Quao, 2003). Few attempts have been made to combine these two streams into a multidimensional positional framework (Christensen, 1993). Missing or inadequate communication is often the root cause of the failure and termination of interorganizational partnerships (Lindberg-Repo & Grönross, 2004). Ensuring communication flows among partners is also a prerequisite for efficient coordination and relationship governance (Mohr & Nevin, 1990). For example, in terms of adjusting and negotiating changes, the importance of established communication channels and arenas comes to the fore. Relationship managers can draw on some notions of how to monitor and evaluate the stability and operation of relationships from the customer relationship management literature. In it, several metrics have been applied, including customer lifetime value (CLV) and the break-down of relationship activities in a modular fashion, to measure value and enhance some degree of routinization in relationships (Storbacka, 1997).

2c: Development of Social Capital

In line with the previous discussions, the ability to create personal relationships must be matched with an organizational effort to maintain these relationships in order to develop all the social capital potentially available to the firm. There has recently been a focus on the ability of employees to create social capital, defined as the potential value of other actors' feelings, trust, collaborative intent, and expectations for individuals and the companies they represent (Nahapiet & Ghoshal, 1998). The development of social capital supports the infusion of new and different forms of knowledge into the organization, alleviating hierarchical silo effects by facilitating the sharing of relevant knowledge held by individuals with a larger community of potential users in the organization. Supporting the development and maintenance of social networks is an important relationship management activity. Several investigations have identified the importance of social relationships within and across organizational boundaries (Burt, 2005). One case of companies seeking to support the formation of social capital is that of Deloitte Touche Tohmatsu in Sydney, Australia. In it, management sought to establish facilities, traditions, and norms supporting information sharing, including mentoring agreements, social gatherings (e.g., business lunches with colleagues from other departments), and various clubs and events (Townley, 2002). Such initiatives need not only be taken within the organization: opening up social capital-developing activities to external participants may be central to attracting external talent and competencies. Employee exchanges, teamwork, and social functions are important means for creating fora in which organization members can exchange ideas and experiences. Physical co-location and face-to-face interaction are often necessary to advance these processes. For example, in the case of Jamo, an international producer of speakers located in Denmark, a group of engineers is located at their main Chinese supplier to support knowledge exchange and communication. Likewise, Airbus asks its risk-sharing partners to locate engineering resources in its R&D test center when developing new aircraft.

Developing social capital also hinges on the creation of connections that cross organizational boundaries, in order to support communication channels among departments located in different organizations. Research findings suggest that, while top management is often most active when relationships are being formed, the personal networks in the middle management level are responsible for the ongoing dialogue as well as the adjustment and routinization of activities (Donaldson & O'Toole, 2002; Kumar & Andersen, 2000). An important task of relationship managers is to ensure that these networks are facilitated and that managers also draw in relevant key people from departments other than their own in the organization.

Both types of social networks are important for the formation of operation routines within and between organizations, ensuring efficient coordination with a minimum of adjustments and communication. As shared or transactive memory systems develop in an organizational setting, the ability to act and react in a coordinated fashion is strengthened (Argote, McEvily, & Reagans, 2003). Over time, this may lead to the formation of relationship-specific skills or competencies in an organization, which is an important aim of relationship management. At the same time, however, such relationship-specific skills may become rigidities calling for organizational unlearning and relearning, linked to the managerial tasks of unlearning and reorganizing. This also relates to the distinct issue of balancing existing patterns of thoughts and shared ideas with novel and challenging notions, which may destroy existing notions and harbor new ones in order to avoid narrow specialization and competence traps (March, 1991).

CHANGING ORGANIZATIONAL COALIGNMENT WITH RELATIONSHIPS AND NETWORKS

Besides creating and stabilizing relationships, the ability to change or even terminate relationships provides the third important pillar for relationship management efforts. Networks consist of relationships with individual economic actors, each pursuing its own aspirations. This also means that networks are constantly changing and that relationship management must develop and adapt the network position of a company to accommodate these changes. Normann and Ramirez (1993) describe this as a process of creating network constellations, in which value creation is contingent on the mobilization of new actors and/or activities. As the strategizing efforts of business actors unfold, existing relationships and network positions must also develop in order not to become obsolete.

3a: Configuration of Activities and Resources

Aligning network positions with network dynamics is an important task of relationship managers. Miles and Snow (1992) point out that business networks can be more or less dynamic in the sense of their configuration durability. The dynamics and reconfigurability of a network must reflect the pace of change in its task environment. There are several examples of hyper-mobile networks that are established to pursue one specific project and are dismantled and reconfigured in other contexts after a given run. These are referred to as opportunity networks by Achrol and Kotler (1999), that is, networks organized around servicing the unique need of a single actor. One example of this type of network is found in Li and Fung, a leading supplier of textiles operating from Hong Kong. This firm has no production facilities of its own. It creates links between 7,500 suppliers and customers. The company takes care of design, development, production planning, internal logistics and delivery, quality inspections, raw material procurement, and so forth, in principle generating a new, custom-tailored delivery system for every order (Fung, 1998).

One task of relationship management in terms of reconfiguring activities and resources relates to identifying and selecting the potential and current partners that are best aligned with the company's strategic focus. This issue is closely related to the definition of the business scope and activities of the relationship, that is, what activities are considered critical and what activities may be left to specialized suppliers or buyers.

Network configuration tasks also include the continuous evaluation of potentially new forms of collaboration available from a given network position and how alterations in the present setup may affect existing resource constellations. Resource constellations between actors may be strongly or loosely coupled, and the constituent relationships may be positively, negatively, or potentially connected (Blankenburg Holm & Johanson, 1992). They may be connected in the sense that an existing relationship increases or decreases the possibility of creating value in other relationships. The existence of positive interconnectedness is also discussed in terms of positive network externalities, related to the increased value associated with increased use of a specific resource, such as the Linux kernel. The expanding number of users and programmers using Linux or other open-source programs increases the number of applications available to all other users. Market creation processes, in which firms seek to attract still more users to a specific platform, also reflect this mechanism, as described in relation to innovation communities (Miles, Miles, Snow, Blomqvist, & Rocha, 2009).

Relationships may also become negatively interconnected; this leads to the loss of interpartner trust and eventually to the termination of activities, possibly caused by the changing strategic dispositions of other actors. For example, when the Norwegian fund Orkla took over Carlsberg, an international beverage producer domiciled in Denmark, it came close to losing Coca-Cola, one of its key customers. This was because Orkla had strong interests in distributing Pepsico, and it is a Coca-Cola company policy not to share distributors with their main international competitor. This example indicates that other forms of linkages than actor linkages enforced through ownership can lead to negative interconnections.

Finally, interconnectedness may be latent, meaning that actors have an opportunity to create positive or negative network externalities through network reconfiguration. One example of a latent positive effect is illustrated in a case study of the building and construction companies involved in building the Sydney Olympic Village. Here the main contractor realized potential positive network externalities by introducing fairly simple relationship-specific standards for construction and for interaction with other actors, which were acceptable to all actors involved (Andersen et al., 2004).

Reconfiguration of resources on the network level concerns fundamentally changing a firm's current business model and realizing a new one (Christensen & Raynor, 2003). Envisioning new business models and redesigning the configuration of activities and resources have been discussed in various contexts of the strategy literature as blue ocean strategies, rule breaking (Hamel, 1996), or disruptive innovation (Christensen & Raynor, 2003). However, these frameworks do not detail how relationship management efforts should be carried out in order to disentangle existing activities, while in some cases remolding them into new form.

3b: Development and Termination of Relationships

A central challenge concerns the ongoing development of incentives to maintain and develop relationships with other actors on the dyadic level. The sharing and distribution of value created through collaboration is important in order to ensure continued support from the relationship partners. One key issue is the reinvestment or repatriation of profits. This problem is particularly significant in relationships in which firms conduct joint marketing efforts and share marketing costs. For example, subcontractors developing system solutions for customers frequently dispute the distribution of costs and revenues and whether potential income should be reinvested or cashed out. In this context, the role of relationship management as providing distributive justice comes to the fore (Kumar & Andersen, 2000).

As relationships are not static, relationship managers must continuously adjust relationship management efforts to meet the changing strategic priorities and dispositions of their partners. Moreover, they must include considerations for managing the fundamental reconfiguration or termination of relationships. Few companies seem to incorporate the dynamic and evolving nature of relationships in their relationship management efforts. One case is KE-Burgmann, a small Danish producer and exporter of specialized ventricles and technical fittings for industrial use in large process plants. The behavior of buyers of these products is rather complex and calls for a substantial problem solving effort by salespeople. Therefore, to operate efficiently on this market, salespeople receive a substantial amount of technical training, and then transfer knowledge to KE-Burgmann's foreign intermediaries. Over time, this equips the intermediary with the necessary skills to develop a consulting business of its own in similar or complementary business areas, serving the customer segment it can reach because of its acquired skills. Previously, this caused many abrupt terminations of relationships, as intermediaries acted opportunistically and abandoned ship. This behavior was often costly to both parties and led to disruptions on the export market. To accommodate this relationship development pattern, KE-Burgmann has developed a partnership program, which includes an option for intermediaries to establish themselves as independent consultants. Through this process, they may change their status from that of close partners to more distant distributors of KE-Burgmann's product range. Moreover, KE-Burgmann often forges continued collaboration with these new partners, which will typically be motivated to involve KE-Burgmann in larger projects on a collaborative basis. At the same time, this policy serves two other aims: First, KE-Burgmann has been able to minimize the imitation of its products, as intermediaries are less inclined to start up their own production. Second, KE-Burgmann has been able to challenge much larger producers of competing products for this highly specialized market.

3c: Develop, Unlearn, Reorganize, and Include New Employees

Firms develop their skill base by acquiring new employees or by facilitating learning and unlearning activities among present employees. Changing the skill base in accordance with the changing requirements of network coalignment is an important task of relationship managers. One example is that of Ribe Maskinfabrik, a company that transformed itself from a traditional supplier of machined components into a global sourcing hub. For this change to be possible, existing personnel had to revamp their skill base, learning new ways of dealing with external partners such as Chinese suppliers and customers. Moreover, they also had to unlearn the notion of being a traditional manufacturing company, learning the new concept of manufacturing through a network of suppliers in other countries.

The labor market is changing rapidly, and an increasing share of employees is knowledge workers, who are not hired on standard terms. The increased flexibility of markets, combined with the opportunities afforded by IT to integrate processes and interaction between people across vast geographical distances, have created the basis for a series of innovations in employer-employee contracts. People working from home, freelancing, and temporary employment on specific projects are some examples of how changing business conditions have affected the organization and management of personnel. Consequently, the organization of the labor market, including the role of unions, is in upheaval. Companies specialized in mediating these new needs are growing rapidly. The multinational company Adecco specializes in temporary assignments and has more than 750,000 freelancers in the U.S. alone (Drucker, 2002). This has consequences for employee management as well. As the sanction mechanisms inherent in markets become increasingly integrated into business organization, they assume the role of controlling the efforts of individual employees. Individual employees, on the other hand, increasingly look for ways to improve their own market value through the work tasks they take on; knowledge workers in particular are increasingly demanding with respect to the type of work they are looking for, seeking to balance fields in which they have some experience with projects that may provide new learning opportunities.

Research is also examining the need for organizational development in terms of establishing new organizational functions. One suggestion is to create positions for organizational architects whose function is to ensure ongoing adaptation and coordination among business network actors inside and outside the firm (Sauer & Willcocks, 2002). One example is that of organizations such as RTX Telecom, in which the entire organizational structure is organized around the initiation, management, and dissolution of collaborative product development and manufacturing projects involving suppliers and customers. On average, this firm hosts more than 30 groups working on the development and launch of new versions of existing products, adding wireless functionality to existing products, or developing entirely new products in which wireless communication provides a central functionality. There is a limited number of offices in the RTX buildings. Instead of being in offices, RTX employees are physically located in project rooms organized in up to five time zones, equipped with the newest virtual meeting technology in order to support collaborative projects involving people not physically present in the buildings, and to facilitate shifting between working groups.

In light of the growing importance of knowledge in value creation, the control of critical production resources is increasingly shifting hands – from firms to employees (Drucker, 1993; Martin & Moldoveanu, 2003). Creating the boundary conditions for networking also includes the social contract between employers and employees, understood as the explicit and implicit expectations with respect to obligations and benefits. The social contract in relationship management-oriented firms differs substantially from that of firms characterized by conventional management. In relationship-oriented firms, there is a strong focus on the abilities of individual employees as the foundation for value creation, since personal relationships and trust-building are prerequisites for gaining access to resources and activities controlled by others (Drucker, 2002).

The fundamental orientation of the employee has changed, from having a job, clearly defined in terms of working hours and obligations, to pursuing an individual project, in which fostering the creation of ongoing self-development is at the core of the work orientation agreed on in the social contract. In addition, job descriptions have become more variable and short-term. They might better be described as projects that may advance the organization and lead individual employees to gain knowledge, which in turn may increase their personal market value. Social skills —understood as the skills underpinning the ability to get along with others and get them to cooperate—have become increasingly important. Situational awareness, social presence, trustworthiness, communication abilities, and empathy are all aspects of human behavior highly rated in the relationship-oriented firm. Following on the increased importance of human talent, employees also expect to be regarded more as partners, related to the firm through employee-owned share schemes.

These changing values are echoed in the case of RTX, as pointed out by Niels Henning Olesen, development manager at RTX:

> I believe that our employees belong to a culture, where shopping around is common. It is the projects that bind you to your employer, more than the job. People are very loyal to their project, but they also move on. They are good at timing these shifts when they are no longer involved in projects. Typically, they will not stay on in a similar type of project more than two to three times. After that they move to another company or maybe to a different type of project in house.

The above quotation outlines the porous nature of social capital. It emphasizes that a stronger focus on employees as partners with which the company has relationships (even after they may have left the organization) must be incorporated into the principles guiding managers seeking to optimize their management of relationships with organizational personnel.

INTERLINKING THE LEVELS AND TASKS OF NETWORK MANAGEMENT: TOWARD A HOLISTIC FRAMEWORK

The preceding sections have discussed a conceptual model for addressing nine key tasks of relationship management. However, as described in Figure 9.1, these tasks are clearly also interrelated, suggesting that there are synergy effects among the individual areas of managerial responsibility identified. In this sense, the framework for network management suggested here is holistic. In Figure 9.2, these interrelationships are described as four "platforms" or benchmarks for achieving system fit: collaboration design, collaboration alignment, relationship creation and management, and relationship development and reconfiguration.

In this section, these interrelationships will briefly be discussed. On the network level, *collaboration design* concerns the fundamental task of

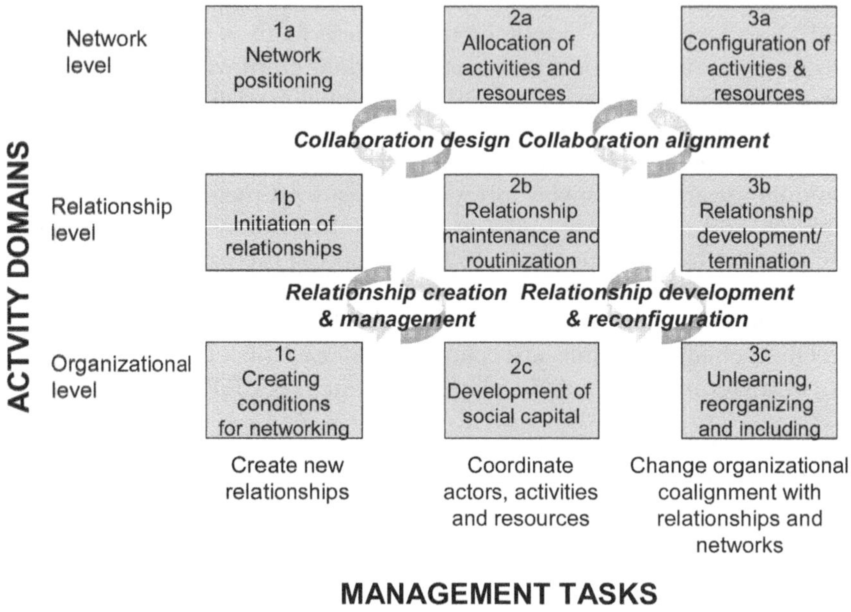

Figure 9.2. Interrelationships among management tasks: a holistic perspective.

ensuring that relationship initiation and maintenance correspond to the intended positioning. Hence, a critical benchmark for management is to assess whether the initiation and design of relationships corresponds with the overall strategic intention of the firm in terms of achieving a specific network position and ensuring that the activities unfolding in the relationship correspond to this aim. On the other hand, as opportunities continuously emerge in relationships, the ability to communicate this knowledge and inform strategists of emerging opportunities is equally important. This link describes the fundamentally dynamic and dialectic nature of network positions and corresponding roles (Anderson, Havila, Andersen, & Halinen, 1998). A network position provides opportunities to marshal and allocate resources. At the same time, however, efforts to create a particular position will alter how this allocation process develops. Strategizing efforts in terms of reconfiguring organizational co-alignment in the network will affect configurations of resources and activities.

Moving to the relationship level, the role of *relationship creation and management* has been discussed to some degree in the literature on buyer-seller relationships (see, e.g., Dwyer, Schurr, & Oh, 1987; Ford, 1980). Clearly, as business relationships unfold in a historical context in which actor bonds play an important role in the unfolding of relationships, creating adequate conditions for individual networking ability is important for both the initiation and daily management of relationship-oriented activities. On the other hand, it is also important that management ensure some fit between the interactions among individuals and the tasks to be carried out in the relationship. The network-managing firm may lose crucial information and affect its opportunities should the personal network not correspond to the activities at hand.

Collaboration alignment deals with the interdependent activities for continuously ensuring a fit between network positions, on one hand, and relationship management and development activities, on the other, corresponding to management's strategic intentions. Networks are stable, not static. The network structure evolves continuously, as actors to whom the firm is related make new strategic dispositions and act on them. These changes affect the firm both directly, through its relationships with other actors, and indirectly, as third-party actors may change configurations of activities and resources. Hence, carefully monitoring the strategic fit between overall network positions on the network level and how activities unfold on the relationship level is crucial when combining network management responsibilities.

Finally, *relationship development and reconfiguration* inside and across firm boundaries precludes the development of social capital in the firm; it is also quite clear, however, that the development of social capital can foster the conditions for further networking, as shared interests emerge. This has, for example, been discussed in the literature on communities of practice (Wenger & Snyder, 2000). In addition, unlearning, reorganizing, and including new actors are both a consequence of the creation of social capital and may also lead to the expansion of the social capital base.

The interlinking of activity domains in each of the principal relationship management tasks underlines how decisions and activities initiated on one level must have consequences throughout all areas of management responsibility within the organization. For example, network positioning decisions clearly outline the conditions for initiating new relationships (the link between 1a and 1b in Figure 9.1), which in turn may frame policies for networking—particularly outside the organizational realm, as indicated by the arrow linking 1b and 1c in Figure 9.1. Likewise, decisions on how to allocate resources and activities on the network level (2a) will set standards for the governance of relationships (2b), which will in turn influence policies for creating social capital in the firm. Finally, strategizing efforts to change configurations of activities and resources may lead to the revitalization or termination of relationships, and this will in turn affect the social network activities on the organizational level.

DISCUSSION AND CONCLUDING REMARKS

This chapter has sought to outline a new management perspective given the changing organizational conditions in terms of increasing interdependency with other firms, linking relationship marketing to the notion of social exchange rather than control. This idea that management is contingent on organizational form is far from new. However, so far, few have attempted to substantiate how the fundamental nature of management must change given these changing conditions.

Developing and presenting the integrative model of nine interrelated management tasks in the networked enterprise provides an opportunity to unite contributions from a variety of research disciplines that have worked partially with these issues. These research disciplines tend to reflect the industrial-age form of organization, in which managers were trained to perform predictably within strictly defined areas of specialization, rather than being able to take initiatives and configure business networks. In a management framework suited for the networked enterprise, the need to de-compartmentalize these disciplines and take a more holistic view of management is greater than ever. While the limited space in this chapter does not permit more detailed discussion of how managerial concepts may be developed, drawing on the various strands of literature that have themselves already draw together various aspects of business relationships and networks, the main aim has been to provide an overview of this literature. Clearly, several streams of literature have been disregarded, and developing the framework is an ongoing process. The question here is whether the framework qualifies as an adequate and managerially useful framework for examining specific management explanations. One future research avenue that may help address this issue would be to ground the framework empirically. This can be achieved through several routes of enquiry. The traditional approach would be to expose the framework to qualitative questioning and debate among managers, possibly using focus groups. This would undoubtedly provide valuable input that would strengthen the framework. Another and perhaps complementary perspective would be to use an action-oriented framework to address how companies might implement management in the networked enterprise as a practice, and develop the framework in interaction with managers seeking to grasp these managerial realities by focusing on the initiation, management, and development of network connections, rather than on control.

REFERENCES

Achrol, R. S., & Kotler, P. (1999). Marketing in the network economy. *Journal of Marketing*, *63*(Special Issue), 146–163.

Andersen, P. (2008). Generic rivalry strategies in business networks: Towards a conceptualization. *Journal of Business Market Management, 2*(2), 99–117.

Andersen, P. H. (2005). Relationship marketing and brand involvement of professionals through web-enhanced brand communities: The case of Coloplast. *Industrial Marketing Management, 34*, 285.

Andersen, P. H. (2006). Listening to the Global grapevine: SME Export managers' personal contacts as a vehicle for export information generation. *Journal of World Business, 41*, 81–96.

Andersen, P. H., Christensen, P. R., & Damgaard, T. (2009). Diverging expectations in buyer–seller relationships: Institutional contexts and relationship norms. *Industrial Marketing Management, 38*, 814–824.

Andersen, P. H., Cook, N., & Marceau, J. (2004). Dynamic innovation strategies and stable networks in the construction industry: Implanting solar energy projects in the Sydney Olympic Village. *Journal of Business Research, 57*, 351–360.

Andersen, P. H., & Ellegaard, C. (2010, September). *Start making sense again: A framework for restoring personal relationships in business networks*. Paper presented at the International Marketing and Purchasing (IMP) conference, Budapest, Hungary.

Andersen, P. H., & Kumar, R. (2006). Emotions, trust and relationship development in Business Relationships: A conceptual model for buyer–seller dyads. *Industrial Marketing Management, 35*, 522–535.

Anderson, H., Havila, V., Andersen, P. H., & Halinen, A. (1998). Position and role: Conceptualizing dynamics in business networks. *Scandinavian Journal of Management, 14*, 167–186.

Argote, L., McEvily, B., & Reagans, R. (2003). Managing knowledge in organizations: An integrative framework and review of emerging themes. *Management Science, 49*, 571–582.

Barnard, C. I. (1938). *The functions of the executive*. Cambridge, MA: Harvard University Press.

Barney, J. B., & Hesterly, W. S. (2006). *Strategic management and competitive advantage: Concepts and cases*. Upper Saddle River, NJ: Pearson/Prentice Hall.

Bartlett, C., & Ghoshal, S. (1998). *Managing across borders: The transnational solution*. Boston, MA: Harvard Business School Press.

Blankenburg Holm, D., & Johanson, J. (1992). Managing network connections in international business. *Scandinavian International Business Review, 1*(1), 5–19.

Blau, P. M. (1964). *Exchange and power in social life*. New York: Wiley.

Bourdieu, P. (1986). The forms of social capital. In J. C. Richardson (Ed.), *Handbook of theory and research for the sociology of education* (pp. 241–258). New York, NY: Greenwood Press.

Burt, R. S. (1992). Structural holes: The social structure of competition. In N. Nohria & R. G. Eccles (Eds.), *Networks and organization: Structure, form and action* (pp. 42–87). Boston, MA: Harvard Business School Press.

Burt, R. S. (2005). *Brokerage and closure: An introduction to social capital*. Oxford, England: Oxford University Press.

Castells, M. (1996). *The rise of the network society*. Malden, MA: Blackwell.

Chandler, A. D., Jr. (1977). *The visible hand: The managerial revolution in American business*. Cambridge, MA: Harvard University Press.

Chesbrough, H. W., & Teece, D. J. (2002). Organizing for innovation: When is virtual virtuous? *Harvard Business Review, 80*(8), 127–135.

Christensen, C. M. (1993). The rigid disc drive industry: A history of commercial and technological turbulence. *Business History Review, 67*, 531–588.

Christensen, C. M., & Raynor, M. E. (2003). *The innovators solution*. Boston, MA: Harvard Business School Press.

Cox, A., Lonsdale, C., Watson, G., & Quao, H. (2003). Supplier relationship management: A framework for understanding managerial capacity and constraints. *European Business Journal, 15*(3), 135–145.

Das, T. K., & Kumar, R. (2010). Interpartner sensemaking in strategic alliances: Managing cultural differences and internal tensions. *Management Decision, 48*, 17-36.

Das, T. K., & Teng, B. (1998). Between trust and control: Developing confidence in partner cooperation in alliances. *Academy of Management Review, 23*, 491-512.

Das, T. K., & Teng, B. (2000). A resource-based theory of strategic alliances. *Journal of Management, 26*, 31-61.

Demsetz, H. (1992). *The emerging theory of the firm*. Uppsala, Sweden: Uppsala Universitet.

Donaldson, B., & O'Toole, T. (2002). *Strategic market relationships: From strategy to implementation*. West Sussex, England: Wiley.

Drucker, P. F. (1993). *Post-capitalist society*. New York, NY: Harper Business.

Drucker, P. F. (2002). They're not employees: They are people. *Harvard Business Review, 80*(2), 70–77.

Dwyer, R. F., Schurr, P. H., & Oh, S. (1987). Developing buyer–seller relationships. *Journal of Marketing, 51*(April), 11–27.

Ehret, M. (2004). Managing the trade-off between relationships and value networks: Towards a value-based approach of customer relationship management in business-to-business markets. *Industrial Marketing Management, 33*, 465–473.

Ford, D. (1980). The development of buyer–seller relationships in industrial markets. *European Journal of Marketing, 14*, 339–354.

Ford, D. (2003). *Understanding business markets and purchasing* (3rd ed.). London: Dryden.

Fung, V. (1998). Fast, global, and entrepreneurial, supply chain management, Hong Kong style. *Harvard Business Review, 76*(3)102-108

Gadde, L.-E., Huemer, L., & Håkansson, H. (2003). Strategizing in industrial networks. *Industrial Marketing Management, 32*, 357–363.

Greenwald, J., & Pascual, A. (1998, July 13). Is Boeing out of its spin? *TIME*. Retrieved from http://www.time.com/time/magazine /article/0,9171,988702,00.html

Gulati, R., & Kletter, D. (2005). Shrinking core, expanding periphery: The relational architecture of high-performing organizations. *California Management Review, 47*(3), 77–104.

Gummesson, E. (1991). Marketing-Orientation revisited: The crucial role of the part-time marketeer. *European Journal of Marketing, 25*(2), 60–75.

Hallén, L., & Sandström, M. (1991). Relationship atmosphere in international business. In S. J. Paliwoda (Ed.), *New perspectives on international marketing* (pp. 14–37). London: Routledge.

Hamel, G., & Prahalad, C. K. (1994). *Competing for the future*. Boston, MA: Harvard Business School Press.

Hamel, G. (1996). Strategy as revolution. *Harvard Business Review, 74*(4), 69–82.

Handfield, R. B., Ragatz, G. L., Petersen, K. J., & Monczka, R., M. (2000). Involving suppliers in new product development. *California Management Review, 41*(2), 59–82.

Holmen, E., & Pedersen, A.-C. (2003). Strategizing through analyzing and influencing the network horizon. *Industrial Marketing Management, 32*, 409–418.

Holmlund, M. (2004). Analyzing business relationships and distinguishing different interaction levels. *Industrial Marketing Management, 33*, 279–288.

Håkansson, H., & Snehota, I. (1989). No business is an island. *Scandinavian Journal of Management, 5*, 187–200.

Håkansson, H., & Snehota, I. (1995). *Developing relationships in business networks*. London: Routledge.

Johnson, M. D., & Selnes, F. (2004). Customer portfolio management: Toward a dynamic theory of exchange relationships. *Journal of Marketing, 68*(2), 1–17.

Kragh, H., & Andersen, P. H. (2009). Picture this: Managed change and resistance in business network settings. *Industrial Marketing Management, 38*, 641–653.

Kumar, R., & Andersen, P. H. (2000). Inter firm diversity and the management of meaning in international strategic alliances. *International Business Review, 9*, 237–252.

Kumar, R., & Das, T. K. (2007). Interpartner legitimacy in the alliance development process. *Journal of Management Studies, 44*, 1425-1453.

Lei, D., Slocum J. W., Jr., & Pitts, R. A. (1997). Building cooperative advantage: Managing strategic alliances to promote organizational learning. *Journal of World Business, 32*, 203–223.

Lindberg-Repo, K., & Grönross, C. (2004). Conceptualising communications strategy from a relational perspective. *Industrial Marketing Management, 33*, 229–240.

March, J. G. (1991). Learning from experiences in ecologies of organizations. *Organization Science, 25*, 2–9.

Martin, R. L., & Moldoveanu, M. (2003). Capital versus talent: The battle that is reshaping business. *Harvard Business Review, 81*(July), 36–41.

Masciarelli, J. P. (1998). Are you managing your relationships? *Management Review, 87*(4), 41–45.

Mathews, J. A. (2006). *Strategizing, disequilibrium, and profit*. Stanford, CA: Stanford University Press.

Miles, R., Miles, G., Snow, C., Blomqvist, K., & Rocha, H. (2009). The I-form organization. *California Management Review, 51*(4), 59–74.

Miles, R. E., & Snow, C. C. (1992). Causes of failure in network organizations. *California Management Review, 34*(4), 53–72.

Miles, R. E., Snow, C. C., Mathews, J. A., Miles, G., & Coleman, H. J. J. (1997). Organizing in the knowledge age: Anticipating the cellular form. *Academy of Management Executive, 11*(4), 7–20.

Miles, R. E., Snow, C. C., & Miles, G. (2000). TheFuture.org. *Long Range Planning, 33*, 300–321.

Mintzberg, H., & McHugh, A. (1985). Strategy formation in an adhocracy. *Administrative Science Quarterly, 30*, 160–197.

Mohr, J. J., & Nevin, J. R. (1990). Communication strategies in marketing channels: A theoretical perspective. *Journal of Marketing, 54*(4), 36–51.

Möller, K. K., & Halinen, A. (1999). Business relationships and networks: Managerial challenge of network era. *Industrial Marketing Management, 28*, 413–427.

Nahapiet, J., & Ghoshal, S. (1998). Social capital, intellectual capital and the organizational advantage. *Academy of Management Review, 23*, 242–267.

Nooteboom, B. (2000). Learning by interaction: Absorptive capacity, cognitive distance and governance. *Journal of Management and Governance, 4*(1), 69–92.

Normann, R., & Ramirez, R. (1993). From value chain to value constellation: Designing Interactive Strategy. *Harvard Business Review, 71*(July/August), 65–78.

Ojasalo, J. (2004). Key network management. *Industrial Marketing Management, 33*, 195–206.

Parvatiyar, A., & Sheth, J. N. (2001). Customer relationship management: Emerging practice, process and discipline. *Journal of Economic and Social Research, 3*(2), 1–34.

Pels, J. (1999). Exchange relationships in consumer markets. *European Journal of Marketing, 35*(1/2), 4–37.

Piore, M. J., & Sabel, C. (1984). *The second industrial divide: Possibilities for prosperity.* New York, NY: Basic Books.

Prahalad, C. K., & Hamel, G. (1990). The core competence of the corporation. *Harvard Business Review, 68*(3), 79–91.

Ritter, T., Wilkinson, I. F., & Johnston, W. J. (2004). Managing in complex business networks. *Industrial Marketing Management, 33*, 175–183.

Sauer, C., & Willcocks, L. P. (2002). The evolution of the organizational architect. *MIT Sloan Management Review, 43*(3) (Spring), 41–49.

Scott, W. R. (1995). *Institutions and organizations*. Thousand Oaks, CA: SAGE.

Shenhar, A. J., & Reiner, J. (1996). How to define management: A modular approach. *Management Development Review, 9*(1), 25–31.

Spekman, R. E., Salmond, D. J., & Lambe, C. J. (1997). Consensus and collaboration: norm-regulated behaviour in industrial marketing relationships. *European Journal of Marketing, 31*, 832–856.

Squires, G. (2001). Management as a professional discipline. *Journal of Management Studies, 38*, 473–487.

Storbacka, K. (1997). Segmentation based on customer profitability: Retrospective analysis of retail bank customer bases. *Journal of Marketing Management, 13*, 479–492.

Thompson, J. D. (1967). *Organizations in action*. New York, NY: McGraw-Hill.

Townley, C. (2002). People plus knowledge at Deloitte Tohmatsu. *KM Review, 5*(1, March/April), 21–25.

Ulaga, W., & Eggert, A. (2006). Value-based differentiation in business relationships: Gaining and sustaining key supplier status. *Journal of Marketing, 70*(1), 119–136.

Wagner, S. M., & Johnson, J. L. (2004). Configuring and managing strategic supplier portfolios. *Industrial Marketing Management, 33*, 717–730.

Weber, M. (1968). *Economy and society*. New York: Bedminster.

Weick, K. E. (1991). The nontraditional quality of organizational learning. *Organization Science, 2*, 116–124.

Weick, K. E. (1995). *Sensemaking in organizations*. Thousand Oaks, CA: SAGE.

Wenger, E. C., & Snyder, W. M. (2000). Communities of practice: The organizational frontier. *Harvard Business Review, 78*(1), 139–145.

Workman, J. P., Jr., Homburg, C., & Jensen, O. (2003). Intraorganizational determinants of key account management effectiveness. *Journal of the Academy of Marketing Science, 31*, 3–21.

Zheng, J., Johnsen, T. E., Harland, C. M., & Lamming, R. C. (2001, April 8–11). *A taxonomy of supply networks*. Paper presented at the 10th Annual Conference of International Purchasing and Supply Education and Research Association, Jönköping, Sweden.

CHAPTER 10

SENSEMAKING IN CROSS-NATIONAL ALLIANCES

T. K. Das and Rajesh Kumar

In this chapter we propose a framework for understanding interpartner sensemaking in cross-national strategic alliances, and discuss how to manage the problems arising from the cultural differences and internal tensions that are inherent in such alliances. Alliance partners embedded in different national cultures rely on interpretive schemes to make sense of the conflicts, contradictions, and internal tensions that emerge in strategic alliances. We describe the two fundamental interpretive frames that relate to sensemaking, that of sensemaking *of* and *in* chaos, and examine how an appreciation of these interpretive frames enable us to better manage cultural differences and internal tensions. Briefly, the two types of the interpartner sensemaking calls for different strategies for managing alliances. As interpartner sensemaking occurs at all stages of alliance evolution, research attention is needed to assess the impact of conflicting interpretive schemes (a) in the stages of formation, operation, and outcome, (b) concerning issues of appropriation and coordination, and (c) in learning processes. The framework proposed in this chapter should prove useful to managers with alliance responsibilities, helping them to identify and exploit the most effective ways of accounting for the role of interpartner sensemaking in alliances for productive interactions and performance.

Strategic Alliances in a Globalizing World, pp. 219–242

INTRODUCTION

Strategic alliances have come to play an increasingly prominent part in the contemporary global economy. Although partner firms are increasingly entering into these alliances due to the intensification of global competition, many of these alliances are failing to meet partners' expectations (Gill & Butler, 2003). Cross-national alliances in particular often experience difficulties stemming from lack of trust (Das & Teng, 1998; Ring & Van de Ven, 1994), deceit and opportunism (Das, 2005; Das & Rahman, 2010), strategic incompatibility (Ariño & de la Torre, 1998), poor organizational integration (Gulati & Singh, 1998), ineffective management of internal tensions (Das & Teng, 2000), or cultural distance (Brown, Rugman, & Verbeke, 1989; Lane & Beamish, 1990). The central theme in this literature is that divergent expectations among alliance partners stemming from differences in strategic objectives, culture (national and corporate), organizational practices or trust may either lead to opportunistic behavior on the part of alliance partners or make the task of achieving interorganizational coordination difficult.

In this chapter we explore the role of interpartner sensemaking in understanding the impact of national cultural differences and internal tensions on the dynamics of strategic alliances. We begin with brief observations on the conflicting interpretive reference frames of alliance partners. We then propose two interpretive schemes in alliance functioning, namely, "sensemaking *of* chaos" and "sensemaking *in* chaos." Next we outline the importance of national culture in shaping the evolution of cross-national alliances, and discuss the role of national cultural values in the use of interpretive schemes. In the final part, we elaborate upon the linkages between the sensemaking of interpretive contradictions among alliance partners and the internal tensions in alliances.

The starting point of our analysis is the recognition that alliance managers who have been socialized in different national cultures are likely to interpret and respond to their partners' behavior in conflicting ways. As most researchers agree today, reality is socially constructed and is subject to multiple interpretations (Berger & Luckmann, 1966; Morgan, 1979). We thus need to understand how alliance functioning is interpreted in different ways by alliance partners in different national cultures and the role of these interpretations in shaping their subsequent behaviors.

The recognition that differences in frames of reference among alliance managers socialized in different national cultures may lead to interactional conflict is not a novel one (Brislin & Yoshida, 1996; Hofstede, 1980). But the idea that interactional conflicts have an interpretive significance is an underdeveloped notion and it is this idea that we seek to develop in this chapter. While conflicts existing at the lower levels in the alliance firm may directly or indirectly influence the interpretive conflicts existing at the upper echelons of management, it is only what transpires at the upper levels that is the most determinative of alliance evolution.

THE DYNAMICS OF ALLIANCE EVOLUTION

It has been argued that an alliance may experience pragmatic, moral, or cognitive conflict stemming from conflicting frames of reference among the alliance partners (Kumar & Andersen, 2000). Pragmatic conflict occurs at the level of the functional specialists, moral conflict falls within the domain of alliance level managers, and cognitive conflict involves the top level managers, that is, the individuals who are responsible for initiating and managing the alliance based strategy of the firm. Pragmatic conflict centers on issues of operational coordination among partner firms, moral conflict revolves around the appropriateness of behaviors among the partner firms, while cognitive conflict focuses on issues pertaining to the strategic rationale for continuing with or exiting from the alliance.

An alliance may survive the existence of pragmatic and moral conflicts so long as top-level managers are able to effectively manage the cognitive conflicts. Cognitive conflicts stand at the apex of hierarchy inasmuch as they provide the determinative lens for viewing alliance functioning. Cognitive conflicts among top-level managers are interpretive conflicts for they focus on the critical issue of whether it makes sense for the alliance partners to continue or deepen their cooperation notwithstanding the myriad difficulties that the alliance may be experiencing.

What factors condition the interpretation made by top-level managers among partner firms? According to Daft and Weick (1984), "Interpretation processes are not random. Systematic variations occur based on organizational and environmental characteristics" (p. 286). In other words, there are large numbers of variables that may influence the interpretation processes, including those relating to the individual manager's perceptions of the strategy milieu and subjective time perspectives (Das, 1986). For strategic alliances, the interpretation processes may be conditioned by the experience of top managers in managing alliances, degree of consensus within the top management team, the criticality of the alliance to organizational performance, and the capability of the top management team in managing cross-national diversity. We will of course focus on the impact of national cultural differences on the interpretation process. While we do not wish to assert that national culture is the only determinant of these interpretations, culture does provide the institutional context for alliance decision making.

The question confronting top-level managers when the alliance is experiencing difficulties, whether at the pragmatic or moral level, is a sensemaking question focusing on the fundamental issue of whether to continue with or exit from the alliance. It is the essential argument of this chapter that when the top level managers answer that fundamental question, they may choose among two alternative interpretive schemes which we label as "sensemaking *of* chaos" and "sensemaking *in* chaos." The choice of one as opposed to the other interpretive scheme is influenced to a large degree by the top managers' implicit assumptions, shaped primarily by their national cultural backgrounds.

INTERPRETIVE SCHEMES AND ALLIANCE FUNCTIONING

We will discuss the two interpretive schemes in some detail in this section. An interpretive scheme is a perspective for making sense of interruptions that prevent the alliance partners from achieving their goal. As Bartunek (1984) notes, "Interpretive schemes operate as shared, fundamental (though often implicit) assumptions about why events happen as they do and how people are to act in different situations" (p. 355). Implicit in this definition is the idea that interpretive schemes are key tools in coping with ambiguity and uncertainty that are ever-present when interruptions occur. Mandler (1975) points out that there are two types of interruption: (a) the failure of an expected event to occur and (b) the occurrence of an unexpected event. It is these interruptions that provide the foundation for the emergence of pragmatic and moral conflicts among the alliance partners. A good example of both kinds of interruption can be seen in the alliance between MCI and Telefonica. The two telecommunication companies (one American, the other Spanish) had entered into an alliance to expand their market coverage. MCI was strong in Western Europe while Telefonica was strong in Latin America. The expectation was that the alliance would help MCI extend its coverage in Latin America while Telefonica would be able to extend its reach in North America, where it was hardly visible. Yet, none of this came to pass. As Rocks (1999) notes, "Of the dozen or so initiatives the companies have announced virtually none has come to pass." (p. 87). The negotiated agreement "called for Telefonica to distribute MCI's services in Spain" (p. 88). This has not materialized. By contrast, in Brazil MCI has bought a controlling stake in the long distance carrier Embratel, an action that puts it in direct competition with Telsp, the network operator in Sao Paulo owned by Telefonica. In sum, not only have the expected outcomes not occurred but, perhaps more significantly, unexpected outcomes (in the sense of partners acting in a competitive way) have become salient in this alliance.

How are these interruptions to be interpreted? We argue that the interruptions can be appreciated in terms of an interpretive scheme that can be labeled as "sensemaking *of* chaos." We will outline the implicit assumptions about alliance functioning that are entailed in these schemes and the dominant national cultural values.

The term chaos is traditionally used in the sense of disorder or unpredictability that characterizes social systems. In recent years, chaos and complexity theories have begun to be applied to the study of organizations (Andersen, 1999; Stacey, 1995; Thietart & Forgues, 1995; Tsoukas, 1998). The central theme in this literature is that organizations are chaotic systems characterized by the existence of forces that are simultaneously sources of order and disorder. It has also been argued that the greater the number of countervailing forces in an organization, the greater the likelihood of the emergence of a chaotic state (Thietart & Forgues, 1995). Chaotic systems are extremely sensitive to initial conditions, generate order out of chaos through the existence of attractors, are time irreversible, evolve from one state to another through a bifurcation process, and possess the property of scale invariance (Thietart & Forgues, 1995). The implications of this form of organization are well spelled out by Stacey (1995), who notes that in such a system there are no clear-cut cause-effect linkages, behavior is subject to both negative and positive feedback, the long-term outcomes are partly intentional and partly emergent, and conflict and ambiguity are ever-present in the organization.

Here we take an interpretive perspective on the issue of chaos and complexity. Whatever be the chaotic or the complex dynamics in a social system, one must recognize that chaos and complexity have to be interpreted as such by the agents who are participants in the social system. In other words, as Chia (1998, pp. 343–344) notes, "complexity is more about experiencing of seemingly complex phenomena and the amount of effort required to articulate this experience into transmissible form rather than about objective complex states of affairs existing independent of the observer system." The interpretation of chaos by the agents is shaped by their cultural backgrounds, leading to the emergence of the two interpretive schemes: "*sensemaking* of *chaos*" and "*sensemaking* in *chaos*."

Sensemaking of Chaos

The interpretive scheme labeled as "sensemaking *of* chaos" assumes implicitly that predictability is and should be the system's operating norm. Chaos is an aberration that needs to be eliminated. Applied in the context of alliance functioning, this implies that the interaction among the alliance partners should be predictable. Interruptions should be infrequent, if any at all. Furthermore, even if interruptions occur their causes should be easily definable and the emerging difficulties ought to be managed in a relatively smooth way. It also assumes that the alliance partners are seeking to attain an adaptive equilibrium among themselves. This would be a state, for example, where pragmatic and moral conflicts would be nonexistent or exist at a very minimal threshold among the alliance partners. The behavior of the alliance partners is assumed to be driven by negative feedback. Thus, if one's alliance partner fails to comply with its stated obligations, this would be communicated to it and its future behavior monitored more explicitly. In other words, even if chaos emerges it needs to be controlled or eliminated in a timely fashion through explicit or implicit modes of control. From a normative standpoint the implicit assumption in this interpartner sensemaking exercise is that chaos is disruptive. By fostering unpredictability chaos impedes the effectiveness of the alliance partners in achieving their objectives.

The interpretive scheme "sensemaking *of* chaos" is grounded in the logic of instrumental rationality (Chaffee, 1985). Firms enter into alliances to achieve certain aims, and to be successful in this regard they must structure their interaction in a way that is effective. Information flows must be timely, the managerial mechanism appropriate to the task at hand, and the external environment monitored to ensure an alignment between the task requirements and the internal structure of the alliance. In sum, this is an interpretive scheme that operates through the principle of complexity reduction (Boisot & Child, 1999), that is, the agents seek to understand the drivers of complexity and act upon it directly.

Sensemaking *in* Chaos

The interpretive scheme "sensemaking *in* chaos" does not assume that predictability is inevitable or, for that matter, even desirable. Chaos is viewed as normal, and it is within this context that order has got to be discovered and maintained. Applied in the context of alliance functioning, this implies that the alliance partners must seek to thrive in ambiguity. Alliance partners need to enact their own environment. As Daft and Weick (1984) note, "they experiment, test, and stimulate, and they ignore precedent, rules, and traditional expectations" (p. 288). Another critical aspect of this interpretive scheme is that even if some order were to be attained, the underlying order will always have a tentative quality to it, that is, it will always be boundedly unstable (Stacey, 1995). It is also likely to be the case that the temporal frame for attaining this order, albeit a boundedly unstable one, is equally unpredictable. In an alliance context, this means that an alliance will always have a certain quality of fragility to it, with the added proviso that the path through which the fragility is enhanced or lessened is also variable. An interesting implication of this is that while this interpretive scheme emphasizes experimentalism, it is balanced with the need for incrementalism (Quinn, 1980), that is, the experimental actions ought not to be too radical as that may destabilize a boundedly unstable system.

"Sensemaking *in* chaos" emphasizes the importance of symbolism. Although symbolism is a crucial aspect of managerial activity (Pfeffer, 1981), it is particularly important in circumstances that are inherently novel, ambiguous, and decidedly uncertain. Alliance partners need to demonstrate their commitment to the alliance and to their partners in an environment that is boundedly unstable. It is only then that a relationship begins to be institutionalized (Ritti & Silver, 1986). Finally, this interpretive scheme views chaos more positively than the other one. Chaos is viewed as being fundamentally transformative in character. It is chaos that provides the preconditions for the generation of new insights (Brown & Eisenhardt, 1998).

This interpretive scheme is grounded in the principles of symbolic rationality as opposed to instrumental rationality. Symbolic rationality emphasizes the need for alliance partners to engage in a process of joint identity construction through the process of crafting a shared intent (Hamel & Prahalad, 1989) and also, for partner firms in an alliance, through a process of interactive learning about and from each other (Das & Kumar, 2007). In this interpretive mode the agents or actors are engaged in the process of "complexity absorption" by possessing "multiple and sometimes conflicting representations of environmental variety, retaining in their behavioral repertoire a range of responses, each of which operates at a lower level of specialization" (Boisot & Child, 1999, p. 238).

Comparing the Two Interpretive Schemes

In sum, the evolution of a cross-national alliance is determined by the congruency of interpretations as well as the content of interpretation among alliance partners. The degree of congruence may be low, moderate, or high. Likewise, interpretations may focus on threat, an opportunity, or some combination thereof. If both the partners come to interpret the alliance as a source of threat, the level of commitment to the alliance will diminish. On the other hand, if the discrepancies are viewed by both the partners as a source of opportunity the alliance will function smoothly. The alliance partners will put in their best effort to deal with the discrepancies to accomplish and preserve harmony as much as practicable (Das &

Kumar, 2009). Furthermore, the process of rectifying discrepancies will draw the partners even closer as they exchange more information among themselves. The interaction will come to resemble what Browning, Beyer, and Shetler (1995) describe as a "self-amplifying reciprocity." In retrospect, the crisis in the nature of discrepancies may prove to be the best thing that happened in the alliance.

The most ambiguous situation occurs when one of the alliance members either is not concerned about discrepancies, or views the discrepancies as an opportunity, while the other alliance partner views the discrepancies as a source of threat. How is the alliance going to develop under these conditions? Our approach suggests that alliance development will resemble a chaotic system. Chaotic systems, as articulated by Stacey (1995), are "nonequilibrium systems with disorderly dynamics" (p. 481). The long-term outcomes of such a system are only partially controllable by the alliance partners. Furthermore, these are systems that are capable of "spontaneous self organization and creative destruction" (p. 481). It is the interpretation of the "disorderly dynamics" and the reaction of the alliance partners to these dynamics that defines the critical threshold for alliance functioning.

The interpretive question centers on the conception of "disorderly dynamics." If the disorderly dynamics is viewed as exemplifying chaos the key question confronting alliance managers is: How is sense to be made of chaos? If, on the other hand, the "disorderly dynamics" is viewed as a context within which sensemaking is to occur the key question is: How is sense to be made within chaos? Sensemaking is essentially a processual activity driven more by plausibility rather than by accuracy (Weick, 1995). As Weick notes, "sensemaking is about plausibility, coherence, and reasonableness. It is about accounts that are socially acceptable and credible" (p. 61). The two interpretive schemes construe alliance functioning in two radically different ways. They are predicated on different assumptions, they differ in their strategic response to chaotic situations, and they metaphorically interpret chaos in very different terms. The contrasts between the two interpretive schemes are outlined in the Table 10.1

A major point of departure for the interpretive schemes is the fundamental difference in their core assumptions. The interpretive scheme labeled as "sensemaking *of* chaos" assumes implicitly that predictability is and should be the system's operating norm. "Sensemaking *in* chaos," by contrast, does not assume that predictability is either inevitable, or for that matter even desirable. The schemes also differ in their strategic response to chaotic situations. The interpretive scheme "sensemaking *of* chaos" is grounded in the logic of instrumental rationality. Information must be gathered and analyzed to determine the appropriate strategic response. The focus is on cognition and the assumption that cognition precedes

Table 10.1. Interpartner Sensemaking of and in Chaos in Cross-National Alliances

	Sensemaking of Chaos	*Sensemaking in Chaos*
Key Assumption 1	Predictability is the system's operating norm	Although predictability may be desirable, it is not inevitable
Key Assumption 2	Fluidity and ambiguity are the hallmarks of the operating system	Lack of predictability is the operating norm
Strategic Response to Chaos	Controlling or eliminating chaos through: (a) information acquisition (b) analysis/planning (c) explicit/implicit modes of control (d) closure	Managing chaos through: (a) experimentation (b) incrementalism (c) symbolism
Interpreting Chaos	Chaos is "disruptive"	Chaos is "transformative"

behavior. Implicit in this framework is a linear-rational model of strategy (Chaffee, 1985; Das & Teng, 1999). "Sensemaking *in* chaos" operates in a very different framework. Chaos is viewed as normal, and it is within this milieu that order has to be discovered and maintained. In an environment lacking predictability, and experimental spontaneity is an essential precursor for discovering order. Experimental spontaneity is defined as the tendency to engage in experimentation in a non-programmatic way. Experimental spontaneity promotes flexibility, variety, and responsiveness. It may also provide the foundation for generating insights. The ability to act insightfully in complex and ambiguous situations is a critical skill (Langley, Mintzberg, Pitcher, Posada, & Saint-Macary, 1995). Related to experimentalism is incrementalism. If experimentalism provides the foundation for new behaviors, incrementalism suggests that the new behaviors ought not to be too radical in content. (This is not to say that there is no room for radical experiments. Indeed, in a crisis-like situation, there may very well be no alternative. However, in the early stages of the evolution of a relationship, too radical or dramatic a change may be destabilizing.)

A further difference is that sensemaking *of* chaos compels managers to reduce ambiguity and uncertainty expeditiously. They may do this by making decisions expeditiously and decisively. Sensemaking *in* chaos, however, allows managers the luxury to postpone or equivocate in making the necessary decisions, thereby permitting the situation to resolve itself in due course rather than through an intervention that is direct or clear-cut. Finally, sensemaking *of* chaos may exacerbate the problematic among the partners as a direct consequence of the actions undertaken by the partners to resolve a situation. In contrast, sensemaking *in* chaos may prevent that eventuality inasmuch as it prevents the kinds of actions that may automatically create an escalatory cycle.

NATIONAL CULTURE AND ALLIANCE EVOLUTION

There is no one all-encompassing definition of national culture. As Porter and Samovar (1994) note, "Culture is ubiquitous, multidimensional, complex, and all pervasive" (p. 11). Culture can be conceptualized as consisting of two dimensions, namely, a cognitive and a behavioral. The cognitive dimension of culture focuses on the meaning that the different situations hold for actors, while the behavioral dimension focuses on interactional patterns extant in a particular culture. Different definitions of culture emphasize different aspects of culture, although each definition contains elements of both the dimensions. For example, Geertz's (1973) notion of culture as a "control mechanism," which defines the rules for behavior, has a strong cognitive content although the behavioral dimension is not altogether absent. The cognitive dimension of culture, besides focusing on meaning, also implies a series of rules by which the meaning is to be ascertained. These rules may be likened to what Abelson (1976) calls a "script," that is, a set of sequential and interrelated steps that lead to the completion of an activity. These rules provide the basis for making interpretations as well as for outlining the nature of that interpretation. Hofstede's (1980, 1991) work has been increasingly used in the international and comparative management literatures. He classifies cultures in terms of five dimensions: individualism-collectivism, power distance, uncertainty avoidance, masculinity-femininity, and Confucian dynamism. The dimensions proposed by Hofstede are more behavioral than cognitive in content. As Redding (1994) notes,

> Although Hofstede's dimensions provide a useful beginning to an empirical approach to the social construction of reality as classically described by Berger and Luckmann (1966) we are still left with only the broadest hints about the mental frameworks of leaders in different cultures and there is a clear need for much more indigenous specification of meaning structures of the kind offered by Pye on authority in Asia. (p. 336)

Interpretive conflicts arise from conflicting interpretive systems. Interpretive systems, in turn, are rooted in the cognitive component of cultures. To fully understand the origins and the consequences of interpretive conflicts it is, therefore, useful to focus on a definition of national culture that has a strong cognitive slant.

Triandis (1995) suggests that the choice of a definition of culture depends on the goals of the investigator. Our goal, as mentioned earlier, is to assess the impact of culture on alliance functioning. Culture shapes the behavior of alliance managers as well as the interpretations imposed by alliance managers on alliance functioning. Our discussion will analyze the impact of culture on alliance functioning at both cognitive and behavioral levels. This discussion will be framed within the context of the model of alliance functioning elaborated earlier.

One definition of culture is offered by Kluckhohn and Strodtbeck (1961). These authors develop a value orientation framework that articulates the parameters for decision making. The framework is based on the premise that while all societies are confronted with similar sets of problems, their approach to managing these problems is culturally variable. The different approaches are reflective of different preferences, with the different preferences being described as "variations in value orientations." Kluckhohn and Strodtbeck identify five major value orientations: (a) Relationship of humans to nature: Is the desirable goal to achieve mastery over nature, live in harmony with it, or be subjugated to it?; (b) Time orientation: Is it desirable to have a past, present, or future orientation?; (c) Assumption about human nature: Are individuals primarily evil, good or are they a little bit of both?; (d) Activity orientation: Is it desirable to have a doing as opposed to a being orientation?; and (e) Relationships among people: Is it desirable to be responsible for others or should one primarily look after oneself? An implicit assumption is this framework is that what is variable across cultures is the dominance of different orientations and not the absence of any one particular orientation. The framework assumes that while all of the variations may be present in all cultures the relative salience of such variations differs across cultures.

International alliances necessarily involve crossing national boundaries, so that the differences in the national cultures of alliance partners become a salient factor in alliance management. Various recent studies have examined the impact of national and corporate cultural differences in international strategic alliances, with insightful analyses and findings concerning the differences in the roles of trust, commitment, legalisms, and satisfaction (Das & Teng, 1998; Dong & Glaister, 2007; Gill & Butler, 2003; Kauser & Shaw, 2004; Kwon, 2008; Lin & Wang, 2008; Robson, Katsikeas, & Bello, 2008). A number of studies have also concluded that national culture is important (e.g., Barkema & Vermeulen, 1997; Meschi & Riccio, 2008; Steensma, Marino, Weaver, & Dickson, 2000), although some others question this importance vis-à-vis corporate and professional culture (e.g., Sirmon & Lane, 2004). In this context, Leung, Bhagat, Buchan, Erez, and Gibson (2005) have observed: "scholars have argued that instead of addressing whether national culture makes a difference it is more useful to address the issue of how and when it makes a difference" (p. 368). What is relevant for us to note is that, because of the inherent ambiguities of the relationships among the partners, cross-national alliances constitute a potentially fruitful arena to examine the impact of national culture (Kumar & Das, 2009).

Theorists concur on the importance of national culture in shaping managerial behavior (Earley, 1993; Hofstede, 1980). Scholars have explored the interlinkages between national culture and such topics as strategy formulation (Schneider, 1989), alliance evolution (Kumar & Nti, 2004), licensing versus foreign direct investment decisions (Shane, 1994), and self-managing work teams (Kirkman & Shapiro, 1997). These illustrative research areas indicate how widely national culture has been studied for its relevance in understanding different managerial issues.

What role does culture play in the evolution of alliances? Alliance scholars point out that every alliance potentially faces problems of appropriation and coordination (Gulati & Singh, 1998). Appropriation problems revolve around the concern that one of the partners may appropriate greater value for itself at the expense of its counterpart whereas coordination problems revolve around the concern that the partner may not be able to effectively coordinate their activities. It has also been argued that when appropriation is the central strategic issue differences in trust and strategic objectives may be the primary drivers of interaction, whereas when coordination is the primary strategic issue differences in national or corporate culture may be the primary drivers of interaction. Differences in culture (national or corporate) are likely to be reflected in differences in organizational routines or standard operating procedures and it is these differences that create problems of coordination. It is possible, and may indeed be likely, that coordinative difficulties, if not appropriately addressed by the alliance partners, may lead to problems of appropriation, whether real or subjectively perceived. The original problems experienced by the partners, as well as other variables, may become salient during the course of the interaction. One would surmise that in any cross-national alliance both sets of problems are likely to be present, although the relative salience of appropriation and coordination concerns may well be variable.

If culture is important, as it is indeed, then the question arises as to why are we privileging national culture over corporate culture? To address this issue it is important to recognize that national cultural differences reflect differences in core assumptions across cultures while corporate cultural differences are indicative of differences in organizational practices across cultures (Hofstede, Neuijen, Ohayv, & Sanders, 1990). Differences in core assumptions reflect cultural differences that are relatively enduring whereas differences in organizational practices have a transient character (Laurent, 1986). A major implication of this is that while corporate culture may readily modify the behavior of organizational members, it is unlikely to be able to redefine the basic assumptions of national culture. As Laurent (1986) notes, "it would probably be illusionary to expect that the recent and short history of modern corporations could shape the basic assumption of their members to an extent that would even approximate the age-long shaping of civilizations and nations." (p. 98). The relatively enduring character of national cultural differences has been underscored in a study of international joint ventures in Hungary (Meschi & Roger, 1994). Their study demonstrated that national cultural differences had a greater impact on the evolution of international joint ventures than corporate cultural differences.

Our discussion suggests that while there may be a number of variables that affect the evolution of cross-national alliances, national culture is an important variable whose impact has not been fully analyzed in the context of alliance functioning at the interpretive level.

NATIONAL CULTURAL VALUES AND THE USE OF INTERPRETIVE SCHEMES

Kluckhohn and Strodtbeck's (1961) conception of culture as reflecting differences in value orientation provides a useful framework for assessing how national culture shapes the interpretive scheme used by a particular cultural group. As outlined earlier, there are five major value orientations that the authors propose. We consider that of the five value orientations proposed by these authors, three have a direct bearing on the use of a particular interpretive scheme. Those three are (a) relationship of humans to nature; (b) activity orientation; and (c) relational orientation.

The other two dimensions (time orientation and assumption about human nature) do not directly impact on the choice of the interpretive scheme, although they may relate to the timing of the use of a particular interpretive strategy or influence the specific behaviors adopted by the participants as they act on the basis of their interpretive schemes. The temporal orientation, that is, the attitude towards past, present, or future, is more likely to have influence when a particular interpretive scheme is used to make sense of interruptions rather than directly affect the choice of the interpretive scheme per se. Cultures characterized by a present or future orientation will make use of a particular interpretive scheme sooner vis-à-vis cultures characterized by a past orientation. Whether the dominant value orientation views human nature as good or evil is more likely to influence the strategies adopted by managers in dealing with other individuals rather than directly affect the choice of the interpretive scheme.

Relationship of Humans to Nature

Cultures where the dominant value orientation is one of attaining mastery over nature will subscribe to the "sensemaking *of* chaos" interpretive scheme. Chaos, in this conceptualization, prevents the actors from attaining consistent and continuous control over the environment, and surely this is not the preferred state of affairs. Where chaos prevails, the desired goals are either not attained or are attained and sustained only irregularly. For managers socialized into this value orientation maintaining predictability and control is crucial. Alliance managers subscribing to this interpretive scheme will do what it takes to minimize the occurrence of any interruptions and, even when these are unavoidable, have back-up strategies to lessen their disruptive impact.

Cultures where the dominant value orientation is one of being in harmony with nature will subscribe to the interpretive scheme "sensemaking *in* chaos." Since humans cannot exert control over the environment they must learn to cope with its quirkiness. They must be prepared to cope with any threats posed by the environment and to exploit any opportunities that nature presents. The threats and opportunities may appear and disappear in an unpredictable manner and the linkages between actions and outcomes may be far from readily apparent. For managers socialized in this interpretive scheme adaptability is the *sine qua non* for successful strategic behavior.

Activity Orientation

Cultures where the dominant value orientation is one of doing will follow the interpretive scheme of "sensemaking *of* chaos." In a doing culture there is "a demand for the kind of activity which results in accomplishments that are measurable by standards conceived to be external to the acting individual" (Kluckhohn & Strodtbeck, 1961, p. 17). A chaotic situation for this reason invites a natural intervention by managers who have been socialized within this value system. These managers will want to make sense of chaos by controlling it through managerial intervention. If the chaotic situation proves intractable to managerial intervention they may even consider exiting from the alliance but even that is not an attempt to bring order to a problematical situation.

Cultures where the dominant value orientation is one of being will follow a different logic. They may choose either of the two interpretive schemes depending on what they spontaneously feel at that point in time. There is a certain volatility or unpredictability in the logic utilized by managers socialized within this being frame of reference, a volatility that may aggravate the problems with their alliance partner.

Relational Orientation

The relational orientation draws attention to the importance of the goals of the individual vis-à-vis the goals of the larger group. Cultures that give preeminence to individual goals over collective goals will rely on "sensemaking *of* chaos" as the interpretive scheme. Alliance managers socialized in cultures where individual goals are accorded prominence will be discomfited by interruptions that threaten their goal attainment. For them the failure to attain the desired goals is tantamount to a chaotic situation that needs to be corrected expeditiously.

By contrast, cultures that give preeminence to collective goals over individual goals will rely on "sensemaking *in* chaos" as the dominant interpretive scheme. Alliance managers socialized in such cultures will tend to view situations in more nuanced terms. The critical question for them is one of attaining and maintaining alignment between their individual and group goals. It is the need to balance the two in a harmonious manner that invites viewing the situation through the lens of "sensemaking *in* chaos."

INTERPRETIVE CONTRADICTIONS AND INTERNAL TENSIONS IN ALLIANCE EVOLUTION

Alliances contain within themselves the seeds of behavioral contradictions (cooperation vs. competition), structural contradictions (rigidity vs. flexibility), and temporal contradictions (short term vs. long term) (Das & Teng, 2000). In the event the alliance partners are unable to effectively manage the interpretive contradictions, the alliance is likely to enter an unstable phase. While the nonresolution of interpretive contradictions may not lead to an instant demise of the alliance, it may set in motion a chain of events that may exacerbate the already existing interpretive contradictions. In particular, nonresolution of interpretive contradictions may make salient contradictions that may have been only latent till that point in time. Consider, for example, the inherent tension between cooperative and competitive behavior, a tension that lies at the heart of behavioral contradiction. If partner firms are unable to manage this contradiction effectively, they will become wary and, in so doing, may modify their behavior and reevaluate their partner's behavior. A behavior that was viewed as exemplifying cooperation may now be viewed in a neutral or a self-serving manner. When both the partners begin to act in this way, they make explicit the behavioral contradiction and create the preconditions for the emergence of a vicious circle. Vicious circles arise in interorganizational dynamics because the actors are biased against perceiving vicious circles (Masuch, 1985). The consequence of this is that ever so small a change in behavior may lead to potentially large consequences as one or both of the partner firms decides to exit from the alliance.

A similar dynamic may be operative in the context of structural contradictions, that is, a tension between rigidity and flexibility (Das & Teng, 2000). The failure to effectively manage interpretive contradictions means that alliance partners may hold conflicting views concerning the appropriate balance between the two structural attributes. Thus, while one of the alliance partners may be concerned about "insufficient details on how to collaborate, little irreversible commitment, unclear property rights, and weak authority structure" (p. 87), the other partner may be more concerned about modifying the structural arrangements so as to more effectively function in changing environments. Structural contradictions may become highly salient under these conditions, with an alliance firm beginning to question the motives and the underlying intentions of its partners. There is the danger here of a self-fulfilling prophecy, with the emergence of a vicious circle a strong possibility.

The temporal contradiction, that is, the conflict between the short-term and the long-term is a very critical contradiction in alliances (Das, 2006; Das & Teng, 2000). Interpretive contradictions, if not managed effectively, may sensitize the alliance partners to this otherwise latent contradiction. Where one of the partners focuses on the short-term while the other partner focuses on the long-term appropriation concerns may intensify, leading the partner with a longer term strategic focus to sharply limit or curtail the pattern of interaction with its partner. This will affect the ability of the alliance to realize its strategic goals, further calling into question the meaningfulness of the alliance for either partner.

In sum, the framework posits that an ineffective management of interpretive contradictions may give rise to behavioral, structural, and temporal contradictions. The emergence of these contradictions is likely to further intensify the nature of the interpretive contradiction among the alliance partners. Vicious circles once again are likely to be very prevalent under these circumstances.

An example of a cross-national alliance where the interpretive contradiction was not effectively managed is provided by Ariño and de la Torre (1998). This was an alliance between NAMCO, a US-based company, which was active in the household products industry and Hexagon, a French company, whose primary interests were in chemicals, cosmetics, and pharmaceuticals. These firms had developed a joint venture to exploit the market for ecological cleaners. The two firms had complementary strengths—Hexagon was strong technologically but did not possess a worldwide distribution network; NAMCO had a good distribution network but did not possess the requisite technical capabilities to develop their products globally.

When the alliance experienced an interruption, i.e., the expected outcome did not occur (the market for ecological cleaners turning out to be much less promising than what was thought originally), the alliance partners were confronted with the necessity of making sense of this interruption. This was a task in which they were not particularly successful.

As outlined in the development of this chapter, the partners needed to be clear about whether the alliance is functioning well, demanding reasonable efforts, and has prospects of further cooperation. Although at first the alliance partners were in agreement about the changed strategy following the less than promising results in the market for ecological cleaners, this agreement did not endure for very long. (The new agreement had called for the alliance to try to market hypoallergenic soaps and skin care products.) NAMCO became particularly concerned about the impact that the new strategy was having on the "cannibalization of NAMCO products" by the joint venture. Although an agreement was reached among the alliance partners, the implementation of the agreement was marked by continuous tension among the partners. As Ariño and de la Torre (1998) note, the partners' "inability to reach consensus about the interpretation of their respective obligations, and modify them if necessary in the face of significant external change, is allowed to fester and make their positions diverge" (p. 321). This conflict reached a climax when NAMCO was perceived to have allowed one of Hexagon's competitors to reestablish a position in the hypoallergenic market and not lose competitive position to Hexa-Care, the product being promoted by the joint venture.

It also became increasingly apparent that the partners were finding it hard to restore the alliance to a state of equilibrium. Whatever one partner desired, the other partner had objections. This obviously made the task of managing the alliance a costly process leading both the partners to lessen their commitment to the venture. In due course the partners made a negative assessment on the possibility of maintaining or deepening the cooperation among themselves. A negative assessment on this score led to the dissolution of the joint venture in December 1993.

The case highlights the consequences of the failure of the partner firms to effectively manage interpretive contradictions. At a behavioral level, both partners did not consistently maintain a cooperative mode of behavior. As an example, while NAMCO may have allowed one of Hexagon's competitors to enter the market, Hexagon on its part did not transfer the rights to a specific diet product to the venture as had been agreed upon. On the structural level, both partners were not sufficiently flexible in coping with the contingencies posed by the failure of the market for ecological products to develop. While the partners agreed on the choice of a new product for the joint venture, they were unable to satisfactorily resolve the operational challenges that this posed. Adjustments needed to be made but the partners were either unwilling or unable to make the requisite changes.

CONCLUSIONS

The chapter has explored the implications of conflicting interpretive schemes on the evolution of cross-national alliances. It had been argued that there are two alternative interpretive schemes through which the alliance partners may seek to make sense of the interruptions that they may encounter in alliance functioning. The first scheme, "sensemaking *of* chaos," copes with interruptions through a process of complexity reduction, whereas the second interpretive scheme, "sensemaking *in* chaos," copes with interruptions through the process of complexity absorption. Conflicting interpretive schemes generate an interpretive contradiction that, if not appropriately managed, may lead to the emergence of behavioral and structural contradictions that make it difficult for an alliance to yield the desired outcomes.

The interpartner sensemaking framework developed in the chapter makes several contributions. Although there have been a number of different theoretical perspectives that have been put forward to explain the problem of alliance instability, Das and Teng (2000) observe that "there is as yet no general framework that explains why strategic alliances are inordinately unstable" (p. 84). These authors do attempt to explain the instability of alliances in terms of what they describe as an "internal tensions perspective", and while this certainly extends the literature, the perspective they offer is not an interpretive one. The framework proposed here attempts to do just that. It is not the mere existence of internal tensions (important as they are) that is crucial to understanding alliance instability; it is also how these tensions are interpreted and acted upon by the alliance partners that help shape the dynamics of alliance evolution.

Second, the chapter articulates the challenges faced by managers in cross-national alliances. Although there are many who now argue about the importance of cultural differences in shaping alliance dynamics (Child & Faulkner, 1998; Johnson, Cullen, Sakano, & Takenouchi, 1996), the management of the interpretive aspects of these alliances has not been stressed by these and other writers to any degree. This chapter thus provides a complementary perspective to the existing literature on alliance functioning.

Interpartner sensemaking occurs at all stages of alliance evolution. Future research may therefore seek to assess the impact of conflicting interpretive schemes in a number of ways. First, we know that alliances proceed through the stages of formation, operation, and outcome (Das & Teng, 2002). It might be helpful therefore to explore how these interpretive contradictions unfold at these different stages. Second, alliances may be prone to conflicts centering on issues both of appropriation and coordination (Gulati & Singh, 1998). Appropriation concerns revolve around the ability of the partner firms to extract value from the venture while coordination cost concerns center on the ability of the alliancing firms to engage in effective coordination. How do the different interpretative schemes condition the evolution of these conflicts? The interpretive schemes may also be particularly relevant in learning-related alliances where there is ambiguity both about the learning intent of one's partner (Das & Kumar, 2007; Hamel, 1991) and one's own ability to absorb learning (Cohen & Levinthal, 1990). Conflicting motivations and ambiguity regarding learning processes and outcomes no doubt have the potential of accentuating conflict, in which case these interpretive schemes become especially relevant.

A further aspect of the framework highlights the importance of conducting longitudinal studies for studying alliance evolution. If the evolution of a cross-national alliance is dependent on the interpretive schemes used by alliance managers as well as on how congruently the interpretive schemes mesh with each other, then longitudinal studies would enable one to capture the dynamics of the interpretive process. Although studying an alliance as it unfolds may be difficult, it will surely be insightful; in any event, it is our belief that in conceptual endeavors such as in this chapter the more significant goal is to discover potentially fruitful concepts and insights rather than be overly concerned about the practicalities of immediate empirical investigations (Das, 1984, 2003). One could also, of course, study the evolution of alliances retrospectively in a manner attempted by Ariño and de la Torre (1998) or Doz (1996). In both of these studies the authors conducted in-depth interviews as a prelude to conducting an inductive analysis of alliance evolution.

The interpartner sensemaking framework also has significant managerial implications. In particular, the framework emphasizes the importance of the implicit assumptions that guide each partner's behavior. Managers are often unaware of their own assumptions, much less the assumptions of their counterpart. Divergent interpretations over which the partners are unable to negotiate a consensus are for that reason often attributed to the presence of hidden agendas than due to conflicting assumptions. This may lead one or both of the partners to pursue actions that are more likely to aggravate rather than lessen conflicts. An awareness of the implicit assumptions shaping one's own behavior and that of one's partner is for that reason crucial in alliance management.

This awareness can be heightened through cross-cultural training. A key component of many cross-cultural training programs is to help the managers get a better appreciation and awareness of their own assumptions and that of their partner. Heightened awareness may override the managers' natural tendency to process information in an automatic fashion, preventing these managers from making instantaneous judgments about their partner's intentions. Better awareness will also sensitize managers to their own interpretive schemes as well as that of their partners'. Cross-cultural workshops that bring together participants from both of the alliance firms prior to the commencement of the alliance should be immensely useful. This should be supplemented by ongoing cross-cultural workshops once the alliance has commenced operation. This will solidify managerial understanding in both partner firms and will allow them to resolve conflicts constructively. Role plays, simulations, case studies, and small group discussions are often key components of these workshops, and these can go some distance in sensitizing alliance firms to the interpretations of their opposite numbers. A related implication is that partners must become skillful in the management of conflicts as and when they occur. Conflicts are bound to arise many a time in alliances, given the conflicting interpretive schemes, but effective management of conflict implies that conflicts are prevented from escalating needlessly.

In sum, this chapter has attempted to highlight the contradictions inherent in strategic alliances and the factors that give rise to the emergence of these contradictions. Interpartner sensemaking—"sensemaking *of* chaos" and "sensemaking *in* chaos"—need to be appreciated as interpretive frames of alliance partners in an arena intrinsically fraught with contradictions. Studying alliances from an interpretive perspective seems to have rarely been attempted. An initial attempt has been made here to highlight the benefits of such a perspective, and especially so in the context of cross-national alliances, where the divergence of meaning may be particularly acute. It is our hope that researchers will pay greater attention to this perspective in the future in studying strategic alliances.

ACKNOWLEDGMENT

This chapter, save some minor changes, was earlier published as Das, T. K., & Kumar, R. (2010). Interpartner sensemaking in strategic alliances: Managing cultural differences and internal tensions. *Management Decision, 48*, 17–36.

REFERENCES

Abelson, R. P. (1976). Script processing in attitude formation and decision making. In J. S. Carroll & J. W. Payne (Eds.), *Cognition and social behavior* (pp. 33–45). Hillsdale, NJ: Erlbaum.

Andersen, P. (1999). Complexity theory and organization science. *Organization Science, 10*, 216–232.

Ariño, A., & de la Torre, J. (1998). Learning from failure: Towards an evolutionary model of collaborative ventures. *Organization Science, 9*, 306–325.

Barkema, H. G., & Vermeulen, F. (1997). What differences in cultural backgrounds of partners are detrimental for international joint ventures? *Journal of International Business Studies, 28*, 845–864.

Bartunek, J. M. (1984). Changing interpretive schemes and organizational restructuring: The example of a religious order. *Administrative Science Quarterly, 29*, 355–372.

Berger, P., & Luckmann, T. (1966). *The social construction of reality.* New York, NY: Doubleday.

Boisot, M., & Child, J. (1999). Organizations as adaptive systems in complex environment: The case of China. *Organization Science, 10*, 237–252.

Brislin, R., & Yoshida, T. (1996), *Intercultural communication training: An introduction*. Thousand Oaks, CA: SAGE.

Brown, L. T., Rugman, A. M., & Verbeke, A. (1989). Japanese joint ventures with Western multinationals: Synthesizing the economic and cultural explanations of failure. *Asia Pacific Journal of Management, 6*, 225–242.

Brown, S. L., & Eisenhardt, K. M. (1998). *Competing on the edge: Strategy as structured chaos.* Boston, MA: Harvard Business School Press.

Browning, L. D., Beyer, J. M., & Shetler, J. C. (1995). Building cooperation in a competitive industry: Sematech and the semiconductor industry. *Academy of Management Journal, 38*, 113–151.

Chaffee, E. (1985). Three models of strategy. *Academy of Management Review, 10*, 89–98.

Chia, R. (1998). From complexity science to complex thinking: Organization as simple location. *Organization, 5*, 341–369.

Child, J., & Faulkner, D. (1998). *Strategies of cooperation: Managing alliances, networks and joint ventures*. New York, NY: Oxford University Press.

Cohen, W. M., & Levinthal, D. A. (1990). Absorptive capacity: a new perspective on learning and innovation. *Administrative Science Quarterly, 35*, 128–152.

Daft, R. L., & Weick, K. E. (1984). Toward a model of organizations as interpretation systems. *Academy of Management Review, 9*, 284–295.

Das, T. K. (1984). Portmanteau ideas for organizational theorizing. *Organization Studies, 5*, 261–267.

Das, T. K. (1986), *The subjective side of strategy making: Future orientations and perceptions of executives*. New York, NY: Praeger.

Das, T. K. (2003). Managerial perceptions and the essence of managerial world: What is an interloper business executive to make of the academic-researcher perceptions of managers? *British Journal of Management, 14*, 23–32.

Das, T. K. (2005). Deceitful behaviors of alliance partners: Potential and prevention. *Management Decision, 43*, 706-719.

Das, T. K. (2006). Strategic alliance temporalities and partner opportunism. *British Journal of Management, 17*, 1–21.

Das, T. K., & Kumar, R. (2007). Learning dynamics in the alliance development process. *Management Decision, 45*, 684–707.

Das, T. K., & Kumar, R. (2009). Interpartner harmony in strategic alliances: Managing commitment and forbearance", *International Journal of Strategic Business Alliances, 1*, 24–52.

Das, T. K., & Rahman, N. (2010). Determinants of partner opportunism in strategic alliances: A conceptual framework. *Journal of Business and Psychology, 25*, 55–74.

Das, T. K., & Teng, B. (1998). Between trust and control: Developing confidence in partner cooperation in alliances. *Academy of Management Review, 23*, 491–512.

Das, T. K., & Teng, B. (1999). Cognitive biases and strategic decision processes: An integrative perspective. *Journal of Management Studies, 36*, 757–778.

Das, T. K., & Teng, B. (2000). Instabilities of strategic alliances: An internal tensions perspective. *Organization Science, 11*, 77–101.

Das, T. K., & Teng, B. (2002). The dynamics of alliance conditions in the alliance development process. *Journal of Management Studies, 39*, 725–746.

Dong, L., & Glaister, K. W. (2007). National and corporate culture differences in international strategic alliances: Perceptions of Chinese partners. *Asia Pacific Journal of Management, 24*, 191–205.

Doz, Y. L. (1996). The evolution of cooperation in strategic alliances: Initial conditions or learning processes? *Strategic Management Journal, 17*, 55–83.

Earley, P. C. (1993). East meets West meets Mideast: Further exploration of collectivistic and individualistic work groups. *Academy of Management Journal, 36*, 319–348.

Geertz, C. (1973). *The interpretation of cultures*. New York, NY: Basic Books.

Gill, J., & Butler, R. J. (2003). Managing instability in cross-cultural alliances. *Long Range Planning, 36*, 543–563.

Gulati, R., & Singh, H. (1998). The architecture of cooperation: Managing coordination costs and appropriation concerns in strategic alliances. *Administrative Science Quarterly, 43*, 781–814.

Hamel, G. (1991). Competition for competence and interpartner learning within strategic alliances. *Strategic Management Journal, 12*(S1), 83–103.

Hamel, G., & Prahalad, C. K. (1989). Strategic intent. *Harvard Business Review, 67*(3), 63–76.

Hofstede, G. (1980). *Culture's consequences: International differences in work related values*. Beverly Hills, CA: SAGE.

Hofstede, G. (1991). *Cultures and organizations: Software of the mind*, London: McGraw-Hill.

Hofstede, G., Neuijen, B., Ohayv, D. D., & Sanders, G. (1990). Measuring organizational cultures: A qualitative and quantitative study across twenty cases. *Administrative Science Quarterly, 35*, 286–316.

Johnson, J. L., Cullen, J. B., Sakano, T., & Takenouchi, H. (1996). Setting the stage for trust and strategic integration in Japanese-US cooperative alliances. *Journal of International Business Studies, 27*, 981–1004.

Kauser, S., & Shaw, V. (2004). The influence of behavioral and organizational characteristics on the success of international strategic alliances. *International Marketing Review, 21*(1), 17–52.

Kirkman, B. L., & Shapiro, D. L. (1997). The impact of cultural values on employee resistance to teams: Toward a model of globalized self managing work team effectiveness.. *Academy of Management Review, 22*, 730–757.

Kluckhohn, F. R., & Strodtbeck, F. L. (1961). *Variations in value orientation*. New York, NY: Row Peterson.

Kumar, R., & Andersen, P. (2000). Inter firm diversity and the management of meaning in international strategic alliances. *International Business Review, 9*, 237–252.

Kumar, R., & Das, T. K. (2009). Strategic alliances and culture in a globalizing world. In J. Ulijn, G. Duysters, & E. Meijer (Eds.), *Strategic alliances, mergers and acquisitions: The influence of culture on successful cooperation* (pp. 13–29). Cheltenham, England: Edward Elgar.

Kumar, R., & Nti, K. O. (2004). National cultural values and the evolution of process and outcome discrepancies in international strategic alliances. *Journal of Applied Behavioral Science, 40*, 344–361.

Kwon, Y.-C. (2008). Antecedents and consequences of international joint venture partnerships: A social exchange perspective. *International Business Review, 17*, 559–573.

Lane, H. W., & Beamish, P. W. (1990). Cross-cultural cooperative behavior in joint ventures in LDCs. *Management International Review, 30*(Special Issue), 87–102.

Langley, A., Mintzberg, H., Pitcher, P., Posada, E., & Saint-Macary, J. (1995). Opening up decision making: The view from the black stool. *Organization Science, 6*, 260–279.

Laurent, A. (1986). The cross-culture puzzle of international human resource management. *Human Resource Management, 25*, 91–102.

Leung, K., Bhagat, R. S., Buchan, N. R., Erez, M., & Gibson, C. B. (2005). Culture and international business: Recent advances and their implications for future research. *Journal of International Business Studies, 36*, 357–378.

Lin, X., & Wang, C. L. (2008). Enforcement and performance: The role of ownership, legalism, and trust in international joint ventures. *Journal of World Business, 43*, 340–351.

Mandler, G. (1975). *Mind and emotion*. New York, NY: Wiley.

Masuch, M. (1985). Vicious circles in organizations. *Administrative Science Quarterly, 30*, 14–33.

Meschi, P. -X., & Riccio, E. L. (2008). Country risk, national cultural differences between partners and survival of international joint ventures in Brazil. *International Business Review, 17*, 250–266.

Meschi, P. -X., & Roger, A. (1994). Cultural context and social effectiveness in international joint ventures. *Management International Review, 34*, 197–212.

Morgan, G. (1979). *Sociological paradigms and organizational analysis*. Beverly Hills, CA: SAGE.

Pfeffer, J. (1981). Management as symbolic action: The creation and maintenance of organizational paradigms. *Research in Organizational Behavior, 3*, 1–52.

Porter, R. E., & Samovar, L. A. (1994). An introduction to intercultural communication. In L. A. Samovar & R. E. Porter, R. E. (Eds.), *Intercultural communications: A reader* (pp. 4–26). Belmont, CA: Wadsworth.

Quinn, J. B. (1980). *Strategies for change*. Homewood, IL: Irwin.

Redding, S. G. (1994). Comparative management theory: Jungle, zoo or fossil bed. *Organization Studies, 15*, 323–359.

Ring, P. S., & Van de Ven, A. H. (1994). Development processes of cooperative interorganizational relationships. *Academy of Management Review, 19*, 90–118.

Ritti, R. R., & Silver, J. M. (1986). Early processes of institutionalization: The dramaturgy of exchange in interorganizational relations. *Administrative Science Quarter*ly, *31*, 25–42.

Robson, M. J., Katsikeas, C. S., Bello, D. C. (2008). Drivers and performance outcomes of trust in international strategic alliances: The role of organizational complexity. *Organization Science, 19*, 647–665.

Rocks, D. (1999, October 11). A failure to communicate: Will mistrust doom the MCI-Telefonica global alliance. *Business Week*, pp. 88-89.

Schneider, S. (1989). Strategy formulation: The impact of national culture. *Organization Studies, 10*, 157–176.

Shane, S. (1994). The effect of national culture on the choice between licensing and foreign investment. *Strategic Management Journal, 15*, 627–642.

Sirmon, D. G., & Lane, P. J. (2004). A model of cultural differences and international alliance performance. *Journal of International Business Studies, 35*, 306–319.

Stacey, R. D. (1995). The science of complexity: An alternative perspective for strategic change_processes. *Strategic Management Journal, 16*, 477–495.

Steensma, H. K., Marino, L., Weaver, K. M., & Dickson, P. H. (2000). The influence of national culture on the formation of technology alliances by entrepreneurial firms. *Academy of Management Journal, 43*, 951–973.

Thietart, R. A., & Forgues, B. (1995). Chaos theory and organization. *Organization Science, 6*, 19-31.

Triandis, H. C. (1995). *Culture and social behavior.* New York, NY: McGraw-Hill.

Tsoukas, H. (1998). Introduction: Chaos, complexity and organization theory. *Organization, 5*, 291–313.

Weick, K. E. (1995). *Sensemaking in organizations*. Reading, MA: Addison Wesley.

CHAPTER 11

NATIONAL CULTURE AND LEGITIMACY IN INTERNATIONAL ALLIANCES

Rajesh Kumar and T. K. Das

In this chapter we explore the interrelationship between national cultural values and the dynamics of legitimacy management in international alliances. Alliances are prone to instability and international alliances may suffer the additional problem of a cultural gap that may further enhance such instability. The idea that interpartner legitimacy is crucial in shaping alliance success is now being increasingly recognized in the literature but there is as yet little systematic work that demonstrates the linkages between national culture and legitimacy management in international alliances. The chapter discusses how national cultural values may impact different types of legitimacy (pragmatic, moral, cognitive) in an international alliance. The concept of national culture has been operationalized in many ways but for the purposes of this chapter we draw upon the construct of individualism-collectivism that has garnered much attention in the literature. Individualistic and collectivistic cultures are known to differ on a number of dimensions and these differences have significant implications for legitimacy management in alliances. These differences have an impact on the process by which legitimacy is attained, the relative importance of different types of legitimacy, and the issue of legitimacy repair. We also discuss the legitimacy

Strategic Alliances in a Globalizing World, pp. 243–261

dynamics at the different stages of alliance development. A number of propositions are derived for each of these alliance development stages to facilitate empirical testing. We conclude by discussing the key managerial implications of the framework proposed in the chapter regarding the interrelationship between national cultural values and the dynamics of legitimacy management.

INTRODUCTION

The growing popularity of strategic alliances is often accompanied by heightened instability. Scholars have begun to explain this puzzle drawing upon a variety of theoretical perspectives that seek to understand the roles of opportunism (Das & Rahman, 2010), internal tensions (Das & Teng, 2000), bargaining power (Inkpen & Beamish, 1997), learning asymmetry (Hamel, 1991), a perceived lack of fairness (Luo, 2008), and cultural differences (Kumar & Nti, 2004).

Implicit in all these perspectives on alliance instability is the argument that alliances fail either because of poor governance arrangements or clashing expectations, the origins of which could be many. We recognize that these theoretical perspectives have gone some way in advancing our knowledge of alliances but we would also have to make the broader argument that, with few exceptions, these perspectives have failed to adequately consider the microdynamics of alliance management. It may be argued that microdynamics are irrelevant to understanding alliances, as they do not provide a parsimonious explanation of alliance failure. We suggest, by contrast, that microbehavioral dynamics are critical in explaining alliance performance because without an understanding of this one would be hard pressed to appreciate how alliances work in practice.

A microbehavioral perspective sensitizes us to the fact that managerial perceptions, cognitions, and behavior are crucial in understanding how alliances evolve over time. A wide body of literature in strategic management and organizational behavior has reinforced the importance of managerial perceptions and cognitions in influencing decision making (e.g., Das, 1986, 2003; Das & Teng, 1999), and this is indeed beginning to be recognized in the field of strategic alliances (e.g., Das & Kumar, 2007, 2010a, 2010b; Kumar & Das, 2010a). In general, as many scholars have noted, understanding alliance practice remains an under-researched area in the alliance literature.

The microbehavioral perspective looks at the dynamics of interorganizational interaction, using as its building block the impact of different variables such as emotions, culture and regulatory focus on how the relationship between the partners evolves over time. Alliance managers are confronted with the necessity of making decisions and this by definition implicates the relevance of the human agency (Kumar & Das, 2010a). It is for this reason that variables that impact managerial decision making are crucial in understanding how alliances develop over time. For example, the presence of negative emotions such as frustration or anger has the potential of undermining trust and creating a negative vicious circle (Kumar, 1997, 2008). In a similar vein, differences in national culture may also give arise to misunderstandings, distrust, and prevent the partners from effectively dealing with the problems at hand (Kumar & Nti, 2004; Pak, Ra, & Park, 2009). Recent work (Das & Kumar, in press) has also highlighted how differences in alliancing firm's regulatory focus may both condition their willingness to commit opportunistic acts as well as their willingness to tolerate opportunistic actions of their partner. This stream of research has been very useful in providing a useful corrective to the more macroperspectives that remain dominant in the study of alliances, but it does remain the case that the existing microbehavioral work still remains somewhat partial, and has not been developed to its maximal potential.

How do we address this limitation in the extant alliance literature? We propose that the concept of interpartner legitimacy as recently articulated by Kumar and Das (2007) may play an influential role in this regards. The concept refers to how the partner firms evaluate each other with the implicit recognition that the attainment of interpartner legitimacy "can facilitate cooperation, lower transaction costs, and enhance the reputational capital of the partners" (p. 2). A recent study by Gulati, Lavie, and Singh (2009) notes that alliancing firms learn more from "partner specific experience" as opposed to a "general partnering experience." We would suppose and draw the conclusion that "partner specific experiences" are more enriching as opposed to a "general partnering experience" because they permit the alliancing firms to establish legitimacy. This is not to say that such legitimacy will always be created; it is only to make the argument that "partner specific experiences" provide the apposite context for the creation of such legitimacy. It is therefore not surprising that "partner specific experiences" are more enriching from the standpoint of learning.

We would suppose that interpartner legitimacy is a concept that is macrolevel in character but has microlevel foundations. It is a macrolevel concept in that it exists at a firm level, but the roots of it lie in the interpersonal interactions that occur among alliance managers. As such, this concept can be quite useful in integrating both the micro- and the macroperspectives in the study of alliance evolution. The starting point of our analysis is the recognition that while all alliancing firms are faced with the strategic imperative of attaining legitimacy, their ability to do so and their ability in sustaining it might be crucially dependent on the national culture that they emanate from (Kumar & Das, 2010a). Although this insight has been recognized earlier, it has not been fully developed, and it is this imbalance that we are seeking to redress in this chapter. The chapter begins by sketching out first of all the notion of culture. We then outline the concept of legitimacy and demonstrate the linkages between culture and legitimacy. The chapter concludes by outlining future directions for research and discussing managerial implications.

CONCEPT OF NATIONAL CULTURE

In a globalizing world, national culture has come to play an important role. International alliances bring together managers socialized in different cultures. A wide body of work most clearly suggests that national cultural differences can impede cross-border cooperation (e.g., Gibson, 1999; Hofstede, 1980; Kumar & Nti, 2004). National cultural differences among other things impede effective communication (Hall, 1959) and exacerbate the difficulties of successfully concluding a negotiation agreement (Graham & Lam, 2003; Kumar 1999a, 1999b) and resolving conflicts (Kozan, 1997). This is by no means an exhaustive list of all of the ways in which national cultural differences can affect cross-border cooperation but it is clearly suggestive of the kinds of difficulties alliance managers must be prepared to deal with. Most importantly, these differences can not only be distracting but may also have the potential of creating a poisonous atmosphere among the alliance partners.

National culture refers to the dominant values and beliefs that exist in a given society. It is to be noted, however, that no culture is completely consistent in regard to any particular set of values and beliefs. That said, there are clusters of values and beliefs that are more dominant in one culture as opposed to another culture. North American and European cultures are primarily individualistic, while Confucian-based cultures of East Asia are primarily collectivistic. It is also to be noted that national cultures are often dynamic and not static (Leung, Bhagat, Buchan, Erez, & Gibson 2005). A dynamic conception of national culture presumes that changes in values and beliefs may be more commonplace than what has assumed to be the case so far.

A number of cultural typologies have appeared in the literature (e.g., Hofstede, 1980; House, Hanges, Javidan, Dorfman, & Gupta, 2004; Schwartz, 1994). One of the most influential of these typologies is that developed by the Dutch social psychologist Geert Hofstede. Based on an empirical study of IBM employees, Hofstede (1980) identified four fundamental dimensions along which cultures vary. The dimensions are individualism-collectivism, power distance, uncertainty avoidance, and masculinity-femininity. The dimension of individualism-collectivism refers to the degree to which individuals give priority to their own goals as opposed to the larger collective. The dimension of power distance refers to the degree to which power is distributed unequally in a society. Uncertainty avoidance refers to the degree to which people are troubled by ambiguity. Masculinity-femininity refers to the degree to which the dominant values in the society are masculine or feminine. The fifth dimension (Confucian dynamism) was added later to the list. Although Hofstede's work has been influential, it has had its share of criticism (e.g., McSweeney, 2002).

Notwithstanding this controversy, it does remain the case that Hofstede's work has been very influential both among scholars and practitioners (Ailon, 2008). We suspect that many, if not all, of Hofstede's dimensions have an intuitive appeal and are empirically well-supported in the literature. This remains particularly true for the construct of individualism-collectivism, which has been extensively relied upon by cross-cultural researchers (Brewer & Chen, 2007). We will therefore be relying primarily upon the construct of individualism-collectivism to demonstrate the linkage between culture and legitimacy management in international alliances.

The dimension of individualism-collectivism is particularly germane to understanding legitimacy management in international alliances for a wide range of reasons. It has direct implications both for the kinds of goals that alliancing firms seek to pursue, and also for the best way they might pursue these goals (Kumar & Das, 2010a). In turn, the nature of the goals as well as the means by which they are attained have direct implications for the partner firms' ability in both attaining and maintaining legitimacy. Second, the construct of individualism and collectivism has direct implications for how alliancing firms embedded in these different cultures view the concept of partnering. Although partnering has become a popular concept, it remains the case that, for individualistically oriented firms, it may not be as natural or commonplace a phenomenon as it is for a more collectivistically-oriented firm. This is so for the fundamental reason that in individualistic cultures individual interests take priority over group interests. This may have implications also for how the partnering firms seek to manage legitimacy, and how successful they are likely to be. Finally, a firm in an individualistically- oriented culture, as opposed to a collectivistically-oriented culture, may be less adept in dealing with ambiguity with corresponding implications for legitimacy management. Individualistic cultures are often less tolerant of ambiguity compared to their collectivistic counterparts (Kumar & Worm, 2004). Scholars note that alliances are often characterized by ambiguity and the effective management of ambiguity therefore becomes a salient issue (Walter, Lechner, & Kellermanns, 2008).

CONCEPT OF INTERPARTNER LEGITIMACY

The concept of legitimacy is intrinsic in much of social science theorizing. It has more recently been imported into organizational studies, with Suchman's (1995) article being an influential contribution. Suchman defines legitimacy as "a generalized perception or assumption that the actions of an entity are desirable, proper, or appropriate within some socially constructed system of norms, values, beliefs, and definitions" (p. 574) Legitimacy judgments, as Kumar and Das (2007) note, are "made by the constituents or the societal groups to which the organization must be responsive" (p. 1427). Legitimacy evaluation is a subjective process in which the actions of the focal entity are evaluated within the context of the existing dominant set of values.

Kumar and Das (2007) build upon the work of Suchman and suggest that alliancing firms are faced with the necessity of evaluating the actions of their partners. The product of this evaluation is either the attainment or non-attainment of interpartner legitimacy. Interpartner legitimacy is defined as "*the mutual acknowledgement by the alliance partners that their actions are proper in the developmental processes of the alliance*" (Kumar & Das, p. 1430). If the alliancing firms are able to attain and maintain interpartner legitimacy they are likely to effectively deal with both internal and external challenges that they may be confronted with. By contrast, where interpartner legitimacy is lacking, the alliance is likely to be much less successful and may not be able to prosper or thrive over time.

Suchman (1995) also draws a distinction between three alternative types of legitimacies that he labels as pragmatic, moral, and cognitive. Pragmatic legitimacy has the derivative implication that the alliancing firms see their involvement in the alliance as beneficial. The evaluation of moral legitimacy is predicated on how the alliancing firms view the actions of their partner. If their partner is seen to behave in an appropriate way, the alliance is seen to be exhibiting moral legitimacy. If, by contrast, an alliance firm acts in an opportunistic way or is insensitive to its partner's concerns the alliance will lack moral legitimacy. Finally, cognitive legitimacy, as Suchman notes, is probably the highest level of legitimacy and is indicative of a situation where the alliancing firms do not question the wisdom of entering into an alliance. This judgment overrides the judgment that may be based on pragmatic or moral legitimacy concerns.

In their conceptualization, Kumar and Das (2007) have shown that different types of legitimacy are relevant at different phases of alliance development. Scholars note that alliances evolve through the stages of formation, operation, and outcome (Das & Teng, 2002). At the formation stage pragmatic legitimacy takes center stage. If the alliance partners cannot at this stage see any tangible benefit from the alliance they will refrain from entering it. At the operation stage, moral legitimacy becomes vitally important. The behavior of the partner firms is crucial. If, for example, a firm reneges on its commitment, or is unwilling to share information, it will have acted in ways that may have compromised the moral legitimacy of the alliance. Cognitive legitimacy takes on major significance at the outcome or evaluation stage of the alliance. It is at this stage that the allancing firms will make the decision if alliancing is indeed the way to go for them. Their article explores the determinants of pragmatic, moral, and cognitive legitimacies at different stages of alliance development. These authors also note that moral legitimacy has the greatest salience for joint ventures and a minimal salience for minority equity and nonequity alliances. The argument is also made that joint ventures require the greatest amount of effort to attain pragmatic and cognitive legitimacies while nonequity alliances require the least amount of effort.

INDIVIDUALISM VERSUS COLLECTIVISM

Scholars have theorized about the distinction between the two constructs of individualism and collectivism on the basis of four key dimensions (e.g., Chen, Chen, & Meindl, 1998; Triandis, 1995). The four dimensions are: (a) nature of the self; (b) goal orientation; (c) relative importance of attitudes/norms; and (d) relational orientation. Individualists are known to possess an independent self whereas the collectivists possess an interdependent self (Markus & Kitayama, 1991). Individuals with an independent self make decisions on the basis of their own self-interests and needs whereas individuals with an interdependent self are bound to explore the consequences of whatever decisions they make on other individuals who are part of their group. Individualists are solely preoccupied with achieving their own goals while collectivists give greater weightage to group goals over their own goals. Collectivists' behavior may be heavily constricted by attitudes and norms whereas the behavior of individualists is subject to few constraints of this kind. Finally, individualists emphasize goal attainment over relationships, while the collectivists prioritize relationships over goal attainment.

In a more recent conceptualization, Brewer and Chen (2007) differentiate between individualism and collectivism on the basis of three dimensions, namely, the locus of identity, the locus of agency, and the locus of obligations. The identity dimension focuses on the uniqueness of the self. This uniqueness could either be in relation to others, or in relation to the group as a whole. From this perspective, individualism is related to the uniqueness of the self, whereas collectivism is related to relationships with significant others. The agency dimension relates to the locus of responsibility for generating any outcome. The individualists assume that outcomes are a product of individual action whereas collectivists believe that outcomes are a consequence of group effort. The obligations dimension defines whether individuals are acting to achieve their own goals or whether their effort and actions are constrained by the need to conform to group norms. As is to be expected, individualists are primarily motivated to attain their own goals while collectivists have the motivation to conform to the group norms. A key insight from Brewer and Chen's work is that researchers have to be sensitive both to the fundamental distinction between relational and group collectivism as also to the aspect of individualism-collectivism (self-representation, agency, values) that may be most relevant to explaining behavior.

INDIVIDUALISM-COLLECTIVISM AND LEGITIMACY DYNAMICS IN INTERNATIONAL ALLIANCES

Alliances evolve through the stages of formation, operation, and outcome (Das & Teng, 2002). At the formation stage the alliance partners are tasked with assessing their partner and concluding a negotiated agreement. The operation stage of the alliance begins when the partners put into practice the commitments and the agreements that they had agreed to at the negotiation stage. Finally, at the outcome stage, the alliance partners evaluate the performance of the alliance to date and come to a judgment as to whether or not they wish to persist with the alliance. We will discuss how national culture as operationalized in terms of individualism-collectivism plays an important role at all three stages of alliance development.

Formation Stage

At the formation stage it is critical that the alliance partners be successful in establishing interpartner legitimacy. If such legitimacy is not attained, the alliance may not even come into existence. A successful negotiation between the alliance partners implies that pragmatic legitimacy has been attained. Attaining negotiation success is not easy, however, for several reasons (see Kumar & Das, 2010b, for a comprehensive discussion of inter-partner negotiations in alliances). First of all, the partners are tasked with the need to forge an agreement in a mixed-motive situation. This makes negotiation difficult because it induces uncertainty about how their potential partner might behave over time. As Kumar and

Das (2007) note, "The mixed-motive character of the interaction makes it difficult for the top management in either firm to persuade its alliance managers about the motives of the top management of its partner firm" (p. 1436). The problem is no doubt compounded by cultural differences, because in addition to the uncertainty about partner's motives and behavior, there is the added problem that the process of negotiation varies across individualistic and collectivistic cultures (Kumar 1999a). Individualists, as opposed to the collectivists, are contract-focused, do not care much about building relationships, and are very sensitive to time. If investing in particular partnership is time-consuming and the results uncertain they may withdraw. They may also tend to be direct, aggressive, and less consensually inclined in their decision making process. This is very much at variance with the collctivistic spirit. Collectivists are relationship-oriented, seek to build consensus, and are wary of committing themselves to the other party, unless they are able to establish affective trust (Chen, Chen, & Meindl, 1998).

Differences in negotiation styles are therefore likely to lead to script incongruence (Kumar, 1999b). Script incongruence refers to the expectational inconsistency among the alliance partners as to how the negotiation is going to unfold. Script incongruence generates negative emotions, and prevents the emergence of trust (Kumar, 1999b). It may also generate frequent interruptions as each partner acting on the basis of its norms and values violates the expectations of its partner. Negotiators embedded in individualistic cultures are likely to experience dejection-related emotions while negotiators embedded in collectivistic cultures are likely to experience agitation-related emotions (Kumar, 1999b). Dejection related emotions are indicative of an absence of a positive outcome while agitation-related emotions signify the potential presence of a negative outcome. It has been maintained that dejection-related emotions will foster aggressive behavior on part of the individualists, while agitation-related emotions will lead the collectivists to withdraw (Kumar, 1999a). This may intensify the frustration of the individualists who may begin to wonder if they can conclude the agreement. A vicious circle is likely to develop, and the alliance partners, instead of coming together, are likely to drift further apart, and this makes it even less likely that the negotiations will be successful. Impasses may be frequent and not easily bridged, absent a trusted third party.

Second, even in the circumstance that negotiation style differences do not generate excessive negative emotions, the alliance partners will nevertheless face a protracted negotiation process due not only to differences in negotiation styles but also for the extra time and effort required to bridge the differences. Finally, given the differences between the individualistic and the collectivistic cultural orientations, it is by no means clear that, even if the actors perceive to have successfully established pragmatic legitimacy, they will necessarily have complete clarity about what they have negotiated. Cultural differences may be bridged successfully but this does not necessarily imply that complete clarity has been attained. Notwithstanding the intentions of either party, this may be impeded by contractual incompleteness, time constraints, and conflicting cognitions. In other words, cultural bridging while essential for the attainment of interpartner legitimacy, does not necessarily imply an accurate understanding as to what the alliance entails. This will be particularly true if the alliancing firms are both new to alliances as also to cross cultural interactions. Most often, it is only at the implementation stage that the alliance partners begin to determine the veracity of their assumptions. This leads us to the following propositions:

Proposition 1(a): Alliancing partners embedded in differing cultures, individualistic and collectivistic, will encounter frequent interruptions as they negotiate to establish interpartner legitimacy.

Proposition 1(b): Alliancing partners embedded in individualistic cultures will seek to speedily establish interpartner legitimacy, relative to their collectivistic counterparts; the slowness of the negotiation process in collectivistic cultures will only fuel frustration among their individualistic counterparts.

Proposition 1(c): In the event that the partners are able to bridge their differences, interpartner pragmatic legitimacy will no doubt be established, but nonetheless it may still remain unclear as to whether the partners have a good and accurate understanding of their agreement.

Operation Stage

At the operation stage the alliance partners start making the alliance a concrete reality. A new entity is established, employees seconded to the venture from the partners, new hires brought in from the outside. It is conceivable that everything proceeds smoothly. If so, then there are no issues for the alliance partners to address. In actual fact such a condition may often be a rarity for several reasons. First of all, as Luo (2002) suggests, "Alliances vary in the levels of engaged risk and interdependence" (p. 690). The higher the risk and interdependence between the partners, the greater the task difficulty confronting them. Cultural distance will not only aggravate this problem, it may create problems of its own. The partners may experience communicative difficulties and this may prevent trust from being strengthened. The decision styles of the partners may also be variable, and this too may create additional problems. Consensus decision making is the norm in collectivistic cultures whereas in individualistic cultures this is not the dominant practice. Then too, the alliance partners may differ in the types of attributions that they make about any deviation from the expected performance (Kumar & Nti, 2004). Attributional reasoning refers to the rationale for a given outcome. If, for example, an alliance has fared poorly, an internal attribution would suggest that it is either one's own fault or the fault of one's partner. A situational attribution, by contrast, would suggest that perhaps external forces may account for the alliance's poor results. Scholars note that collectivists (e.g., East Asians) are often prone to making situational attributions whereas the individualists (Europeans, North Americans) tend to make internal attributions (Nisbett, Peng, Choi, & Norenzayan, 2001). This may give rise to an "attributional conflict" (e.g., Kumar & Nti, 2004).

Whatever be the specific nature of the problem, associated with each of these problems is likely to be an unfavorable process or outcome discrepancy (Kumar & Nti, 1998). An unfavorable process discrepancy means that the partners are dissatisfied with the manner they are interacting with each other. An unfavorable outcome discrepancy means that the alliance has been ineffective in attaining its goals over a period of time. The existence of unfavorable process and outcome discrepancies poses a grave challenge to both moral and pragmatic legitimacy of the alliance. Moral legitimacy comes into play because the existence of process discrepancies suggests that the partners have not behaved in the manner that they ought to. Of course, this judgment is being made from the cultural standpoint of the partner concerned. Pragmatic legitimacy comes into play because an unfavorable outcome discrepancy suggests that the alliance has not been able to attain its goal.

Alliance management becomes challenging if both pragmatic and moral legitimacies come to be challenged during the operation of the alliance. The necessity of dealing with both types of legitimacy simultaneously may result in an excessive amount of managerial burden. The process becomes even more challenging because both types of legitimacy may not have the same resonance in individualistic and collectivistic cultures. It has been maintained that moral legitimacy is more important in a collectivistic culture while pragmatic legitimacy is more important in an individualistic culture (Kumar & Das, 2010a). A key reason for this differential importance is the difference in the locus of obligations in an individualistic as opposed to a collectivistic culture (Brewer & Chen, 2007). In a collectivistic culture it is incumbent upon the participants to act in ways that will maximize group welfare, whereas in an individualistic culture the pursuit of self-interest is dominant. A key implication of this is that when the alliance is not doing well the collectivistic partner will expect that its counterpart subordinate its self-interest to that of the larger alliance. The individualistic partner, by contrast, will have the obligation to pursue its interest in an untrammeled way. Thus, not only do we have the fact that the alliance has a problem, but the situation is made worse by the fact that the partners may not even agree as to what is the dominant problem in the alliance. It may also be worth noting that in an individualistic culture there may be less of a consensus about the need to attain moral legitimacy, and even in the case where such a need is acknowledged, there may be less of a consensus as to whether such legitimacy exists at any given point in time. This too stands in sharp opposition to the scenario in a collectivistic culture, where not only is there likely to be a strong consensus about the need for moral legitimacy, but there will also be a strong consensus as to the existence or the non existence of moral legitimacy.

A related problem revolves around the fact that when legitimacy is violated, the repair of legitimacy is far from a straightforward process. This is so for several reasons. First is the issue of responsibility: Who is to blame? Second is the issue of determining what actions needed to be taken, the scope of the actions, and how they should be implemented in resolving the impasse. This is not an easy issue, given especially the large cultural distance between the parties. The problem is aggravated by the fact that in all alliances there is an inherent tension between value creation and value appropriation, and this may simultaneously create a tension between and within the partners as they seek to balance the use of integrative with the use of distributive strategies (Ness, 2009). Finally, and perhaps most crucially, the collectivistic cultures differ from individualistic cultures in the steps that they require for the reestablishment of moral legitimacy. Face plays a key role in collectivistic cultures (Chen, Chen, & Meindl, 1998; Earley, 1997) and when moral legitimacy is lost, then so is face. Moral legitimacy implies that the partners have behaved inappropriately. The nonfulfillment of obligations or adopting inappropriate behaviors may reflect negatively on an individual's character. This requires face repair strategies from the individualistically-oriented firm, and apart from the fact that they may not know how to repair face, they may also question the wisdom of doing so, as this practice is likely to be culturally alien to them. It is also a process that takes time, and the individualists are unlikely to be pleased by this. This only exacerbates the problem. The challenge facing the collectivistically-oriented firm is altogether different. It will need to cater to the demands of its individualistic counterpart who is, above all, interested in pragmatic legitimacy. This collectivistic firm must be swift in its response so as to cater to the heightened time sensitivity that is a characteristic feature of individualistic cultures. It must also be proactive and convince its individualistic counterpart that it is undertaking actions which will help to rectify the problem.

Another issue has to do with the managerial levels that might be involved in the management of legitimacies. We would surmise that in individualistically-oriented cultures legitimacy management will be largely dependent on the discretion of the alliance managers. By contrast, in collectivistic cultures, legitimacy management is likely to be a top down process. Hofstede's work shows that collectivism by and large goes hand in hand with a high power distance. This raises the problem that in collectivistically-oriented cultures legitimacy management may be a drawn-out process, given the fact that the top management is likely to be intimately involved. At the same time it raises the other problem, namely, that there might be a conflict between the managerial levels involved in legitimacy management, and this internal conflict may further aggravate the problem.

It is also conceivable that the methods used by the alliancing firms to resolve unfavorable pragmatic legitimacy may further exacerbate the crisis. As we mentioned earlier, firms embedded in an individualistic societal context are more sensitive to the presence or absence of pragmatic legitimacy. When they find that such legitimacy has been eroded, they will undertake a variety of actions to reverse this condition. They may influence their partner, put pressure on it, use threats, and in the ultimate instance may withdraw from the venture. These are face-threatening actions and will not go down well with their collectivistic counterparts for whom process may be even more important than the final outcome. The collectivistic firm is likely to react negatively to this and may feel that its trust in its partner has been misplaced. This can only accelerate the demise of the venture. This leads us to the following propositions:

Proposition 2(a): Pragmatic legitimacy will be more valued by a partner embedded in an individualistic culture whereas moral legitimacy will be more valued by a partner embedded in a collectivistic culture.

Proposition 2(b): In alliancing firms from individualistic cultures, as opposed to collectivistic cultures, there will be less of a consensus about the presence or absence of moral legitimacy.

Proposition 2(c): In repairing moral legitimacy with their collectivistically- oriented partner, the individualistically-oriented alliancing firm will have to engage in face management strategies.

Proposition 2(d): In repairing pragmatic legitimacy with their individualistically-oriented alliance partner, the collectivistically-oriented firm will need to be proactive and flexible.

Proposition 2(e): An alliancing firm embedded in an individualistically-oriented culture will find that repairing legitimacy with a collectivistically-oriented partner will be a drawn-out process.

Proposition 2(f): An alliancing firm embedded in a time-sensitive individualistically-oriented culture may employ strategies to reestablish legitimacy that may ironically further undermine the legitimacy.

Outcome Stage

At a certain point in time alliance partners are faced with the necessity of evaluating alliance performance. Is the performance satisfactory or is it unsatisfactory? Should they persist with or, alternatively, withdraw from the alliance? These are important questions that may have a significant impact on how the alliance evolves over time. The constructs of individualism and collectivism have an important bearing at the outcome stage in a variety of ways. First, the individualists, as opposed to the collectivists, are likely to be much more hard-nosed about the evaluation. In other words, if the alliance does not deliver the expected results, they will be among the first both to note this possibility and to communicate it to their partner. They will also not be reluctant to pull the plug on the venture if, in their judgment, there do not exist realistic alternatives for enhancing alliance performance. Given their focus on attaining and maintaining pragmatic legitimacy, these conclusions should by no means surprise us.

The individualists, as opposed to the collectivists, will also differ in the metrics that they use for assessing alliance performance. For the individualists, the metrics will have to be tangible, be it the development of new technology, the attainment of certain profitability levels, and so on. Tangible metrics are useful because they provide a clear-cut benchmark for evaluating pragmatic legitimacy. The collectivists, while not necessarily opposed to financial metrics, will also make an assessment of the nature of their relationship with their alliancing partner. Is the relationship developing in the right direction? Is an appropriate level of trust being established? The focus on the relational dimension and on whether they are developing the partnership with the right kind of partner highlights the importance of moral legitimacy to them. Put differently, the collectivists will use multidimensional measures, as opposed to unidimensional measures in assessing alliance performance. Again, this is not surprising, given the relational orientation and the focus on moral legitimacy that is so often a characteristic feature of collectivistic societies.

If the alliance has succeeded in attaining moral legitimacy, then the collectivists, as opposed to the individualists, are more likely to transfer that legitimacy to other alliances involving the same partner. We would suppose that this is so for the fundamental reason that the establishment of moral legitimacy implies that the partners have come to trust each other. If, on the other hand, the alliancing partners do not have any other alliance in which they are connected before hand, they may well seek to initiate new ventures with their existing partner. This leads to the following propositions:

Proposition 3(a): Alliancing firms embedded in individualistic, as opposed to collectivistic, cultures will be faster in assessing pragmatic legitimacy, and as a consequence thereof, will be more expeditious in deciding whether to persist with or withdraw from the venture.

Proposition 3(b): Alliancing firms embedded in individualistic, as opposed to collectivistic, cultures will be more prone to using financial metrics in assessing whether an alliance has succeeded in attaining pragmatic legitimacy.

Proposition 3(b): If the alliance has succeeded in attaining moral legitimacy, the collectivists, as opposed to the individualists, will be much more inclined in transferring this legitimacy to other alliances involving the same partner.

CONCLUSION

In this chapter we have attempted to highlight the impact of national culture on legitimacy management in international alliances. The issue of interpartner legitimacy and that of the impact of national culture remains an under-researched area in the alliance literature.This is a surprising omission given that many alliances cross national boundaries, and while doing that, they must also motivate their partner to act in ways that facilitate interpartner legitimacy. This is by no means an easy undertaking but at the same time it is vital if the alliance is to survive and prosper.

The framework articulated in this chapter has important theoretical as well as managerial implications. It first of all extends the existing literature on interpartner legitimacy by showing how national cultural differences can impact legitimacy dynamics in international alliances. Second, it bridges the national culture and legitimacy literatures that have to this date remained distinct and disparate. This is surprising inasmuch as that at the root of the national culture construct is the notion of legitimacy. National cultures determine through their own prisms of values and beliefs what is legitimate and what is not. Third, the chapter articulates a series of propositions that link national culture (individualism-collectivism) to the different facets of legitimacy management. These propositions can be empirically tested either through case studies, survey based investigations, or some combination there of. To our knowledge, there is no study as yet that has explicitly made the attempt to link national culture with legitimacy management in alliances. We would suggest that this is long overdue and our chapter hopefully provides some impetus for further work in this area. At a broader level the chapter contributes to extending the microbehavioral paradigm for studying alliances by linking the concepts of national culture and legitimacy.

The framework outlined here has important managerial implications. Alliancing firms need to be well aware of the cultural assumptions on which they operate as well as the cultural assumptions of their partner, and especially so because of the fact that these assumptions do not operate in any overt or concrete manner. Although this is not a novel insight and the point has been made before, it has not been previously linked to the legitimacy literatures (for an exception, see Kumar & Das, 2010a). This is vital to effectively bridging the culture gap between the parties. It needs to be noted of course that while the culture gap can be bridged it cannot be eliminated altogether. Alliancing firms must recognize this because, in its absence, unrealistic expectations may prove to be another potent source of problems. They must also recognize that, notwithstanding good intentions, problems are still likely to arise and till the time they are able to develop information about the intentions of their partner, they must not overreact even if they remain unhappy with the actions of their partner. The issue of finding the right balance between temperance and action is essential for effective alliance management. The framework also suggests the need for cultural training for managers at all levels of the organization. This may not be easy or cheap, but is nonetheless essential. Alliances have become commonplace but, as the literature suggests, they have often been far from successful. It is our hope that the arguments set forth in this chapter will prove useful both for extending the literature and providing useful managerial guidance.

REFERENCES

Ailon, G. (2008). Mirror, mirror on the wall: Culture's consequence in a value test of its own design. *Academy of Management Review, 33,* 885–904.

Brewer, M. B., & Chen, Y. -R. (2007). Where (who) are collectives in collectivism? Toward conceptual clarification of individualism and collectivism. *Psychological Review, 114,* 133–151.

Chen, C. C., Chen, X. P., & Meindl, J. R. (1998). How can cooperation be fostered? The cultural effects of individualism-collectivism. *Academy of Management Review, 23,* 285–304.

Das, T. K. (1986). *The subjective side of strategy making: Future orientations and perceptions of executives.* New York, NY: Praeger.

Das, T. K. (2003). Managerial perceptions and the essence of the managerial world: What is an interloper business executive to make of the academic-researcher perceptions of managers? *British Journal of Management, 14,* 23–32.

Das, T. K., & Kumar, R. (2007). Learning dynamics in the alliance development process. *Management Decision, 45,* 684–707.

Das, T. K., & Kumar, R. (2010a). Interpartner sensemaking in strategic alliances: Managing cultural differences and internal tensions. *Management Decision, 48,* 17–36.

Das, T. K, & Kumar, R. (2010b). Interpretive schemes in cross-national alliances: Managing conflicts and discrepancies. *Cross Cultural Management: An International Journal, 17,* 154–169.

Das, T. K., & Kumar, R. (in press). Regulatory focus and opportunism in the alliance development process. *Journal of Management,* DOI:10.1177/0149206309356325

Das, T. K., & Rahman, N. (2010). Determinants of partner opportunism in strategic alliances: A conceptual framework. *Journal of Business and Psychology, 25,* 55–74.

Das, T. K., & Teng, B. (1999). Cognitive biases and strategic decision processes: An integrative perspective. *Journal of Management Studies, 36,* 757–778.

Das, T. K., & Teng, B. (2000). Instabilities of strategic alliances: An internal tensions perspective. *Organization Science, 11,* 77–101.

Das, T. K., & Teng, B. (2002). The dynamics of alliance conditions in the alliance development process. *Journal of Management Studies, 39,* 725–746.

Earley, P. C. (1997). *Face, harmony, and social structure: An analysis of organizational behavior across cultures.* New York, NY: Oxford University Press.

Gibson, C. B. (1999). Do they do what they believe they can? Group efficacy and group effectiveness across tasks and cultures. *Academy of Management Journal, 42,* 138–152.

Graham, J. L., & Lam, N. M. (2003). The Chinese negotiation. *Harvard Business Review, 81*(10), 82–91.

Gulati, R., Lavie, D., & Singh, H. (2009). The nature of partnering experience and the gains from alliances. *Strategic Management Journal, 30,* 1213–1233.

Hall, E. T. (1959). *The silent language.* New York, NY: Doubleday.

Hamel, G. (1991). Competition for competence and inter-partner learning within international strategic alliances. *Strategic Management Journal, 12*(Summer Special Issue), 83–103.

Hofstede, G. (1980). *Culture's consequences: International differences in work related values.* Newbury Park, CA: SAGE.

House, R. J., Hanges, P. J., Javidan, M., Dorfman, P. W., & Gupta, V. (2004). *Culture, leadership, and organizations: The GLOBE study of 62 societies*. Newbury Park, CA: SAGE.

Inkpen, A., & Beamish, P.W. (1997). Knowledge, bargaining power, and international joint venture instability. *Academy of Management Review, 22*, 177–202.

Kozan, M. K. (1997). Culture and conflict management: A theoretical framework. *International Journal of Conflict Management, 8*, 338–360.

Kumar, R. (1997). The role of affect in negotiations: An integrative overview. *Journal of Applied Behavioral Science, 33*, 84–100.

Kumar, R. (1999a). A script theoretical analysis of international negotiating behavior. *Research on Negotiation in Organizations, 7*, 285–311.

Kumar, R. (1999b). Communicative conflict in intercultural negotiations: The case of American and Japanese business negotiations. *International Negotiation, 4*, 63–78.

Kumar, R. (2008). Contested meanings and emotional dynamics in strategic alliances. In N. Ashkanasy & C. Cooper (Eds.), *Research companion to emotion in organizations* (pp. 561–574). London: Edward Elgar.

Kumar, R., & Das, T. K. (2007). Interpartner legitimacy in the alliance development process. *Journal of Management Studies, 8*, 1425–1453.

Kumar, R., & Das, T. K. (2010a). Strategic alliances and culture in a globalizing world. In J. Ulijn, G. Duysters, & E. Meijer (Eds.), *Strategic alliances, mergers and acquisitions: The influence of culture on successful cooperation* (pp. 13–29). London: Edward Elgar.

Kumar, R., & Das, T. K. (2010b). Inter-partner negotiations in the alliance development process. In T. K. Das (Ed.), *Researching strategic alliances: Emerging perspectives* (pp. 207–257). Charlotte, NC: Information Age Publishing.

Kumar, R., & Nti, K. O. (1998). Differential learning and interaction in alliance dynamics: A process and outcome discrepancy model. *Organization Science, 9*, 356–367.

Kumar, R., & Nti, K. O. (2004). National cultural values and the evolution of process and outcome discrepancies in international strategic alliances. *Journal of Applied Behavioral Science, 40*, 344–361.

Kumar, R., & Worm, V. (2004). Institutional dynamics and the negotiation process: Comparing India and China. *International Journal of Conflict Management, 15*, 304–334.

Leung, K., Bhagat, R. S., Buchan, N. R., Erez, M., & Gibson, C. B. (2005). Culture and international business: Recent advances and their implications for future research. *Journal of International Business Studies, 36*, 357–378.

Luo, Y. (2002). Building trust in cross-cultural collaborations: Toward a contingency perspective. *Journal of Management, 28*, 669–694.

Luo, Y. (2008). Procedural fairness and interfirm cooperation in strategic alliances. *Strategic Management Journal, 29*, 27–46.

Markus, H. R., & Kitayama, S. (1991). Culture and self: Implications for cognition, emotion, and motivation. *Psychological Review, 98*, 224–253.

McSweeney, B. (2002). Hofstede's model of national cultural differences and their consequences: A triumph of faith—a failure of analysis. *Human Relations, 55*, 89–118.

Ness, H. (2009). Governance, negotiations, and alliance dynamics: Explaining the evolution of relational practice. *Journal of Management Studies, 46*, 451–480.

Nisbett, R. E., Peng, K., Choi, I., & Norenzayan, A. (2001). Culture and systems of thought: Holistic vs analytic cognition. *Psychological Review, 108*, 291–310.

Pak, Y. S., Ra, W., & Park, Y. -R. (2009). Understanding IJV performance in a learning and a conflict mediated context. *International Business Review, 18*, 470–480.

Schwartz, S. H. (1994). Beyond individualism/collectivism: New cultural dimensions of values. In U. Kim, H. C. Triandis, C. Kagitcibasi, S. C. Choi., & G. Yoon (Eds.), *Individualism and collectivism: Theory, methods, and applications* (pp. 85–119). Newbury Park, CA: SAGE.

Suchman, M. C. (1995). Managing legitimacy: Strategic and institutional approaches. *Academy of Management Review, 20*, 571–610.

Triandis, H. C. (1995). *Individualism and collectivism.* Boulder, CO: Westview.

Walter, J., Lechner, C., & Kellermanns, F. W. (2008). Disentangling alliance management processes: Decision making, politicality, and alliance performance. *Journal of Management Studies, 45*, 530–560.

ABOUT THE CONTRIBUTORS

Rutger Alberink holds an MSc in business administration (2010) from the University of Twente. For his master's thesis, he focused on the impact of contractual roles on alliance performance. At the moment, he is studying for the MSc in Business analysis and consulting at the Strathclyde Business School. E-mail: r.h.a.alberink@utwente.nl

Poul Houman Andersen is a professor and head of the Center for Design of Global Enterprise at the Aarhus School of Business and Social Sciences, University of Aarhus. His current research concerns the organization and management of interfirm and network relationships in international business contexts, and relates to international management, strategy, and marketing issues. His work has appeared in *International Marketing Review, California Management Review, Journal of Business Research, Strategic Organization, Industrial Marketing Management, Research Policy,* and *Journal of World Business*. E-mail: poa@asb.dk

Reinhard Bachmann is professor of strategy at the University of Surrey, School of Management. He published in journals such as *Organization Studies, Cambridge Journal of Economics, British Journal of Sociology* and *European Societies*. With Christel Lane he edited *Trust Within and Between Organizations* (Oxford University Press, 1998/2000); and in 2006 he edited the *Handbook of Trust Research* (together with Akbar Zaheer). He is currently deputy editor-in chief of the *Journal of Trust Research* and serves on the editorial board of *Organization Studies*. E-mail: r.bachmann@surrey.ac.uk

Xavier Castañer is an assistant professor, Strategy Department, University of Lausanne. Professor Castañer holds a Licenciatura and MBA from ESADE (Barcelona, Spain), and a PhD in business administration from the Carlson School of Management (University of Minnesota). Prior to his studies in Minnesota, he was assistant professor at both the Department of Business Policy and the Institute of Public Management at ESADE. Before joining the University of Lausanne, he was assistant professor at HEC (Paris) where he developed and taught several courses on strategy at all levels, including the *Grande Ecole*, the MBA, the PhD and executive education programs. At Lausanne he teaches corporate strategy in the master's program and interorganizational relations and strategies in the PhD program, and is also the co-director of the arts management executive program. Professor Castañer's research revolves around corporate strategy and development (including alliances and acquisitions) as well as on organizational innovation and integration. He has received several awards and distinctions for his academic work; among them, he was a finalist of the 2003 Best Dissertation Award of the Business Policy and Strategy (BPS) Division of the Academy of Management (AOM). In addition to several books and book chapters, his work has been published (or is forthcoming) in the *Administrative Science Quarterly,* the *Strategic Management Journal,* the *Journal of Management,* the *Journal of Management Studies,* and the *Journal of Cultural Economics,* among other journals.. Professor Castañer is an active member of several scientific associations, including the AOM for which he was the representative of its BPS Division in France for 2003–2007, and served on the BPS research committee between 2008–2010. He also serves on the editorial review board of *Organization Science* and the *Strategic Management Journal.* He was recently elected Representative at Large of the Strategy Process interest group of the Strategic Management Society (SMS), and previously was Representative at Large of the Corporate Strategy and Governance Interest Group of SMS. Professor Castañer has also consulted in the area of strategic evaluation and planning for both for-profit and not-for-profit organizations. E-mail: Xavier.Castaner@unil.ch

T. K. Das is professor of strategic management and area coordinator (strategic management and business & society) at the Zicklin School of Business, Baruch College, City University of New York. He is concurrently a member of the University's Doctoral Faculty. Professor Das received his PhD in organization and strategic studies from the Anderson Graduate School of Management, University of California at Los Angeles (UCLA). He also has degrees in physics, mathematics, and management, and a professional certification in banking. Prior to entering the academic life,

Professor Das had extensive experience as a senior business executive. He has research interests in strategic alliances, strategy making, organizational studies, temporal studies, and executive development. Professor Das has published several books and monographs, and his research has appeared in over 45 journals of which some of the later ones include *Academy of Management Executive, Academy of Management Review, British Journal of Management, Journal of International Management, Journal of Management, Journal of Management Studies, Organization Science, Organization Studies,* and *Strategic Management Journal*. Professor Das currently serves as a senior editor of *Organization Studies,* and is or has been associate editor or editorial board member of a number of other journals. He is the founding series editor of *Research in Strategic Alliances* (Information Age Publishing). E-mail: TK.Das@baruch.cuny.edu.

Gjalt de Jong is associate professor at the Department of International Economics & Business. He holds a PhD in business administration (1999) and an MSc in economics (1993) from the University of Groningen. He worked as senior management consultant for PricewaterhouseCoopers and KPMG Consulting. His research interests focus on determinants and consequences of institutions at different levels of analysis. E-mail: g.de.jong@rug.nl

Ard-Pieter de Man is professor of knowledge networks and innovation at the VU University Amsterdam. He also is principal consultant at Atos Consulting, the Netherlands, where he specializes in alliances and innovation management. Key themes in his consulting are designing alliance governance structures, building up alliance capabilities, alliance evaluation and open innovation. He has acted as a consultant in both the private and public sector. At Atos Consulting he is responsible for the Atos Consulting Open Innovation research project and he is the service leader in the area of strategy & innovation. His academic research also concerns alliances, networks and innovation. He is a prize-winning author and a coauthor of about 40 articles and 10 books, mainly on alliances and innovation. Current research projects include research into alliance mindset, trademarks as an indicator for innovation, alliance capability building, mergers and acquisitions. Ard-Pieter holds a number of other functions among others member of the Global Board of Directors of the Association of Strategic Alliance Professionals. He is a regular keynote speaker at conferences across the world. Previous employers include KPMG, Nolan Norton & Co and the Technische Universiteit Eindhoven. He obtained his PhD from the Rotterdam School of Management. E-mail: ard-pieter.deman@atosorigin.com

Dries Faems is associate professor at the Department of Operations, Organizations, and Human Resources in the Faculty of Management and Governance, University of Twente and affiliated researcher at the Research Center for Organization Studies in the Faculty of Business and Economics, Katholieke Universiteit Leuven. He obtained his PhD in applied economics from Katholieke Universiteit Leuven. His current research focuses on governance processes in alliances and acquisitions, innovation strategies and performance implications of alliance portfolios. E-mail: d.l.m.faems@utwente.nl

Robert Gannon is an instructor, professor of business and MBA program coordinator at at Alvernia University, Reading, PA. For 21 years, he served as the president and CEO of Pathcom, Incorporated, a regional telecommunications company. Prior experience included management functions for Ericsson Information Systems. He holds an MBA in accounting management from Saint Joseph's University, and received his BS degree from Auburn University. He is currently pursuing a doctorate in professional studies at Pace University's Lubin School of Business in New York City. His research interests include strategic alliances and small business, social network theory, top management teams, international corporate governance and entrepreneurship. E-mail: robert.gannon@alvernia.edu

Mehmet E. Genç is an assistant professor of management at Baruch College, and is interested in how institutional environments affect the strategic behavior and performance of firms. Specifically, he studies the implications of home and host country institutional environments for firms' international expansion strategies and subsequent performance, competition between multinationals from developed and developing countries, and the impact of foreign direct investment on local firms. His other major area of interest is the role of complementarity in corporate strategy. Professor Genç's research has appeared in the *Journal of International Business Studies*, and the *Journal of Management Studies*, among others. Originally a native of Turkey, he holds a PhD in Strategic Management from the University of Minnesota. E-mail: mehmet.genc@baruch.cuny.edu

Aard Groen is professor of innovative entrepreneurship and scientific director of NIKOS, the Dutch Institute for Knowledge Intensive Entrepreneurship at the University of Twente, the Netherlands. Professor Groen's research interest is focusing on knowledge intensive entrepreneurship in networks. NIKOS research contributes to the IGS, Institute for Innovation and Governance Studies, where he is leading the research on "Innovation & Entrepreneurship." E-mail: a.j.groen@utwente.nl

Michael A. Hitt is a distinguished professor and holds the Joe B. Foster Chair in Business Leadership at Texas A&M University. He has authored or coauthored over 280 publications, including 26 books. A recent article listed him among the top 10 most cited management scholars over a 25 year period. He is a past president of the Academy of Management and the current past president of the Strategic Management Society. He is a former editor of the *Academy of Management Journal* and is the current coeditor of the *Strategic Entrepreneurship Journal*. He received the 1996 Award for Outstanding Academic Contributions to Competitiveness and the 1999 Award for Outstanding Intellectual Contributions to Competitiveness Research from the American Society for Competitiveness. He is a Fellow in the Academy of Management and a Fellow in the Strategic Management Society. He received an honorary doctorate (Doctor Honoris Causa) from the Universidad Carlos III de Madrid. He has received awards for the best article published in the *Academy of Management Executive* (1999), *Academy of Management Journal* (2000) and *Journal of Management* (2006). He has also received the Irwin Outstanding Educator Award and the Distinguished Service Award from the Academy of Management. E-mail: mhitt@mays.tamu.edu

Sean Tsuhsiang Hsu is a strategy doctoral candidate at the University of Pittsburgh. His research interests include industry convergence, interfirm-relationship network, co-opetition, and technology standard competition. His dissertation focuses on industry convergence and how firms leverage and convert strategic alliance into acquisitions. Additional research interests center on how firms' copetition networks contribute to their performance, the relationship between homophily dynamics and network evolution the influences of social network effects on technology sponsors' strategy in standard battles. Prior to joining the PhD program, he was a senior marketing manager in one of the top LCD manufacturing companies. E-mail: thsu@katz.pitt.edu

Rosalinde Klein Woolthuis studied business economics at the Erasmus University in Rotterdam and the Wirtschaftsuniversitat Wien. She started her PhD with the European Doctoral Program for Small Business Management and Entrepreneurship at the Universita Autonoma de Barcelona (Spain) and Vaxjo University (Sweden). She finished her PhD at the University of Twente. Her PhD was on interorganizational collaboration between high-tech firms, and focused on the roles of trust, contracts and dependence. After her PhD, she broadened her research to include networks, clusters and innovation systems, and she broadened her horizon by also being active in policy advice in The Netherlands, United Kingsom, Denmark and for the European Commission. She currently works for the VU University Amsterdam and the TNO strategy department. E-mail: rkleinwoolthuis@feweb.vu.nl

Rajesh Kumar is an associate professor of international business strategy at the University of Nottingham. His expertise lies in the management of alliances, international negotiations, and managing in emerging markets with a specific focus on India. Professor Kumar has a PhD degree from New York University. He has taught at Penn State, Ohio State, and Babson College in the United States and in numerous institutions throughout Europe. Prior to moving to Nottingham in January 2008, he was an Associate Professor at the Aarhus school of business, University of Aarhus. Professor Kumar's work on alliances has looked at the microbehavioral processes involved in alliance development. Past work has highlighted the importance of interpartner legitimacy, emotions, process and outcome discrepancies, and more recently regulatory focus on alliance evolution. Professor Kumar has published in leading international journals such as *Journal of Management, Journal of Management Studies, Organization Science, Journal of World Business, Industrial Marketing Management, Journal of Applied Behavioral Science, International Marketing Review,* and *International Journal of Conflict Management,* and continues to maintain an active research agenda. E-mail: Rajesh.Kumar@nottingham.ac.uk

Ravi Madhavan is an associate professor of business administration at the Joseph M. Katz Graduate School of Business, University of Pittsburgh, and a faculty associate at the Center for Industry Studies there. He earned his PhD in strategic management at the University of Pittsburgh in 1996. Professor Madhavan's research has two themes: one, by studying alliance networks and M&A, he seeks to understand recombinant resources as performance drivers; two, by studying firm strategies in rapidly globalizing industries, he seeks to understand strategic and organizational responses to sudden-onset globalization. Empirical contexts of primary interest have been Steel and Venture Capital, two very dissimilar industries that have both been relatively slow to globalize. Professor Madhavan has published papers in premier journals including *Academy of Management Review, Journal of International Business Studies, Strategic Management Journal*, and *Academy of Management Journal*, and has received research grants from the National Science Foundation and the Alfred P. Sloan Foundation, among other funding agencies. E-mail: rmadhavan@katz.pitt.edu

Kerstin Neumann is assistant professor at the Department of Strategic Management and Innovation at WU Vienna University of Economics and Business. Her research focuses on issues of organizational design and evolution. Specifically, questions on corporate activities regarding interorganizational relationships (IORs) and merger and acquisitions (M&A) are emphasized in her work, for example, factors influencing boundary decisions, the role of formal mechanisms and trust in IORs (more generally, factors affecting ex ante governance implementation and ex post cooperation in IORs), postmerger integration, factors affecting M&A performance. E-mail: kerstin.neumann@wu.ac.at

Mike Nevin is a highly experienced international strategic alliance consultant, coach and trainer. He was the founding chairman of the Association of Strategic Alliance Professionals in Europe which he launched in March 2003. Current membership is over 500 with active chapters in: the United Kingdom, France, Germany, Netherlands, and the Nordics. He has consistently espoused the virtues of best practices in alliance instigation and management and it was this approach that inspired a 7 year research program into the critical success factors of business to business partnerships. To date over 300 of the world's leading partnering organizations in Europe, the United States, Australia, and India have benchmarked themselves against Mike's best practice database. He has worked closely with many leading alliance companies over the last 7 years including: IBM, Bank of America, Siemens AG, Capgemini, CSC, Nortel, Microsoft, Oracle, Vodafone, Starbucks BT plc, Computacenter, Micro Focus, HP, Eli Lilley, GSK (Healthcare), GSK (Pharma), Cardinal Health, Bax Global, Exel, Reckitt Benckiser, AstraZeneca, Marconi, Alcatel, McAfee and Cognos. It is this rigorous research and deep knowledge that allows him to present with authority and keen insights into the critical success factors of business to business partnerships thus ensuring that they are performing to their optimum. He is an accomplished and much sought after international presenter and has delivered both internal and external keynote presentations, workshops and speeches. E-mail: mike.nevin@alliancebestpractice.com

John E. Prescott is the Thomas O'Brien Chair of Strategy and past Director of the Doctoral Program in the Katz Graduate School of Business at the University of Pittsburgh. Professor Prescott was a founder of The Society of Competitive Intelligence Professionals (SCIP.org), the 1991–1992 President, served 10 years on the board of directors and 3 years as a Trustee of the CI Foundation. He is a fellow, the 1994 meritorious award winner, a finalist for the Fay Brill Service Award and International Advisor of the Society of Competitive Intelligence, China. John was the executive editor of the Competitive Intelligence Review for 8 years and the coeditor of the *Journal of Competitive Intelligence and Management* for 2 years. Most recently he chaired the CI Professionals' Competency Framework task force which developed SCIP's competency framework. John is the author and/or editor of five books, the most recent being *Establishing a World-Class Competitive Intelligence Function* and has published over 90 articles. Professor Prescott designed the first MBA course in competitive intelligence and in 1986 was awarded the Valley Forge Honor Certificate for Excellence in Economic Education. In 1996 he designed and implemented the first web-based CI course. Professor Prescott's research focuses on dynamic competitive rivalry, alliance networks, governance structures and technology strategy. He is the CI content expert at the American Productivity and Quality Center (APQC.org). He was the dean of the Business Analyst Program at Texas Instruments. Professor Prescott consults internationally. E-mail: prescott@katz.pitt.edu

Noushi Rahman is an associate professor of management at Pace University's Lubin School of Business. He received his PhD in Business (Strategic Management) from the Graduate Center/Baruch College, City University of New York. He has published in *Business & Society, Journal of Business and Psychology, Management Decision, International Journal of Strategic Business Alliances, Journal of Hospitality & Tourism Research, Asia Pacific Business Review, Small Enterprise Research, Journal of American Academy of Business, Current Topics in Management*, and *Journal of General Management*. His research interests include strategic alliances, corporate strategy, corporate governance, corporate social responsibility, and social entrepreneurship. E-mail: nrahman@pace.edu

Nadine Roijakkers obtained her PhD degree on inter-firm collaborative innovation from United Nations University-MERIT (Netherlands) in 2002. For 2 years she worked as a policy researcher for the European Commission. The goal of her studies was to determine the value of inter-firm R&D networks within the EU region. From 2004 to 2007 she was an assistant professor of Open Innovation at Eindhoven University of Technology (Netherlands). For the past 2½ years she was working as a strategy consultant at Atos Consulting (Netherlands) advising large companies in utilities and telecommunications on how to profit from their innovation/alliance strategies. Since November 2009 she has been working in Belgium alongside Wim Vanhaverbeke to further develop the theory and practice of Open Innovation. Outlets for her research include *Long Range Planning, Harvard Business History Review*, and *Research Policy*. E-mail: nadine.roijakkers@uhasselt.be

Qingjiu (Tom) Tao is an assistant professor of management in college of business and economics in James Madison University, Harrisonburg, VA. He received his PhD in strategic management and international business from University of Pittsburgh in 2004. His research on alliance portfolio and competitive intelligence has been published in *Strategic Management Journal* and *Competitive Intelligence Review*. Starting from 1998, his research has been focused on the automobile market in China. His early effort was on the market entry and postentry development of multinational auto firms in China's emerging market. More recently, his research interests rest on the outward auto FDI from China to external markets. He is also an active researcher of the IMVP (International Motor Vehicle Program) hosted by MIT and Wharton School. As a dedicated researcher and independent observer of the Chinese automobile market, Professor Tao has been traveling extensively in China and has established contacts with auto executives, industry experts, and auto-focused research centers as well as universities. Over time, he has built a significant data archive regarding the history as well as the current developments of China's auto market. He has spoken at Wharton School, Dartmouth, University of Tokyo, University of Michigan, and AutoUni-VW, and has testified before the congressional U.S.-China Economic and Security Review Commission on China's auto industry. He is also a regular expert commentator on economic issues for Voice of America and Netease Finance. E-mail: taoqx@jmu.edu

Bing-Sheng Teng is an associate professor of strategic management and Associate Dean for MBA at Cheung Kong Graduate School of Business in Beijing, China. He was previously an associate professor of strategic management with tenure at George Washington University (GWU), as well as the lead professor of the departmental doctoral program at GWU. Professor Teng's research has been published in a variety of top academic journals including *Academy of Management Review* and *Organization Science*. Professor Teng also serves on the editorial boards of *Journal of Business Research* and *International Entrepreneurship and Management Journal*. He was awarded the Wendell and Louis Crain Research Scholarship at GWU. Professor Teng's current research interests include strategic alliances, mergers and acquisitions, business model innovation, and international strategies (especially of Chinese firms). His expertise on Chinese management led to frequent interviews by the popular media such as *Wall Street Journal* and *Business Week*. E-mail: bsteng@ckgsb.edu.cn

INDEX

Abelson, R. P., 228
Achrol, R. S., 204
Acquisitions, 1, 3, 5, 9–19, 53
Activity orientation, 231–233
Adaptive equilibrium, 224
Agency theory, 95
Ailon, G., 247
Airbus, 203
Airline industry, 94, 160, 162, 169
Akerlof, G. A., 14
Aldrich, H. E., 33
Alliance agreement, 102
Alliance Analyst, 102–103
Alliance Best Practice, 118, 120, 122, 126–127, 130
Alliance capability, 117–118, 129, 132–133, 135–136
Alliance development stages, 219, 237, 244, 248–250, 252, 256
Alliance diagnosis, 120, 126
Alliance experience, 135
Alliance instability, 236, 243–244
Alliance management experience, 93–95, 99, 101, 103–104, 106–111
Alliance objectives, 78, 95, 97, 102, 109
Alliance performance, 94–95, 101, 110
Alliance structure, 94–97, 100–101, 103–106, 109–111, 224
Alliance success, 76–77
Alliance types, 95–97, 102
Alliances, balanced, 1–2, 15–16
Alliances, domestic, 102
Alliances, dyadic, 72–73, 78, 102
Alliances, equity, 1, 3, 12, 15, 18–19
Alliances, international, 101–102, 104, 108–109, 111, 243, 246–247, 250, 257–258
Alliances, multipartner, 102
Alliances, nonequity, 12, 15
Alliances, prior, 95, 100, 103, 105
Alliances, unbalanced, 2, 15–16
Allocca, M. A., 141
Alon, I., 140, 143
Amit, R., 166
Anand, B. N., 100, 117–118
Andersen, P. H., 192, 194-198, 201, 203, 205–206, 210
Andersen, P., 221, 223
Anderson, E., 143, 161
Anderson, H., 210
Anderson, J. C., 150
Anderson, S. W., 69, 71
Andersson, S., 140–142, 147
Ang, S., 12, 18
Anthony, S., 30
Appropriation concerns, 94, 237
Argote, L., 203
Argyres, N. S., 73, 166

Argyris, C., 119
Ariño, A., 17, 69–70, 72–74, 76–78, 88, 160, 163, 220, 234–235, 237
Arregle, J. -L., 34, 101
Arrighetti, A., 167, 175, 180
Arrow, K., 10
Ashby, W. R., 166
AT&T, 98
Atabay, I., 148
Athanassiou, N., 97, 101
Aulakh, P. S., 164–166, 177, 179
Auster, E. R., 64
Authority, 189
Autio, E., 146

Bachmann, R., 162, 164, 167, 175, 180
Baetz, M. C., 142
Bagozzi, R. P., 7
Baker G., 162–163, 165
Balakrishnan, S., 14
Banks, J. C., 39
Baratta, J. E., 40
Barden, J. Q., 5, 28, 31
Barkema, H. G., 4, 8, 100, 229
Barnard, C. I., 189
Barney, J. B., 32-33, 143, 165, 177, 199
Bartlett, C. A., 4, 7, 186
Bartunek, J. M., 222
Baughn, C. C., 96, 98, 109
Baum, J. A. C., 150
Beamish, P. W., 8, 18, 32–33, 39, 160–161, 220, 244
Behavioral uncertainty, 94
Behrens, D., 95
Bell, J. H. J., 3–4, 8, 100
Bell, J., 140–141, 144–146, 148–149
Bello, D. C., 229
Bengtsson, L., 97
Bensaou, M., 160
Berger, P., 220, 228
Berry, A. J., 169
Beyer, J. M., 226
Bhagat, R. S., 229, 246
Bierman, L., 37
Bijlsma-Frankema, K., 78
Bilderbeek, J., 121
Birley, S., 148
Blankenburg Holm, D., 205
Blau, P. M., 72, 190
Bleeke, J., 68, 98
Blomqvist, K., 205
Blomstermo, A., 143, 145–147
Bloodgood, J. M., 140
Boeing, 54–55, 63, 187
Boisot, M., 224–225
Bonache, J., 143
Boonstra, J. J., 135
Born global firm, definition, 142
Borza, A., 34, 101
Bouchikhi, H., 160
Bourdieu, P., 191
Bouwen, R., 78
Bradach, J. L., 100
Brand name integration, 98–99
Brazil, 222
Brewer, M. B., 247, 249–250, 253
Brewer, T. L., 182
Brislin, R., 220
British Telecom, 98
Brouthers, K. D., 5, 9, 11, 101
Brouthers, L., 5, 9, 11
Brown, L. T., 220
Brown, S. L., 225
Browning, L. D., 226
Bryk, A. S., 40
Buchan, N. R., 229, 246
Buckley, P. J., 28, 97, 102
Bucklin, L. P., 95, 98, 161
Burt, R. S., 69, 143, 195, 198, 203
Butler, R. J., 220, 229
Buyer-seller partnerships, 94

Calabrese, T., 150
Calori, R., 13
Camerer, C., 69
Camp, S. M., 143, 150
Cannella, A. A., 13
Capron, L., 14
Carlsberg, 205
Carpenter, G., 30
Carson, S. J., 95, 100
Casson, M., 28
Castañer, X., 8, 11, 19
Castells, M., 187

Caves, R., 11
Cavusgil, S. T., 140, 142, 145–146, 149, 151, 163, 165–166, 177, 179
Chaffee, E., 224, 227
Chandler Jr., A. D., 189
Chang, J. J., 11
Chaos, 223–227
Chen, C. C., 249, 251, 254
Chen, H. L., 142, 147
Chen, X. P., 249, 251, 254
Chen, Y. -R., 247, 249–250, 253
Chesbrough, H. W., 142, 145, 201
Chi, T., 99
Chia, R., 223
Child, J., 224–225, 236
Child, P., 4
Chinese auto industry, 27, 34, 37
Choi, I., 253
Choi, S. C., 261
Christensen, C. M., 30, 200, 202, 206
Christensen, P. R., 196
Chu, W., 100, 164
Chung, S., 165
Clegg, S. R., 181
Coase, R. H., 143
Coca-Cola, 98, 205
Code-sharing, 94
Cognitive institutions, 3
Cognitive legitimacy, 243, 248–249
Cohen, W. M., 7, 12, 237
Coleman, H. J. J., 186
Coleman, J. S., 165
Collaborative know-how, 95, 100, 109–110
Collis, D. J., 11, 32
Coloplast, 201
Communities of practice, 211
Complexity absorption, 225, 236
Complexity reduction, 224
Confidence in partner cooperation, 100, 110
Conflict, cognitive, 221
Conflict, moral, 221, 224
Conflict, pragmatic, 221, 224
Contract complexity, 78
Contract roles, 75
Contract, 68
Contractor, F. J., 184
Contractual alliances, 96–97, 100, 103–105, 108
Contractual safeguards, 100
Control function, 70, 72
Control mechanisms, 98, 110
Control, 55, 63–64
Cook, N., 195, 205
Cool, K., 6, 33
Cooperation vs. competition, 233–234
Coordination and control, 96
Coordination costs, 94
Coordination function, 73
Core competence, 187
Corporate culture, 220, 229–231
Costa, A. C., 78
Coviello, N. E., 140–141, 143–145, 147, 149, 151
Cowan, R., 143
Cox, A., 202
Cropper, S., 180
Cross-alliance evaluation, 121
Cross-cultural training, 238
Cross-national alliances, 219–221, 225, 227, 230–231, 234, 236–238
Cross-national diversity, 221
Cuervo-Cazurra, A., 9
Cullen, J. B., 236
Cultural differences, 219–221, 229–231, 236
Cultural distance, 220
Cultural training, 258
Cultural typologies, 246–247
Culture dimensions, 228
Currall, S. C., 72, 164

D'Aveni, R. A., 94
Dacin, M. T., 34, 101
Daft, R. L., 221, 224
Damgaard, T., 196
Dana, L. P., 142
Danone, 98
Das, G., 7
Das, T. K., 13, 16, 17–18, 28, 33, 64, 70–74, 94–95, 97–98, 100, 109, 111, 119, 143–144, 161, 164, 188, 193–194, 199, 202, 220–

221, 225, 227, 229–230, 233–234, 236–237, 244–248, 250–251, 253
Davidsson, P., 146
Davis, J. H., 163
Day, D. L., 35
De Jong, G., 68
de la Torre, J., 220, 234–235, 237
De Man, A. P., 117–121
De Rond, M., 160
De Winne, S., 79
Deakin, S., 167, 175, 180
Debackere, K., 78
Deeds, D. L., 78, 141, 144, 150
Dekker, H. C., 69, 162–163, 168–169
Delmotte, J., 79
Deloite & Touche, 203
Demsetz, H., 198
Denekamp, J. G., 98
Desai, M. A., 53, 56–57, 64–65
Deshpande, R., 164
Developed countries, 2, 7, 9
Dhanaraj, C., 5, 28, 31
Dicken, P., 140
Dickson, P. H., 143, 229
Dierickx, I., 6, 33
Dimitratos, P., 140, 149
Discrepancies, 225–226
Disorderly dynamics, 226
Diversity, 2, 7–8
Donaldson, B., 203
Dong, L., 229
Dorfman, P. W., 2, 9, 246
Double loop learning, 119, 133, 135
Douma, M., 121
Doz, Y. L., 7, 17, 68, 94, 142–143, 151, 237
Draulans, J., 117–118
Dreamliner, 54–55, 63
Drew, C., 54–55
Drucker, P. F., 207–208
Dunne, T., 35
Dussauge, P., 11, 98
Duysters, G. M., 100, 117–121, 241
Dwyer, R. F., 210
Dyer, J. H., 17, 64–65, 71–72, 74, 97, 100, 117–118, 140, 144, 150, 164, 175

Earley, P. C., 230, 254
Ebers, M., 72, 180
Eccles, R. G., 100
Echambadi, R., 163, 165–166, 177, 179
Eggert, A., 197
Ehret, M., 196
Eisenhardt, K. M., 72, 143–144, 147, 162–163, 225
Eisenmann, T. R., 29–30, 34–35
Ellegaard, C., 198
Embratel, 222
Emerging market, 28, 33, 48
Enterprises, small and medium size, 140, 142
Entrepreneurial behavior, born global firms, 143, 149, 151
Entrepreneurial firms, 141, 143, 145–146, 148
Entry mode, 1–3, 5–6, 8–10, 12, 18–20
Erez, M., 229, 246
Ernst, D., 68, 98
Erramilli, M. K., 3
Etemad, H., 140, 141, 148, 150
Evans, J., 6
Experimental spontaneity, 227
Exploitative innovation projects, 78
Explorative innovation projects, 78
Exporter, instant, 142

Faems, D., 68–69, 71, 74, 77–79
Faulkner, D., 236
Fichman, M., 164
Finkelstein, S., 7, 15, 147, 151
Firm size, 110
Firm-specific knowledge, 98
First mover, 29
Flexibility, 55, 64
Foley, C. F., 53, 56–57, 64–65
Ford, D., 195, 210
Foreign direct investment, 2, 28
Forgues, B., 223
Formal contract, 73, 159, 161–167, 174, 179

Formal institutions, 1–3, 5, 11, 14, 16, 18–20
Formation stage and legitimacy, 250–252
Forrier, A., 79
Friesen, P. H., 147
Frynas, J. G., 28, 30–31
Fung, V., 204
Futrell, D., 120

Gadde, L. -E., 194
Galbraith, C. S., 97
Galbraith, J. K., 142, 145
Galbraith, J. R., 70
Gal-Or, E., 30
Game theory, 95
Garcia-Canal, E., 72, 74, 77, 96
Garrette, B., 11, 98
Gatignon, H., 143
Geertz, C., 228
Genç, M., 8–9, 13, 19
George, G., 146
George, J. M., 72
George, V. P., 164
Geringer, J. M., 39, 76
Ghemawat, P., 6–7
Ghoshal, S., 4, 7, 186, 202
Gibbons, R., 162–163, 165
Gibson, C. B., 229, 246
Gill, J., 220, 229
Gilpin, R., 140
Glaister, K. W., 97, 102, 229
Global mindset, 7–8, 14
Globalization, 56
Goerzen, A., 8, 18, 95, 104
Golder, P. N., 29
Gomes, L., 40
Gomes-Casseres, B., 11, 16, 143–144
Gong, Y., 72, 74, 76
Governance structure choice, 93–115
Governance structures, 95, 102, 108
Govindarajan, V., 4, 7–8, 14
Graham, J. L., 246
Granovetter, M., 143
Grant, R. M., 143
Gray, B., 170
Greenwald, J., 186
Griffith, D. A., 3, 6
Grönross, C., 202
Guillén, M., 14
Gulati, R., 11, 18, 73, 77, 94–97, 101–104, 109, 143–144, 150, 161, 164, 166–167, 187, 220, 230, 237, 245
Gummesson, E., 197
Gupta, A. K., 4, 7–8, 14
Gupta, V., 2, 9, 246

Hagedoorn, J., 68–69, 97, 100
Håkansson, H., 192, 194, 199–200
Haleblian, J., 7
Halinen, A., 190, 210
Hall, E. T., 12, 246
Hallén, L., 197
Hambrick, D. C., 13, 147, 151
Hamel, A., 186, 206
Hamel, G., 11, 17, 34, 68, 94, 98, 199, 225, 237, 244
Handfield, R. B., 200
Hanges, P. J., 2, 9, 246
Harland, C. M., 190
Harmony, interpartner, 225
Harris, J., 163–164
Hart, J. A., 9
Havila, V., 210
Haykansson, H., 150
Hebert, L., 39
Heide, J. B., 162–163
Heimeriks, K. H., 117–118
Henisz, W. J., 11
Hennart, J. -F., 3, 4, 6, 8–11, 13, 16, 17–18, 96
Henriksson, K., 97
Herbert, L., 76
Hesen, G., 68–69
Hesterly, W. S., 165–166, 177, 199
Hexa-Care, 235
Hexagon, 235
Hierarchical control, 96
Hierarchical linear modeling (HLM), 40
High tech start-ups, 140–141, 145, 147, 149, 152
Hill, C. W. L., 141, 144, 150

Hillebrand, B., 68–70, 73
Hines Jr., J. R., 53, 56–57, 64–65
Hirschman, A. O., 168
Hite, J. M., 143, 145, 149
Hitt, M. A., 34, 101, 143, 150, 161
Hoang, H., 95, 100
Hobson, E. L., 35
Hoffman, D., 120
Hoffmann, W. H., 164, 182
Hofmann, D. A., 41
Hofstede, G. H., 3, 220, 228, 230, 246
Holmen, E., 195
Holmlund, M., 201
Homburg, C., 197
Honig, B., 146
House, R. J., 2, 9, 246
Huang, Y., 142, 147
Huemer, L., 194
Human, S. E., 143
Huxham, C., 180
Hymer, 2, 6–7

Idenburg, P., 121
IJV entry modes, 36
Immelt, J. R., 7
Incomplete contracts, 100
Incrementalism, 227
Individual evaluation, 119
Individualism-collectivism and legitimacy, 250–257
Informal institutions, 1–3, 5, 10, 16, 18–19
Informal mechanisms, 175
Information and communication technology, 186
Information processing, 95
Inkpen, A. C., 12, 18, 72, 98, 160–161, 165–166, 244
Innovation, 140, 142–143, 146, 150–151
Institutional environments, 101
Institutions, 1–3, 5, 10–11, 14, 16, 18–20
Instrumental rationality, 226
Intellectual capital, 98
Intellectual property, 101
Interdependencies, 160, 162, 166, 178
Internal tensions, 219–220, 233–236, 244
International entrepreneurship, 142, 149
International expansion, 7–8, 10, 19
International experience, 1, 4, 18
International exploitation, 7–8
International exploration, 7–8
International joint ventures, 27, 53
International new venture, 140, 142
International partners, 95, 101, 104, 109
International risk, 101
Internationalization, 142–143, 147–149
Internationalizer, instant, 142
Interorganizational relationships, (IORs), 159
Interpartner legitimacy, 243, 245, 248, 250, 252, 257–258
Interpartner negotiations, 246, 250–252
Interpartner sensemaking, 219–220, 224, 227, 236–238
Interpretive contradictions, 233–235
Interpretive schemes, 219–220, 222–226, 231–233, 236–238
Interruptions, 222–224, 235–236
Ireland, R. D., 143, 150, 161
Isabella, L., 118
Isobe, T., 28

Jacobs, R., 40
Janssens, M., 68–69, 71, 74, 77–78
Jap, S. D., 161
Jarillo, J., 18
Javidan, M., 2, 9, 246
Jemison, D. B., 13, 15
Jensen, O., 197
Johanson, J., 6, 140, 148, 150, 205
John, G., 95, 100
Johnsen, T. E., 190
Johnson, J. L., 200, 236
Johnson, M. D., 196, 201
Johnston, W. J., 190
Joint bidding, 94, 96

Joint evaluation, 119–120, 131, 133, 136
Joint marketing, 93–95, 97–99, 103, 105–111
Joint production, 94, 103
Joint R&D, 93–95, 97–98, 103, 105–111
Joint ventures, 53, 56, 65, 93–100, 103–110, 140
Jonard, N., 143
Jones, G. R., 72
Jones, M. V., 140, 145, 149
Judge, T. A., 164

Kagitcibasi, C., 261
Kale, P., 64–65, 68, 97, 100, 117–118
Karakaya, F., 30
Katsikeas, C. S., 229
Kaufmann, D., 2
Kauser, S., 229
Kekic, L., 2
Kellermanns, F. W., 247
Kerin, R. A., 29–31, 34, 39
Kessler, E. H., 141
Khanna, T., 7, 9, 97, 100, 117–118, 161
Killing, J. P., 94
Kim, U., 261
Kirkman, B. L., 230
Kitayama, S., 249
Klein Woolthuis, R. J. A., 68–70, 73
Klein, B., 165
Kletter, D., 187
KLM, 98
Kluckhohn, F. R., 229, 231–232
Knight, G., 140, 142, 145–146, 149, 151
Knowledge accumulation, 118, 129–130, 133–134
Knowledge acquisition, 97, 110
Knowledge diffusion, 118, 129, 134
Knowledge integration, 118, 129–130, 134
Knowledge storage, 118, 129–130, 134
Knowledge transfer, 97–98, 101, 110
Knowledge, intangible, 140, 142–147, 151–152
Knowledge-based view, 141, 151
Kobrin, S. J., 11
Kochlar, R. 37
Kogut, B., 3, 7–9, 15, 17, 65, 96, 98–99, 160
Koput, K. W., 97, 118
Kostova, T., 5, 18, 101
Kotler, P., 204
Koza, M. P., 14, 78
Kozan, M. K., 246
Kraay, A., 2
Krackhardt, D., 95
Kragh, H., 192
Krishnan, R., 100
Kumar, R., 16, 18, 97, 193–194, 198, 203, 206, 221, 225, 230, 237, 244–248, 250–251, 253
Kwon, Y. -C., 229

Lam, N. M., 246
Lambe, C. J., 201–202
Lamming, R. C., 190
Lane, C., 164, 180
Lane, H. W., 220
Lane, P. J., 95, 132, 229
Langley, A., 227
Lanzolla, G., 29, 30–31, 34, 48
Larimo, J., 3, 8, 11
Larson, A., 96, 148
Larsson, R., 15, 97
Laurent, A., 231
Lavie, D., 78, 245
Lawrence, P. R., 73
Learning races, 98
Learning, 4, 7, 10, 18–19
Learning-by-doing, 118
Lechner, C., 247
Lee, J. Y., 9
Lee, K., 165
Legitimacy and national culture, 243–261
Legitimacy, 5, 11–12, 16, 18
LEGO, 186
Lei, D., 196
Lenway, S. A., 7
Leonard, D., 143
Leung, K., 229, 246
Levinthal, D. A., 7, 12, 164, 237

Levitas, E., 34, 101
Lewin, A.Y., 78
Li & Fung, 204
Liability of foreignness, 2, 5, 12
Liability of newness, 140, 147
Lieberman, M. B., 29–31, 34, 39, 47
Lin, X., 229
Lindberg-Repo, K., 202
Linux, 205
Lofstrom, S., 164
Lonsdale, C., 202
Looise, J. K., 121
Lorange, P., 184
Lorsch, J. W., 73
Lu, J. W., 33
Lubatkin, M., 13, 132
Luckmann, T., 220, 228
Lui, S. S., 100
Luo, Y., 6, 7, 18, 28–29, 33–34, 38–40, 69, 74, 76, 87, 252
Lyles, M., 5, 28, 31, 95
Lyons, B., 68–69

MacMillan, I. C., 35
Madhok, A., 68–69, 73–74, 77, 88, 95, 100, 161
Maes, J., 79
Makino, S., 5, 9, 11, 16, 18, 28
Malhotra, D., 69
Managerial mechanism, 224
Mandler, G., 222
Mankin, E., 10, 17
Mansfield, E., 9
Marceau, J., 195, 205
March, J. G., 6–7, 18, 204
Marino, L., 143, 229
Markus, H. R., 249
Martin, R. L., 208
Martin, X., 100
Martínez, J. I., 18
Mascarenhas, B., 29, 35–36, 39
Masciarelli, J. P., 198
Mason, P. A., 147
Mastruzzi, M., 2
Masuch, M., 234
Mathews, J. A., 10, 186, 194
Mauri, A. J., 140–141
Mavondo, F. T., 6
Mayer, K. J., 68-69, 73
Mayer, R. C., 163
McAuley, A., 142
McDougall, P. P., 140–142, 145, 150–151
McEvily, B., 17–18, 164, 203
McGill, J. P., 64
McHugh, A., 193, 198
MCI, 222
McMahan, G. C., 143
McQuade, K., 16
McSweeney, B., 247
McWilliams, A., 143
Mehra, S., 11
Mehta, J., 68–69
Meijer, E., 241
Meindl, J. R., 249, 251, 254
Mellahi, K., 28, 30–31
Mellewigt, T., 69, 73, 77, 88, 98
Mergers & Acquisitions, 53, 57–58, 63, 65
Merz, G. R., 147
Meschi, P. -X., 229, 231
Metrics, 120
Meyer, K. E., 5, 9, 11
Microbehavioral perspective, 244–245, 258
Miles, G., 142, 186–187, 205
Miles, R. E., 186–187, 199, 201, 204–205
Milgrom, P., 166
Miller, D., 57, 147
Miller, K. D., 95, 102
Minority equity alliances, 93–97, 99, 103–109
Mintzberg, H., 73–74, 147, 193, 198, 227
Minute Maid, 98
Mitchell, W., 98
MNEs, 1–5, 7–9, 11, 14, 19
Mohr, J. J., 202
Moldoveanu, M., 208
Möller, K. K., 190
Monczka, R. M., 200
Montgomery, C. A., 11, 32
Montgomery, D. B., 28–31, 34, 39, 47

Moorman, C., 164
Moral legitimacy, 243, 248–249, 253–257
Morgan, G., 220
Morosini, P., 6, 10, 12-13
Morrison, R. M., 35
Mowery, D. C., 98
Multilateral alliance, 72–73, 78
Munro, H. J., 140, 144–145, 147, 149
Murnighan, J. K., 69
Murphy, K. J., 162–163, 165
Murtha, T. P., 7
Mutual hostage, 98

Nahapiet, J., 202
Nakamoto, K., 30
NAMCO, 234–235
National culture and legitimacy, 243–261
National culture, 219–221, 228–231, 243, 245–246, 250, 257–258
Ness, H., 254
Network perspective, 141, 144, 148
Network theory, 95
Network ties, 199
Networks, 143–144, 146–150, 152–153
Neuijen, B., 230
Neumann, K., 163–164, 167, 169, 180, 182
Nevin, J. R., 202
New York Times Index, 102
Neyens, I., 120–121
Ngo, H., 100
Nielsen, B., 28
Nigh, D., 97, 101
Nisbett, R. E., 253
Nohria, N., 97, 161
Nonaka, I., 143
Noorderhaven, N. G., 100
Nooteboom, B., 68–70, 73, 96, 199
Norenzayan, A., 253
Normann, R., 204
Normative institutions, 3, 5
North, D. C., 311
Northwest Airlines, 98
Nowak, P., 143
Nti, K. O., 230, 244, 246, 253
Nummela, N., 143
Nyaw, M. -K., 72, 74, 76

O'Toole, T., 203
Oh, S., 210
Ohayv, D. D., 230
Ohmae, K., 56
Ojasalo, J., 195
Olleros, F. J., 35
Olsen, C. P., 74, 160
Operation stage and legitimacy, 252–256
Operational integration, 96
Opportunism, 70, 94, 96, 98, 100, 159, 220
Order entry effects, 32–33
Osborn, R. N., 96, 98, 109
Otley, D. T., 169
Ouchi, W. G., 72, 162–163
Outcome stage and legitimacy, 256–257
Oviatt, B. M., 140–142, 145, 149–151
Oxley, J. E., 94, 98, 102

Pak, Y. S., 245
Palepu, K., 7, 9
Paliwoda, S. J.,
Park, S. H., 4, 8, 160–161, 165, 167, 179
Park, Y. -R., 10, 245
Parkhe, A., 31, 69–70, 73, 78, 87, 94–95, 101, 103, 161, 166
Partner cooperation, 73, 76
Partner nationality, 101
Parvatiyar, A., 202
Pascual, A., 186
Pearce, R. J., 160, 162–163
Pedersen, A. -C., 195
Pels, J., 196
Peng, K., 253
Peng, M. W., 6, 18, 28–29, 33, 37, 49
Pennings, J. M., 3–4, 8
Performance risk, 95
Performance trends, 38, 45–46
Perlmutter, H. V., 7
Perrone, V., 17–18, 164
Petersen, K. J., 200

Peterson R. A., 29–31, 34, 39
Pfeffer, J., 143, 225
Phiri, T., 140, 149
Pigman, G. A., 28, 30–31
Piore, M. J., 186
Pisano, G. P., 94, 96, 151
Pitcher, P., 227
Pitts, R. A., 196
Poppo, L., 69, 78, 87, 165, 175
Porter, M., 21
Porter, R. E., 228
Posada, E., 227
Powell, W. W., 97, 118
Pragmatic legitimacy, 243, 248–250, 252–257
Prahalad, C. K., 34, 186, 199, 225
Predictability, 223–224, 226–227, 232
Preece, S. B., 142
Prisoner's dilemma, 95
Procedures and policies, 96
Provan, K. G., 143

Quao, H., 202
Quinn, J. B., 225

Ra, W., 245
Ragatz, G. L., 200
Rahman, N., 141–142, 161, 164, 220, 244
Ramaswamy, K., 40
Ramirez, R., 204
Rangan, U. S., 94, 96
Raudenbush, S. W., 40
Raynor, M. E., 206
Reagans, R., 203
Redding, S. G., 228
Reddy, S., 9, 18
Regulatory focus, 244–245
Regulatory institutions, 3
Reich, R., 10, 17
Reiner, J., 189
Relational capital, 187
Relational embeddedness, 148
Relational orientation, 231, 233
Relational risk, 95
Relationship management tasks in strategic alliances, 191–209
Relationship management, 190–191
Relationship norms, 196
Relationship of humans to nature, 231–232
Rent appropriation, 10, 12
Residuals, allocation, 99
Resource commitment, 34, 36, 47
Resource compatibility, 101
Resource complementarity, 159, 162, 165, 177, 179
Resource heterogeneity, 101
Resource integration, 101
Resource-based theory, 32, 48
Resource-based view, 95
Resources, financial, 99
Resources, human, 99, 101
Resources, in born global firms, 140, 144, 146, 150–151
Resources, marketing, 99
Resources, organizational, 101
Resources, physical, 99, 101
Resources, technological, 101
Reuer, J. J., 17, 69–70, 73, 78, 88, 95, 102, 119, 160, 163
Riccio, E. L., 229
Richardson, J. C., 213
Rigidity vs. flexibility, 233–234
Ring, P. S., 18, 72, 160, 162–165, 168, 180, 220
Risk perception, 95
Risk, 5–7, 9, 11–13, 15, 18, 20
Risk-sharing, 54–55, 63
Ritter, T., 190
Ritti, R. R., 225
Roberts, J., 166
Roberts, M. J., 35, 229
Rocha, H., 205
Rocks, D., 222
Roehl, T. W., 99
Roger, A., 231
Rosenkopf, L., 78
Roth, E., 30
Roth, K., 18
Rothaermel, F. T., 78, 95, 100
Rousseau, D. M., 69
Rowley, T., 95
RTX, 208–209

Rugman, A. M., 182, 220
Rumelt, R. P., 28
Russell, C. J., 3, 6
Russo, M. V., 160–161, 167, 179

Sabel, C., 186
Safeguarding clauses, 70–71
Saint-Macary, J., 227
Sakano, T., 236
Salk, J. E., 95
Salmond, D. J., 201–202
Samovar, L. A., 228
Sampson, R. C., 95, 100
Samuelson, L., 35
Sanders, G., 230
Sandström, M., 197
Santoro, M. D., 64
Santos, J., 7, 142–143, 151
Sapienza, H. J., 140, 146
Sarkar, M. B., 163, 165–166, 177, 179
Sauber, M. H., 147
Sauer, C., 208
Schendel, D. E., 28
Schneider, S., 230
Schoemaker, M., 13
Schoemaker, P. J. H., 166
Schon D. A., 119
Schoonhoven, C. B., 143–144, 147
Schoormann, F. D., 163
Schurr, P. H., 210
Schwartz, S. H., 246
Scott, R. W., 3
Scott, W. R., 200
Script, 228
Seabright, M. A., 164
Self-amplifying reciprocity, 226
Selnes, F., 196, 201
Sels, L., 79
Sengupta, S., 95, 98, 161
Sensemaking in alliances, 219–242
Sensemaking *in*, 219–220, 222–228, 232–233, 236, 238
Sensemaking *of*, 219–220, 222–224, 226–227, 232–233, 236, 238
Sensiper, S., 143
Sexton, D. L., 143, 150
Shan, W., 40
Shane, S., 6, 10, 12–13, 145, 230
Shanley, M., 65
Shapiro, D. L., 230
Shared ownership, 96, 98, 100
Sharma, D. D., 143, 145–147
Shaw, V., 229
Shenhar, A. J., 189
Shenkar, O., 33, 72, 74, 76, 100
Sheth, J. N., 202
Shetler, J. C., 226
Shimizu, K., 37
Short term vs. long term, 233–234
Shrader, R. C., 140–141
Shuen, A., 151
SIC codes, 110
Siegel, J. I., 11
Silver, J. M., 225
Silverman, B. S., 98, 150
Simonin, B. L., 100, 109
Singh, H., 3, 6, 8–13, 15, 17, 64, 68, 71–74, 94–97, 100, 102–104, 109, 117–119, 140, 144, 150, 160, 165–167, 175, 220, 230, 237, 245
Single loop learning, 119
Sinha, J., 7
Sirmon, D. G., 229
Sitkin, S. B., 13, 15, 69
Slocum Jr., J. W., 196
Slugay, M., 120
SMEs (see Enterprises, small and medium size)
Smith-Doerr, L., 97, 118
Snehota, I., 192, 199–200
Snow, C. C., 186–187, 199, 201, 204–205
Snyder, W. M., 211
Social control, 72
Sparks, J., 97
Speckbacher, G., 164, 182
Spekman, R. E., 118, 201–202
Spence, M., 148
Squires, G., 189
Stacey, R. D., 223–224, 226
Stage models, 140, 145, 148–149
Stahl, M. J., 30
Starr, J. A., 148

Staw, B. M., 17
Steensma, H. K., 5, 28, 31, 143, 229
Stephens, C. H., 120
Stevens, J. H., 98
Storbacka, K., 196, 202
Strauss, S., 143
Strodtbeck, F. L., 229, 231–232
Structural choice, 94–97, 103
Structural decisions, 94–95
Structural integration, 97
Structure and control mechanisms, 94
Structure and exit possibilities, 94
Structure and operational process, 94
Stump, R. L., 162, 163
Suarez, F. F., 29–31, 34, 48
Suchman, M. C., 248
Supply chain, 54, 64
Sydow, J., 180

Takenouchi, H., 236
Tallman, S. B., 74, 161
Technological knowledge, 97
Teece, D. J., 13, 28, 68–69, 94, 99, 143, 151, 167, 201
Telefonica, 222
Tellis, G. J., 29
Teng, B., 13, 17, 28, 33, 64, 70–74, 94–95, 100, 109, 111, 119, 143–144, 164, 188, 199, 202, 220, 227, 229, 233–234, 236–237, 244, 248, 250
Thietart, R. A., 223
Thomas, J. B., 95
Thompson, J. D., 70, 73, 166, 186
Tihanyi, L., 3, 5, 6, 28, 31
Time perspective, 221
TMT (see Top Management Team)
Tomkins, C., 166, 168
Top Management Team, 141, 146–153
Townley, C., 203
Transaction cost economics, 94
Transaction cost theory, 70
Trevino, L. K., 95
Triandis, H. C., 229, 249, 261
Trimble, C., 7
Trust, 10–13, 17–18, 69, 100–102, 159, 162–165, 167, 175, 179, 220, 229–230
Trustful collaboration, 72–74, 77
Tsoukas, H., 223

Ulaga, W., 197
Ulijn, J., 241
Ungson, G. R., 4, 8, 161
Uppsala model, 148

Vahlne, J. -E., 6, 140, 148
Vaidyanath, D., 161
Valdés-Llaneza, A., 72, 74, 77
Value chain, 141, 145
Value orientations, 229, 231
Van de Ven, A. H., 18, 72, 143, 160–162, 164–165, 168, 220
Van der Meer-Kooistra, J., 169
Van Looy, B., 68–69, 71, 74, 77–78
Varadarajan, P. R., 29–31, 34, 39
Varman, R., 95, 100
Veiga, J., 13
Venkatraman, N., 160
Verbeke, A., 220
Vermeulen, F., 4, 8, 100, 229
Very, P., 13
Vicious circles, 234
Volberda, H. W., 117–118
Vosselman, E. G. J., 169

Wagner, S. M., 200
Walker, G., 161
Wall Street Journal Index, 102
Walsh, J. P., 13
Walter, J., 247
Wang, C. L., 229
Wang, L., 65
Watson, G., 202
Weaver, K. M., 143, 229
Weber, M., 189
Weibel, A., 69, 73, 77, 88
Weick, K. E.. 193, 197, 201, 221, 224, 226
Wenger, E. C., 211
Werner, S., 5
Wheeler, C., 140, 149

Wholly owned greenfield, 9
Wictor, I., 140–142, 147
Wiersema, M., 161
Wilkinson, I. F., 190
Willcocks, L. P., 208
Williamson, O. E., 15, 69–70, 140, 163
Williamson, P., 7, 142–143, 151
Wooster, R. B., 30–31, 33, 35, 39
Workman Jr., J. P., 197
Worm, V., 247
Wright, P. M., 143
Wright, R. W., 140, 142, 148

Yan, A., 170
Yin, R. K., 169, 170
Yin, X., 65
Yiu, D., 5, 9, 11, 16, 18
Yoon, G., 261
Yoshida, T., 220
Yoshino, M. Y., 94, 96
Young-Ybarra, C., 161

Zaheer, A., 17, 18, 162–164
Zaheer, S., 2, 13
Zahra, S. A., 146
Zajac, E. J., 65, 74, 160
Zaltman, G., 164
Zander, U., 7
Zárraga, C., 143
Zeng, M., 3–4, 11, 16, 18
Zenger, T., 69, 78, 87, 165–166, 175
Zheng, J., 190
Zollo, M., 119, 160
Zucker, L. G., 164

Printed and bound by CPI Group (UK) Ltd, Croydon, CR0 4YY
15/09/2026
14962373-0002